TWILIGHT
at the
WORLD OF
TOMORROW

TWILIGHT
at the
WORLD OF TOMORROW

GENIUS, MADNESS, MURDER,

AND THE 1939 WORLD'S FAIR

ON THE BRINK OF WAR

JAMES MAURO

BALLANTINE BOOKS

NEW YORK

Published in the United States by Ballantine Books, an imprint of
The Random House Publishing Group, a division of
Random House, Inc., New York.

BALLANTINE and colophon are registered trademarks of Random House, Inc.

LIBRARY OF CONGRESS CATALOGING-IN-PUBLICATION DATA
Mauro, James.
Twilight at the world of tomorrow: genius, madness, murder, and the
1939 World's Fair on the brink of war / James Mauro.
p. cm.
Includes bibliographical references and index.
ISBN 978-0-345-51214-7
eBook ISBN 978-0-345-52178-1
1. New York World's Fair (1939–1940)—History.   I. Title.
T785.B1M393   2010   907.4'747243—dc22   2010012709

Printed in the United States of America on acid-free paper

www.ballantinebooks.com

2 4 6 8 9 7 5 3 1

First Edition

Book design by Susan Turner

For Heather,
who so quickly became my muse

And for Madelyn,
who will always be my World of Tomorrow

*Anyone who thinks about the future must
live in fear and terror.*

—From "To Posterity,"
Einstein's letter placed inside the
Westinghouse time capsule
at the 1939 New York World's Fair

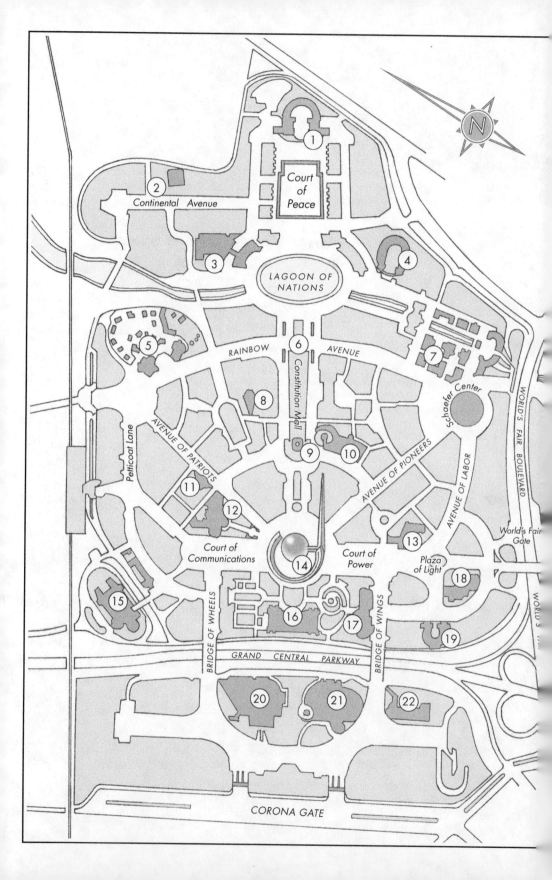

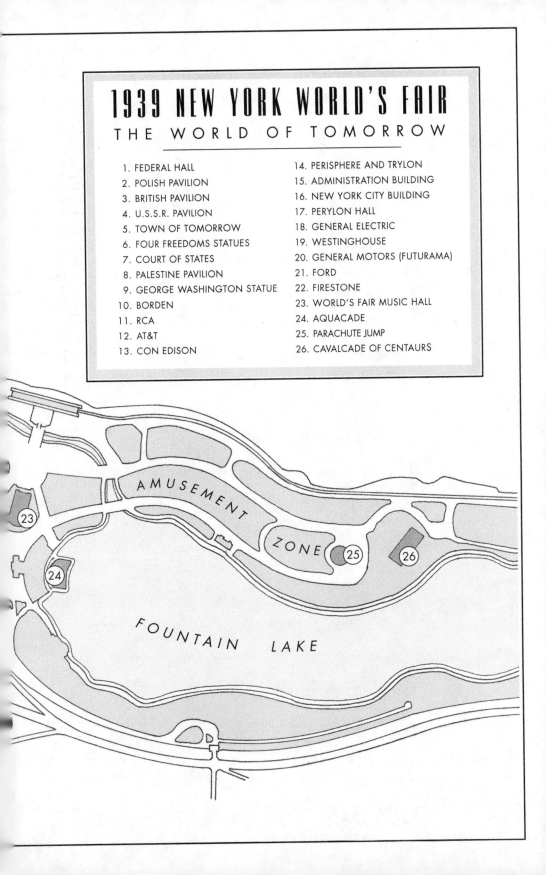

1939 NEW YORK WORLD'S FAIR
THE WORLD OF TOMORROW

1. FEDERAL HALL
2. POLISH PAVILION
3. BRITISH PAVILION
4. U.S.S.R. PAVILION
5. TOWN OF TOMORROW
6. FOUR FREEDOMS STATUES
7. COURT OF STATES
8. PALESTINE PAVILION
9. GEORGE WASHINGTON STATUE
10. BORDEN
11. RCA
12. AT&T
13. CON EDISON
14. PERISPHERE AND TRYLON
15. ADMINISTRATION BUILDING
16. NEW YORK CITY BUILDING
17. PERYLON HALL
18. GENERAL ELECTRIC
19. WESTINGHOUSE
20. GENERAL MOTORS (FUTURAMA)
21. FORD
22. FIRESTONE
23. WORLD'S FAIR MUSIC HALL
24. AQUACADE
25. PARACHUTE JUMP
26. CAVALCADE OF CENTAURS

AMUSEMENT ZONE

FOUNTAIN LAKE

CONTENTS

AUTHOR'S NOTE

"The trouble with intellectuals is that they don't know what a World's Fair is all about," wrote George R. Leighton in *Harper's Magazine*. "A World's Fair is an art form, a combination of beauty and bombast . . . and the universal hankering for a holiday."

Mr. Leighton visited the 1939 New York World's Fair, and later the 1964 version, and sums up one of the most important questions this book attempts to answer: "What makes a World's Fair a 'success'—money or love?" There's something enduringly magical about a World of Tomorrow built on an ash heap and poised directly between two of the most catastrophic, and self-defining, events in twentieth-century American history: the Great Depression and World War II. No matter the cost, the result was a promise that life would soon be brighter, easier, and filled with more leisure time than anyone had ever known. And in that way the World of Tomorrow looked hopeful to a degree that it hasn't ever since.

This book came about as the result of an accidental finding one day as I was strolling around the grounds of Flushing Meadows–Corona Park, the site of both the '39 and '64 World's Fairs. There, buried in the ground outside of the only remaining building from the 1939 Fair (which now houses the Queens Museum of Art), is a historical marker detailing the events of July 4, 1940. And yet, of the numerous visitors to the Fair that I spoke to, no one remembered anything about it. Several of them assured me that I must be mistaken.

But it's true. In fact, every detail of this book is nonfiction; all of the quotes come from a letter, speech, or other documented source, and I have cited as many facts as seems reasonable without going overboard. There's a temptation in research to footnote every sentence. But that's impossible and, I feel, unnecessary. You can't write history without filling in the blanks or you'll leave a lot of blanks. For advice, I turned to a former professor, a true mentor and noted historian, Edward Chalfant. In the first of his three-volume biography of Henry Adams, he offers this perfect summation of the process:

"What the biographer does is tirelessly imagine story after story until a story comes to mind which is in every respect sustained and in no respect undermined by all the available evidence, precisely understood. Then the biographer tells that story."

That is what I have done in this book. If there are nagging questions that arise in the reader's mind: "How does he know what Grover Whalen's mood was?", suffice it to say that the answer lies in the body of evidence as a whole. That is, if attendance at the Fair was below expectation, I find it justified to state that its president was worried. The minutes of the Fair Corporation's board meetings support that assumption.

In any case the reader can rest assured that I have analyzed the research, have documented as much as possible, and then taken a step back and filled in the pieces where necessary. To my knowledge, those pieces are as accurate, and as few, as possible.

This Brief PARADISE

A world's fair is its own excuse. It is a brief and transitory paradise, born to delight mankind and die. . . . International expositions do not *prevent* wars; they go on *despite* wars. They don't solve the problems of depression and unemployment; they persist in the face of depressions. The world's fair idea is tough and durable, and the reason is this: people think they're just wonderful.

—George R. Leighton,
Harper's Magazine

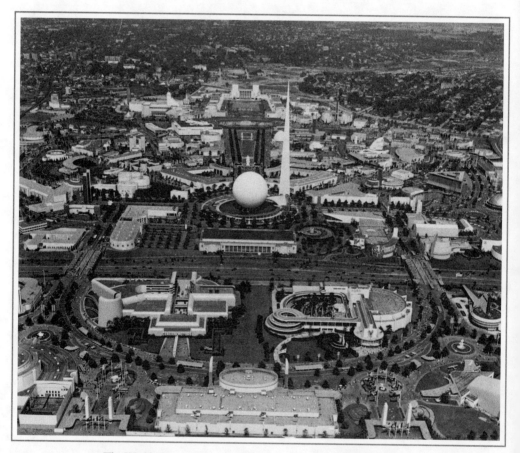

The World of Tomorrow, 1939 *(Courtesy of the New York Public Library)*

FROM ASH HEAPS
TO UTOPIA

On the Fourth of July 1940, Detective Joe Lynch was enjoying a rare Thursday afternoon at home. Given the current situation, any day off from his frenzied routine with the NYPD's Bomb Squad was a bonus. Ordinarily, on a big holiday like this, he might have treated his family to a picnic out at Rockaway Point Beach. He had his eye on a nice little cottage out there that he hoped to someday buy as a summer retreat for his wife and five children.

But not today. Although he was officially on duty, the department had allowed him to spend the afternoon at home as long as he was available via telephone if something came up. Not that it mattered much; a miserable stretch of rain had been soaking the city for days and pretty much canceled out anyone's plans for a summer outing. Despite the weather, Lynch, sitting in his cramped two-bedroom apartment in the Kingsbridge section of the Bronx, listened to the rumble of the elevated train outside his window and thought of the ocean.

This summer especially was not the time for leisurely fun, holiday or no holiday. The second season of the World's Fair was in full swing, and every New York City cop knew what it meant to have something so large and so popular going on right in his backyard. There was a tremendous influx of tourists, for one thing—millions of them, if you believed the newspapers. And along with them came the usual cast of characters who made it their business to rob the rubes of their money and anything else they could think of. There were security issues, safety issues, vagrant issues, and vice issues: More crowded city hotels meant more men seeking more women who wanted company, both legitimate and otherwise. It was no secret that the Fair featured nude and nearly nude models cavorting in several shows in the Amusements Area. And that sort of thing couldn't help but promote some inherent desire for an after-hours liaison between spectator and performer.

Lynch knew all this, but he had more pressing concerns on his mind. A World's Fair of this magnitude attracted all kinds of agitators who would go to any extreme to make a political statement, especially now that war had broken out in Europe. And it had been just his luck that right before the Fair opened, he and his partner, Freddy Socha, had been assigned to the seemingly dichotomous duties of what was known as the Bomb and Forgery Squad.

It was easy duty at first. They spent most of their time studying endless documents for signs of fakery—a repetitive and mind-numbing task. But it was also considered a good path for promotion, and at the time, Joe had been glad to get the assignment. Chasing down crackpot bomb threats was only a sideline, and thankfully they almost always turned out to be false alarms. On the few occasions when a suspicious package was found, especially if it happened to be ticking, standard procedure was to immerse the object in motor oil in order to defuse it. The squad's most memorable moment had come when they'd successfully deactivated a cuckoo clock.

The two detectives got along well. Lynch, lantern-jawed and handsome, had more the look of a Hollywood star than a street cop. In fact, he bore a striking resemblance to manly actor John Payne, the singing boxer in that year's hit *Kid Nightingale* but better known a few years later as the defender of Santa Claus in *Miracle on 34th Street*. Socha, from Greenpoint, Brooklyn, was less than two years older but had five years' more experience on the force than Joe and was nowhere near as good-looking. With his round face, receding hairline, and double chin, he reminded his fellow officers of Mayor Fiorello La Guardia.

To each man's pleasant surprise, the Fair's inaugural season the previous summer had passed without a major incident. Earlier that year, however, the partners began investigating a string of bomb threats against ocean liners, bridges, and foreign consulates. Lynch and Socha were kept busy in the scramble to investigate every claim, however dubious the source. Despite the fact that as winter turned to spring no actual bombs were found, their boss, Lieutenant James Pyke, was clearly concerned. He urged Police Commissioner Lewis Valentine to double the security around all piers, convinced that it was only a matter of time before the threats became acts.

He wasn't wrong. In May 1940, the World's Fair reopened. By June, the bombings turned deadly.

It began as a waste-management project. From the turn of the century through the early 1930s, the Brooklyn Ash Removal Company, owned and operated by a tightfisted Tammany man named John "Fishhooks" McCarthy,* dumped more than a hundred railroad cars of ash, trash, and even animal carcasses a day into its repository in a Queens neighborhood called Flushing Meadows Corona Park. From 1909 to 1935, the area became known as "the Corona Dumps"—a fetid, foul-smelling swamp of decay that stank in summer and choked in winter. Mountains of ash were known to rise as high as one hundred feet.

In a novel he had originally called *Among the Ash-Heaps and Millionaires* (until his editor, Max Perkins, convinced him to change it to *The Great Gatsby*), F. Scott Fitzgerald described the scene as "a valley of ashes—a fantastic farm where ashes grow like wheat into ridges and hills and grotesque gardens."

And then, something just short of a miracle happened. An out-of-work Belgian engineer named Joseph Shadgen suggested the site as the perfect location for a World's Fair, and the idea caught on like wildfire. Mayor La Guardia banned all privately owned dumping grounds within city limits; Fishhooks sold his dump to the city for $2.8 million; and out of

---

* Although "Fishhooks" sounded like an appropriate nickname for a garbage dump owner, it actually stemmed from his famous inability to reach for his wallet whenever a dinner check arrived at his table.

the ash heaps, City Parks Commissioner Robert Moses saw a new kind of Promised Land: a World's Fair that would build a dream city quite literally out of garbage.

Groundbreaking ceremonies were held on June 29, 1936, and even the officials who attended were shocked by the stench and squalor of the site. Nevertheless, in three years' time the Fair would open, and it would be bigger, grander, and more spectacular than any exposition to date— more than three times the size of Chicago's "A Century of Progress" World's Fair just six years earlier.

More important to the people of 1930s America, it boldly, bravely presented a mind-boggling vision of the Future (usually with a capital "F"). General Motors spent a whopping $7 million (around $100 million in today's dollars) on its Futurama exhibit, a fantastic ride through the wondrous world of 1960. In fact, the Fair presented an astounding number of inventions and new technology that would change the culture in decades to come. Television made its debut on Opening Day with a speech by President Franklin D. Roosevelt;* AT&T introduced "Pedro the Voder," a synthetic human speech device; and over in RCA's "Radio Living Room of Tomorrow," the *New York Herald Tribune* was transmitted over a "facsimile" device at the rate of one page every eighteen minutes.

But of course not every futuristic prediction would come true. The Westinghouse exhibit paraded a seven-foot-tall cigarette-smoking robot named Elektro who "talks, sees, smells, sings and counts with his fingers." Westinghouse also buried a time capsule containing millions of pages of microfilm along with such everyday objects as a pair of Mickey Mouse ears and a pack of Camel cigarettes. And at what point in the future was this time capsule to be opened? Not in the year 2039, or 2539, or even 2939. No, this "cross-section of today's civilization" was buried with the intention of its being unearthed in 6939—a full five thousand years hence.

In 1939, when they said the Future, they *meant* the Future.

---

* More accurately, regularly televised programming made its American debut that day. Television itself had been around in various forms for approximately three decades by 1939, and in Great Britain, the BBC had begun regularly televised programming three years earlier. The use of the word *television* here and on Opening Day is intended to mean the publicly accessed medium as we know it today.

It was called many things: the Mad Meadows, the Whalensian Wonderland (after its grandiose president, Grover Whalen), and the Flushing Follies. Some described it as "a dream city of the future," others as "a nightmare of design gone bad." Visitors to the Fair remembered it as either "one of white enchantment that extended my knowledge of the world" or "the twilight of darkness that would encompass the world and my own life for the next six years." One astute witness noted it simultaneously as both "a vision and a warning."

The Dickensian dilemma that was the 1939 New York World's Fair is perhaps best summed up by writer Sidney Shalett in an essay for *Harper's Magazine*:

> It was the paradox of all paradoxes: It was good, it was bad; it was the acme of all crazy vulgarity, it was the pinnacle of all inspiration. It had elements of nobility, features so breathtakingly beautiful you could hardly believe they were real. It also had elements of depravity and stupidity, features that were downright ugly. It proved that Man was noble . . . then it turned right around and proved that Man could also be a simpleton.

In other words, it ran the gamut of civilization—the intended and unintended result of five years' planning, unprecedented expense, and the contribution of a multitude of creative geniuses and the talents of Grover Whalen, "the greatest salesman alive." It gave the American people "an unforgettable opportunity this summer to see themselves as they would wish to be," while at the same time it was "a better Fair than the American people deserve, and probably a better one than they wanted." That these last two observations came from the pen of the same critic, in only the third month of its existence, shows just how puzzling this great Fair was from its very beginning. No one, it seemed, knew what to make of it.

Grover Whalen did. By 1939, he had made a name for himself as New York's dandiest police commissioner, a top-hatted top cop who loved racing after fires in his specially outfitted touring car that allowed him to gleefully blare the siren from his backseat perch. But he was better known as the city's "official greeter," practically inventing the ticker tape parade for visiting celebrities, including Albert Einstein and Howard Hughes. When Charles Lindbergh made his historic flight from New York to Paris in 1927, Grover Whalen was the last man to shake his hand before takeoff at the Roosevelt Field airstrip on Long Island and the first man to welcome him upon his return to the city.

For Whalen, this World's Fair was the culmination of a career defined by maximum public exposure and grandiose spending (though never with his own money). It also capped a life filled with odd coincidences and crosscurrents, an intersection of lives and biographical happenstance that had led him to believe he was living a charmed life. It was almost, he sometimes mused, as if the whole thing—his career thus far, those he had chosen to befriend and model himself after, the odd trajectory of fate that had put him in charge of this Fair—had been planned out in advance.

His singular devotion to bettering himself, and his unflinching surety that greatness was his birthright, had led him out of a life of ordinary hardship and into the realm of the truly exalted. Through hard work and obsessive glad-handing, he had built a World's Fair beyond anyone's wildest dreams. And now, at fifty-two years old, nothing less than the measure of his life depended on its success. His legacy was leveraged solely on the spinning of its turnstiles, and he was never more keenly aware of that fact than on April 30, 1939, Opening Day of the Fair.

True, he had been a New York celebrity for years. In 1930, Cole Porter had immortalized him in his song "Let's Fly Away":

> *I'm tired of having Texas Guinan greet me;*
> *I'm tired of having Grover Whalen meet me.* *

Even Groucho Marx had gotten into the act, adding a line to his famous "Lydia, the Tattooed Lady" and singing, "Here's Grover Whalen unveilin' the Trylon . . ."

---

* Guinan ran a bawdy speakeasy called the 300 Club and was known for her famous greeting, "Hello, suckers!"

He was, according to one journalist, "recognized on the street by more persons than any other New Yorker except Al Smith, Babe Ruth, and Jack Dempsey." But with his leadership of the Fair, Whalen was finally getting the national recognition he felt he so richly deserved.

The whole thing lasted a mere eighteen months, from the end of April 1939 to late October 1940, but during its brief life span the New York World's Fair could be considered the most extravagant folly of its age: a $160 million "World of Tomorrow" built on twelve hundred acres of primeval bog. That it was constructed on a notorious garbage heap stood as a prime example of unintended irony and unbridled optimism for the future, despite the looming certainty of war. That such an undertaking could be conceived at all during the height of the Great Depression is staggering, but no less indicative of the acute hope for a better life to come. And that such enormous sums of money ($2.3 *billion* today) could be spent for its construction seems callous, rather like throwing a party while your neighbor's house is burning down. Nevertheless, its purpose was pure: More than a billion Depression-era dollars was expected to flow into the local economy via tourism.

Unfortunately, things didn't work out as planned. A rain-soaked Opening Day afternoon seemed to portend the Fair's dismal fortunes over the next two seasons. Early morning sunlight and promise faded to evening shadows and misgivings: The Fair opened as a glorious vision of a better life to come and closed in bankruptcy.

It was partly a matter of timing. The difference between September 1938 and that same month just one year later—from British prime minister Neville Chamberlain's "Peace for Our Time" speech to his country's declaration of war against Germany—provided a timeline to the collapse of hope. There was simply no denying that before construction was completed, the World of Tomorrow was already outdated. By Opening Day, two of its pavilions represented countries that, for all practical purposes, no longer existed: Austria and Czechoslovakia. Before the Fair's end, Belgium, Denmark, France, Luxembourg, and the Netherlands, among others, would be added to the list—each nation's collapse ringing like a death knell in the ears of the American public. During the second season, the Polish exhibit would be draped in black, marking exactly half of the Fair's major European pavilions as now under the control of Nazi Germany.

During the Fair's lifetime, the real world of tomorrow would degenerate from something toward which one looked courageously, with no small measure of hope and promise, into a bleak and blank question mark. The national mindset would tilt drastically from optimism to dread, from hopeful emergence out of the Great Depression to saddened acknowledgment of what lay ahead. By early December 1941, a little over a year after the Fair had closed its doors for good, most of its young male visitors would be lining up for induction into war.

The year 1939 also marked a turning point in the life of Albert Einstein. On March 14, he turned sixty at a time when the number meant old age. He celebrated the milestone quietly at home with only his stepdaughter Margot and his longtime secretary, Helene Dukas. Their private family dinner was an altogether different affair from the hoopla that had accompanied the scientist's fiftieth birthday in 1929, when the occasion was marked by a national celebration throughout Germany. Those days were a distant and disturbing memory to him now, but there was still so much more to do.

After a lifetime marked by fame and marred by anti-Semitism, Einstein had immigrated to America and settled in at the Institute for Advanced Study in Princeton, New Jersey. And this year, he had finally applied for naturalization and was looking forward to becoming an American citizen. No doubt his life had changed dramatically. Any thought of returning to his native country was now out of the question. His politics were changing, and the "Hitler problem" weighed heavily on his mind.

A lifelong pacifist, he had on that national occasion a decade earlier announced that he would "unconditionally refuse to do war service, direct or indirect," regardless of the cause. Now he wasn't so sure.

By the summer of 1939, Einstein was happily enjoying an extended vacation at his rented home in Peconic, Long Island. He had been appointed honorary chairman of the Science Advisory Committee to the

World's Fair, and his proximity to Flushing Meadows allowed him to take part in several major events there: He gave a notorious speech on Opening Day that ended in a spectacular power failure; he wrote a message for the time capsule that was both prophetic and terrifying; and most significant, he was chosen over key Zionist leaders to dedicate the opening of the Palestine Pavilion, an honor that propelled him out of the quiet privacy of scientific study and into the stormy political arena as a de facto leader of the Jewish people.

(His name had one more connection to the Fair: In a midway show called the Congress of Beauties, model Yvette Dare had trained a macaw named Einstein to remove her bra in time with the beating of tom-toms.)

That year, he also apparently failed to see the connection between his most famous work and the development of a new kind of weapon that he would have almost nothing to do with, but with which his name would forever be associated. As recently as his sixtieth birthday, he had written, "Our results so far concerning the splitting of the atom do not justify the assumption of a practical utilization of the atomic energies released in the process."

The "utilization" would come to Einstein that summer, brought to him by a friend and former colleague who interrupted an afternoon sail with a theory that would change the world. Fifteen years later, close to death, Einstein would recall his actions during 1939 and 1940, the course of the World's Fair, as the "one great mistake in my life."

At a little after four o'clock on the Fourth of July, Joe Lynch got the call he was dreading—another bomb threat at the World's Fair. He listened with only faint interest; a few weeks earlier, he had investigated a phony claim that had been called into the Italian Pavilion. Yet this was a weird one: An electrician working at the British Pavilion had found a suitcase tucked away in a utility room that was off-limits to the general public. Without thinking, he had picked it up and carried it to his boss's office, where the two of them discovered it was "ticking like a clock."

Joe promptly hung up and called Freddy Socha's house. He was in luck; Freddy was off that day, but the rain had kept him at home as well.

The two of them made plans to hustle out to the fairgrounds and check this thing out. With any luck, Joe told his wife, they could do the job quickly and he'd be home in time for supper.

What neither man counted on was that the ticking suitcase in Queens would grip the city in a manic manhunt, a bomb frenzy, and a fury of anti-Nazi paranoia for the next year and a half. At one point, Commissioner Valentine placed every police officer on twenty-four-hour duty and added to the fear and furor by warning the public, "This is only the beginning."

It was, and it would not stop until December 7, 1941, capping a historic series of events that began in 1934 with a man on a mission and a little girl's recitation of what she had learned in school that day.

PART ONE

The DEVIL TO PAY

When a fair is over, there is frequently the devil to pay. For often as not World's Fairs result in thumping deficits.

—*Time* magazine, 1939

The Flushing Meadows site, pre-construction *(Courtesy of the New York Public Library)*

1

"WHY DON'T YOU DO IT, DADDY?"

By all accounts, 1934 was a remarkable year: Flash Gordon made his first appearance in the comic strips, and Frank Capra's *It Happened One Night*, starring Clark Gable and Claudette Colbert, would go on to win every major Academy Award. In May, one of the worst storms of the Dust Bowl swept away massive heaps of Great Plains topsoil; in August, Adolf Hitler became Germany's new Führer. Pretty Boy Floyd, Baby Face Nelson, Bonnie and Clyde, and John Dillinger were all gunned down in spectacular, tabloid-titillating fashion. On Broadway, Ethel Merman opened in Cole Porter's big new hit, *Anything Goes*; while farther uptown, in Harlem, seventeen-year-old Ella Fitzgerald made her singing debut at the recently christened Apollo Theater.

But savvy New Yorkers, sophisticated or streetwise, had something much more important on their minds. The repeal of Prohibition the previous December had made it easier and cheaper, if somewhat less fun, to spend an evening socializing over a glass of beer or a highball. Almost overnight, some thirty thousand–plus speakeasies in the city closed their doors for good, to be replaced by everything from the neighborhood saloon to the tony, upscale supper club. In the late summer of that year, at a cocktail party held in an unremarkable tavern in Kew Gardens, Queens, that was neither saloon nor salon, a small group of would-be swells mingled and chatted amiably. They were by no means the cream of society (the Kew Gardens location could attest to that), but some could claim proximity, or at least relation, to it.

One in particular was Edward Roosevelt, a stout, balding, bespectacled man whose round face and weak chin gave him the look of an elementary school principal or a henpecked husband. He was, however, a second cousin of Eleanor Roosevelt and a sixth cousin of her husband, the president. The association wasn't doing him much good at the moment, though; like a lot of other people in the country at that time, he was looking for work. He'd spent most of his adult life in Europe as an executive at Ford and International Harvester, but now that he was back in New York, he was living at a YMCA on West Twentieth Street that catered mostly to the merchant marine. Despite his portly physique, he paid for his room and board by working as a recreational instructor. Leading ancient, long-retired sailors in meaningless exercises seemed like the depths of misery, and Roosevelt kept mostly to himself and waited for something better to come along.

The party was in full swing when a friend tapped Roosevelt on the arm and introduced him to an energetic, sophisticated-looking man who seemed particularly anxious to meet him. Edward squinted over his wireless glasses and tried to decide exactly who would benefit whom over this introduction.

"Mr. Roosevelt, this is a Mr. Shadgen," his friend stated, adding, "Who has some distinct ideas about fine wines."

Edward, having lived for quite some time in France, had developed an interest in wines and decided to give this stranger his full attention. At forty-three years old, Joseph Shadgen was broad-shouldered and stood six feet tall, a somewhat impressive figure compared with Roosevelt. Moreover, he was neatly dressed and impeccably well groomed. With the high sweep of his neatly combed, distinguished gray hair and the little swoosh of a silvering mustache that barely exceeded the width of his nose, he looked like a middle-aged Charles Boyer. Before Shadgen opened his mouth to speak, Roosevelt probably sensed he was European. The little bow he gave as they shook hands confirmed it.

The two men, approximately the same age, shared a remarkable economic history, each having achieved an impressive degree of success early in life, only to find themselves thrust into financial uncertainty as a result of the Depression. The major difference between them was that Roosevelt was an American who had sought his glory in Europe, while Shadgen was a European who had tried to seize the day in America.

As they spoke, casually at first, Roosevelt must have noticed that Shadgen carried with him, in his manner and his carriage, something of an aristocrat, deserved or not. Although raised as a citizen of Belgium, Shadgen had been born in the Grand Duchy of Luxembourg, and when one has had a grand duke as monarch, a little touch of nobility remains. In 1915, he had immigrated to America, and for the last ten years he'd worked as a civil and mechanical engineer for the firm of C. H. Smoot & Company. He liked to describe himself as an "idea man" and often boasted that he had once made as much as $150,000 a year.

This, unfortunately, was not one of those years. When Charles Howard Smoot died in 1933, Shadgen abruptly left the company and moved his wife and young daughter from their oceanfront home in Brooklyn to a modest house in Jackson Heights, Queens—a sparsely populated area hard hit by hard times. He drove an old Packard that he kept in cold storage because it had recently refused to run.

When the conversation finally got around to wine, Shadgen's Belgian accent added a distinctly continental air of sophistication to his pitch. For the last few months, he said, he had been working as a technical consultant for the Rockefeller Liquor Study, which had been anticipating all sorts of calamities now that the public was allowed to drink themselves silly again. And with the repeal of Prohibition, the trading and purchasing of fine wines would surely regain its popularity with the Manhattan elite. But since most of them lived in apartments, however large, where on earth were they going to store it?

His idea was to form a company; rent a large, underground space somewhere on Manhattan's Upper East Side (around twenty-five thousand square feet, he reckoned); and divide the area into mini–wine cellars. Then all he had to do was rent the units, make sure the proper temperature was maintained, etc., etc., and he could sit back and rake in the money. All he needed, Shadgen said, was a partner who could help him rope in a few key investors to get it off the ground.

Edward nodded and listened intently. The fundamentals of Shadgen's wine storage idea seemed sound. With sufficient start-up money, there was indeed no limit to the number of subterranean wine lockers they could sublease.

From the start, it was an unlikely partnership. Shadgen was a good talker who needed a door opener; Roosevelt was a (currently, at least) poor relation who needed a project to which he could attach himself and the meager connections his name brought with it. Miraculously, when the effect of their drinking wore off the next morning, Roosevelt still thought it was a good idea, and one that required immediate action. Shadgen and his new partner spent the better part of the next several weeks almost inseparable—scouring suitable storage locations, sketching out plans, and hunting down investors to fund the whole thing. They even rented desks in a cramped real estate office from which they would run their little company until the profits started flowing in. It was all going well except for one small detail: Nobody else thought the idea had merit, and no one would invest.

After weeks of frustration, watching his savings dwindle and his hopes of turning his friendship with a bona fide Roosevelt into his much-deserved fortune, Shadgen decided to give the partnership one more try. Privately, he had another idea in mind—one much larger in scope and scale than the wine storage concept. In fact, it was so huge that he'd been reluctant to share it with anyone, let alone his new partner.

It had come to him earlier that year, on a warm spring evening while he waited for dinner and made small talk with his twelve-year-old daughter, Jacqueline, who had just returned home from school. As she entered the room, still wearing her uniform from the nearby Blessed Sacrament Convent, Shadgen pulled her up next to him and asked, "Well, what did you learn in school today?"

Jacqueline was probably too old for the question, but she answered it anyway. "I learned that the United States is a hundred and fifty-eight years old this year," she told him.

Her father simply stared at her in silence. "Because the Declaration of Independence was signed in 1776," she explained.

Shadgen thought this over. He had a surprising grasp of American history for a foreigner, or perhaps because of it. This didn't make sense to him. The Declaration of Independence was merely that, he told her—a *declaration*, the signing of a document that spelled out only what the Founding Fathers *intended* to do. The nation, he believed, wasn't really "born" until it elected its first president, George Washington, in 1789.

Jacqueline gave him a suspicious look, and the two began to argue. It was the word of the sisters at Blessed Sacrament versus her father, who hadn't even been born here and who still spoke with an accent. The Fourth of July 1776 had been drummed into her head for as long as she could remember as the nation's birthday.

"Oh no," he answered firmly. "The United States would be only a hundred and fifty years old in 1939."

When Mrs. Shadgen called out that dinner was ready, the two of them dropped the discussion and headed quietly for the dining room. Still, something had clicked in that stubborn, persistent brain of his.

The idea to host a World's Fair in order to boost New York City's economy at the end of the 1930s should have come from the minds of its great community leaders. It didn't. "Don't get the idea that I was doing any of this for civic good will," Shadgen would later remark. "I was working for two things—money and reputation."

To date, there had been exactly fourteen officially recognized World's Fairs, and all but four of them had lost money. The very first, London's Crystal Palace in 1851, had been managed by Prince Albert himself and advertised its global status as "the Great Exhibition of the Works of Industry of All Nations." *Punch* magazine described it as "the only National Building that an Englishman is not ashamed of." More than six million people visited from all over the world, and the idea caught on—in no small part due to the fact that it had also managed to turn a profit of over $500,000.

The French tried to top it just four years later at their Exposition Universelle of 1855, which introduced the Singer sewing machine, then went hog wild with World's Fair fever, repeating the effort in 1867, 1878, and, most notably, 1889—the Fair most famous for its construction of the Eiffel Tower.

America had gotten into the act when New York copycatted London and held its own Crystal Palace Exhibition in 1853. Although it was housed in a single iron-and-glass building on a four-acre plot of land,* there were four thousand exhibitors when it opened on July 14, and before it closed in November of the following year, more than one million people came to see it. Yet despite the mass influx of tourism into the city, the Fair was a financial flop, losing about $300,000 and leaving a visible legacy of failure when the structure burned to the ground in 1858.

In 1876, Philadelphia (supporting young Jacqueline's assertion) commemorated the nation's birth with its Centennial Exposition, erecting seven magnificent palaces and outspending New York by six times. But America's crown jewel was Chicago's Columbian Exposition of 1893 (named in honor of Columbus's so-called discovery of America four hundred years earlier), more famously known as "the White City." Looking to "out-Eiffel Eiffel," this Fair presented George Ferris's magnificent wheel and became famous as a symbol of architectural classicism that influenced a generation of builders and designers to come. It also had a profound effect on the country's breakfasting habits, introducing Aunt Jemima pancake mix, Shredded Wheat, and Quaker Oats, and on its snacking preferences with Cracker Jack and Juicy Fruit gum.

At over six hundred acres and featuring nearly two hundred buildings, the White City for a time served as a model for the 1939 New York World's Fair: Most of its buildings were temporary structures, there were specially constructed canals and lagoons, and the entire enterprise served to show the world that beauty could be built upon ashes, in this case those left from Chicago's Great Fire, which had destroyed so much of the city some two decades earlier. At a time when the country's total population was sixty-five million, more than twenty-seven million visitors passed through its gates, netting the Fair a handy profit of more than $1 million.

The United States continued its elaborate celebrations with the Louisiana Purchase Exposition of 1904. No longer content to have its expo-

* The area would eventually become known as Bryant Park.

sition be considered merely a *World's* Fair, the city of St. Louis decided to up the ante by calling its Fair a "Universal Exposition." Although it was indeed huge—at twelve hundred acres, it was almost twice the size of the White City—and while sixty-two foreign nations and forty-three (out of forty-five) of the United States participated, there is no documentation to support the fact that any other representatives of the universe actually showed up.

The Fair also contributed to the world one of the most brain-sticking tunes of all time, "Meet Me in St. Louis, Louis," and claimed to be the birthplace of American staples such as the hamburger and hot dog, peanut butter, and cotton candy. It wasn't, but it was nice to think so, and somehow the myth stuck.

Yet the World's Fair that was on everyone's mind in the 1930s was Chicago's second triumph—the Century of Progress exposition of 1933 and 1934. Its signature attractions were the Sky Ride, built in part by the Otis Elevator Company, and a scandalous fan dancer named Sally Rand. Chicago also boasted to its brethren on the Hudson that its Fair had paid off all of its investors and even turned a modest profit, and that a good many hotels along the city's famous Loop had been rescued from receivership by the reigniting of its Depression-starved economy.

Those numbers were key ingredients that lay behind the audacious dreams of Joseph Shadgen. They would also spur the even more feverish visions of the dreamers yet to come.

The next morning, Jacqueline and her father continued to debate the anniversary issue. Shadgen decided to end the debate once and for all by taking her to the one spot he thought would settle the matter. After breakfast, they rode the Second Avenue elevated train down to Federal Hall on Wall Street, to the very place where Washington had been inaugurated. Together, they read the inscription at the base of his statue, miraculously unharmed in the Wall Street bombing fourteen years earlier:

ON THIS SITE IN FEDERAL HALL, APRIL 30, 1789,
GEORGE WASHINGTON TOOK THE OATH AS THE
FIRST PRESIDENT OF THE UNITED STATES OF AMERICA.

Shadgen felt his point had been made, and the little girl probably didn't feel like arguing anymore. Nevertheless, on the ride back to Jackson Heights, Jacqueline innocently asked her father whether there was going to be any kind of celebration to mark this anniversary. After all, in five years' time the country would be one hundred and fifty years old; there ought to be some sort of commemoration.

The idea was no doubt already spinning in his head as he answered that "as far as he knew," there were no plans for any such thing. It all came together: Not only should the country plan something, but the occasion should take place here, in New York City, where the original event had actually occurred.

"Why don't you do it, Daddy?" Jacqueline asked. That single, innocent suggestion set the wheels in motion for a project so large in size and scope, one that would eventually cost so many millions of Depression-era dollars and would forever change the landscape of New York, that neither of them (nor anyone else at the time) would scarcely have believed it was possible.

That it would also have serious and destructive effects on her father's life and reputation could similarly not be imagined.

By the time they exited the Queens Boulevard line at Roosevelt Avenue, Shadgen's mind was already off and running. A few stations past their stop, the subway would eject passengers in a neighborhood called Corona, where the world's most infamous garbage dump sat festering in the muggy afternoon air.

"I first began to think seriously of this idea of a World's Fair for New York," Shadgen recalled, " . . . about July 1934. Working independently at first, my idea became concrete and I carried out surveys and researches covering the five boroughs of New York. I completed all my thought on this idea before telling anyone about it. And when my mind had finished working on it, well, to put it frankly, I was scared. I did not discuss it with anyone for at least six weeks, until I regained the courage of my convictions."

When "the idea was really ready for submission to anyone," he said, "I spoke of it to some business associates."

Whether or not Shadgen was ready to present a project of such magnitude to his partner, the failure of his wine storage company gave him the fortitude to approach Edward with this mind-boggling idea, however ludicrous it might seem to him. To support his case, he had deduced that the best location for the eventual fairgrounds would be the site that had so damaged his neighborhood, all of Queens, and, by extension, New York City itself for decades: the Corona Dumps.

On a bright fall morning in 1934, Shadgen hurried into their makeshift office to tell him the news. "Ed, this wine storage idea isn't going to work out," he said. "But I've got another idea. Let's put on a World's Fair."

"New York lives because of its great port," he explained. Without the port, New York "would be just a burg." The city needed business; it needed tourism, money. What could bring in money better than a World's Fair? Chicago's Fair had just closed its doors for good, after two successful seasons. And what could be done in Chicago could be done right here in New York. Bigger, even, and better, with greater financial reward.

Shadgen hurried on, filling in the details, the occasion of Washington's inauguration in 1789 and the upcoming anniversary in April 1939. Chicago's Fair had taken exactly five years from concept to opening; they had almost as much time to create a New York version. After all, New York had a larger population and a better occasion to celebrate. Chicago's Century of Progress theme had marked the Second City's centennial, but that was merely a statewide anniversary. This one commemorated the birth of the entire nation and therefore, he reasoned, would attract more people.

"I firmly believe that the holding of the World's Fair here will augment New York's civic pride and city-mindedness, as well as stimulate business," he said. It was a difficult point to dispute.

The more Roosevelt heard, the less skeptical he became. The idea had merit. After a few more conversations and prolonged arguments about the details, Roosevelt thought he knew who could get the ball rolling for them.

Ironically or not, the man Edward Roosevelt chose to advance Shadgen's World's Fair idea was also named Roosevelt, and like Edward, he was a second cousin to Eleanor and sixth cousin to the president. He was also Edward's first cousin, and his name was Nicholas. Shadgen must have felt his head spinning.

This Roosevelt, however, had fared somewhat better in life than his counterpart. Nick Roosevelt, a Harvard graduate, was an editorial writer for both *The New York Times* and the *Herald Tribune,* two of the most respected daily newspapers of their day. As such, he had access to that particular breed of people who got things done in New York. Nick, who probably felt some sort of familial pangs for his down-on-his-luck cousin, agreed to take a meeting.

After making the proper introductions, Edward sat back and let Shadgen give his speech. He went into great detail about his qualifications as an engineer and his diligent survey of the region, anticipating that Nick might find it a ludicrous idea, considering the source.

As it turned out, he was impressed; moreover, he knew exactly the best person to present it to. He picked up the telephone and started dialing. Shadgen, elated that the team had progressed up another rung of the ladder, prayed for two things: that the man on the other end was indeed a bona fide ball roller, and that he wasn't named Roosevelt.

He wasn't. After a brief conversation, Nick made an appointment for them to go and see, as he described him, a "banker" named George McAneny, a man he knew personally since McAneny was also an executive manager of the *Times*. Nick hung up the phone and smiled at them. After offering a few words of advice, he armed the partners with a letter of introduction and sent them on their way. Grateful and terrified, they left his office, knowing they had their work cut out for them.

For one thing, George McAneny was no ordinary banker. At sixty-five he was, in fact, president of the Title Guarantee and Trust Company. In the second decade of the century, he had served as Manhattan borough president, president of the New York City Board of Aldermen, and chairman of the Transit Commission of the State of New York. Most important to the cause of a World's Fair, since 1929 (the year of its founding) McAneny had been president of the Regional Plan Association.

Here at last, Shadgen realized, was the man who could indeed spin one of his ideas into gold. When the day of their meeting finally came, Roosevelt and Shadgen were ready—perhaps a little over-ready. They had even taken the liberty of drawing up a few "rough plans" for their vision of this World's Fair.

The two men entered McAneny's impressive office and steeled themselves. McAneny, with his close-cropped hair parted in the middle and his old-fashioned, high-collared suit and pince-nez, looked every bit the high-powered executive he was. He greeted them formally, sat with his hands folded politely on his desk, and waited for them to begin.

With typical audacity Shadgen stood up, laid his makeshift sketches across the banker's desk, and dug into the backbone of his vision. For nine months, he said, he had been studying a nasty situation not far from his home in Jackson Heights, knowing that something had to be done about the abomination known as the Corona Dumps. He watched as carload after carload of coal dust and carcasses unloaded from the train tracks of the Brooklyn Ash Removal Company, quietly fuming, as did every one of his neighbors, at the fumes.

McAneny shrugged but seemed interested. The Corona Dumps had been considered a blight on New York City since the turn of the century, but the site had grown so large and so intractable that the funds needed to clear it would total in the tens of millions. Given the current economic situation, the project was unthinkable.

Nevertheless, Shadgen carefully described a method for "reclaiming the land, pumping up new land [and] dredging channels." When McAneny failed to see the connection, Shadgen repeated almost verbatim the sales pitch he had given both Roosevelts regarding his idea for a World's Fair, then delivered his ace. After he had eliminated seven possible locations for the Fair, he'd found one "which had more space than anything near the center of the city, and better traffic conditions than anything else available in outlying districts.

"Flushing Meadows," he stated proudly, "was a good place to hold the Fair."

McAneny leaned back in his tall banker's chair and nodded at the two men.

"My dear Mr. Roosevelt and Mr. Shadgen," he began, "a number of us have been sitting around talking off and on for three years, trying to figure out what to do about the commercial situation in New York."

He waited, savoring the moment. Roosevelt and Shadgen held their breath. "I think you gentlemen have found the solution," McAneny said, with an uncharacteristic smile.

The ball, finally, was rolling.

In fact, it began to roll with more power than either Shadgen or Roosevelt could compete with. As it turned out, this meeting with George McAneny had been the high point of Shadgen's involvement with the Fair; faster than he could have imagined, his role in its development became secondary and almost meaningless.

Yet despite the urgency of a deadline, McAneny took his time getting things officially started. Speed was never one of his virtues (newspapers often referred to him as "Mañana Mac"); careful planning was. Over the next few months, he organized a seemingly endless series of luncheons with what he considered to be the city's appropriate business and civic leaders. Most of these he held at the Oval Room of the Ritz-Carlton Hotel, of which he was conveniently a director. His primary cohorts in these affairs included Percy S. Straus, president of Macy's; William Church Osborn, a prominent attorney; Henry Bruere, president of the Bowery Savings Bank; Matthew Woll, president of the Building and Construction Trades Council of the American Federation of Labor; and Grover Whalen, by then chairman of the board of Schenley Distillers Corporation but better known as the best promotions man in the country.

It was a stunningly impressive group, and by contrast Shadgen and Roosevelt were just a pair of pikers. The first hint of their secondary status in the presence of such captains of industry came from Whalen himself. At one of McAneny's luncheons, he leaned across the table and, in his best ingratiating manner said, "Mr. Shadgen and Mr. Roosevelt, I have great admiration for you. I congratulate you for spending so much time working for the good of our city."

With Whalen's subtle suggestion of the past tense, he might as well have ended his statement with, "Thank you. And goodbye."

As winter turned to spring and spring into summer, McAneny kept up the pace of these meetings, until at one time or another he had met with and subsequently fed every merchant, banker, lawyer, and architect he deemed worthy of an invitation. Privately, he also met with Mayor La Guardia, Governor Herbert Lehman, and even FDR himself, each of whom expressed a "lively interest" in the Fair and, without committing to anything, offered to "try to see that it got the backing, both moral and financial," of their respective government branches.

Finally, on September 23, 1935, with three and a half years to go until the anticipated opening, McAneny formally announced a plan for the city of New York to host a World's Fair in 1939. No fewer than sixty mucketymucks were present, and the dinner was once again held at the Ritz. Both Lehman and La Guardia attended. Shadgen and Roosevelt were there as well, but if the Belgian still didn't imagine the degree to which he was being dismissed, he must have sensed something was up when he read the list of names that made up the Fair's newly formed steering committee in the papers the next day: Nicholas Roosevelt was on it; he and Edward were not.

At the dinner, McAneny boldly stated that the Fair's opening would have to be April 30, 1939, in order to mark the inauguration anniversary. The shortened deadline was met with a few harrumphs, but when he declared its intended location, in Flushing Meadows, not a few of his surprised guests slurped their soup in shock. About the only detail he got wrong was his original estimate of the cost, which he figured would be somewhere in the neighborhood of $40 million total.

Both the mayor and the governor spoke, and McAneny read a telegram from President Roosevelt in support of the idea. And when a few questions arose about the logistics of converting the horror that was the Corona Dumps and the surrounding Flushing Meadows area into anything remotely resembling parkland, McAneny dropped a name that silenced the detractors.

"The subject of the site was taken up some weeks ago," he reassured them, "with Parks Commissioner Robert Moses, who also examined the various possibilities and declared emphatically in favor of the Flushing plan."

An exchange of raised eyebrows and hushed whispers ensued. Moses was already enjoying his reputation as a man who got things done despite impossible odds.

It was Moses's belief, McAneny went on, "that a development of great beauty may be worked out both on the shore and through the meadow area, and that the picture of a new White City on the edge of the bay would prove a fascinating one."

Suddenly, all were in agreement. Flushing Meadows it would be. After all, what was good enough for Moses was good enough for them.

When McAneny had first brought the concept of a World's Fair to the attention of Robert Moses, he told him, "We have a great idea and we want your help."

Moses, as if seeing the answer to all his problems, pounded on his desk and shouted, "My God, that *is* a great idea!"

Instantly, he recognized the plan for what it was: a means to an end. By his own account, from the very beginning Moses cared less about the Fair than its aftermath. "I am waiting for another and less dramatic event," he admitted, "the night when the Fair closes. . . . In another quarter of a century, old men and women will be telling their grandchildren what the great Corona Dump looked like in the days of F. Scott Fitzgerald . . . and how it was all changed overnight."

His vision was that of a park to end all parks, one and a half times the size of Central Park, that would be known as "the Versailles of America." In fact, he had been trying to get the thing built for years. The site he had in mind was the exact location McAneny had suggested for the World's Fair—a square-mile patch of land that had been subjected to the most extreme degrees of decay despite its prime location at the geographic center of New York City's five boroughs.

Moses, never one to underestimate himself, took his inspiration from the Bible: "Give unto them beauty for ashes." In 1931, he had begun construction on the Grand Central Parkway, connecting the city with Nassau

County in order to provide better access to Jones Beach, his most famous state park to date.* His decision to build the new parkway through the western edge of the Corona Dumps also carried the secondary goal of reclaiming the land around it.

"This was the logical place for it," he explained, "but only on the assumption that there was to be a general reclamation of the entire surrounding area."

Once the parkway was completed, Moses felt sure that when city government officials saw all that traffic cutting right through an unsightly garbage dump, they would allocate the funds to allow him to clean it up. They didn't. He got the money for the road and nothing more.

"An agreement was made," Moses insisted. "Construction on the parkway began. But the state work was limited strictly to work within an ordinary parkway right of way. The artery was, therefore, driven through the dump in the form of a chute, with great mountains of ash and refuse on each side."

Clearly, this was not what Moses had in mind. Although he had cleared away fifty million cubic yards of ash, the parkway did little more than cut a tiny swath through the muck. "We fondly hoped to cover [the garbage] with a thin layer of topsoil and to plant, at a price which would not subject us to indictment," Moses said. He couldn't even get the money for the topsoil.

"This dream," he realized, "seemed too big for the vision and means of the city in the face of competition of so many other urgent enterprises."

But then, as he later put it, "The miracle happened—the idea of a World's Fair."

Even as McAneny's words were falling from his lips, Moses heard the word *Fair* but thought of the word *park*. The World's Fair was a hurdle, a two-year blip that would be gone in the snap of a finger. His park, on the other hand, would be one for the ages. Immediately, he drew up a lease for the land that contained the provision "from the beginning the project was planned so as to insure a great park" once the Fair was over and torn

---

* In an oddly familiar assessment, Moses described the original beach site as "a mosquito-infested tidal swamp full of stagnant pools." When Moses first brought the idea of a state park to his architects, one of them reportedly asked him, "Are you crazy?"

down. The improvements, including the infrastructure—the sewers and pipes and electrical cables—would all be constructed not for the Fair, but for what came after.

"Everything of a permanent nature must be part of the plan for the ultimate park which was to be completed once the Fair was over," he repeatedly insisted. He also included plans for fountains, boat basins, and not one but two man-made lakes. After all, what would Versailles be without fountains?

Undeterred by the site's squalor, Moses immediately began surveying the land, noting that he would have to transform "thirty years of the off-scourings, tin cans, cast-off baby carriages and umbrellas of Brooklyn." The rats, as he described them, were "big enough to wear saddles."

McAneny knew what he was doing when he approached Robert Moses with the proposed location. Transforming it would be a tremendous job, and no ordinary person, seeing the density of refuse and the sheer vastness of such a wasteland, would believe it could be done. Moses thought otherwise. He knew how government worked. He understood that all it took was money, but that in order for the money to be committed there had to be a clear explanation of why the public was spending that money. McAneny gave it to him.

And once Moses came on board, the whole thing had a grander purpose to it. The World's Fair would help create a permanent park for the residents of New York City; the park itself would make the expense of a Fair seem somehow more palatable to the taxpaying public. It was the perfect storm of needs and wants on behalf of the city itself. And since La Guardia had now delegated the dumps as parkland, it all came under the supervision of Robert Moses, its new landlord.

Not that there weren't lingering doubts, even among the leaders of this steering committee. In October, Moses took the mayor and a couple of city officials out to look the site over. "All my predecessors have something to answer for," La Guardia said. "[It] is the most remarkable thing I've ever witnessed," with "landscaping possibilities that challenge the imagination."

As they circled the swampy tract in an open car, La Guardia expressed his concern that the land couldn't possibly provide a solid foundation for all the buildings to be erected. The mayor, it was reported, "did not appear to be particularly pleased at what he saw there."

When a reporter asked Moses what *he* had seen, the parks commissioner smirked, held his hands about a foot apart, and replied with one word: "Rats."

The site notwithstanding, by the end of the month incorporation papers had been drawn up and filed, and New York World's Fair, Inc., was born. In November, its board of directors voted George McAneny as president and another banker, Harvey Gibson, president of Manufacturers Trust Company, as chairman. Waiting in the wings, content for the time being to be elected to the executive committee, was Grover Whalen. It was a secondary and practically powerless position in the company; and, as with most of the other appointments in his career thus far, he did not stay in the background for long.

To his unending regret, Robert Moses saw to that.

Grover Whalen (in top hat) escorts Charles Lindbergh in his ticker tape parade, June 14, 1927.
(© Bettmann/Corbis)

2

MR. NEW YORK

Grover Aloysius Whalen had spent his early years nurturing a singular conviction: that his life would matter. He sought the spotlight, but not in ways that others imagined for themselves. He was a born promoter, and because promotion requires something other than oneself to point out its greatness, his place, his niche, would be carved out of the secondary spotlight thrown by those around him whose aura shone greater than his own. Yet by catching those reflected rays, he instinctively knew he would manage to create a cone of his own luminescence. He was comfortable with that, and the knowledge allowed him entrance into levels of wealth and societal standing that he might not otherwise have reached if left to his own limitations.

Whalen also possessed two extraordinary gifts: He was a social climber, and he didn't care who knew it. In the annals of American history, there may never have been a man so comfortable in his skin, with an exact working knowledge of how to use his Irish blarney and bullheadedness to get ahead in life. He was often laughed at, frequently made the butt of public jokes, and for most of his life endured left-handed digs from the press at his dapper appearance.

In an era that reveled in nicknames, reporters dubbed him "Gardenia" Whalen for the ever-present flower pinned to his finely tailored suits (though a white carnation was his preferred boutonniere). His credentials for achieving certain positions—most notably as New York City police commissioner, a position he held for just eighteen months at the close of the 1920s—were constantly questioned and sneered at, as was his effectiveness at his job. None of it mattered to him, nor did it change his outlook or his steadfast resolve to live up to what he considered his birthright. During a meteoric climb through the upper reaches of Manhattan's power circles, Grover "Gardenia" Whalen shrugged off public opinion. He knew what he was, he knew he was right, and not caring what others thought propelled him ever further into greatness.

His was a curious boyhood. Born on the Lower East Side of New York on June 2, 1886, he was named after President Grover Cleveland, whose White House wedding that day made the front pages of every newspaper. His father, Michael Henry Whalen, was a prominent Civil War veteran and an enthusiastic supporter of Tammany Hall, a loyalty that served him well in his own quest for success.

"My father started out in the general contracting business with one horse and a cart," Grover stated. "When he died his business kept seventy-five horses and trucks busy."

At forty-three, Michael Whalen was already on his second family by the time Grover came around. After his first wife died and left him with three children, he married Esther DeNee, a vibrant and vivacious French Canadian who gave him hell about his Irish roots as often as she could get away with it. Before Grover was born, she promptly shipped off Michael's two daughters, Mary and Laura, to neighborhood convents. The third child, a boy named Harry, was left to his own devices. In the short span of five years, Esther bore three children of her own—Gertrude, Grover, and Stephen, named after Cleveland's *vice* president, Adlai Stevenson. Michael was a Democrat through and through, and he wanted his sons' names to reflect that.

Grover's upbringing was neither privileged nor poor; in fact, he seemed to have spent his youth on the cusp of the American Dream. The family home was a brick tenement owned by his father, at 275 East Broadway, not far from the Fulton Fish Market and in the shadows of the

Williamsburg Bridge. Proximity to the waterfront had a profound effect on the young boy; he spent hours watching cargo and passenger ships arrive, imagining the wondrous places they had come from and the exotic passengers and crew they carried. He attended public schools with the children of other immigrant families, but even then he showed signs of the dandy he was to become. In later years, he recalled the "ragging" he took at the hands of his classmates. At the age of seven, his father bought him a fancy brown derby from the upscale Best and Company store, which he promptly lost to a group of tough newsboys on his way home from school.

"My father was so grieved and disgusted," he said, "that from that time on I don't believe he ever bought an article of clothing for me as a present. He took it for granted I'd . . . have it taken away from me."

To toughen up his son, or maybe to show him the true immigrant roots he had been spared by being part of this second wave of Whalens, his father gave him a job collecting rents at several of the other dilapidated tenements he owned. "I remember one house on Madison and Gouverneur Street that had six families in it as well as some extra boarders," he recalled in his autobiography, *Mr. New York*. "When I went there to collect the rent, I found the bathtub had been filled with coal and a board laid on top of the coal. A mattress placed on top of the board served as an extra boarder's bed."

On a later visit, he found that "a second tier had been built over the tub bed, and our tenant was now able to take in no less than two day and two night boarders."

The boy reflects the man, it has been said, and in Grover's case that appears to go double. For one thing, Michael Whalen had an insatiable love of parades. But he was never content to stand on the sidewalk and watch them; whenever he got word that a group of marchers was gathering, Michael would hitch up two of his smartest horses to his finest wagon, wait until it was too late for anyone to object, and then take his place in the procession, all the while smiling and waving and bowing to the crowd as if he alone were the subject of tribute. He wasn't; it was always someone else's party, but who cared when the throngs were cheering so loud and so lovingly.

For Grover, the message was clear: His father may not have been the guest of honor, but everyone knew his name.

That singular fact made a lifelong impression: Michael Whalen was *popular*. Throughout Grover's childhood and on into his high school years at DeWitt Clinton, he watched the old Irishman sitting with his cronies on the sidewalk in front of their home on warm summer evenings; watched as he accepted handshakes from passing city workers, always offering a cigar and greeting them by name; watched as his Tammany connections allowed his father to buy building after building in the neighborhood, growing his wealth and his reputation.

But somewhere he must have known there was a limit to the old man's potential. An Irish immigrant, Michael Whalen was six feet tall and sported a handsome handlebar mustache, but he also carried the essence of his roots as a one-horse street peddler. Grover felt no such limitation, and he vowed that none would ever be placed upon him. He learned from his father the importance of friendships, of relationships with people in power, but his reach would be further, higher. To accomplish this he needed a mentor, a benefactor, someone who not only could introduce him to a world beyond his own experience, but who would guide him in his quest, whispering in his ear the secrets of attaining favor among the rich and powerful.

He found it in the son of another successful businessman, one whose wealth went way beyond a stable of horses, trucks, and multiplanked tenements.

The man he chose was Rodman Wanamaker, and the choice he made was deliberate. After graduating high school, Grover was impatient for the future to deliver on its promises of wealth and fame. In 1904, he entered New York Law School, and it was there that destiny delivered. In need of pocket money, he took a job as a part-time clerk at Wanamaker's, the largest department store in the world at the time. Its owner and founder, John Wanamaker, was nearing seventy years old, but Whalen set out to impress him anyway. Almost immediately, he began a campaign to befriend his son.

"I came to know Mr. Wanamaker well through his son Rodman, who became my friend and sponsor," Whalen said. "Mr. Rodman used to send me books that he knew his father was reading."

More likely, Whalen pressed him for the information, wanting to make an impression on the old man. The ruse worked. The founder, Whalen recalled with obvious glee, "remarked that I seemed to be exceptionally well read! Perhaps this was one of the little things . . . that helped me move up from clerk to executive, then to Director of executive administration, and eventually to General Manager of John Wanamaker, New York, in the next few years."

There was no "perhaps" about it. Before he even entered the political arena, Whalen apparently knew how the game was played. In fact, he was already a master at it. Law school exited the picture when Michael Whalen died in 1907, but by then it didn't matter. His star was rising fast at Wanamaker's, as was his salary and his taste in clothes. In forty-four-year-old Rodman, the twenty-something Grover had found the father figure who would take him out of the Lower East Side and into the palatial store on Broadway and Ninth Street. Still, he needed another ticket to get farther uptown, "into the social stratum that used to be known as lace-curtain Irish."

This time, Anna Dolores Kelly fit the bill. He married her on April 23, 1913, at the Tiffany glass–domed Church of St. Ignatius Loyola, on upper Park Avenue. At twenty-six, Grover Aloysius Whalen had officially arrived.

There was more to do. In 1917, Rodman's influence forced Preston Lynn, the fussbudget general manager of Wanamaker's, to name Whalen as secretary of his Business Men's League—an organization devoted chiefly to ousting John Purroy Mitchel, the current "Boy Mayor of New York." Mitchel had been elected on the Fusion ticket after the murder of an infamous gambler named Herman Rosenthal and the anti-Tammany shake-up that ensued. But that was four years ago, and now Tammany Hall, the once powerful Democratic organization, wanted its influence back. The Business Men's League was determined to get it, and the man they chose to defeat Mitchel was Preston Lynn.

Rodman again interceded, with the help of his father. According to Whalen, "They sent for Mr. Lynn and told him they hoped he would not consider running for mayor, as they needed him to run their New York store." Under the circumstances, it was an astounding request to make: preventing a man from becoming mayor of New York City because you couldn't spare his talents as a floorwalker. Despite the fact that his name had already made the papers as the Democratic choice, Lynn reluctantly declined the offer.

The nomination went instead to a little-known judge named John Francis Hylan, a publicity-shy stooge whose main qualification seemed to be that he would follow orders if elected. Tammany had chosen carefully, sending a glorified garbage man—one Fishhooks McCarthy—to "look over" Judge Hylan. Fishhooks had a reputation as a pretty good "talent scout," and his assessment, approved by the extremely frustrated Preston Lynn, was that "John F. Hylan may not be the most learned and distinguished jurist in the City of New York, but I am sure that if he is nominated for Mayor, he will be elected."

He was. Whalen saw to that. Effectively taking charge of the Business Men's League in the wake of Lynn's rejection, Whalen was put in charge of a secret steering committee that made all the decisions for Hylan. Throughout the campaign, Whalen used his sartorial skills to polish the self-conscious candidate "till he glistened." Shortly before taking office, the mayor-elect asked Lynn for one more favor—that Grover be allowed a leave of absence from Wanamaker's in order to serve as his secretary. Lynn threw up his hands and agreed, and in this case Rodman apparently had no qualms about losing one of his trusted executives.

"He advised me to take the post of Secretary and promised it would not change his plans for my future in the Wanamaker organization," Whalen said.

By the end of World War I, Whalen's admiration for Rodman had grown into a desire to be just like the man. In 1918, Rodman was named chairman of two committees, one to organize a series of massive celebrations for General John J. Pershing and the returning doughboys, the other to greet distinguished guests from around the world. He wasted no time naming Grover as executive vice chairman of both.

"The various parades and celebrations lasted nearly a year," Whalen recalled. "The city turned out en masse."

A familiar image burned in Whalen's mind: Rodman Wanamaker smiling and waving and bowing to the crowd as if he himself were a returning hero. Only this time Grover saw that the cheering throngs weren't made up of the immigrant neighbors of his youth, but numbered in the tens of thousands, and from every level of New York society. Rodman was no doubt Whalen's idol, but this he wanted for himself.

When President Woodrow Wilson returned from a peace conference on July 8, 1919, Grover got his chance at glory. Rodman, a fierce Republican, could not be seen riding in an open car with the Democratic president. Whalen took his place. The son had now come full circle, surpassing both fathers in the admiration of the masses.

Parades quickly became Whalen's forte. When the Prince of Wales visited in November, Grover, having witnessed a handful of clerks throw ticker tape from a couple of office windows in previous celebrations, took the idea an ingenious step or two further.

"I organized a word of mouth campaign along lower Broadway," Whalen boasted. "Some office workers even carried the idea beyond ticker tape. They tore up phone books, waste paper and almost any kind of paper and tinsel they could get their hands on and threw it in great volume from tens of thousands of windows."

He may not have invented the ticker tape parade, but he certainly upped the ante of frenzy, and the blizzard of confetti that has rained down ever since became one of Grover's most famous trademarks. Moreover, since all European visitors arrived by boat, Whalen ordered the municipal fireboats to shoot massive jets of water aloft from their hoses as they docked.

"The Whalen welcomes are always perfectly managed and thumpingly successful," reported *The New Yorker*. Their success, in fact, was partly manufactured. Whalen had wisely decided to stage his parades between noon and one o'clock, when he knew the streets would be full no matter who was being feted: "The visitor is always brought to shore at twelve sharp. Many an honest foreigner's eyes fill with drops of tenderness and gratitude on the ride up Broadway, as he observes the vast throngs which have turned out in honor of lunch."

Added to Grover's genius was the fact that his ceremonial parades just happened to pass right by Wanamaker's store.

B y his second year in office, Mayor Hylan had had enough. Although he had pushed Whalen into the spotlight (a position in which Hylan was never comfortable), Grover was perhaps hogging a little too much of the public's attention. While the papers took to calling the mayor "Red Mike" (referring not just to his flaming hair, but to his notoriously hot temper), Whalen was being referred to as "the brains of the administration." In May 1919, Hylan kicked him upstairs as commissioner of plant and structures, which put Whalen in charge of bridges, ferries, and bus lines. It wasn't far enough. After another year, he approached Rodman Wanamaker and hinted that maybe Grover would like his old job back.

"But I wouldn't want to take him away from you." Rodman grinned, enjoying the mayor's discomfort.

"Never mind me," Hylan replied.

Finally, in 1924, citing the need to make more money for his family, Whalen resigned from politics and returned to Wanamaker's as director of executive administration. His real job was to make sure the parades kept marching past the store, and as usual it didn't last long.

Elsa and Albert Einstein arrive in New York aboard the S.S. *Belgenland*, 1930. (*© Bettmann/Corbis*)

3

A VOLUNTARY EXILE

In December 1932, Albert Einstein and his wife, Elsa, boarded a steamer ship named *Oakland* and set sail for America. They had made the trip on two previous winters, as Einstein preferred the warmer climate of Pasadena, California, where he was a guest lecturer at the California Institute of Technology, to the harsh winters of Berlin. But this time, the trip had greater significance. Einstein's native Germany had become a dangerous place for Jews, and for several years Einstein, perhaps the world's most famous Jew, had been singled out as a particularly nasty target.

In fact, he was in the second decade of anti-Semitic attacks. As early as 1921, a German crackpot named Rudolph Leibus was arrested for offering a reward to anyone who would assassinate Einstein. More than a decade before the Nazis took over, Leibus was fined only $16 for the offense. And now, with what seemed like the inevitable rise to power of Adolf Hitler, the situation turned truly dangerous for Einstein. His life was threatened again, and this time by a more serious faction than Leibus.

Despite his current commitment to Caltech, Einstein had already begun private negotiations with a man named Abraham Flexner, director of the newly created Institute for Advanced Study at Princeton University in New Jersey. Flexner, wanting desperately to have Einstein join his faculty, wooed the scientist with the promise of a "haven where scholars and scientists may regard the world and its phenomena as their laboratory without being carried off in the maelstrom of the immediate."

To Einstein, Flexner's offer seemed irresistible: He was to become the most famous member of a very small but prestigious staff and to have absolutely no duties of any kind whatsoever, except for the occasional lecture. In short, Einstein would be hired merely to do as he pleased, and to think.

When asked how much he would want for such a coveted position, Einstein answered firmly that he required a salary of $3,000 a year.

"Could I live on less?" he asked.

"You couldn't live on that," Flexner replied, counteroffering the impressive sum of $16,000 a year.

Despite the money, Einstein at first demurred. As yet unwilling to leave his homeland for good, he wondered if he could divide his time between Berlin and New Jersey. Finally he settled on a schedule that would require him to be in residence at Princeton from October 1 to April 15 each year. He may still have been unsure of his future as he and Elsa boarded the *Oakland* in Bremerhaven on December 10.

"I am not abandoning Germany," he said as they prepared for their voyage. "My permanent home will still be in Berlin."

Nevertheless, his scientist mind prepared him for any permutation; he and Elsa set sail with thirty trunks stowed in the ship's storage. Einstein was looking forward to their trip. He enjoyed his visits to the United States and was perpetually fascinated by the customs and nature of its people. He also found it particularly amusing that they treated him like a movie star.

"Sometimes the Americans are just children," he said. "You should see them flocking to see me, as if I were a miraculous animal. All this interest is very pleasant, but still sometimes it can be inconvenient."

There were inklings that this voyage from Germany would be their last. A few days earlier, as they were closing up their home, Einstein turned to his wife and said, "Before you leave our villa this time, take a good look at it. You will never see it again." Elsa thought he was just being silly.

Their repeated visits to California, the land of celebrity, had solidified Einstein's reputation as a bona fide star in America. He regretted it, but all the attention seems to have had a positive effect. "Gone was the flustered and bewildered German scientist," one reporter noted after his first three-month stay at Caltech, "who early in December first met a crowd of news gatherers and cameramen . . . and then fled from them in dread. In his place today was a gentleman who was smilingly at ease."

He also found a way to deal with what he considered to be the inane practice of autograph seekers: He began charging them a dollar a pop.

Although Einstein gradually accepted his fame, for the rest of his life he never understood the public's fascination with him. When a popular magazine offered to pay him a large sum of money for an article, he was dumbfounded. "What?" he deadpanned. "Do they think I am a prize-fighter?"

Slowly, Einstein began to accept the idea that all the interest and ballyhoo had less to do with his work than with his own eccentricities. Moreover, he began to suspect that the incomprehensibility of his theories was part of what had made him so popular to begin with. And once that was understood, he began to enjoy it a little more.

"The Einstein of 1933 has become fairly reconciled to the occupation of popular idol," stated *The New Yorker*. "He has developed into a mixer, a wit, an authority on things in general."

Not that America was making it any easier. Before his final departure in 1932, the American Women's Patriotic Organization lodged a complaint against him with the State Department, demanding that the United States deny him an entry visa and calling him a Communist. In response, Einstein joked, "Never before have I experienced from the fair sex such energetic rejection of all advances. Or if I have, never from so many at once!"*

* As with many of Einstein's quotes, there exist several variations of this statement, as American newspapers translated his German using different sources. "Never before has any attempt of mine at an approach to the beautiful sex met with such an energetic rebuff; even should perchance such have ever been the case, then certainly, not by so many all at once," wrote *The New York Times*, which must have consulted a high school textbook for that one. The above seems less literal, certainly more in agreement with Einstein's conversational intention, and undoubtedly funnier.

Unfortunately, the situation grew more serious than at first he was willing to believe. Two days after his off-the-cuff rebuke, the United States Consulate General demanded his presence in order to determine his fitness to visit America. Einstein was incensed; on every other voyage to California, officials of whatever shipping line he traveled on had handled the issuance of visas and other formalities. At first he refused the order; then, accompanied by his wife, he reluctantly appeared at the consulate. They questioned him for forty-five minutes.

"What is your political creed?"

Unable to stop himself, Einstein suddenly burst out laughing. "I don't know," he said when he had finally regained himself. "I can't answer that question."

"Are you a member of any organization?"

Einstein ruffled his hair and turned to Elsa in astonishment. "Oh, yes! I am a War Resister!"

He grew more and more impatient as the minutes, and the interrogation, ticked on. The questions were so inane that Einstein began to believe it was all an elaborate practical joke.

"Gentlemen, are you trying to kid me?" he asked. "Are you doing this to please yourselves or are you acting upon orders from above?"

Finally, when he was asked, "What party do you belong to or sympathize with?" his normally genial expression turned cold and stern. His voice broke.

"What's this?" he cried. "An inquisition? Is this an attempt at chicanery? I don't propose to answer such silly questions. I didn't ask to go to America. Your countrymen invited me; yes, begged me! If I am to enter your country as a suspect I don't want to go at all!"

With that he grabbed his hat and coat, pulled Elsa to her feet, and left the office. That night, they abandoned the thorough packing of their belongings and left Berlin, heading for their country home in Caputh, where despite inquiries Einstein refused to comment on the matter. Elsa spoke for him to a crowd of reporters who had invaded their property.

"If we don't get that visa by noon tomorrow," she said, delivering the ultimatum her husband had dictated for her, "that's the end of our ever going to America again."

Einstein, who had been listening to the commotion from another room, gleefully joined the party now that the fireworks had started. The shocked faces he saw put him back in his old mischievous mood.

"Wouldn't it be funny if they didn't let me in?" He grinned, rubbing his hands together and delighting in the brouhaha he was stirring up. "Why, the whole world would laugh at America!"

The ultimatum did the trick. At eleven a.m. the following morning, Einstein got a call from George Messersmith at the United States Consulate General. He would personally issue a visa that afternoon; there would be no more questioning. Einstein thanked him, hung up the phone, lit his pipe, and smiled broadly. He would submit to all the stupid questions of the world for a victory as sweet as this one.

That afternoon, he and Elsa returned to Berlin and resumed packing. His mood could not have been brighter.

In the 1930s, Einstein himself could be called "the paradox of paradoxes." Perhaps most puzzling of all was the turbulent conflict of his fervent pacifism, which he had confirmed over and over again in public, with his recent militarism regarding Adolf Hitler.

This inner struggle plagued Einstein. He had once described himself as an "absolute pacifist." Now he was becoming a "convinced pacifist," he stated, struggling to define the difference in his own mind as well as for his confused admirers and followers. "That means there are circumstances in which in my opinion it is necessary to use force. Such a case would be when I face an opponent whose unconditional aim is to destroy me and my people."

Despite his dual feelings of nationalism vs. Nazism, the timing of Einstein's departure in December 1932 could not have been better. The following month, Adolf Hitler was sworn in as chancellor of the German government. Had Einstein not left the country seven weeks earlier, he might have spent the remainder of his life in a concentration camp. That is, if they'd allowed him to live at all.

On January 9, they arrived in the Port of Los Angeles. Two weeks later, Einstein attended a public symposium at Caltech that was in part intended to improve relations between Germany and the United States. Einstein's speech, entitled "America and the World Situation," was broadcast world-wide. Oddly, although the occasion certainly called for it, he elected to basically ignore the issue of rising anti-Semitism in his native country.

Instead, he blamed the current tension on economic resentment stemming from World War I: "It has been assumed, namely, that the world Depression for the most part had its origin through war debts," he said. To avoid war, there must be a "moral disarmament . . . through international agreement." America could help make this happen, "if she had not become accustomed to such great aloofness in the field of international politics."

As for America's Depression, which was now entering its fourth and most severe year, Einstein asserted that its roots could be traced back to "the improvement in the apparatus of production through technical invention [that has] decreased the need for human labor . . . and thereby caused a progressive decrease in the purchasing power of the consumer."

And that pretty much summed it up. The rise of Nazism had its roots in economic depression and might lead to war if the newly elected president of the United States, Franklin Roosevelt, continued along his isolationist path. Clearly the great scientist was acting as peacemaker, holding in check, for the time being, his violent hatred for the party that now ruled his homeland.

After their brief sojourn in California, on March 15, 1933, Einstein and Elsa were scheduled to sail from New York back to their home on board an ocean liner ominously named *Deutschland*. But now the voyage, and the question of his ever returning to Germany while Hitler was in power, was doubtful. On March 10, his last day in California, he gave a public statement of his intentions to reporter Evelyn Seeley of the *New York World Telegram*.

"As long as I have any choice in the matter," he said, "I shall live only in a country where civil liberty, tolerance, and equality of all citizens before the law prevail. . . . These conditions do not exist in Germany at the present time."

When Seeley asked where the scientist would go if not to his native homeland, Einstein said he would probably choose to live in Switzerland, where he also held citizenship. He ended the interview, politely explaining that he had one final lecture to present in his commitment to Caltech. Seeley noticed something strange was happening. At that very moment, a massive earthquake was rumbling beneath Los Angeles, a mere twenty miles or so from where they stood.

"As he left for the seminar," Seeley reported, "walking across the campus, Dr. Einstein felt the ground shaking under his feet."

By the time they arrived in New York, Einstein had apparently made up his mind—he reluctantly canceled the homecoming trip aboard the *Deutschland*. In their suite at the Waldorf-Astoria, in case there was any doubt in the matter, he made his position clear: "[I do] not intend to put foot on German soil as long as conditions in Germany are as at present."

In response, the *Berliner Lokal-Anzeiger* (*Berlin Local Advertiser*) commented on the news with the statement "Good news from Einstein—he's not coming back."

Nevertheless, Einstein took no joy in renouncing his country. "Germany's contribution to the culture of mankind is so vital and significant that you cannot imagine the world without it," he said solemnly. Moreover, he hoped the situation was only temporary.

During one of his ocean voyages, Einstein had made an entry in his private diary in which he mused poetically, "I decided today that I shall essentially give up my Berlin position and shall be a bird of passage for the rest of my life. Gulls are still escorting the ship, forever on the wing. They are my new colleagues. . . . How dependent man is on external things, compared to such creatures!"

But Einstein knew he was dependent on such important matters as home, and that even the seagulls he admired eventually gave up the pursuit of flight and turned back toward land. Now Einstein also understood that he was in permanent flight, perhaps with no hope of ever returning to the shore.

As the *Deutschland* sailed for home without them, Einstein and Elsa sat alone in their hotel, the sum total of their belongings packed in crates in the Waldorf's basement. What would become of their town house in

Berlin and their idyllic cottage in Caputh? What would be the fate of their adult children: Albert's two sons, Hans and Eduard; and Elsa's two daughters, Margot and Ilse? And what of the Jews throughout Germany and neighboring Poland and Czechoslovakia and all the countries of Eastern Europe—what was to become of them as well?

It was all a great mystery, a puzzle more unsolvable to the scientist than the mathematics of the universe he had worked his entire life to decipher. The threat, Einstein felt, was "not imminent. But where the danger comes in is that Hitlerism is contagious. This form of political thought and action has unfortunately become fashionable, for there are too many ignorant human beings in the world."

The *Deutschland* had left. Einstein and Elsa remained.

From that moment on, he was a voluntary exile.

With three extra days added to their sojourn in America—Einstein elected to sail for Antwerp on March 18 on the liner *Belgenland* as opposed to the *Deutschland*, to Belgium instead of Germany, aboard ships bearing their destination as titles—he and Elsa attended a reception thrown for them in support of a group of international pacifists. He gave a short speech reaffirming his belief in war resistance, after which an audience member asked him, "What do you think of pacifists who are pacifists in times of peace but not in times of war?"

The scientist, for a moment, had no answer. Finally he smiled—a reluctant acceptance of the circumstances—and ever the mathematician added a ratio to the equation: "I am sorry to say that ninety percent of pacifists belong to this category."

Whether or not he included himself in that majority, there was no doubt that his views on the matter were changing drastically. Fascism, he was coming to believe, had to be stopped; even pacifists could no longer ignore Hitler. He had already begun urging the United States to abandon its firm stance on isolationism; now he went a step further, convinced that the only way to abolish war was the development of an international military force. He went so far as to suggest that conscientious objectors should be given special dispensation to fight the Nazis.

These remarks earned him banishment from the pacifist circles of Henri Barbusse, head of the World Committee Against War and Fascism.

Although he ordinarily enjoyed any free time, the three-day delay at the Waldorf made him restless, impatient, and angry. He sought comfort by playing the violin, but in his frustration he improvised ugly melodies to vent his feelings of betrayal.

Finally, on March 18, he and Elsa boarded the *Belgenland*, where he found a crowd of approximately one hundred female admirers waiting for him. Einstein was horrified; he rushed past the throng and locked himself in his cabin, ordering the master-at-arms to guard the corridors and prevent anyone from disturbing his privacy. He refused to come out until someone informed him that the ladies-in-wait represented the Women's Peace Society. Reluctantly, he brushed down his windswept hair and agreed to make a few statements to the gathering—one of which was astounding in light of the devastation that would be attributed to that great mind of his.

"A conflict between the United States and Japan should not be thought of seriously," he said presciently. "I doubt very much whether it really is."

With that he left the group and locked himself in again, this time in his bedroom, and refused to appear until the ship had sailed. Then he climbed back up to the deck and stood at the rail, waving at the crowd of admirers who cheered him and, looking up, at the skyline of Manhattan as it drifted slowly from view. He remained there, his smile gently collapsing into a frown of thought, waving as though in a halfhearted salute at the country to which he knew he would return, perhaps for good, after one last voyage to his beloved Europe.

He stayed there, in silent contemplation, until the *Belgenland* had straightened out into the Hudson River and headed for the Atlantic.

The question of what was to become of his homes and property began to be answered after only two days at sea. On March 20, members of the Nazi "brownshirt" brigade raided Einstein's summer home in Caputh under the stated pretense that the scientist had stored a quantity of arms and ammunition there. The charge was as ridiculous as what the search yielded: nothing more dangerous than a bread knife. From the radio room of the *Belgenland*, Einstein issued a statement:

"The raid on the home of my wife and myself in Caputh by an armed crowd is but one example of the arbitrary acts of violence now taking place throughout Germany . . . by a raw and rabid mob of the Nazi militia."

His concerns about family members were eased when news came that both of Einstein's stepdaughters had fled Germany in secret; Elsa learned of their departure only when she telephoned Margot and was informed by a weeping servant that "her mistress had fled for the frontier."

At the end of the month they arrived in Antwerp, welcomed by a cheering crowd shouting, "Long live Einstein!" His plan was to spend the summer in the seaside resort village of Le Coq sur Mer. Any hope of quiet contemplation with his assistant, Walther Mayer, quickly dissipated, however. Two days after raiding his country home, the Nazis seized his bank accounts, appropriating the 30,000 marks (about $9,600) "to prevent their use for treasonable purposes." Perhaps most stinging of all, they would later confiscate his beloved sailboat, as well as a motorboat that had in better times been a gift to him from the city of Berlin.

In response, Einstein promptly resigned from the Prussian Academy of Science, a centuries-old establishment of which he had been a member since 1914, and renounced his Prussian citizenship, effectively ending his official designation as a German national. He described the current situation as "a psychic malady of the masses" and "a mass psychosis which had manifested itself in Germany in so dreadful a way."

The academy, in turn, accused him of "participation in atrocity propaganda in America" and demanded an explanation of his anti-German statements. Einstein was aghast at the betrayal shown at the hands of his former country. The very idea that Germany could now consider him a traitor left a gaping, emotional wound in his enduring native spirit, one he hoped would be rectified in the years to come.

"Surely there will come a time when decent Germans will be ashamed of the ignominious way in which I have been treated," he wrote his friend, the German physicist Max Planck.

From his villa on the Belgian coast, Einstein stated, "All I ask is a little peace and quiet."

The next few months would offer anything but. At first, he began speaking of the formation of an "international police force" to secure peace. Gradually, this grew into a virtual renunciation of the practice of pacifism altogether.

"What I shall tell you will greatly surprise you," he wrote to Belgian pacifist Alfred Nahon in July. "Were I a Belgian, I should not, in the present circumstances, refuse military service."

This was in direct conflict with his earlier assertion that he would "unconditionally refuse to do war service" regardless of the cause. The repercussions resounded worldwide. A Dutch newspaper editorial stated that Einstein "now thinks he can save European civilization by means of fire bombs, poison gas and bacteria." The International League of Fighters for Peace were stunned, and questioned whether Einstein had in fact even made the statements.

Einstein did what he could, assuring his critics that his views had not changed but the situation in Europe had. "It is beyond me why the entire civilized world has failed to join in a unified effort to make an end to this modern barbarism," he said in a July interview. "Can it be that the world does not see that Hitler is dragging us into war?"

That no one else, it seemed, was taking the Führer seriously was completely baffling to him. Lord Arthur Ponsonby, a former member of Parliament and one of England's foremost pacifists, wrote to him in August and affirmed his belief that "Hitler's methods may be insane and criminal, but I am firmly convinced he is not such a fool as to think he could gain anything for Germany by waging war against another country."

Einstein's response was incredulous. "Can you possibly be unaware of the fact that Germany is feverishly rearming and that the whole population is being indoctrinated with nationalism and drilled for war?" he wrote back. "What protection, other than organized power, would you suggest?"

To avoid the firestorms of protest, Einstein agreed to a number of obligations in order to keep busy. He accepted a chair at the Sorbonne in Paris and gave a lecture at the University of Madrid. Wherever he went, whichever country he visited, he listed his address as *"ohne"* ("without") in the official guestbooks.

His desire to live as freely as the gulls was now an unfortunate reality.

One happy coincidence of his stay in Belgium was the opportunity to visit with his good friend and fellow German, Queen Elisabeth of Belgium. The papers had a field day with it, reporting that both he and Elsa had ignored the official welcoming party and had instead trudged to the royal home on foot, carrying their own luggage.* But when word quickly came that the *Fehme*, a Nazi organization, had sent a team of assassins to kill him, Einstein was forced to endure the company of twenty-four-hour bodyguards for the remainder of his stay. Again, he decided to see the humor in it. When he read that a $5,000 bounty had been placed on his head, Einstein remained unfazed.

"I didn't know my head was worth so much," he said.†

Elsa was not quite as nonplussed. She especially worried since her husband refused to give up his morning walks in the Belgian countryside. He pooh-poohed her concerns. "When a bandit is going to commit a crime," he told her, "he keeps it secret."

Every morning he went on his way, effortlessly pondering whatever problem attacked his brain without a thought of Nazi bullets. Nevertheless, the situation grew dangerous enough for him and Elsa to leave Belgium and seclude themselves in a log cabin in Roughton Heath, in England's low-lying county of Norfolk, the exact location of which was kept secret. Yet despite the fact that police were under orders to shoot any

---

* Elsa, apparently, was no stranger to peculiarity herself. *The New Yorker* once reported that at a dinner in Cleveland, "Mrs. Einstein, shrugging her shoulders at what appeared to be an elegant American eccentricity, ate a bouquet of orchids which she found on what seemed to be a salad plate."

† Again, the quote here has been translated into various incarnations, as was the actual size of the bounty. Some reports put it at 20,000 German marks (around $6,800). The *London Daily Herald* reduced it to England's more familiar currency of 1,000 pounds (about $4,550). In the *New York Times* account of his statement, Einstein is quoted as saying, "I didn't know my head was worth 20,000 marks." Clearly he thought the higher sum was more suitable.

unauthorized persons, Einstein insisted on tempting fate by driving around the countryside, hatless, in an open car and walking for hours on end, "talking to the goats."

On the eve of his return to the United States in the fall of 1933, Einstein gave a speech in front of an audience of ten thousand at the Royal Albert Hall in London. It was his first major public appearance in months, and the atmosphere was filled with tension. That afternoon, Scotland Yard had received a message stating, "Be on your guard—there's a plot to assassinate Einstein tonight."

He was closely watched by police and plainclothesmen, but to the audience and news reporters he looked as nonplussed and casual as ever, speaking "as if he were lecturing in a classroom." In a statement that would echo throughout the world, he issued a challenge to his listeners:

"We must realize how much we owe to that freedom which our forefathers won through bitter struggle. Without this freedom there would be no . . . decent homes for the mass of people, no railways or radios, no protection against epidemics, no low-priced books, no culture, no general enjoyment of the arts. There would be no machines to relieve people of the drudgery required to produce the necessities of life. . . .

"One can only hope that the present crisis will lead to a better world."

In a few short years, Grover Whalen would echo those sentiments in laying out the basic premise for his World of Tomorrow.

"I do not know where my future lies," Einstein told a London reporter. "I am European by instinct and inclination. I shall want to return here."

A few days later, Einstein, along with Elsa and Walther Mayer, boarded yet another aptly named ship, the *Westernland*, and set sail from England for New York. For most of the journey he remained in his cabin, often leaving the dining room mid-meal after complaining of illness. No doubt he was sick in his heart. At one of his rare appearances on deck, the scientist and celebrity was asked if he would submit to even a single question. Dejectedly, he shook his head no. Not even that.

On October 17, 1933, the Einsteins arrived in America and immediately released a public statement that from then on, he would give no further interviews. His one desire, he stated, was to be left alone.

"He and Mrs. Einstein have been upset for several months over recent events," said Abraham Flexner.

Wearing a black, broad-brimmed hat and a dark suit and overcoat, Einstein arrived by special tugboat at the Battery. Reporters crowded around, taking pictures and shouting questions at them. Elsa, shaken, appealed for them to leave their little party in peace. Einstein held up his violin case to shield his face from their cameras. Without a word, they hurried into a waiting limousine and sped off for Princeton.

It would be Einstein's home for the rest of his life. Elsa would enjoy one last trip to Europe to visit her ailing daughter in France, but Einstein, despite his instincts and inclinations, would never return.

Detective Joseph J. Lynch

4

THE GARDENIA
OF THE LAW

J oe Lynch had never wanted to be a cop in the first place. For one thing, he had grown up in a municipal family and had spent countless evening hours listening to the elder Lynch men grumbling about their jobs as New York City patrolmen. His father, John J. Lynch, had entered the force at a time when most New Yorkers hated cops or, at the very least, distrusted them intensely.

In 1915, a police lieutenant named Charles Becker was sent to the electric chair for his supposed role in the murder of Herman "Beansy" Rosenthal, a Manhattan gangster. Although Becker had gone to his death proclaiming his innocence, he did admit to accepting large amounts of graft from Rosenthal and a number of other criminals throughout his career. The tabloid newspapers denounced not only Becker, but also the entire police department and the city government as being under the control of Tammany Hall and its various rackets. They weren't entirely wrong.

In the early stages of his career, a pall hung around John Lynch and the force in general. What had once been a noble and respected career now infected him with the suspicion that he, too, must be corrupt. Never mind that the Lynches lived in a modest home in the Bronx or that the family's only known luxury was the quality of their children's education. John Lynch struggled to instill in his sons the belief that public service still stood for something.

Although his eldest boy, John junior, eagerly followed in his father's footsteps and became a police officer, Joe would have none of it. In fact, his brother's induction was marred by an eerie replay of the scandal that had plagued his father. In 1928, another notorious gangster, a gambler named Arnold Rothstein who was famous for having supposedly fixed the 1919 World Series, had been shot in a Manhattan hotel and died the next day. And while this time the murder wasn't ascribed to any particular officer, once again allegations of graft and corruption erupted after weeks went by without an arrest.

Up for reelection the following year and therefore desperate to turn attention away from Rothstein's murder, Mayor Jimmy Walker fired his police commissioner, Joseph Warren, and turned to a bombastic public relations genius who he hoped could take the pressure off. His name was Grover Whalen, and his chief qualification for the job was that Walker knew if anyone's name made the headlines in the coming weeks, it would be Whalen's and not Rothstein's or any one of his suspected killers.

By 1928, Grover had earned the title of New York City's "official greeter," succeeding Rodman Wanamaker, who had become gravely ill. After resigning from the Hylan administration, Whalen had organized a spectacular series of parades and receptions for visiting dignitaries and returning heroes, including Admiral Richard Byrd, Queen Marie of Romania, and, most famously, Charles Lindbergh. Nevertheless, despite his lack of experience in any form of law enforcement, Whalen was considered the best man for the job. In December of that year, Walker paid a visit to his office at Wanamaker's and offered it to him.

"Grover," the mayor said, "I've got to make a change of police commissioners. This Rothstein murder has raised hell. I'm afraid Joe Warren must go. Police morale is shot to pieces and a change has to be made—and soon! So, Grover, I'm here this afternoon to ask you to be the 'top cop.' "

John Lynch Jr. and Sr. would agree with that statement, but when they heard the name of his replacement, they could hardly believe their ears. To add insult to injury, now they had a window dresser as boss. They weren't alone in their skepticism.

"It takes more than a silk hat and a pair of spats to make an efficient police commissioner in the city of New York," noted then congressman Fiorello La Guardia.

Whalen took office in late December, just in time for his supposed "investigation" into Rothstein's murder to have a positive effect on Walker's bid for reelection. Well-known as a dandy, Whalen had taken the oath of office in semiformal morning clothes; and displaying one of his more fastidious quirks, he installed his own personal chair in the barbershop at headquarters, "the best on the market, in which he was shaved every morning and in which nobody else was ever shaved at all."

On his first morning as commissioner, Whalen walked into his office carrying an antique inkwell and a parchment-shaded lamp—fancy-pants carryovers from his decorative suite at Wanamaker's. Scowling at the room's appearance, he fussily ordered that a brass cuspidor be removed: "I'll have no use for that; take it out!" A bronze statue of Napoleon, another of his trademarks, was delivered shortly thereafter, along with the ornate mahogany desk upon which it stood. Within two hours, Whalen found the written resignations of seven deputy police commissioners piled neatly next to Napoleon.

By the end of his third day in office, magistrate David Hirshfield summed up the popular opinion of him: "The city is in for a reign of terror by a snobbish, self-centered, would-be society Police Commissioner in high hat, long-tail coat, striped trousers and light spats. God help the plain people of our city."

A newspaper cartoon pictured Whalen greeting a well-dressed criminal with familiar pomp and circumstance at the entrance to City Hall. In the public's eye, it seemed, he had made the entire department a joke. No one in John Lynch's family thought it was funny.

The criticisms stung, but they didn't stick. One of Whalen's first official orders of business was to call upon his flair for fashion by personally designing new police uniforms complete with snappy Sam Browne belts. ("He loves to design uniforms," one reporter noted.) Then he sprang into action, firing his chief inspector, William Lahey, and his chief of detectives, John D.

Coughlin, "the two men responsible for the investigation of the Rothstein case," he said. On the day after Christmas, he revived the city's "strong-arm squad," recruiting the "hardest hitting men in the department" to use "blackjack reasoning" in dealing with members of the underworld.

"I told them that there is a lot of law in the nightstick," Whalen said. "And I told them they need have no hesitation in using whatever means they found necessary in dealing with gangsters and thugs."

Almost immediately, he declared an all-out war on organized crime. "I want every underworld character to have it impressed upon him that New York is an unhealthy place in which to live," he stated.

He also got rid of the central office of the Homicide Squad, making it publicly known that out of two hundred and twenty-eight murders in the last year, the police had arrested exactly two suspects. "A record of that kind doesn't deserve any consideration," he sniffed. "Therefore the homicide squad is abolished and a [new] squad will be established in each borough under a competent officer."

Once everything was settled, he promised to begin focusing on the Rothstein murder. Then he reversed himself, stating that there were "certain major cases" left over from the Warren administration that "have been put at the head of the list for immediate action."

When asked what those other cases were, "Commissioner Whalen did not say," the papers were delighted to report.

Since he couldn't get away with doing absolutely nothing, Whalen devoted himself to a series of causes that he hoped would divert the public's attention away from the Rothstein case. "There are certain types of places which are breeding places of crime," he said at a press conference, "and I want the city to be rid of them."

"Speakeasies, too?" asked one concerned reporter.

Reluctantly, Whalen answered yes. Privately, like everyone else in the city, he knew the speakeasies were too popular and too numerous to shut down. By some estimates, as many as thirty-two thousand establishments were selling illegal liquor in the city in 1928. And nobody, not even the U.S. government, was taking the law seriously. New York's Prohibition administrator, a man named Maurice Campbell, was a former movie director with several dubious films to his credit, including *She Couldn't Help It*, *The Speed Girl*, and *An Amateur Devil*.

But rather than institute a citywide raid on the illegal sale of liquor, Whalen focused primarily on those dives that sold "poison liquor." Just after New Year's, he instituted a raid on some fifty-five joints where traces of wood alcohol had been found in the drinks. Despite the well-meaning premise behind it, Whalen's crusade, it was reported, tended to focus on "those that sold a drink for a quarter, whereas the far more numerous establishments that sell a drink for seventy-five cents escaped, with rare exceptions, untouched."

Then he turned his attention elsewhere.

"It seemed evident that New York was becoming a hotbed of Communism," as he described the situation. "There may not have been many in the Party then, but they were all real Tartars, making up for any lack of numbers by their energy and ability to outshout others. It was here in New York that their far-reaching program for the future of the Party in America was being prepared."

Why not? Red-baiting was always good for a little news, and who cared about a dead gangster when anarchists and Socialists were taking over the city?

Perhaps noticing the extraordinary amount of publicity a Chicago treasury agent named Eliot Ness was getting, Whalen formed his own gang of "untouchables": fifty probationary officers who would actually join the Communist Party undercover, infiltrate their meetings, and secretly send daily intelligence reports back to Whalen. "Red infiltration was the greatest enemy of this country and our city," Whalen insisted repeatedly. Forget the speakeasies. Forget Rothstein. The campaigns against Communists were frequently so violent that his police force was nicknamed "Whalen's Cossacks," most notoriously after they stormed a march on City Hall by more than a hundred thousand demonstrators.

And it worked. "Mr. Whalen declared so often and so loudly that he was going to solve [the Rothstein case] that half the people in New York probably think he did solve [it], and most of the others do not care," wrote *Harper's*. For the time being, Walker was pleased.

I f he'd had any doubts before, Joe Lynch was now more than ever determined not to follow in his father's and brother's footsteps. For the last four years, he had been working toward a bachelor's degree in pharmaceutical science at nearby Fordham University; after graduation, he accepted a position there as an assistant professor. If all went well, if the economy continued to boom, he could count on opening his own neighborhood drugstore in a few years.

Fate, disguised first as a pretty young girl and then, more significantly, as the collapse of Wall Street, intervened.

Born and raised in the Bronx, Joe had a love of and fascination for Manhattan that his father and brother, as enforcers of the law and therefore witnesses to the city's worst elements, could not appreciate. Perhaps it was the by-product of his education, or maybe one of his former classmates or fellow professors persuaded him, but in the fateful year of 1928, Joe Lynch ventured into that colorful section of the city known as Greenwich Village to attend a simple church dance.

That evening, a pretty, dark-haired girl with the unfortunate name of Easter Hore caught Joe's eye. Tall, slender, and pretty, she had the delicate features of an Irish Myrna Loy, with reddish brown hair to match. It took a while, but he finally summoned the courage and asked her to dance. That, apparently, was all it took. In between dances they chatted easily; Joe was astonished when Easter told him that she, too, was from the Bronx. The coincidence put him instantly at ease. She'd come to the dance after working in her parents' little candy and sandwich shop in the West Village, over on Greenwich Street near the Hudson River, but in fact she lived with them up on Naples Terrace. The address was not far from Joe's family home; clearly, it was destiny after all that had brought them together in a neighborhood so far from their own.

They spent the rest of the evening talking only to each other, and by the time they rode the subway together back to the Bronx, Joe Lynch was more than smitten; he was hooked. The following year they were married, and before their first anniversary a daughter, also named Easter, was born. They called her Essie.

Her arrival was a blessing, but it coincided with the second injection of fate into Joe's life. In October the stock market crashed, and with it the dreams he had shared with Easter on those warm summer evenings a year ago—of owning his own store and running his own business, just as her parents did; of their little family buying a home in Riverdale, the more affluent, almost countrified borough just north of Joe's neighborhood—collapsed as well. Over the next few years, a second child, a boy they named John, after Joe's father, was born; and then a third, another son they called Robert.

With three children in tow, the Lynch family moved into a two-bedroom apartment in the Kingsbridge section of the Bronx. It was a working-class neighborhood, but at least it was Irish Catholic. It certainly wasn't Riverdale. In 1935, they were already outgrowing their home when Easter announced she was pregnant again. Joe had just turned thirty, and suddenly his degree and his teaching job weren't enough anymore. Like every family he knew, the Lynches were barely getting by. The little drugstore seemed a distant pipe dream, his pre-Depression plans blown away as swiftly and completely as a Dust Bowl pasture. Something had to be done, and he had to do it quickly.

Joe Lynch didn't like the solution that came to mind, but he didn't see much choice in the matter. He called a family meeting and informed his father and brother that, reluctantly and at an age when most men were a good ten years on the job, he wanted to join them on the police force. In the grand scheme of things, considering the shape the country was in, he was lucky to have that option. That so many Lynches wore the uniform practically guaranteed him a place in the department.

John Lynch clapped his son on the back; John junior shook his hand and grinned. By the end of the evening, they had practically hung a badge on his shirtfront. Joe returned to his children and gave his expectant wife the news, summoning up all the joy and hope he could muster. He was, indeed, lucky. It just didn't feel that way at the moment.

"Banker" George McAneny *(Courtesy of the New York Public Library)*

NEW YORK
WORLD'S FAIR, INC.

By 1930, the long associations that had aided Grover Whalen throughout most of his life suddenly failed him. Rodman Wanamaker, who had been suffering from kidney disease throughout the last decade, died in March 1928. And after only a year and a half as police commissioner, Whalen resigned and returned to the family store. Mayor Jimmy Walker, like his predecessor Hylan, had grown tired of Grover's constantly stealing the show. He wasn't used to sharing the spotlight with anyone, let alone another good-looking, dandy Irishman.

"Well, we won the election. Now Grover can go," Walker said after thoroughly trouncing La Guardia in 1929, and the remark got back to Whalen.

In truth, Whalen had meant to serve a term of only one year. He had stated so in a list of conditions he had presented to the mayor before agreeing to take the job in the first place. Despite the fact that he had insisted he "would tolerate no interference in cracking down on professional gambling, including any that might be going on in Tammany clubhouses," and that he would hire and fire whomever he pleased "without consulting the mayor," Walker had agreed to everything.

And while Whalen noted that Walker "never violated any of the terms of the agreement," he added regretfully, "I lost his friendship."

That much was evident at the press conference in City Hall, where

Whalen formally announced his resignation. Walker chastised the crowding journalists by mocking Whalen's future plans: "Now, now," he said. "This isn't Wanamaker's bargain counter."

It was a low blow, and no doubt Whalen deeply felt the sting of his ex-boss's joke. And as if that weren't enough, Walker had chosen Assistant Chief Inspector Edward Mulrooney to succeed Whalen, telling his new commissioner, for the record, "It was your devotion to duty which led you away from spectacle and sensation that prompted me to select you for this position."

In other words, the very qualities that Whalen possessed and that had caused Walker to appoint him just eighteen months earlier were now reviled by the mayor as being exactly what the job didn't need.

The press conference was a public embarrassment for Whalen, and he didn't deserve it. True, he had spent countless hours in his office working and reworking the patterns for traffic regulation in the city. Some of his sillier suggestions had even included altering the curtain times for various Broadway shows (musicals versus dramas) in order to ease crowding along Times Square. And the press may have been justified in making fun of his notorious delight in personally blaring the siren of his official car as he raced toward fires and other calamities, real or imagined.

But during his run, he also reduced the rate of major crimes in the city; he reorganized the structure of the department and improved its overall efficiency; he established what would become the Police Academy; and he instituted social service considerations in the prevention of crime at its roots. Yet despite all this, he would carry his reputation as "Gardenia of the Law" for the rest of his life.

As it turned out, however, Whalen's resignation was, yet again, a fortuitous and timely decision. On September 1, 1932, Jimmy Walker was essentially booted out of office after testifying in front of the Seabury Commission, which was investigating charges of corruption in the police department, among other things. Grover had gotten out just in time.

But Rodman's death cast a pall over Whalen's renewed executive position at Wanamaker's and made his triumphant return a rather hollow experience. From mid-1930 to late 1934, he led a relatively calm and stable life, but it was a frustrating existence for a man of ambition—his wants and needs thwarted by what now seemed to him a dull career in retail haberdashery. There were fewer headlines, for one thing, and despite the fact that a good deal of the press coverage about him had been negative, he missed being in the spotlight.

When Prohibition ended in 1933, the Schenley Distillers Corporation offered to appoint him as chairman of its board of directors—partly, perhaps, as payback for his work in seeing that "poison liquor" got out of the speakeasies. He had never shut down very many of those establishments, and at the time he rarely touched a drop of liquor himself. But eager to move on from Wanamaker's, he accepted the offer and quickly forced the federal government to enact a law forbidding the reuse or resale of any liquor bottles.

For the first time in his life, he traveled for pleasure, spending protracted vacations reacquainting himself with his wife and three children. His boy, Grover junior, especially welcomed the attention, but the time away from the hubbub of New York only fueled his hunger to get back in the game. He accepted a sideline job as head of the National Recovery Administration in Manhattan and, recalling some of his past glory, organized an immense NRA-boosting parade with a quarter-million marchers; but it was little more than a showy title despite his return to civic duty.

This slow period had gone on long enough; Whalen was rapidly becoming bored at the lack of stimulation and even controversy. He needed a new challenge, so much so that when, as he put it, "nineteen thirty-four . . . brought me into another job, which turned out to be the biggest—both in scope and problems—I had ever been faced with," he jumped at the chance.

George McAneny brought it to him, by way of Joseph Shadgen and Edward Roosevelt.

In the summer of 1935, after long months of lunches and meetings and speeches and discussions, Whalen and McAneny traveled to Chicago to see for themselves exactly how that city's World's Fair had fared financially. McAneny met with former vice president Charles Dawes, who had served under Calvin Coolidge and later became chairman of the finance committee of the Century of Progress Corporation. Whalen, still unable to shake his Wanamaker roots, called on various business and retail interests like Marshall Field.

The trip provided the final confirmation that a World's Fair in New York would succeed greatly. McAneny and Whalen returned with the news that Chicago's Fair had, after paying back more than $11 million to its investors, even managed to turn a small profit. More than that, it had also brought about $770 million worth of new business to the city. They quickly estimated that, based on population and economic differences, the New York World's Fair would generate at least $1 billion in possible revenue.* And when a report by independent statisticians added another $500 million to that number, the race was on to make a formal announcement by summer's end.

On October 22, the steering committee known as New York World's Fair 1939 formally became a corporation. Its first six directors included five of the original insiders: McAneny, William Church Osborn, Percy Straus, Matthew Woll, and Grover Whalen. The only new face was Mortimer Buckner, chairman of the New York Trust Company, who replaced the Bowery Bank's Henry Bruere. In all, the newly formed company listed one hundred and thirty-one incorporators—including such notables as Pierre Cartier, Harry Guggenheim, and David Sarnoff, president of RCA—representing twenty-three banks, thirty corporations, fifteen white-shoe law firms, and a variety of business interests. It was, according to one account, "probably the most eminent group in the aggregate that ever signed papers of incorporation in New York."

Those papers, drawn up by Frank Polk, former undersecretary of state, spelled out the company's function: "The corporation is not organized for any pecuniary profit . . . and no part of its net earnings shall inure to the benefit of any member, director or individual. The balance, if any, of all money received . . . shall be used and distributed exclusively for charitable, scientific and educational purposes."

---

* Their calculations were startlingly specific: $250 million for food and drink; $250 million for entertainment; $200 million for hotels; $140 million for merchandise; $100 million for transportation; and $60 million for what they called "personal services and communication."

It was both a noble and an impressive beginning. But from the start the directors knew they had a huge task on their hands. First and foremost was establishing a theme: What will this World's Fair stand for? Will it be dedicated to the prospect of world peace? Education? Science and technology? One fact was understood completely—that a World's Fair held in New York City could not possibly be a compendium of many ideals merged together, a crazy quilt of principles and messages lacking a single, underlying purpose. Something that would fit nicely into a slogan, for instance.

"We had to find an idea on which to peg the Fair," Whalen explained. "We wanted something different from any Fair that had ever been undertaken before. It was at one of our first conferences that someone suggested that, instead of tying up the Fair with the past, we should connect it with the future. And it was proposed that we should call it 'The World of the Future.' "

So now the Fair had a theme; its overall message, in the sense of what exactly was being promoted, was harder to define. Any World of the Future, and indeed any World's Fair, lived and died by its corporate sponsors. Lord knows Chicago's Fair, despite its stated purpose as celebrating a century of science, had seen its share of company logos, including such down-home, middle-American brands as Kraft, Walgreens, and that city's own Sears, Roebuck. Even the automotive assembly line, considered one of the best shows at that Fair, was criticized as "Chevrolet all the time."

The difficulty was that any Fair held in New York, that most cynical of cities, couldn't possibly get away with such shameless corporate promotion without a thunderstorm of protest and war cries of hucksterism from its all-too-savvy and sophisticated press. Not to mention its citizens. "If the Galoshes Hall were to do no more than push row after row of attractively priced My-T-Dry Galoshes," *The New Republic* warned, "the fickle audience would soon wander off."

Of the Chicago Fair, *Harper's* sniffed, "You had to have the soul of a yokel on a visit to town to take it at the pitch of perfect enjoyment its sponsors intended." And New Yorkers were anything but yokels. Yet the Fair desperately needed their support; according to the numbers, some fourteen million visitors were expected to attend from the metropolitan area alone—about a quarter of the desired minimum of fifty million fair-goers in total.* Without them, the Fair couldn't possibly hope to succeed financially.

The bankers may not have seen a problem with crass commercialism; nor would the store owners and other captains of industry that made up the World's Fair Corporation. For them, promotion was key, the newspapers and critics be damned. But Whalen thought he knew the mind of the average city dweller, and, perhaps as a direct result of his experience with them, he understood the cunning ability of reporters to recognize a scam when they saw one. His job, as he perceived it, was to sell the companies on the idea of sponsoring a Fair without actually permitting them to blatantly sell their product lines—a seemingly impossible task.

In short, he believed he needed a new sales technique that would allow his commercial exhibitors to promote their goods while at the same time avoiding the stigma of having the entire Fair labeled as a strictly promotional endeavor.

"After we had the basic idea," Whalen explained, "came the job of carrying it out. We were sold on it, but we had to sell it to the people who were going to work for us first, so that they in turn might sell it to the people who would put up the money to make it possible."

It was here at last—after so many frustrating years as Mayor Hylan's secretary, his ill-deserved ridicule as police commissioner, the long shadow of Tammany Hall, and the countless barbs he had taken personally since he first set foot in the public spotlight—that Whalen's true genius began to shine through.

"That word, 'future,' bothered me," he said, recalling an early breakthrough in his thought process. "I kept thinking of fortune-telling and crystal-gazing, and one day as I was riding over to the site in Flushing it suddenly occurred to me that we might call it 'The World of Tomorrow.' That's how the name originated."†

---

* This estimate included repeat visitors, each of whom it was hoped would return at least three times.
† The official theme was actually "Building the World of Tomorrow." But most failed to understand its larger implications—that the Fair was created as a model for future America to build on continually after its gates were closed. Once the Fair was constructed, it seemed

It may seem a subtle difference, but what Whalen was beginning to formulate in his mind was the idea that the Fair should promise not only new gadgets and technology, but that those gadgets would deliver on the hope of a better life to come. Not in some ethereal, distant "future," but just around the corner for a country whose populace had had it pretty rough for the past decade. And by focusing on that promise over the means of delivery (the products themselves), it was hoped that Corporate America could perhaps regain some of its lost trust in the eyes of its buying public.

In a radio address spelling out his vision, Whalen hit on the keynote of this issue: "It is evident that the large corporations know that when they exhibit at a Fair they are vividly depicting the vital role played by them in the nation's life. . . . [They] also know that during these days of economic trials, the weight of public opinion is all-important—that the consuming public is becoming more and more educated to values.

"That is why, today," he continued, "we find in most successful firms a special department devoted to public relations."

And when it came to good PR, there was no man better than Grover Whalen. He understood early on that the companies who sponsored his Fair would not just be selling their brands; they were going to have to sell an *idea*. And the biggest idea they could sell, even the businessmen would agree, was that the corporations weren't the bad guys everyone was making them out to be. Big business was getting a bad rap in the 1930s. With so many people out of work, it was easy to blame Corporate America for creating the problems of the little guy. What was needed was a little old-fashioned goodwill and "a renewing and compelling cause for hope," as Bernard Lichtenberg, president of the Institute of Public Relations and later one of Whalen's own PR men, put it. "The New York World's Fair of 1939 will be the medium through which industry . . . is determined to tell its story and present its case to the public."

And if anyone had any doubts about that, the *Public Opinion Quarterly* spelled it out for them: Business, it stated, needed to recognize "the ne-

---

more appropriate for most journalists and visitors to shorten it to simply "the World of Tomorrow."

cessity of defending itself in the eyes of a hostile public. The history of business in the last ten years has proved that its particular public relations problem cannot be solved effectively on a competitive basis. . . . It is as much the lack of confidence in capitalist democracy itself that must be overcome in the public eye."

Of course there was a little more to it than that. Goodwill was one thing, but by showcasing exactly how well a company's new products and inventions performed in making life easier and more efficient for the average citizen, you could also create a lot of demand for all the new gadgets. And the public, in turn, would hopefully rush out to buy them.

"I wouldn't engage anyone who did not believe in the functions that the Fair was going to perform and in the service that it would render," Whalen stated firmly.

And with that key word, *service*, he set in motion exactly what the Fair's purpose would be. Others would define it more clearly in the months to come, but it was Whalen's original direction, from the master public relations man himself, they would be following.

Still, there were other, more serious concerns to deal with. One of the most pressing was how to ensure that the Fair would not only turn a profit, but actually deliver on its magic billion-dollar infusion of cash into the city's coffers. Statistics compiled by Chicago merchants and hotel owners showed that for every dollar spent at that Fair, $13 was spent in the city itself. But there were also lots of folks, most notably the exhibitors themselves, who had felt let down by the relatively meager profits the Fair had generated, considering its cost. Part of the problem was that its sponsors had practically guaranteed that fifty-five million people would attend; fewer than forty million did. Whalen and the other directors were determined not to make such a glaring miscalculation themselves.

On top of that, there was the deplorable condition of the Flushing Meadows site. Whalen had even stated that the project was so vast that nothing short of a "world war or World's Fair" could clean it up. Despite the involvement of Holy Robert Moses, no one was really sure that such a massive undertaking could be completed in just three and a half years' time.

There was first of all the question of who exactly owned the remaining land. When asked, McAneny had stated without hesitating, "I haven't the slightest idea."

In fact, the city owned only about half of Flushing Meadows, most of it acquired by Moses to build his Grand Central Parkway through the Corona Dumps a few years earlier. After condemning the surrounding property, Moses insisted he could scoop up the remaining six hundred acres "at reasonable cost."

As such, only two days after the corporation had been legalized, the New York City Board of Estimate approved an astounding $200,000 to begin preliminary work on the site. La Guardia, also quick to act, authorized a resolution designating Flushing Meadows Park (and whatever surrounding land Moses could gobble up) as officially now the property of the New York World's Fair. His goal, the mayor said, was "to keep the engineers one step ahead of the lawyers."

Although McAneny insisted that "there has not been a dissenting voice since the idea of an exposition in New York was first advanced," it wasn't true. There were many who simply refused to believe that Flushing Meadows could be turned around in time for the proposed Opening Day in 1939. Most of the dissenters, however, were quickly dissuaded from their skepticism, most likely as a result of either financial or political pressure. New York had its heart set on the site in Queens; those who disagreed with the plan had better get on board or risk missing out on the greatest show the city had ever seen.

Edward Loomis, president of the Lehigh Valley Railroad, stated that he "had not been enthusiastic about the idea." Then, within weeks, he quickly reversed himself, assuring everyone that he was now a "wholehearted convert.

"The more I have thought it over," he said, "the more enthusiastic I have become. And as for the site, I consider it the ideal location in New York."

There were more. Brooklyn's borough president, Raymond Ingersoll, wanted the Fair to be held in his district and had offered up several site suggestions. So did Bronx borough president James Lyons. La Guardia shushed them all. "This is to be a World's Fair of the city of New York," he chastised them. "So let us not hear any more talk about individual boroughs."

The mayor did admit, however, that three and a half years was a "very short time" to construct a Fair of this magnitude.

Throughout, McAneny remained firm in his commitment to the location. "It was the judgment of both the city officials and of others consulted," he said, "that there should be no invasion of existing parks. . . . The availability of inner water areas capable of conversion into courts of honor or other display features was also held important. It so happens that the Flushing Park territory . . . meets these requirements."

He may have been somewhat overly optimistic when he went on to say that, despite the condition of the land, "the Fair, in short, is off to an excellent start."

No doubt Moses had a hand in all this. He wanted his park, and he didn't give a damn how he got it. From the beginning, he pledged that he "would stop at nothing to help," but if and *only* if the Fair was constructed in Flushing Meadows. On this point he was adamant, going so far as to issue a veiled threat that this particular location "was the only site in New York where they could get any cooperation from the Park Department." In no uncertain terms, he was stating: No Flushing, no Moses. It was that simple.

Building any kind of Fair without the support of the city's parks commissioner was unthinkable. He knew there were challenges; he took particular delight in addressing their concerns regarding "the depth of mud in the meadows" and the "lengths of piles which would have to be used to insure safe foundations even for temporary buildings." He just didn't care. As long as the city was willing to pay for it, he would help create their World's Fair and would personally oversee the development of his eventual park afterward.

Whatever lingering doubts may have remained, shortly after incorporation, everyone, it seemed, was absolutely overjoyed with the seemingly preposterous idea of transforming the Corona Dumps into a World of the Future. Or the World of Tomorrow or whatever. As long as it was cleaned up.

In 1935, Robert Moses was forty-six years old and already famous for having developed Jones Beach into a Long Island haven—for those who had cars, anyway. He was also famous for his impossible temper and the fact that he rarely enjoyed any relationships with city officials that didn't somehow involve angry outbursts, outright threats, and general obstinacy as a means of getting his way.

Cleveland Rogers, in an *Atlantic Monthly* portrait, summed up Moses's confounding demeanor: "A fighter of quick temper, he is ruthless in dealing with self-seekers and those who would obstruct his plans. He flatly contradicts opponents, tells them they don't know what they are talking about, puts them straight as to facts, or sears them with sarcasm and ridicule."

His friends called him Bob, but he made sure that those who worked for him used the more deferential moniker "R.M." He stood over six feet tall and even in middle age retained the broad shoulders and lean body he had developed as a young swimmer at Yale. He had the impossibly large hands of a Michelangelo sculpture and a massive, brooding forehead with thick black eyebrows that frequently folded into a scowl of impatience with what he perceived as the frustrating incompetence of nearly everyone he came in professional contact with.

The son of a wealthy department store owner (which put him in somewhat of the same class as Rodman Wanamaker), he had enjoyed a privileged childhood in dual homes in New Haven, Connecticut, and New York City. His undergraduate success at Yale included membership in the Phi Beta Kappa Society, but his inherent stubbornness and refusal to conform to the rules and regulations of any governed body led to his being ostracized by every fraternity. It was an early pattern he was to repeat throughout his life, continually maintaining a position above those around him and refusing to accept anyone's dictates upon himself. He was elected to the Senior Council, but only after he had a hand in its initial organization.

After Yale he studied at Oxford, where he swam some more and captained the water polo team (clearly preferring the solitude of water to the company of classmates). After graduating with a master of arts in 1913, he earned a doctorate of philosophy at Columbia, and in 1915 he married Mary Sims, granddaughter of a Methodist minister and no doubt the cause of some consternation between Moses and his Spanish Jewish father. With a decent inheritance from his family, he established a life for his wife and two daughters in an apartment overlooking the East River in Manhattan and a country home in Babylon, Long Island.

Nevertheless, he remained an enigma to his friends and patrons. "Bob Moses is the most efficient administrator I have ever met in public life," said former New York governor Alfred E. Smith, on whose staff Moses had served as secretary of state in 1927 and 1928. "I know he went to Yale and Oxford, but he didn't get that keen mind of his from any college. And he was a hard worker. He worked on trains, anywhere and any time. When everyone else was ready for bed he would go back to work."

This tireless energy drove his staff crazy; he reportedly kept a team of secretaries at his disposal, and he often ran them ragged. His long-winded, impassioned speeches confounded even Smith, who once, after listening for what seemed like hours to Moses's pleas for new legislation, dropped out of his chair and pretended to faint.

In 1924, Moses was elected president of both the State Council of Parks and the Long Island State Park Commission, and quickly developed thirteen parks totaling more than ten thousand acres in Nassau and Suffolk counties. The total cost of these, and the parkways he built to provide access to them, exceeded $50 million, and Moses readily admitted that it sometimes took "strong-arm methods" to get them built.*

Even Jones Beach had been no easy task. The town of Hempstead voted decisively against its development, and the owners of Long Island's famed estates were aghast at the idea of a public park along their southern shoreline. "If this Moses scheme goes through," argued a representative of the nearby town of Islip, "Long Island will be overrun with the rabble from the city."

---

* Moses's parkways were no ordinary thoroughfares. He considered them "ribbon parks" and ordered that there were to be no traffic lights, grade crossings, commercial traffic, or signs of any kind other than exit designations. Likewise there could be no hot dog stands or gas stations, and absolutely no left turns.

"Can't you realize," one particularly overwrought landowner confronted him, "that this is the last real fox-hunting country left in New York? If you build a road across it the hounds will lose the scent every time the fox crosses the concrete."

Moses's by now infamous sneer was evident in his retort: "Perhaps we can build a tunnel under the road for the fox."

In the end, he won the battle by threatening to take away the towns' bay bottom rights, a necessary staple to their fisherman economy. The strong-arm tactics taught him an important lesson.

True to his independent, arrogant nature—a trait he supposedly inherited from his mother, Isabella, and especially from his grandmother Rosalie Silverman—Moses drafted the laws and by-rules of every government position he ever held. In 1933, he essentially conceived and created the job for which he was most famously known throughout his life, commissioner of parks under Mayor La Guardia. (He officially assumed the position in January 1934.) Before him, the job had been performed by five borough park commissioners whose salaries totaled $62,000 a year. Moses consolidated them all and took only $13,600 a year for his trouble. Discounting his two-year term as secretary of state, it was the only salary he took in return for what he considered was public service.

"The minute you put a salary on the job," he once told Governor Smith, "it becomes an item for the politicians."

Throughout the Depression, he spent $300 million to increase the number of city parks from one hundred and nineteen to more than four hundred; built ten swimming pools, each costing $1 million, for city families to cool off in during summer; and at the end of 1933 he took over the disastrously managed construction of the Triborough Bridge, which he promised to complete by July 1936. In the end, the bridge would cost the city more than $60 million, but Moses would open it right on time.

Still, there was that fiery temper to deal with, as well as his almost childlike habit of repeatedly resigning from any position whenever he couldn't get his way. In fact, Moses so often threatened to resign as parks commissioner that La Guardia kept a printed pad of forms on his desk that read: "I, Robert Moses, do hereby resign as _____ effective _____."

Whenever Moses began to bluster, La Guardia would simply tear off a sheet and hand it to him, grinning like a kid.

Frances Perkins, the first woman appointed to the U.S. cabinet under Franklin Roosevelt, said, "Robert Moses is a good man, but you have to let him have his own way." He rarely lost a battle, if only because when all the shouting was done, Moses's voice still bellowed loud and strong while his opponents had fallen exhausted and hoarse.

"His most ferocious attacks could be devastating," wrote Herbert Kaufman in the *Political Science Quarterly*. "He could wither his adversaries with contempt, humiliate them with ridicule, harpoon them with invective, and destroy them with innuendo."

B ut 1935, even for Robert Moses, was a record-breaking year for controversy. He got his name in the papers virtually every day, usually in connection with one argument or another involving his numerous park projects.

Since January, he had been embroiled in a particularly nasty battle with Secretary of the Interior Harold Ickes, who wanted Moses fired from the Triborough Bridge Authority. As head of the Public Works Administration, Ickes had issued Administrative Order 129, officially withholding funds from anyone who held both a municipal and a PWA office. And since construction of the Triborough was a PWA project, that meant Moses. In fact, it applied *only* to Moses, who claimed it was a personal vendetta and the result of a grudge FDR held against him.*

A storm of protest ensued; Ickes was reviled in the New York press, and FDR was buried in an avalanche of letters and telegrams from various civic groups. Throughout the battle, La Guardia ran end runs down to Washington until finally the federal government caved. A predated letter was written stating that Order 129 was not meant to be retroactive and therefore did not

---

* As governor of New York, Roosevelt, it was said, refused to reappoint Moses as secretary of state because Moses did not give his personal secretary, Louis Howe, a job in the Council of Parks. Howe was a close friend of both the president and Eleanor Roosevelt and was revered by both as one of the few who supported FDR throughout his political comeback after he had been stricken with polio.

apply to Moses. In the end he was allowed to stay, his influence apparently extending as high up as the office of the president of the United States.

"He acknowledged no one as his superior," Kaufman stated. "In fact, he treated few as equals. For most, he showed only condescension, expecting their homage—and usually getting it."

In March, he appeared at a court hearing to defend his decision to tear down a city landmark, the Central Park Casino, which had been built in 1864, arguing that its charge of forty cents for a cup of coffee was "too expensive to be justified at a public park."

He took the case all the way to the state supreme court, and when they blocked his motion to demolish it, Moses promptly defied a restraining order and began digging up the trees and bushes surrounding the property, leading to a charge of contempt of court against him. In the appellate court, Presiding Justice Francis Martin warned that Moses had to be stopped from destroying public landmarks "before he becomes a Mussolini. Suppose he wanted to tear down City Hall?"

He followed that by decimating Inwood Hill Park at the northern tip of Manhattan in order to make room for the Henry Hudson Parkway, drawing the ire of the City Club. Nathan Straus, one of its members, accused Moses of treating public parks "as if they were his own personal property. Is Commissioner Moses the only wise man in the city?"

In June, Moses again threatened to quit all of his projects unless La Guardia immediately offered him a full three-year reappointment as parks commissioner, casting serious doubts about whether the Triborough Bridge would ever be completed on time.

"You tell him for me that's just baby talk," the mayor responded, calling his bluff. "He's talking big, but all it amounts to is baby talk. If the law requires it, I was prepared to reappoint him. But if he wants to talk baby talk I'll consider the appointment very carefully before I make it."

Two days later, La Guardia reappointed him.

At best, he had a contentious but working relationship with La Guardia;*

---

* In fairness, La Guardia fought with all his commissioners, many of whom resigned in the face of his disrespect. "If you were any dumber, I'd make you a commissioner" was one of his favorite statements, usually employed after he'd berated an underling for one infraction or another.

at worst, they took to rabid name-calling and outright accusations of misconduct in the press. In private, their relationship was even more virulent. Moses called the mayor "the little organ grinder" as a dig at his Italian ancestry. It was one of the nicer racial nicknames he invented for La Guardia; his three other favorites were "that Dago son of a bitch," "that Wop son of a bitch," and "that Guinea son of a bitch." La Guardia responded by referring to Moses as "His Grace."

Nevertheless, whether out of intimidation or awe at his ability to mobilize a wide variety of factions in the planning and building of each of his projects, the mayor respected Moses's ability to get things done. And while La Guardia was a well-known hothead himself, in the end Moses almost always got his way.

The controversy continued. On November 20, 1935, the board of directors of New York World's Fair, Inc., held their first meeting and unanimously elected two bankers, George McAneny and Harvey Gibson, as president and chairman. But by the end of the year, Moses was growing ever more impatient with the corporation when it came to reclamation of the Corona Dumps. In December, he warned that any delay in preparing the site would be "fatal." Then, as the new year came and went and the bulldozing Moses still wasn't getting his way, he took his argument public, issuing a statement that accused the World's Fair Corporation of dragging its feet.

In typical Moses fashion, the warning was paired with another of his trademark threats. In late January, he confronted Mayor La Guardia and presented him with two possibilities: He could proceed with the plans for a World's Fair, or he could "adopt an alternative plan he has [already] prepared for development of the meadows as a park." It didn't matter at all to him one way or the other, he said; he just wanted to get at least one of the projects under way.

Moses was bluffing, of course. He and everyone else in city government knew that no park could be built without the funds the World's Fair would generate. Still, it was an embarrassing situation all around, and even those who were aware of Moses's tactics were surprised that he would shed doubt on the Fair's much-anticipated existence to the public at large. The ultimatum had made the local papers, as Moses knew it would.

Five days later, McAneny reassured the borough of Queens that they needn't worry. The Fair would proceed, he said, and it would draw "many, many more" visitors than Chicago had. The occasion was a dinner, given in McAneny's honor by the local New York Board of Trade at the Kew Gardens Inn, and for good measure he brought along Joseph Shadgen, their neighbor, whom he now described as "the Father of the Fair."

For Moses, the speeches and promises amounted only to words, not to action. Still unsatisfied, he took the fight a step further, asking the Board of Estimate to authorize the lowering of a portion of his Grand Central Parkway in order for it to be ready when the Triborough Bridge opened that summer. Naturally, the move would compromise most of his efforts in restoring Flushing Meadows for the Fair; moreover, it would in fact reduce the Fair's overall size by eighty-five acres—an area just small enough for the planners to think he was serious and just large enough for it to be a real problem.

The bluffing and bullheaded tactics were getting him nowhere, but Moses may have had an alternate motive in mind when he stated over and over again that he was backing away from the World's Fair idea. That same month, Bronx borough president James Lyons, ever the critic and definitely no friend of Moses, revealed some interesting news: Engineers conducting a secret survey of the land on Flushing Meadows had found it so boggy that no buildings could be erected on it safely. Whether or not it was true, La Guardia immediately denied it and insisted that there was "nothing secret" about the report. Moses backed him up, saying that a full technical analysis "had found the Flushing Meadows entirely suitable for proposed World's Fair purposes."

Still, just to be sure, he ordered additional borings into the muck.

To the vast and forceful impatience of Moses, "Mañana Mac" was living up to his name. The World's Fair Corporation was indeed dragging its feet left and right, and something had to be done before the whole situation turned dire. Six full months had elapsed since the Fair was formally announced, and to date nothing more than a few maps and surveys had been conducted. The three-and-a-half-year deadline had collapsed into just three years; what had at first seemed unlikely now seemed utterly unrealistic.

By now completely fed up, Moses alternately watched the days tick off the calendar and his blood pressure rise up the charts. At the end of March 1936, the board of directors of the Fair corporation actually voted unanimously to suspend all meetings until "adequate appropriation by the public authorities has been made for the preparation of the site for the 1939 Fair and the general enabling legislation now pending at Albany enacted."

Essentially, the corporation had declared, in a terse, forty-eight-word statement that had taken them two hours to write, that it was going to sit with its arms folded and hold its breath until some money came through. This childish behavior stemmed from a disagreement between the city and the state as to who would benefit more from this Fair. The state legislature argued against providing funds for an event they felt would strictly benefit the city; the city responded by saying that it wouldn't cough up the agreed-upon $5 million for sewers and landfill until the state came through with an additional $5 million for a boat basin and roadwork leading to and from the fairgrounds.

Reading the resolution, Moses became incensed. Enough was enough; it was time to remove the procrastinators and replace them with someone who was a mover and shaker, a proven executive who could get the job done without sitting on the details for months on end. He knew who that man was, and he knew that his talents were currently being wasted on an underling's job with the executive committee.

So on April Fools' Day, perhaps as a subtle dig at what he perceived as McAneny's and Gibson's utter incompetence, Moses issued a do-or-die challenge. He submitted a letter to the Fair's directors stating in no uncertain terms that he now believed the Fair would not open until 1940.

Moses wrote:

The loss of time, due to . . . weaknesses in the World's Fair management, have raised a serious question in my mind as to whether the Fair can be held in 1939. The original schedule was a very tight one, and I have repeatedly called attention to the fact that only the utmost cooperation from the very beginning on the part of all concerned would make it possible. I think the contingency should be faced now that the Fair may have to be postponed until 1940. I do not say that the 1939 opening is impossible. It is improbable.

The warning set off alarm bells throughout the city. (Although Moses later declared he meant it as a "confidential" letter to the World's Fair Corporation and not intended for public perusal, it had nevertheless "somehow" managed to leak out.)

Acting quickly to soothe the swelling controversy, and Moses's outrage, on April 22, 1936, the directors voted Grover Whalen chairman of the board of New York World's Fair, Inc., replacing Harvey Gibson, who assumed the more appropriate role as chairman of the finance committee. Whalen now had full rein over the Fair's executive decisions. His first duty, he stated, was to get all the city and state difficulties settled; afterward, "nature would take its course."

Whether or not he meant the double entendre, Whalen knew that the main objective for his coup was to solve the land reclamation problems of Robert Moses. A reporter, citing Whalen's reputation, asked if he would be taking charge of the Fair's promotion.

Whalen reluctantly shook his head no. "Execution," he said, "rather than promotion."

At the time Moses was elated with the choice, but still he had no intention of backing down on his threats, despite Whalen's promise to speed things up. He had already switched gears, Moses said, proceeding with his original plans for extending the Grand Central Parkway through the Flushing site, all but giving up on the possibility that the Fair would be completed on schedule. But again he left open at least *some* hope that his mind could be changed, even at this late date.

Moses also laid out an agenda for what must be done in order to get the project back on track—for not only the World's Fair Corporation, but also the city government, the state of New York, and the Queens borough president to follow if they wanted him to remain on board. All he needed, he said, was authorization to spend an initial $7 million. And he needed it right away.

Whalen, living up to expectations, saw that he got it. Before the month was out, the corporation fully approved all of Moses's suggestions: The city would acquire the remaining land for $1.5 million and spend another $2.75 million for the reclamation of it; another million and change would be spent for building sewers, and an extra $1.5 million was even tacked on for construction of the city's exhibit buildings. The total city expenditure approved equaled $7 million, exactly what Moses had asked for.

But it didn't stop there. The state of New York finally caved in and agreed to invest some $4 million to construct bridges and highways, using mostly manpower from its Department of Public Works.

The next day, nearly every major player came out to reassure the wary public that the Fair would open on time in 1939, "despite scare headlines," as La Guardia put it. Moses himself stated that "there was nothing now to impede the opening on schedule."

"Do you mean that the management has since improved?" James Lyons asked.

"Yes," he said, smiling broadly.

Queens borough president George Harvey, understanding what was at stake for his district and attempting to smooth the ruffled feathers of all involved, got in the last word:

"From the beginning I have felt that the World's Fair was too important to the people of the city," he said. "Once the order for full speed ahead is given I am sure that Commissioner Moses will forget his troubles and join with the corporation in securing for New York and its people a Fair worthy of the city's dignity.

"The World's Fair is now on its way," he continued. "Nothing can stop it."

The date was May 1, 1936, exactly three years minus one day from the Fair's opening.

Whalen swearing in graduates of his new "police college" in 1930 (© *New York Daily News LP*)

6

THE $8 MURDER

Reluctant as he may have been to join the police force, Joe Lynch reaped an early benefit from his family's former nemesis, Grover Whalen. In the waning months of his career as police commissioner, Whalen had created a "police college" in order to better train recruits for a career in what he considered to be the future of law enforcement.

"I started that," Whalen said, "because I saw as soon as I took things over that there was a crying need for education of the men in the department. Detective work is a science nowadays. . . . In the old days a plain cop was thought to be good enough, but in these days . . . real executives are needed."

Lynch, with his Fordham University degree, entered the officers training school—a monthlong program that put him on the fast track for promotion—in 1936. Within a year, Joe had been promoted to detective, third grade. Things were going well again as he and Easter celebrated the birth of their fourth child, another girl whom they named Martha, after Easter's mother.

Then, in the late fall of 1937, tragedy struck. On Thanksgiving Day, the Lynches and the Hores gathered in the Bronx to celebrate their growing family and Joe's continued success in the department. Along with his promotion to detective, Joe had been offered a post with the Bronx District Attorney's Office, a plum assignment that allowed him to work near home in order to be closer to his wife and children.

With the exception of Joe's father-in-law, Jeremiah, they were all in a festive mood. The old man was brooding, however; he'd been drawn for jury duty that week, leaving his wife, Martha, to fend for herself in their little luncheon counter in Greenwich Village. It was a two-person operation: One usually made the sandwiches and served the customers while the other manned the cash register and handled the candy, cigarette, and newspaper trade that had lately made up the bulk of their profits.

Jeremiah didn't like leaving his wife alone to handle all the business, especially during the busy lunch hour. Moreover, the meat slicer was on the fritz, which meant that the cold cuts would have to be carved by hand. But since he would have a break for lunch and the courthouse was only a few blocks away, he supposed he could skip out for an hour and help her in the noontime rush.

The next morning, November 27, Easter's parents boarded an early train to take them into Manhattan. They opened the store promptly at eight, and when Jeremiah was satisfied that his wife was settled in for the morning crowd, he left for the Reade Street Municipal Court to spend a long, dull morning performing his civic duty.

At a little after one o'clock, he came back to help with lunch, but there weren't many customers—too many holiday leftovers to be eaten, probably. At five minutes before two, he unlocked the cash register under the counter and checked the day's receipts: only $8 and some small change. It had indeed been a slow morning, so Jeremiah left the store and headed back to court.

It was an even slower afternoon. At three-thirty, Martha Hore had only two customers, one of them a little boy who was enjoying his school holiday by lingering over a soda, the other a neighborhood kid she may have known by name and probably by reputation. He was a familiar figure in the neighborhood, a blond and twitchy teenager named Joe Healy, and Martha most likely regarded him with equal measures of pity and disapproval. Out of work and uneducated, Healy had been the product of a familiar tale of downtown West Side woe: He'd grown up near the corner of Canal and Hudson streets, where first the mighty Hudson Dusters ruled, to be followed by the Marginals and other "Paddy Irish" gangs. After giving birth to ten children, Healy's mother had died when he was only nine years old.

Healy, a short but well-muscled tough, often came in with his girlfriend, a pretty, dark-haired girl named Grace Tanzola. Although both were only seventeen, what Martha may not have known was that Grace had recently become Joe Healy's wife. They had gotten married two months earlier when Grace had informed him she was pregnant. Now, thrown out of his father's house, Healy and his child bride were living with her mother, Anna, and her nine-year-old sister, Rose Marie. With a baby on the way and no obvious means to support his family, Healy was scared and desperate for money.

He lingered in the store, waiting for his chance, but that damn kid kept slurping his drink and wouldn't go away. Healy had been sitting there for a half hour, seeing almost no other customers and eyeing the old lady's purse on the counter by the cash register. When she finally rang up the kid's soda, Healy thought he spotted "a big bill" in the old-fashioned register and then watched as Martha turned her back on him and walked into a rear room.

He saw an opportunity and decided it was worth the risk. Quickly he jumped behind the counter and pulled open the unlocked register just as Martha came back into the store. They stared at each other for a brief, silent moment, both in utter surprise and unable to move a muscle. Then Martha grabbed the first thing she saw—the sharp butcher's knife she had been using to cut meat for sandwiches in the absence of the working slicer. She came toward Healy, terrified but determined. Without her husband and against a wiry and desperate seventeen-year-old, she brandished the knife in his face and ordered him out of the store.

They struggled. Healy acted fast, snatching the knife away from her. And then, in a fit of panic and rage at the denial of his urgent need for cash, he swiped the blade at her throat. Maybe he had meant to kill her out of fear that she could identify him; maybe he was reacting instinctively to the fact that anyone, even a sixty-five-year-old woman, had approached him with a knife. Whatever the motive, he slashed her once, viciously, and when the old woman still wouldn't quit, he continued beating her until she finally fell motionless behind the counter, dying from the severe gash in her throat.

Healy, shocked by his own crime, looked around to see if anyone had witnessed it. The windows of the store faced out onto Greenwich Street, but he saw no horrified faces peering in at him. Panicked, he decided to make a run for it, forgetting about the cash in the register. In his struggle with the old lady, not only had Healy dropped the murder weapon, but somehow the gray cap he'd been wearing had slipped off his head. Unaware of the evidence he was leaving behind, he ran into the afternoon sunlight and kept on running.

At a little after four o'clock, a neighbor who lived on the fourth floor above the store decided to go downstairs to return a pie plate she had borrowed from the friendly Mrs. Hore. Catherine Troy, a teenager herself at fifteen, casually strolled in the front door and called out her name. The place was empty, and there were no customers. She walked to the counter and spotted Martha Hore lying in a pool of her own blood, then ran out into the street and screamed at the first person she saw. Charles Kuhn, a welder, was repairing his car at the curb directly in front of the shop's window. Apparently, he had been so involved in his work that he'd seen neither the crime nor the murderer as he'd raced away.

Kuhn ran inside, saw the body, and called the police. Catherine Troy returned to her family's apartment, too distraught to speak.

At the sound of screeching police cars, a crowd gathered around the familiar little shop. Most were neighbors who had known the Hores for ages. Someone who must have known them very well had taken off for the municipal court in search of the dead woman's husband. Miraculously, only twelve minutes after his wife's body had been found, Jeremiah shoved his way through the heavy throng and entered the store. His worst fears of leaving his wife alone had come true.

It was a brutal scene. After allowing Jeremiah a few minutes to collect himself, Detective Captain Thomas Murray respectfully asked him to search around and see if anything had been taken. Together they looked in the open register; the same $8 and change lay untouched. Jeremiah found his wife's purse on a shelf, opened it, and noted that whatever little money she carried was still there, along with her rosary beads. He dutifully handed them over as evidence.

Murray was stumped. In the first place, who would kill an old lady for $8 and then leave the bounty behind? The crime incensed him, and he turned his fury on Kuhn. The back doors were locked, so the killer must have run right past him. How could he not have seen anything or heard anything when he was standing the entire time not ten feet in front of the shop's entrance? Kuhn shrugged. There was an elevated track overhead; perhaps a train had gone by and drowned out the noise.

Jeremiah was inconsolable. He simply could not fathom why anyone would want to do this to his wife. One detective posited that maybe some drunken customer had gotten in an argument with Mrs. Hore, but when they found Healy's cap, Murray was fairly certain that what he saw was a robbery gone bad. Jeremiah was asked whether the cap looked familiar; he shook his head no, he couldn't place it with any customer in particular. He was fairly certain he'd never seen it before. Worse, the cap held no identifying marks, no store label or name stitched inside. The only clue came from a small tag; now all they had to do was look for someone with a size 7¼ head.

When Murray felt certain that Jeremiah could offer no further help, he asked if there was anyone they could call to help get him home. He had a son, Francis, Jeremiah told them. But maybe they'd better call his daughter, Easter, since she was married to a cop.

The murder tore into Joe's sensibility as an agent of the law. It was the ultimate slap in the face of his career, and it wasn't the first time a Lynch family badge had proved useless. In an odd twist of fate, Joe's own mother had once been attacked in public, though her injuries were not even remotely as serious.

On December 29, 1930, Mary and John Lynch, who was then a police sergeant, were celebrating at a pre–New Year's Eve party held at the Farragut Inn in the upstate village of Hastings-on-Hudson. Apparently, despite Prohibition, there was much drinking going on, and sometime during the evening, a "Broadway figure" (by which it was meant a gambler and gangster) got into an argument with Mary. Before John could intervene, the man, named John Hanley, struck Mary with his cane. She wasn't seriously harmed, but the sting of her husband's pride hurt worse than her bruises.

Unable to attain prosecution for the crime, the Lynches promptly sued Hanley for $100,000. Hanley denied the attack, and when the case finally came to court, a judge awarded Mary Lynch the grand sum of $500.

Now, disgusted with the system, Joe cursed the ineffectiveness of his own uniform in failing to protect his family from harm. And when he wasn't doing that, he spent every ounce of his remaining strength comforting his wife and caring for their children.

Joe Healy wandered the streets for hours. He thought about the horrific crime he had just committed and what the penalty might be if he was caught; then he thought of his new wife and baby on the way. What kind of life could they hope to have if he went to jail? What kind of upbringing would his child experience with a heinous murderer for a father? As twilight fell, he decided on a plan of action.

Steadying himself, he walked into his mother-in-law's apartment on Renwick Street. Even though it was dark, Healy knew it was a risky move; the dingy tenement was only two blocks away from the murder scene. If there had been any witnesses, the cops would surely be waiting for him there. He stood outside in the shadows for a few minutes to make sure the coast was clear.

Convincing Grace to come away with him would be no easy matter. By now the entire neighborhood had heard of the crime, but Healy felt fairly certain he could talk his wife into leaving without having to confess anything drastic. Somehow he did. The next morning the two of them boarded a train to Philadelphia, where Healy hoped to forget his crime and forge a new life.

In this case, however, despite their somewhat unremarkable record in solving homicides, the NYPD reacted quickly. Although initially no murder weapon had been found, once Martha Hore's body had been removed, the bloody butcher's knife turned up. It was sent to the crime laboratory at the Poplar Street station in Brooklyn to be examined for fingerprints. In the meantime, after canvassing the neighborhood and assuring themselves that there were indeed no witnesses to the murder, detectives focused on the single clue at hand: Healy's cap.

It wasn't much to go on. Being so completely nondescript and of such a dark gray shade, the cap could probably be worn without any casual observer even taking notice of it. No one did. Fortunately for the cops, Healy's primary mistake in committing the crime had been not the forgotten hat, but the fact that he had targeted a spot so close to his mother-in-law's home for robbery in the first place.

As quickly as the morning after the murder, Lieutenant Hugh Sheridan, in charge of detectives at the Charles Street police station, knew the identity of the killer. Anna Tanzola identified the cap as belonging to her son-in-law, whom she reported as missing along with her teenage daughter. Whether or not she knew she was implicating Healy in the murder, since it was already the talk of the neighborhood she must have had some inkling of the impact her testimony would have.

Sheridan wasted no time issuing a description of the suspect as seventeen years old, five feet six inches tall, and weighing approximately one hundred and thirty-five pounds. Without naming Healy specifically, he further stated that the suspect "had recently married." Robbery was the suspected motive for the crime, Sheridan stated, since Mrs. Hore "had been in the custom of leaving her pocket book lying around the store in conspicuous places."

The police knew who he was, but they didn't know where to find him. On the off-chance that Healy would return home at some point, to retrieve either clothes or money for a prolonged escape, Sheridan ordered his men to stake out both Anna Tanzola's apartment and the one his father lived in, another tenement just up the block. Joe Healy and Grace Tanzola had been close neighbors growing up, their buildings separated by no more than a hundred feet. If he showed up at either location, detectives would be there to grab him.

Healy didn't show, but on the following Tuesday, just five days after the murder, he sent his father a telegram asking for money, adding an address in Philadelphia where he wanted it to be sent. Had Healy waited a bit for things to cool off and for the detectives to abandon their stakeout, or had he sent the request via regular mail, Joe Healy might never have been found. As it was, the quick-thinking cops, spotting a rare Western Union man in a neighborhood where telegrams were considered a luxury, intercepted the message.

Philadelphia was a quick four-hour drive, and the detectives wasted no time. The telegram had arrived on Tuesday evening, and by Wednesday morning Inspector Michael McDermott had Healy in custody. They brought Grace back as well. The officers completed the arrest in time for the morning papers to announce that the murder of Martha Hore had been solved and that Healy had immediately broken down and confessed. Grace, who protested that she knew nothing about the crime, was held as a material witness.

Two days later, the case was in the hands of Assistant District Attorney Lawrence McManus, who promptly got statements out of both Joe and Grace Healy, then released the pregnant wife from custody. Clearly, among the members of his own family, Joe was not a popular figure. In solidifying the already airtight case against him, McManus also collected testimony from Joe's sister Helen, as well as Anna and Rose Marie Tanzola. Although she could not identify Healy as the murderer, young Catherine Troy was also brought in as a witness.

A grand jury was convened for the following week, and on December 9 they handed in an indictment of first-degree murder against Healy. In all, fifteen witnesses testified for the prosecution, although none had seen the actual crime being committed. The evidence was circumstantial at best, but Healy's teary-eyed confession to Inspector McDermott practically ensured a conviction.

That afternoon, Healy was taken away in handcuffs to the infamous Tombs, a massive and decrepit jailhouse that occupied a full city block in lower Manhattan. Although its official name was the Manhattan House of Detention, the structure more than lived up to its reputation as a mausoleum for the living. At one time or another, the Tombs had housed some of the worst criminals in the city's history. Now Joe Healy was one of them. He would spend more than a year there, sitting alone in a tiny, darkened cell, waiting for his trial. For Joe and Easter Lynch, 1938 was a long, slow, and agonizing wait for justice.

The Board of Design submitted this sketch for a 250-foot-tall "Theme Tower" in 1936, one of many concepts that would eventually become the Trylon and Perisphere. *(Courtesy of the New York Public Library)*

WHY HAVE A FAIR?

While all the controversy surrounding Flushing Meadows was going on, the World's Fair concept itself began taking shape. And, as usual, it would begin with an argument. All the debate would result in an astoundingly clear vision and specific plan for the Fair in a relatively short amount of time, but it would take committee after committee to get them there.

The problem arose almost immediately after the World's Fair Corporation was formed. George McAneny, who had personally provided initial working capital and even secured offices for the board of directors, had taken it upon himself to hire a small group of marketing professionals from the Chicago World's Fair to create an overall plan for New York's. This did not sit well with the city's fussy art scene, who felt that the blueprints for the Fair, including its overall theme, the layout of the grounds, and the presentation of exhibits, should be left to professionals like, for instance, themselves. For this crowd, the very lack of designers on the World's Fair staff spelled trouble. Marketers were by nature concerned only with commercialism, and they pointed to Chicago's criticism as evidence that only designers should be in charge of design. Let McAneny and Grover Whalen worry about how to pay for it all.

In December 1935, a group of ninety-six artists, designers, and architects calling themselves "Progressives in the Arts" got together at a dinner at the New York Civic Club to decide what should be done about this. In charge was Michael Hare of the Municipal Art Society, supported by future Fair designers Gilbert Rohde and Walter Dorwin Teague. Lewis Mumford, a social commentator and curmudgeonly columnist for *The New Yorker*, backed them up.

It was more than a design issue, they argued. What was needed was a new kind of Fair that would address social issues like unemployment and the vast mistrust the public felt toward the very technology the Fair would be presenting in its vision of the future. The problem was that Mumford, along with many other "progressives," had a rather inflated sense of self-importance.

"If we allow ourselves," Mumford boasted, " . . . as members of a great metropolis, to think for the world at large, we may lay the foundation for a pattern of life which would have an enormous impact in times to come."

This kind of New York intellectual superiority would have significant impact on the fortunes of the Fair, just not in ways Mumford could then imagine.

The end result of the dinner was the formation of a "Fair of the Future" committee. Taking the basic subtext of the corporation's ideas for reflecting on the past only as a way to see into the World of Tomorrow, the committee asserted in its proposal, "The world is in chaos, struggling to master its own inventions." Therefore, "Mere mechanical progress is no longer an adequate or practical theme for a World's Fair. Instead we must demonstrate an American Way of Living. We must tell the story of the relationships between objects in their everyday use—how they may be used and, when purposefully used, how they may help us."

Industrial designers such as Teague had enjoyed great success with the new style of streamlining, and because such designs were closely associated with aerodynamics, with more than a touch of science fiction, the public ate it up. Everything from refrigerators to locomotives was suddenly streamlined and bullet-shaped, though why anyone would want a streamlined refrigerator was never pondered. And while Chicago's Fair had presented its new technology as living in the realm of *Popular Science* and its depiction of a future filled with flying cars and rocket packs, Teague and others like Raymond Loewy wanted to make science fiction a practical reality.

Ultimately, the basic recommendation of the Fair of the Future committee was to create another one, the social planning committee, made up of members representing the fields of architecture, design, education, and engineering. This committee, they insisted, should be given total control over the planning and construction of the Fair in place of the marketers and promotions men from Chicago.

Perhaps because the Fair of the Future's suggestions fell in line so well with the corporation's ideas, their proposal was quickly adopted as the overall framework for the World of Tomorrow. It was, in fact, a page right out of the Whalen playbook, marrying the product with the consumer and the consumer with the notion of greater good. And underneath that came the whiff of patriotism—capitalism dressed up as being good for America. The result would also help to rebuild a little of that lost trust in big business. Whether or not they could sell General Motors on the idea was not their concern; that they would leave up to Grover Whalen.

Not surprisingly, many of their key members managed to secure jobs for themselves as the Fair's designers and architects.

In March 1936, the war of the design world reached its critical peak. At what must have seemed a rather posh setting for such a gathering, the Municipal Art Society held a luncheon at McAneny's Ritz-Carlton Hotel to debate the long-standing issues between the so-called modernist and traditionalist schools. Its general stated purpose was to present a plan that would make sure the Fair was "more beautiful, more comfortable and more inspiring than any of its predecessors."

The problem was, no one who attended the luncheon could agree on exactly how that goal should be achieved.

Michael Hare stood up to denounce the idea that the Fair's main focus should be to allow its visitors "to dodge life" by merely having a good time there. "If this World's Fair is to be anything but just another big ballyhoo with a lot of canned art, classic or modernistic, and blatant advertising dished out to an unsuspecting public," he warned, "we must go back to the beginning and ask ourselves, 'Why have a fair?' "

No doubt it was a good question, although Whalen and McAneny would have had something to say in response—something about profits and $1 billion worth of revenue to the city, to be sure. Hare dismissed this with the astounding statement that he believed the Fair's investors would in any case "probably lose their shirts." The only profit he cared about was that of the millions who were to be shown a better and more enriched way of life.

"What are we going to do to prevent the horrible chaotic jumble of exhibitions that reduces the visitor to a state of coma?" he asked. "How are we going to do away with both museum fatigue and architectural eye-wash?"

Then, because he knew which side his bread was buttered on, Hare applied the art of finance as tied directly to the presentation of art at the Fair. "What is going to induce American citizens to spend their money on another Fair . . . ? What is going to make this a paying proposition for the industrialists?"

Although he stated that his viewpoint represented the collective judgment of the eighty architects and industrial designers of the Fair of the Future committee, he may as well have attributed its essence to Grover Whalen. "There is a way for New York City for the first time to present to the world a vivid and well-integrated expression of the possible American life," he said, "and that is by this integration alone that this Fair will achieve significant architecture."

The fireworks started when Royal Cortissoz, a well-known art critic for the *New York Herald Tribune*, stood up and berated McAneny, who had unfortunately been seated next to him at lunch. Cortissoz pointed his finger down at the banker and charged, "If the 1939 Fair is not a landmark in American taste . . . then it will be sunk. I don't care how much money or amusement comes out of it."

He further recommended that a small group of artists be given sole discretion over the Fair's layout and design and warned that they must be "absolutely ruthless" in its presentation of what he considered a "prodigious job."

"Anyone who introduces politics into the 1939 World's Fair, I solemnly think," he sniffed, "ought to be shot."

McAneny reassured everyone that the sponsors' aim was to make the World's Fair "a thing of great architectural beauty" that would attract a worldwide audience. As such, he agreed that a board of control should be established to plan the scope and layout of the grounds and supervise all design work. The artists, for the time being, were mollified.

Impressed with Whalen's speed in solving the Corona Dumps crisis, the board of directors of the World's Fair Corporation called a special meeting and gave him total control on May 4 by making him president. The corporation's bylaws imbued its president with sweeping powers that put him in charge of the overall business of the Fair, including design and construction, as well as sales and supervision. Whalen had been chairman of the board exactly two weeks, after which he and McAneny exchanged titles and McAneny assumed what was now a figurehead position as chairman of the board. To save face, McAneny insisted that most of his work in getting the whole thing started had been accomplished and that the Fair was taking up too much of his time. He needed to get back to the duties of Title Guarantee and Trust.

Whalen, of course, got right down to business, claiming that "headquarters will be established by the end of the week" and that "the permanent organization will be functioning in less than ten days." As far as Flushing Meadows was concerned, "the contractor will actually go to work about June 1." It was eight months after the first announcement of the Fair, but better late than never.

Privately, however, Whalen began to address a larger issue that had been brought up since the very beginning. The original steering committee had been hell-bent on the idea that a World's Fair in New York would do for the city what the Century of Progress had done for Chicago, but they had overlooked a major cause for concern—namely, the notoriously bad reputation that New York City held in the eyes of the rest of the country.

"The big town never had been held in affection," reported *The Saturday Evening Post*. "People in Dubuque and Birmingham pretended to despise New York, called it a foreign city, and said they wouldn't live there if somebody gave them Rockefeller Center."

No doubt the sentiment was true, and had been for quite some time. In 1929, well-known novelist and newsman Elmer Davis had written, "We knew that our town was not popular in the rest of the country. . . . The back country hates all cities, but especially it hates New York."*

At first, Whalen had been startled by the very idea of such loathing. He simply could not believe that anyone wouldn't want to come to New York, which was then one of the safest cities in the country in terms of homicide and other major crimes. As police commissioner, he had stated publicly that there was less open vice in Manhattan than in any other large city in the world. Yet he understood that part of the hatred of New York stemmed from its reputation as a "wicked city" lacking any semblance of morals whatsoever. Another part of it was Middle America's resentment that most of its citizens could never hope to live in Manhattan, "the most expensive spot on earth." Adding fuel to the fire was the belief that New Yorkers didn't care about anything but themselves, and that the rest of the country didn't matter a whit in the minds of the sophisticated city dweller.

Which was probably true. "So of civic pride as America understands it," Davis went on, "New York has almost none."

And that was indeed a genuine concern for all those entrusted with the creation and eventual success of the Fair. Moreover, the planners worried that maybe New York was past its prime; lack of business in the city's ports had been Shadgen's original motivation for getting the whole thing started in the first place. What if New York was no longer "the goal of American dreams"? Would its residents turn out for an exhibition they might actually resent—either because they felt the city needed no advertisement, or they couldn't care less what the rest of the world thought about their beloved city, or they didn't want the invasion of yokel tourists crowding out their summers?

---

* Mr. Davis himself enjoyed a peculiar love-hate relationship with New York. "I have spent eighteen minutes traveling three blocks (about 700 feet) in a Fifth Avenue bus," he wrote. "A few years more, and the actuaries can safely calculate just how many thousand New Yorkers in the course of a year will starve to death in taxicabs on their way home to dinner, while they wait for the red light to turn green."

"A New Yorker is inclined to be complacent about New York," mused *The Saturday Evening Post*. And the *Post* was the chronicler of homespun Americana, the journal of the Everyman whose Norman Rockwell covers featured the very essence of small-town fantasy life. "If you have to fight night and morning for a foot of space and a strap in the subway," the magazine suggested, "you're not likely to cheer for a bigger population."

After a while, even Whalen had to grudgingly admit that this was indeed a problem. Or it could be if they let it go unchecked. What was needed, he said, reassuring the corporation that the Fair would be greeted with open arms, was exactly what the Fair of the Future committee was proposing: a nationwide, if not global, shift in perspective regarding the city.

"It is infinitely more important to think of how the people of this country and the world feel about New York," Whalen stated in a speech to the Foreign Commerce Club. "In short, we must put our city on the map, psychologically."

The Fair would do more to sell New York, he repeated to the Merchants Association, than "anything the city has ever done" by bringing so many people here to see for themselves, firsthand, that it was not a high-handed, overpriced, stuffed-shirt metropolis. The goal, Whalen said, was the same as when he had organized his grand parades as official greeter: "to portray New York in a true light; to show the world that it is not a cold and indifferent city, but has a warm heart and a sympathetic hand."

His idea to "re-glamorize" New York was not met with overwhelming applause. In fact, he recalled, it almost "landed me in the street." The directors thought it was a ridiculous notion at best; at worst they thought he was crazy. Initially, some were worried that the city itself would ignore the Fair, if only out of protest; the rest of the country, despite Chicago's success, "would smell a rat." After all, they reasoned, New York's only other Fair, the Crystal Palace of 1853, had been a financial flop.

And just how was a World's Fair supposed to change the country's long-held perception of an entire city in just two short seasons? Whalen reasoned it this way: Chicago's Fair, without costing a dime, had all but eradicated the lingering association with Al Capone and the lawlessness of its gangster reputation.

Nevertheless, it was written into the backbone of principle thought that the Fair had better be more spectacle and sensation than dreary enlightenment. Regardless of what the Municipal Art Society would suggest, the World of Tomorrow must be eye-popping as well as educational, high-minded but not high-hat. And that meant keeping it affordable to the average Joe while at the same time presenting him with wonders beyond belief. It also meant plenty of hot dogs and free bathrooms, an issue Whalen would comically refer to over and over again as "the Battle of the Turnstiles." Americans would spend their dollars, Whalen knew, as long as they felt they were getting their money's worth.

Actually, it was less a matter of profits than what financial failure would mean to the Fair's overall legacy; bankruptcy would forever shroud the endeavor with questions about its inherent value and subsequent impact on the real world of tomorrow. Future generations would remember only that the 1939 New York World's Fair must not have been very important after all, if no one came; and if no one came, then its very premise must have been erroneous. And that would make the whole thing purposeless. They may as well quit now.

As it turned out, they were right to be concerned. Once reports about the Fair began to spread nationwide, newspapers in the Midwest, including the *Omaha World-Herald* and the *Detroit News*, sniffed that the city was holding a Fair only because "effete, sophisticated New York" didn't want to be shown up by Chicago. Even closer-to-home publications like the *Albany News* warned that Whalen had probably "bitten off a very big chew, and may have a bad case of indigestion before it is swallowed."

And within the city itself, the New York smart set delighted in sneering at it over cocktails as a country fair whose garbage dump odors would be covered only by the manure smell of its livestock. "It is just like New York," said, appropriately, *The New Yorker*, "to invite the world to a big party, and then set up the tables next to the finest garbage dump in town."

And, cruelly for Whalen, all the "high hat" criticism about New York was channeled into the public's long-held image of him as a gardenia-wearing stuffed shirt. Oddly, for all his promotional skill, the one great failure in his life seemed to be that he could not sell the idea of *himself*—at least not in a way that ever satisfied his snickering public.

"The fashion amongst the New York smart-crackers," wrote *The Saturday Evening Post*, "is to ridicule Whalen; a practice that puzzles and pains him. . . . There is a feeling, expressed in the periodicals aimed at the intelligentsia, that Grover is slightly comic, that . . . he doesn't quite know what it's all about."

He didn't make it any easier. At his own insistence, all World's Fair promotional material went out in his name and carried his title first, preferably in the opening paragraph. "We've got just one thing to sell at this Fair—Grover Whalen," said Director of Publicity Perley Boone. And it backfired. The whimsical catchphrase "Will it play in Peoria?" yielded to grim reality when the editor of that city's *Journal-Transcript* stated, "When Grover Whalen smiles it may be news in New York, but we just don't give a damn."

Whalen, it seemed, was the very embodiment of the smug, superior New Yorker he was trying to downplay. Unlike the "glib, fun-loving city," the *Post* admitted, "[Whalen] is a bit inarticulate and solemn. He does have a rather impenetrable front."

It was exactly the portrait of New York they were trying to dispel: the man in the top hat and spats looking down at the average farmer off the fields, taking his money while at the same time snickering at his overalls and pointing out the hay in his hair. On top of that were the "twentieth-century Barnum" comments that kept cropping up here and there and which made Whalen even crazier with the criticism, wishing that the naysayers would pick one or the other complaint: that the Fair was going to be either a stuffy, high-hat affair or a huckster's circus designed to pick the nickels out of unsuspecting visitors' pockets. Either way, it seemed, he couldn't win.

Mayor Fiorello La Guardia swearing in Robert Moses *(Courtesy of the New York Public Library)*

106 DEGREES
IN THE SHADE

Robert Moses was at it again. In June 1936, after compiling several bids by construction firms to begin work on the World's Fair site, Moses raised the ire of the Fair corporation by rejecting the lowest bid—and the next lowest. His decision would cost the city an extra $342,000, and he defended it in familiar terms. "Time is of the essence," he said, "and if there are any further delays the completion of the basic structure so as to permit the opening of the World's Fair in 1939 will be impossible."

The two less costly firms, he stated definitively, "lack the essential qualifications to complete this work on time."

His old nemesis, Bronx borough president James Lyons, citing the city's long-held practice of awarding contracts to the lowest bidder, tried to block the decision at a special meeting of the New York City Board of Estimate. "I refuse to be stampeded into wasting . . . the taxpayers' money just because a speed demon like Mr. Moses comes in here and tells us how important speed is." The board disagreed with Lyons and sided with Moses.

Throughout the meeting, La Guardia remained silent, seemingly exhausted, and buried his face in his hands. His aides said he had been suffering from "severe pains in the back," without making specific reference to the parks commissioner.

In July, the mayor recovered some of his old backbone and was forced to call out the police to stop Moses from tearing down the municipal ferry terminal at Ninety-second Street on the East River. "The city cannot, of course, submit to have any of its services or departments interfered with by force," La Guardia stated firmly. The next day he relented, agreeing to consider immediate termination of the ferry service so that Moses could begin building an extension from the East River Drive to the about-to-open Triborough Bridge.

"All is quiet on the Eastern Front," La Guardia sighed.

And yet. As soon as work began in Flushing Meadows, no one could have a bad word to say about Robert Moses. On June 3, 1936, eleven World's Fair Corporation officials climbed to the top of a seventy-foot tower constructed to enable a bird's-eye view of the proposed fairgrounds. From where they stood, on a small platform, mountains of ash quivered over their heads. For most of them, it was their first trip out to the dumps, and they were not impressed by what they saw.

Whalen had tried to put them in good spirits by journeying to the site in well-appointed yachts across the East River and transporting them by car as far as they could go before being stopped by all the garbage. The rest of the way they had to travel by foot "over rolling hills of ashes to the tower." Still, he made the most of the event, christening the site by swinging a bottle of 1923 champagne against the tower's girders. It was a silly moment, really, and would prove to be a telling one. Whalen had timed it to occur precisely at sunset, when the sky would be lit by the orange glow of a late spring evening—the dusk of the old day before the dawn of a new one.

The trouble was, just as the group reached the platform and stood, transfixed by the difference between what they saw and what they envisioned, "the sun was hidden behind clouds that already had begun to drop rain."

Whalen decided against using that as a photo opportunity. Instead, on June 29 he herded La Guardia, Moses, McAneny, and a handful of other dignitaries out to Flushing Meadows to officially break ground on the site. To ensure that the ceremony held proper historical context, Whalen had gotten hold of a one-hundred-and-fifty-year-old spade from a man named

George Powell, whose farm George Washington was supposed to have visited. It may have been a second- or thirdhand relic twice removed as far as the anniversary was concerned, but at least its age was correct (according to the Flushing Historical Society, anyway).

Whalen invoked Washington's spirit again, if somewhat ludicrously, by solemnly declaring that Flushing Meadows might have actually become the nation's capital, since the first president had inspected "the ground upon which we are standing this minute" when he was looking for a permanent seat of government. Then he lightened it up a bit by joking that Washington himself had complained of all the mosquitoes in the area.

They all gave speeches, and La Guardia declared that the Fair was now as official "as the government can make anything official." The mayor raised the city's flag, Lieutenant Governor William Bray raised the American flag, and Whalen raised the newly designed blue World's Fair pennant. Then one by one they took turns with the spade, which turned out not to be such a good idea after all. "Those who used it did so with evident trepidation," one reporter noted, "which the hardness of the caked soil did not serve to ease."

As he scooped the ceremonial ash into a container for posterity, La Guardia noted, "This is the way they did it a hundred and fifty years ago." Then he pointed to a steam shovel and announced to a delighted audience, "Over there is what we use today." With that he climbed up into the cab, got the thing started, and proceeded to carve out a great chunk of dirt "with gusto."

"My, she's delicate to the touch!" La Guardia smiled as he jumped back down again to laughs and applause. Never one to be outdone, Whalen mischievously grinned back at La Guardia and mounted the steam shovel himself, showing "considerable dexterity at the controls." Most likely, he had been tutored earlier in an effort to show that he, too, could be one of the guys.

Incredibly, a crowd of about a thousand people attended the ceremony, and while Whalen may have been overjoyed at the turnout, most of them were unemployed construction workers who had been milling about all day, hoping to land a job with Moses and his crew.

The ceremony was indeed symbolic. Moses had actually begun work on the site exactly two weeks earlier, ahead of schedule. Just after the city had officially acquired the final five hundred acres of land around Fishhooks' original plot, Moses ordered that the homes and buildings within the area be condemned and evacuated as soon as possible. Residents were given a mere thirty days' notice to clear out. However, when he saw that work could begin without initially tearing down these structures, he magnanimously awarded their owners an extra thirty days. After that, he called out the marshals and forcibly evicted everyone who remained, including one reluctant tombstone manufacturer who complained that he needed more time, since moving his inventory was a little more difficult.

Already, crews of more than one hundred and fifty men were working around the clock, three separate fifty-man groups toiling in eight-hour shifts. When night came, twelve eighty-foot towers carrying giant floodlights lit up the area, creating an eerie daylight glow that could be seen for miles around. Nearby residents began complaining to anyone who would listen that they couldn't sleep because of the glare. Moses ignored them and went right on digging day and night. The process stopped only when all the machinery had to be oiled, and that occurred only once a day. Even the short pauses caused him heartbreak.

From the outset, the dust-covered site was like an anthill of activity: Steam shovels (minus La Guardia and Whalen) attacked the ash heaps at six different locations simultaneously, each dumping a load full of refuse into an endless line of massive trucks that carried the waste to large-scale landfill projects as far away as Staten Island, Pelham Bay, and Jamaica Bay. Enormous clouds of powder and ash flew up under their wheels, whirlpooling so heavily that the drivers had to wear handkerchiefs over their noses and mouths in order to breathe.

"The scene there now is like a no-man's land in a war," *The New York Times* reported, "with the dust, if not the smoke, of battle rising in clouds to blanket the steeples of Flushing beyond the valley."

In other spots, where the ashes were to be spread out across the meadow, the land was so thick and marshy that the trucks had to unload while moving or risk sinking into a hundred feet of slime. Along the routes they traveled to get there, special macadam roadways had been laid out of the gathering of various stones and rocks unearthed from the digging.

Night and day the trucks thundered along, thirty-five hundred of them every twenty-four hours. Single file, they formed an endless convoy rolling across the city, some trailing a steady stream of soot billowing out in their wake and covering whatever happened to be behind them in a fine layer of ash.

But ashes weren't the only problem. Flushing Creek wound a snake-like path through a thick, swampy section of the grounds. Thousands of tons of goopy creek bed had to be scooped out by a slow parade of enormous dragline derricks with seventy-foot booms dredging along its bottom, scraping and storing the slop for later use in processing topsoil. After that, a new channel had to be dug in order to create a pair of freshwater lagoons, each with a tidal dam to keep out the salt water.

And then there was the problem of odor. The grounds themselves were getting a face lift, but the Flushing River had been the unfortunate recipient of the city's raw sewage for decades, and a new drainage tunnel had to be constructed along the west shore. According to Moses's plan, it was to be as large as a tube of the Holland Tunnel. But within a year, he promised, "the decomposition of sludge on the bay bottom will be completed, the generation of gas will stop and the atmosphere of hydrogen sulphide will be only an unpleasant memory."

Moses knew whereof he spoke. Throughout the early stages of reclamation, men complained and then gradually grew used to the stench of rotten eggs and flatulence that seemed to emanate from the very bowels of Flushing Meadows itself.

In July 1936, just as Moses was doubling the size of his work crew, the city suffered its worst heat wave on record. Although the official high temperature reading of 102.3 degrees was measured at a little before three in the afternoon, readings as high as 115 degrees were noted in Times Square, where the baking sun reflected off the sidewalks. Heat waves were rising visibly from the concrete, washing everything in a watery, swirling motion.

In front of the Central Library at Fifth Avenue and Forty-second Street, one of the city's busiest thoroughfares, a blue haze of automobile exhaust hung low and thick; tourists visiting the area waded breathlessly through it, "as if breasting surf." Policemen lining the streets shed their heavy tunics and revealed sweat-soaked blue shirts; Works Progress Administration workers were let off from roadwork duty after three-thirty because the tar had reached a bubbling point. Before the men were excused, the WPA headquarters at Sixth Avenue and Twentieth Street had become so overrun with cases of heat prostration that the emergency squad stopped keeping a record of them all.

The temperature was one thing, but the intense heat produced by the blazing sun was literally broiling New Yorkers. David Morris, a meteorologist at the Central Park Conservatory, reported a reading of 145 degrees at twelve forty-five; the afternoon shade cooled that down to 106. The average high for that date was 89 degrees.

During the evening rush hour, commuters actually stayed in the subway longer than necessary, because the temperature underground was twenty degrees cooler than at street level. Police opened fire hydrants all over the city for kids to splash around in, the kids squealing in delight when they found that adults were joining in the fun. Along some avenues, cars waded through eight inches of accumulated water.

At night there was some relief, but not much. The beaches at Coney Island and Rockaway became large camping grounds for families intending to spend the night there, cooled by ocean breezes. Special police guards were detailed to keep them safe. The previous night, a large number of arrests had been made owing to an ordinance against open-air sleeping, but Mayor La Guardia dismissed all charges and suspended the edict for the duration of the heat wave. Even Robert Moses chipped in and ordered all city swimming pools kept open until midnight instead of their usual ten p.m. closing time.

For ten sweltering days, between July 5 and 15, the temperature in Manhattan hovered above one hundred degrees. Newspapers, regaling the public with some lighthearted moments, reported the tales of a woman in New Jersey who had fried an egg on the sidewalk and a gentleman in lower Manhattan who had left his dentures on a windowsill, only to return a while later and find them melted. But the effect of the heat wave was considerably more serious. The estimated death toll in the city neared one hundred. Throughout the country, record high temperatures remained for the entire summer; in some states, no significant relief was felt until September. When it was over, more than five thousand deaths would be recorded nationwide.

Right in the middle of it all, on July 11, the Triborough Bridge officially opened for business. At one p.m., the concrete barriers blocking entrances from the boroughs of Queens, the Bronx, and Manhattan fell in a formal dedication ceremony attended by President Roosevelt, Governor Lehman, and Mayor La Guardia, who personally collected the first twenty-five-cent toll. Even Harold Ickes showed up; he and Moses had declared an informal truce, no doubt to last only as long as the opening ceremony itself. There was an awkward tension in the air; Moses remained visibly unmoved when the president called him "Bob." Nevertheless the project, which had begun on Black Friday in 1929, and was suspended in 1932, and then revived again in 1934 with Moses at the helm, was finally completed.

Despite the heat, Moses could now turn his full attention to the festering stew pot in Flushing Meadows. By mid-August, his crews numbered more than five hundred, and already they had moved more than a million cubic yards of material. After the land was cleared out and leveled came the immense job of constructing more than seventeen miles of roads, fifteen miles of gas mains, ten bridges, and two artificial lakes.

For construction of the boat basin, a giant seawall was being built and cellular sheet steel piling was sunk seventy feet deep. "No flimsy riprap or cheap half-hearted bulkhead could be depended on to hold back the shoreline," Moses explained. An asphalt plant had to be built on a barge canal at the mouth of the Flushing River. Over- and underpasses had to be created for traffic flow. New bridges and arteries were springing up for all roads leading to and from the Fair. And to top it all off, the nearby North Beach Airport* was undergoing a complete overhaul, should any of its ritzier clientele desire to arrive by air.

All in all, it was a tremendous job just to reclaim the land and make it fit for habitation, if not spectacle, and the deadline for completion was

* Later to be renamed La Guardia Airport in honor of the mayor.

April 1, 1937. After which the builders would go to work. That left only a little over nine months, a fact that was never far from Moses's mind. Before he was through, Moses's original plea for $7 million to begin work would balloon to around $59 million, an amount even he found "staggering." And all of it, every dime, was spent in consideration of the ground design as being developed for what he was privately referring to as Robert Moses Park.

Scheduled opening date: sometime after October 1940.

Detective Ferdinand A. (Freddy) Socha

PANIC IN TIMES SQUARE

As with most other assignments in the NYPD, life on the Bomb and Forgery Squad involved endless cycles of boredom broken up periodically by heart-stopping tension. The division itself was an odd mix of two singular specialties and had been created only in late 1935, when Commissioner Valentine decided that the duties of the two separate squads often overlapped. The Forgery Squad, Valentine believed, largely investigated anonymous or threatening letters, and even when they didn't specifically mention anything about explosives, it was usually the Bomb Squad that was sent out to investigate.

At first, the combined teams came under the command of Lieutenant Charles Newman, who had been head of the Bomb Squad. The individual staffs even shared the same office space, though it was an uneasy transition for both parties: The forgery men were not entirely thrilled with the prospect of defusing explosives; the bomb staff was already overloaded with information regarding the printed word.

For the better part of the previous year, the sixteen men who made up the Bomb Squad had been studying cryptography under the auspices of the United States Army's Intelligence Service. Twice a month they trundled down to the Army Building at 39 Whitehall Street, an imposing chunk of red granite, brick, and sandstone that had been built half a century earlier.

Their instructor was Colonel George Lynch, and the course itself was exhaustive. Newman and his crew were trained in the fine art of handwriting analysis and typewriter identification. They also studied the varying idiosyncrasies of broken English used by foreigners and how to discern the nationality of the sender by common misspellings and grammatical inconsistencies. In addition, there were numerous courses in paper, perforations, and inks and even a thorough rundown of mystic symbols used by religious blackmailers, dislocated anarchists, and other libelous note writers.

This rigorous study was not well received by men who up until that point were more accustomed to their regular, and much more exciting, training in explosives, which was held at the United States Testing Laboratory in Perth Amboy, New Jersey. Those exercises, conducted by a gruff man's man named Harry Campbell of the Bureau of Explosives, were infinitely more pleasurable, despite the nearly constant threat of losing a finger or two.

Newman himself didn't particularly enjoy the forced combination of duties, and within a few months a brawny, brainy character named Lieutenant James Pyke replaced him. The new commander was already something of a legend in the force. Every man in whichever precinct he was assigned quickly learned the tale of how Pyke had been a driver for General Pershing in the Great War. Men of the Bomb and Forgery Squad were awed to learn that he had been severely burned while attempting to dismantle an incendiary device. Whatever disfigurement he carried was not evident, however; it certainly didn't stop him from making flying tackles of fleeing suspects when the situation called for it. Pyke was fearless; the war had taught him respect for but not hesitation when it came to dangerous situations.

Six feet tall, jug-eared, and graying at the temples, he sometimes let forth an explosive temper to match his new duties, but he could just as easily display a generosity, warmth, and fellowship for the citizens he protected, especially those who had fallen on hard times during the straining years of the Depression. Only a few months after he took command of the Bomb and Forgery Squad, one of his detectives, Peter Hayias, introduced a rather pitiful-looking scene into his office.

Hayias had refused to arrest a man who had forged his name on a home relief check and instead brought his entire family back to the squad's headquarters, hoping he had made the right decision under the circumstances. Pyke, sitting at his desk, looked up at the ragtag parade Hayias was ushering in and wondered what the hell was going on. Hayias stood in the doorway and, in addition to the forger, motioned in the man's wife and four children, who ranged in age from a few months to six years old, and then another woman and *her* three children. He had driven them all here from the Emergency Relief Bureau over on Tenth Avenue. Pyke wondered how he'd gotten them all in one car. He listened as Hayias sheepishly explained the situation.

The man who was to be arrested, it seemed, had found a relief check in the amount of $11.30 on a street near his home in Jamaica, Queens. They were on home relief themselves, and eleven bucks and change was a lot of money for a family of six. He took the check home and showed it to his wife. They argued over what to do with it and then, perhaps needing some moral support for their potential crime, called the other woman, a widow, who now stood in Pyke's office with her children. They needed the money, all agreed, so the man signed his name to the check and had it cashed. He gave the widow $5 and kept the rest for his family.

Several days later, the forgery was discovered and both families were called into the accounting office to which Hayias had been dispatched.* He didn't have the heart to arrest them, Hayias told Pyke; they were absolutely hysterical when he'd arrived, he said, and he just couldn't bring himself to do it.

Pyke looked them all over; they were, he noted, in a "really pathetic condition." Hayias held his breath and waited for either calamity at his dereliction of duty or, preferably, some of Pyke's sense of goodwill to come shining through. Typically, Pyke chose the latter. He sent Hayias out to buy four quarts of milk for the children and coffee and sandwiches for the adults. They hadn't eaten in two days, the families told him.

But the lack of arrest made it a sticky situation, so Pyke had another officer look into the man's background and check to see if he was wanted

---

* The details, including the involvement of the widow and why they all appeared at the Emergency Relief Bureau, are sketchy. Pyke, not wanting to embarrass the families, ordered that all names and incidental facts be stricken from the police department record.

for or had been convicted of any crime. He hadn't. Pyke sat with the man and learned his story; he had been a hard worker before the Depression hit, and his tale hit Pyke squarely in that soft heart of his. He patted the man on the shoulder and immediately called up the Emergency Relief Bureau, arguing with an official for more than half an hour over Officer Hayias's actions.

"I wouldn't arrest these people, no matter who ordered it!" Pyke finally shouted into the phone, and promptly hung up. An Emergency Relief Bureau examiner stood in his office and was now demanding either an arrest in the case or repayment of the amount of the forged check. Pyke, by this time enraged by the bureau's lack of sympathy in the matter, pulled out his wallet and handed him $11. The examiner waited. Pyke dug into his jacket and pulled out thirty cents in coin, asking for a receipt just to be obstinate.

Then he smiled at the two families. "You can go home now," he told them. They each in turn thanked him profusely and began bundling up. The food, Pyke noted, seemed to bring each member back to life. Pyke wasn't through. A late summer storm had broken out, and it was raining hard.

"Wait a minute," he said, then called for a police car and detailed one of his men to drive them home.

From their desks in the cramped office, each man in the Bomb and Forgery Squad watched all this in silence, including thirty-two-year-old Freddy Socha, who had recently joined the team.

Socha's real first name was Ferdinand, but nobody called him that. One of five children, he had grown up in Greenpoint, Brooklyn, and now lived literally around the corner from his family home in a small apartment he shared with his wife, Genevieve, known as Jennie, on Leonard Street just off McCarren Park. Like Joe Lynch, Freddy had joined the force a few years later than the average applicant; he was already twenty-seven and had spent a couple of years working in various jobs while attending Columbia University. Before the Depression hit, he'd wanted to become a doctor.

Within three years, he was promoted to detective, third grade, and when the Bomb and Forgery Squad was formed, Pyke wanted him on his team. He'd seen Freddy in action. The previous October, Pyke had led an arrest raid on a group of eight burly members of the window cleaners union who had sprayed muriatic acid on the storefronts of various buildings along lower Broadway during the union's strike. When the vandals tried to escape, Pyke forced their car off the road and pulled out a couple of thugs. Socha, seeing another group sprinting away on foot, tore out after them and chased them down Cortland Street. He came back with three more suspects in tow. Pyke liked what he saw. Socha wasn't big, but he obviously had guts. The men he'd arrested were twice his size.

The boring part of Socha's job involved the scammers, including a raid on the offices of the American Contest Company, who skimmed the profits off of a Knights of Columbus raffle. They also held run-of-the-mill raids at various racetrack tipping parlors, where the popular "Pay If You Win" racket* was divesting innocent gamblers of about $15 million a year, along with what seemed to be an endless effort to curb the number of bogus one-cent cigarette tax stamps. Fortunately, there were very few bomb investigations, and almost all of them turned out to be phony anyway.

Still, like Lynch, Socha knew that the squad was a fast step to promotion; within four months, he'd been advanced to detective, second grade, during a ceremony that marked the first time a "negro" (as the papers announced) achieved the rank of first grade, the highest rank of detectives.

Things looked up a bit at the beginning of 1938, when Joe Lynch joined the squad, eager for another promotion and another raise in pay. Pyke, noting that he now had two college men on his team, immediately partnered Lynch, who had studied pharmacy at Fordham, with Socha, the would-be physician who'd attended Columbia. Perhaps because each had switched careers from medicine to law enforcement, the two men bonded over their dashed aspirations and became fast friends.

---

* The scheme was simple enough: "Experts" would assign the name of every horse in a particular race to individual bettors. Of course one of them was bound to win, and the lucky individual became convinced that the tipster knew his stuff, thereby agreeing to place future bets that rarely paid off.

The murder of Easter's mother continued to haunt Joe's marriage, although they bravely put on a good front for the children. The month of May finally brought some good news: Joe got the promotion he'd hoped for, to detective, second grade, with an accompanying pay raise to $3,200 a year. A few weeks later, Easter announced that she was pregnant with their fifth child; the new baby would require a further shuffling of their family's already creative sleeping arrangements. In October, he got his name in the papers for arresting a gang of three ex-convicts who had stolen a batch of those cigarette tax stamps. Things were looking up again.

Oddly, the most popular targets for bombs in the 1930s were movie theaters. Throughout the city, an assortment of smoke bombs, tear gas bombs, and bottle bombs—usually four-ounce containers filled with benzyl bromide and fitted with a percussion cap and a watch timer—were set to go off at a specific hour. When they exploded, the glass would shatter with the noise of gunfire, scaring the hell out of anyone trying to watch the show and leaving behind a terrific stench. The bombings were, again, the outcome of a nasty dispute between unions, in this case the Motion Picture Machine Operators versus the Allied Motion Pictures Operators. The explosions continued at various locations for more than a year.

On one particular Thursday night, bombs went off in eight different theaters in a one-hour period, injuring sixty-two people and sending more than thirteen thousand stampeding into the street for safety. The following Monday, six more movie houses were targeted, most of them in Times Square, each explosion occurring at precisely nine o'clock. One woman was seriously burned, several others were cut badly by the flying glass, and a minor panic set in among most moviegoers. Attendance at one of the decade's most popular diversions dropped off the cliff.

Throughout that summer, Joe Lynch and Freddy Socha found themselves with the enviable job of going to the movies several nights a week. The squad had grown to more than seventy-five men at that point, each and every one of whom was assigned to a different theater throughout the city. Sometimes they traveled as far as Nassau County to catch a show; on other occasions they sat in movie houses right in their own neighborhoods. They never brought their wives, and most of the bombers were never caught.

Then, almost as soon as the terror campaign of the movie bombs had died down (a truce was brokered by Brandt Theaters and union operators), a fresh battle sprang up between the International Fur Workers Union and the Associated Fur Coat Manufacturers. At three a.m. on September 11, 1938, two huge explosions went off in the fur district along West Twenty-ninth Street. One of them ripped a gaping hole in the front door of a fur shop and cut a six-inch crater into the sidewalk out front; the other shattered the windows of three adjoining buildings across the street. Burglar alarms rang out up and down the block, sending officers from three different police stations racing to see what was happening.

Pyke and several of his men, including Lynch and Socha, scoured the scene. They found small fragments of light metal scattered around, which meant only one thing: dynamite. Pyke found a man named Morris Schwartz checking out the condition of his nearby store and questioned him. He'd been picketed for nine months by the unions, in protest to a lockout and strike by the entire industry's fifteen thousand fur workers. This was the end result, he guessed.

Pyke was incensed. There was too much dynamite floating around the city. Most of it was pilfered from construction sites that not only left the explosives unguarded, but actually advertised their contents in signs idiotically reading, DANGER, EXPLOSIVES! Two days earlier, Pyke had arrested a man named Louis Friedman, who had tried to rob the Emigrant Industrial Savings Bank, again in Times Square, during lunch hour.

"I want thirty thousand dollars, and if you don't give it to me, I'll blow up the bank," he threatened.

Disaster had been avoided by the manager, David Groden, who simply didn't believe it when Friedman told him, "I have a bottle of nitroglycerin up my sleeve."

Groden lunged at him, grabbing his wrists and pinning back his arms. He and several other employees hustled Friedman into a back room while terrified customers ran out onto Forty-second Street. When Pyke arrived, however, he confirmed Groden's suspicion: There was no nitroglycerin. What Friedman had *actually* been carrying was a black bag containing no fewer than thirty-four sticks of dynamite and forty-eight blasting caps. He must have been planning to blow up the entire building.

Friedman, it turned out, was an electric welder. He'd stolen the dynamite out of a shed of supplies at a job he was working on. He was from Poughkeepsie, and he'd been in the city for three months. Pyke did the math. Out in Flushing Meadows, any crackpot could pick up a carload of sticks and drive them back to Manhattan without anyone thinking twice about it. So many men swirled and lifted and hammered and welded out at the World's Fair site, and who knew what their backgrounds were, what political beliefs they held. Or, more important, which goddamn union they belonged to.

Probably because of his own experience in the war and the scars it left on his body, Pyke hated all types of bombs, but he especially hated bombs made by people who had no idea of their killing power.

"These bombs are crudely constructed, but [they are] the most dangerous machines we have ever encountered," Pyke said. "To make any effort to open them might result in an explosion, and any other means of disposing them would eliminate any chance of examination for finger prints."

The current method of disarming a bomb by soaking it in motor oil was no doubt safer, but all traces of evidence were erased in the process. Pyke sought to find a safe way to open unexploded bombs, for instance by cutting a small hole in whatever container they happened to be placed in and then defusing them by hand. To catch those who perpetrated these acts, he began devising a method that would ultimately prove riskier to his squad but that he hoped would aid in identifying suspects.

Throughout the winter of 1939 and into 1940, he trained his men in this new and dangerous procedure.

The Italian Pavilion, courtesy of Il Duce. (*© Bill Cotter, worldsfairphotos.com*)

SELLING THE FAIR

When Grover Whalen took over the World's Fair Corporation in 1936, the project was woefully behind schedule, the corporation itself a frustrating mix of chaos and disorder. There was money to be raised—a lot of it; foreign nations needed to be coaxed into participating (not to mention the forty-eight American states); plans and designs and blueprints had to be finalized for the following April, when Flushing Meadows would be ready for construction to begin. Whalen, still chairman of Schenley, awarded himself a salary of $100,000 a year and almost forgot about the liquor business entirely.

On May 21, a little over two weeks after he'd been made president of the Fair corporation, he announced the formation of the Board of Design to tackle the enormous job of devising a general plan for the Fair. Its chairman was Stephen Voorhees, president of the American Institute of Architects, and together the seven-member committee was responsible for creating, as Whalen himself defined it, "the definition of the main theme, limitations of heights and areas for structures, and the general architectural characteristics, including color and lighting." As if that weren't enough, they were also charged with hiring everyone needed to design it, build it, landscape it, sculpt it, and paint it. Then he gave them a deadline, September 1, which allowed them the luxury of one hundred days to complete their tasks.

For the new president, running a World's Fair was not all that different from running a department store or a police force. "The principal difference is that in an exposition there is a more urgent necessity for speed," he explained. "[An executive] must know how to pick men and, having picked them, he must give them full authority to do what they see fit."

There was one final facet to the sparkle of his leadership: "I wouldn't engage anyone who couldn't visualize the buildings we were going to erect here just as clearly as I could," Whalen stated. "Moreover, he must have enthusiasm and be able to convey that enthusiasm to those who are working for him."

The Board of Design's first order of business was to create a Theme Committee, headed up by two of its members, Walter Dorwin Teague and Robert Kohn. Teague had been on the Fair of the Future committee and had contributed several designs for the Chicago Fair. Kohn had been president of the American Institute of Architects and one of the founding members of George McAneny's Regional Plan Association. Together, borrowing heavily from the Fair of the Future proposal, they laid out the basic cornerstone of the Fair, dividing it into what would eventually become seven* distinct color-coded zones: Amusement; Government; Production and Distribution; Transportation; Communications and Business; Food; and Community Interests.

Moreover, they expanded upon Whalen's and the corporation's World of Tomorrow concept, elongating it into "Building the World of Tomorrow." Somehow, that made it less of a finite statement; this World's Fair would not be a finished product after all, but a flowing, almost organic representation of what America *could* be rather than what it was or would be when the gates opened in a little under three years' time.

Their greatest challenges lay in the inherent irony regarding the future itself: how to present a utopia of machine age wonders, a "supercivilization" based on industry, when the country was nearly crushed under the oppressive weight of the Great Depression? Practically speaking, what was the true hope of average Americans in emerging from their current situation with enough bread in their bellies to enjoy a new vacuum

---

* Their original plan called for nine zones. Budgetary concerns pared it down to seven.

cleaner? And, most important, how could they create a World's Fair dedicated to the bright promise of tomorrow when today looked so bleak and barren, and the future itself wasn't looking all that rosy, either?

It was a lofty goal, perhaps too lofty. Nevertheless, the Board of Design completed their ideas on August 31, one day ahead of schedule, much to the delight of Whalen, who was somewhat fanatical about adhering to schedules. On October 8, Voorhees and Kohn made their formal presentation to the board of directors, stating, "The New York World's Fair is planned to be 'everyman's fair'—to show the way toward improvement of all the factors contributing to human welfare. We are convinced that the potential assets, material and spiritual, of our country are such that if rightly used they will make for a general public good such as never before has been known."

The lofty goals became loftier, adding a hefty dose of spiritualism, human welfare, and public good to the mix. What they could not have anticipated in 1936, however, was that the two years representing the life of the World's Fair would balance those goals against the crushing alternative that was already brewing in Germany. Those two summer seasons were shaping up to be an antidote to the madness yet to come, the "pinnacle of all inspiration" against the stupidity of war.

On the same day Voorhees and Kohn made their presentation, Robert Moses announced his resignation as a member of the corporation's board of directors. It was one of the few threats he carried out. "I have now come to the definite conclusion that so far as the Fair is concerned I ought to give all my attention to the site," he asserted, "and that it would be a mistake for me and my staff to have their attention diverted to the plans for the Fair itself."

Whalen was livid. More bad press was exactly what he didn't need at this point. He was preparing for a trip abroad first to convince the Bureau of International Expositions, the governing body of all World's Fairs, to give him their official approval, and then to charm as many nations as he could to participate in it. At first, Whalen refused to accept Moses's resignation. Then, when word came that his decision was "absolutely final," he reassured the press that there was "no difference of opinion at all in any manner between Commissioner Moses and the officials of the Fair Corporation."

Privately, he still had doubts as to whether the entire project would ever materialize. His worst fears were realized when, after making a formal appeal in Paris, the Bureau of Expositions approved New York's Fair only in what was termed the "limited" category, meaning that European countries could exhibit if and only if the Fair provided free space for them in a uniform area of ten thousand square feet each. Had they designated it as "unlimited," Whalen would have been free to sell whomever and whatever he pleased, for as much money and space as he could wrangle.

It was a serious setback, and Whalen had to report the disappointing news that Great Britain and France had agreed to occupy only a couple of small pavilions for which the corporation would have to foot the bill— hardly the grand showing for New York he had been expecting to deliver.

For the first time in his life, Whalen decided to play dirty. Perhaps his dealings with Moses had taught him that underhanded tactics sometimes won the match, but he quickly decided that no international bureau was going to limit his Fair, rules or no rules. Since the United States was not a member of the bureau, he felt no particular allegiance to its decision. Conveniently, neither was the USSR. So before he left France, Whalen applied for a visa to visit Moscow. If he could sell Russia on the idea of a large, expensive pavilion, he believed the other foreign nations would be forced to follow suit out of fear of being upstaged.

Russia wouldn't even let him in. Whalen's anti-Communist crusade as police commissioner had left him with no friends in the Kremlin. He returned to New York, crestfallen. There was still no money; at the end of 1936, the World's Fair Corporation had been forced to borrow $1.6 million for seed capital simply in order to pay for their makeshift offices in the Empire State Building and a small staff of visionaries putting lofty ideas down on paper.

But Whalen had an ace up his sleeve. Among his old Tammany cronies, there was talk of Grover Whalen for mayor, to run against Fiorello La Guardia in 1937. For the time being, he was content to let them talk; if worse came to worst, his candidacy would provide an adequate excuse out of this World's Fair mess.

On November 23, 1936, the corporation laid out its plans for raising funds at a gala dinner held at the Hotel Astor. More than two thousand guests were invited, and Whalen, Harvey Gibson, George McAneny, and a host of other directors explained that $27,829,500 would be raised by selling World's Fair bonds to the business interests of the city. The debentures themselves would become payable on January 1, 1941, at an interest rate of 4 percent. How they arrived at such an exact figure was left to the imagination, but the man they picked to lead the charge was impressive. Richard Whitney was a past president of the New York Stock Exchange and currently headed up Richard Whitney & Co., a successful Wall Street investment firm.

As chairman of the Fair's bond sales committee, Whitney stressed the fact that Chicago's Fair had paid off its notes in full, with interest and principal totaling more than $11 million. Gibson, as head of the finance committee, made it clear again that New York would be an even safer investment.

"I speak sincerely in stressing the fact that we are not trying to fool ourselves or to fool you when I say that the bonds will be paid in full and with interest," Whitney predicted. And everyone would benefit from the World's Fair's success, he stressed, including hotels, restaurants, retail stores, and theaters. It was as sure a bet as any he had seen or known in his financial career, and each of the investors had a responsibility besides. "We believe," he told a group of eager-eyed prospects, "that it is proper and just that we should ask you gentlemen to finance your own prosperity in 1939."

Before the year was out, he had sold more than $7 million worth. John D. Rockefeller personally bought $250,000 in bonds. Con Edison bought in for $750,000; the New York Telephone Company came in for half a million, as did the Pennsylvania Railroad. Macy's bought almost half a million, led by board member Percy Straus, who was now chairman of the

Fair's committee on architecture and physical planning. Straus honestly believed in the Fair's ability to restore public confidence in business and the city, but he was realistic when it came to recouping his money.

"If by some mischance the full amount invested is not returned," he stated, much to the chagrin of Gibson and Whitney, "the difference will be but a small contribution toward rebuilding the prestige of New York."

By the end of January, more than $17 million had been sold, including a $100 bond purchased by a twenty-three-year-old truck driver named John Weir Jr., who lived near the fairgrounds and had been driving one of Moses's endless caravans of trucks since groundbreaking in June. Recognizing a good story when he saw one, Whalen pounced on the occasion, riding out to Flushing Meadows to hand-deliver the bond and congratulate Weir on his investment. (And, naturally, reap the benefits of a well-timed photo op.)

But there was more to it than good PR. Amid all the large corporations and multimillion-dollar pavilions Whalen had swimming in his head, for him, truck driver Weir represented what this Fair was really all about. He was the average American to whom the Fair would speak, the embodiment of the "Everyman" whose life would be enriched by its message. Moreover, he was one of the thousands who, after years of hardship, had been given the opportunity to work and support his family because of this World's Fair.

In a personal note to Whalen, Weir had written, "Among other things I should like to tell you that I like my job, am filled with enthusiasm and visions of the success of this undertaking and that I am uplifted with the knowledge that I have contributed by eight hours per day since its inception in helping to build it up."

The letter stirred something deep within Whalen's working-class roots. Weir's eloquence in writing may not have been uncommon, even for a truck driver, in 1930s America, but his dedication and spirit to the task at hand renewed Whalen's initial enthusiasm and perhaps reminded him of the struggles he'd had to overcome.

"I have often heard my father speak of you with kindly admiration," Weir had told him.

On a bitterly cold January morning, Whalen leapt over icy puddles to shake the hand of the man driving Truck Number 29 on Dragline 34. Weir, wearing a greasy sailor's cap, was speechless.

By the end of February, the $20 million mark had been met, including another quarter million by second-banana department store moguls the Gimbel brothers. Whalen himself even bought $10,000 worth. Then things started to get tricky. The total estimated cost of the Fair had grown from McAneny's $40 million to upwards of $70 million and then $100 million. With a little over two years left to go, the corporation was now stating that the actual cost would be somewhere in the neighborhood of $125 million; that in fact they needed to spend the aforementioned $40 million before the gates even opened on construction and operating expenses alone.

To reach that figure, the $28 million in bond sales was to be supplemented by over $11 million in pre-Fair revenue, including advance ticket sales and rents from exhibitors and concessionaires. It was all figured out to the penny. The corporation's prospectus stated that "careful estimates by engineering experts" assured a minimum of forty million visitors in 1939, with a "reasonable hope" of fifty million, in which case the Fair would turn a profit of over $1 million in its first season. "An even larger attendance is not an impossibility," the prospectus went on to suggest.

And if the Fair went a second season, with an estimated twenty-four million paid admissions, the profits would soar to more than $8 million even after the debentures had been paid off in full, with interest.

Yet despite the bold assurances, sales of the bonds all but dried up by March 1. Whalen was at a crossroads. He was, as a *Harper's* magazine profile described him, "the man for the moment; but the way had been prepared for him by a sequence of the right men at other moments."* Now, finally at the helm of a great endeavor rather than the puppet master behind the curtain, he knew he had to commit one way or the other. The papers were already naming him as the potential Democratic nominee for mayor; his off-the-cuff response was that he was too busy with the Fair to give it serious consideration at the moment. But he purposefully didn't discourage the idea, either.

---

* Typically, as far as his press coverage went, the profile was titled "Barnum in Modern Dress."

Forced to either take it a step further or risk the ire of his party, he re-considered and accepted an invitation to enter the primary.

With the bond sale stalled at a little over $20 million, Whalen turned to Whitney for help. But for some reason, the man seemed strangely pre-occupied; no one could get him on the phone. In fact, he'd all but disap-peared, and he'd apparently stopped selling the bonds altogether. His behavior was inexplicable; if the measure failed, they might as well have nothing. The bonds were sold on quota; any amount less than the $27 mil-lion and change made them worthless.

Desperate for any incentive to jump-start sales, Whalen came up with a new idea. He created the Terrace Club, an exclusive establishment in an elaborate building on the fairgrounds that would be open only to individ-uals who bought a minimum of $5,000 worth of bonds. Within a few weeks, he sold almost $4 million worth, effectively closing the gap enough for the remaining amount to be swallowed up by the various banks repre-sented by the corporation's board of directors.

Disaster had been averted, but only briefly. In the second week of March, the reason for Whitney's disappearing act became public: Whit-ney & Co. filed for bankruptcy. Worse, Richard Whitney had been sum-moned to face charges of "conduct apparently contrary to just and equitable principles of trade." In a whirlwind of confession, Whitney pleaded guilty to stealing $105,000 from the estate of his father-in-law, George Sheldon, of which he was a co-trustee, as well as from several other customers' accounts. The story of his rise and fall as a financial ge-nius played out in the daily papers like a Wall Street soap opera. Whitney was charged with two counts of grand larceny; his brother, George, a part-ner at J. P. Morgan, was reported as being in on the scam. Even Edward Simmons, current president of the New York Stock Exchange, was men-tioned as a co-conspirator.

On April 11, Judge Owen Bohan sentenced Whitney to five to ten years in prison. Led away in handcuffs, he spent that night in the Tombs, an unlikely jail mate of Martha Hore's killer, Joe Healy. Eventually, the former chairman of the World's Fair bond committee would also share ac-commodations with Healy as an inmate of Sing Sing prison.

Despite the Whitney debacle, once the bond sale was secured Grover Whalen set sail for Europe once more, this time with an even better ace up his sleeve. Undeterred by his lack of admission into the Soviet Union the previous fall, Whalen had traveled to Washington, D.C., for a meeting with Constantine Oumansky, an adviser at the Soviet embassy. The following weekend, Oumansky returned the favor and visited Whalen in his office in the Empire State Building. By now, with $28 million burning a hole in his pocket, Whalen had outdone himself, commandeering an entire floor of the famed building and decorating his own director's room in his signature cream-colored leather chairs and ornate, art deco splendor. The setting was, according to one visitor, a "utopist's dream."

On Friday night, Oumansky was wined and dined by Mr. New York, and all day Saturday, he listened as Whalen pored over the plans and models of the Fair. By Sunday, he was a devoted fan. Whalen was pleased; he now thought he stood a good chance of getting into the USSR and selling them on the idea of a pavilion after all. What he hadn't expected came when Oumansky stood up and asked to use the telephone. He wanted to call the Kremlin directly and tell Premier Stalin the news.

"The telephone operator on duty at our switchboard that day never did get over the shock," Whalen later described it. Amazingly, Stalin got on the phone and listened as Oumansky talked excitedly about the World's Fair. "He told the Premier that the USSR had been offered a most desirable location on the fairgrounds site upon which they could erect a building," Whalen recalled, "and he strongly recommended it to Stalin."

After half an hour of excited chatter, Oumansky held the phone to his chest and asked Whalen rather meekly how much the pavilion would cost. "I told him about four or five million dollars," Whalen said. "He relayed the information to Stalin and after some further discussion closed the conversation and hung up."

Without even haggling over the price, Stalin had agreed to erect a large pavilion for $4 million. It was the Fair's first large-scale foreign contract, and when the official Soviet ambassador, Alexander Troyanovsky, formally signed the contract a short while later, Whalen made sure the press was in attendance. He also not so subtly suggested to them that they'd better get used to such occasions.

"The log jam was broken," Whalen declared, beaming. "Some complained that I had, in effect, upset the apple cart, and now every country would have to participate on a large scale. No one was going to allow the Russians to overshadow them at Flushing."

The next morning, he got a call from the Bureau of International Expositions, inviting him to return to Paris. "I took the next ship over," Whalen said.

Although President Roosevelt had verbally extended an invitation, through an act of Congress, for foreign nations to participate in the World's Fair, the gesture apparently wasn't grand enough for Grover Whalen. Never one to go cheap, he produced an elaborate, nineteen-by-twenty-five-inch prospectus to use as a formal presentation and had them sent out to various foreign ministers. Among the colorful maps and descriptions of the Fair, Whalen oddly chose to include a poem by Christopher Morley. Titled "Sky Line," the ode to Manhattan included several double-edged lines:

Sorceress beyond compare,
City of glory and despair . . .
Symphony fatal and divine
City of mine.

Perhaps it summed up Whalen's feelings about his native metropolis, but nevertheless its recipients could not fail to give the book their full attention: It weighed more than ten pounds.

Buoyed by his victory with Stalin and the USSR, Whalen decided to go on to Italy and see what he could do with Il Duce. "I called on the American ambassador and he said Mussolini wasn't seeing any Americans," Whalen said. "So I went to see a fellow who was the Italian Consul General here in New York in 1929, when I was Police Commissioner. He got on the phone, and then said to me, 'How would tomorrow night at six o'clock be, for a ten-minute interview?' "

Floored but immensely proud of himself, Whalen went out and bought a new pair of shoes for the occasion and "got all dolled up."

"As I entered the Dictator's office I saw a highly polished floor at least two hundred feet long," he said. "At this point my new patent leather shoes reminded me painfully of their existence. . . . I was left alone with a skating rink of polished parquet in front of me."

Off in the distance, Mussolini stood with his back to Whalen, looking through enormous windows at the sunset. Whalen had been warned that Il Duce was a short man and very sensitive about his height. "Then I saw that the desk, behind which he stood, was placed on a foot-high platform," Whalen noted.

Finally, Mussolini turned and broke the silence. "I understand you served as Police Commissioner of New York," he said.

"Yes, I did," Whalen answered.

"How did my people behave?"

"Some good, some bad."

Mussolini looked him straight in the eye and asked, "The bad ones—from Sicily?"

Although the meeting had been slated for only ten minutes, their conversation dragged on for more than an hour as the dictator famously rolled his eyes and droned on about Italy's domestic situation. Finally, sensing that the time was right, Whalen asked about Italy's participation in the World's Fair.

"What, Italy compete with Wall Street?" the dictator responded. "What, for example, would it accomplish?"

"The American people would like to know what fascism is," Whalen stated matter-of-factly.

Mussolini harrumphed. "You want to know what fascism is? It is like your New Deal!"

Feeling as though he were hitting a brick wall, Whalen tried flattery. The theme of the World's Fair, he said, was "Building the World of Tomorrow," which he graciously compared with Mussolini's vision for Italy.

The strategy worked. Mussolini, echoing Stalin, asked how much it would cost to build a pavilion.

"I said that participation in the Fair would cost Italy five million dollars," Whalen said, upping the price tag, "and he told me that he would appropriate this. Altogether, I spent an hour and three quarters with him. After that, it was a cinch to get the other foreign nations."

Before Whalen was done, sixty-two nations would sign on to be represented at the Fair, an astounding twenty-two of which would build individual pavilions, by far the greatest collection of foreign representation any exposition had ever known. In fact, so much space was let out that Whalen had to cable Voorhees and the Board of Design to tell them to tear up their original plan for the Government Zone—space that had previously been assigned for American states would now be needed just to accommodate the foreign pavilions.

Whalen sailed back to New York triumphantly. He had $30 million worth of contracts in his pocket. By June, he had withdrawn his name from the mayoral ballot.

The Trylon and Perisphere under construction. Many considered its steel framework more beautiful without the stark white gypsum board that eventually covered it. *(Courtesy of the New York Public Library)*

"FOLKS, YOU AIN'T SEEN NOTHING YET!"

The next two years were a frenzy of activity and promotion. When Moses and his crew had finished their transformation of the Corona Dumps, construction began and continued night and day. Foundation work for the Theme Center was laid in May 1937, and almost immediately images of the Trylon and Perisphere started popping up everywhere. Designed by the architectural team of Wallace Harrison and J. André Fouilhoux, the Trylon was to be a seven-hundred-foot-tall, tricornered obelisk; the Perisphere—a huge, hollow globe—would rise eighteen stories high and as broad as a city block.*

"We promised the world something new in Fair architecture," Whalen boasted, "and here it is—something radically different and yet fundamentally as old as man's experience."

By summer, the major corporations began signing up, beginning with General Electric in June and continuing on with Kodak, AT&T, Heinz, RCA, and a host of others. They were by no means easy sells for Whalen. One strict rule was that no company could reproduce a trademark or product in its building's design. When the National Cash Register Company submitted plans for a structure in the shape of a giant register,

---

* Official World's Fair literature and most published reports put the Trylon at seven hundred feet high and the Perisphere at two hundred feet in diameter; but by some accounts, the actual dimensions were lowered by about 15 percent owing to budget constrictions.

Whalen banished them to the Amusement Zone. Howard Heinz demanded that his exhibit be shaped like a pickle; Whalen told him to forget it and promptly sold their space to Borden while Heinz was vacationing in Europe.*

In the end, the problems became less a matter of who would or wouldn't participate than where the Board of Design was going to put them all. Early on, they had decided to place the Transportation Zone in a large area across from the main exhibit grounds, separated by the Grand Central Parkway but easily accessible by a pair of footbridges. Whalen had imagined Detroit's Big Three automotive companies would fill up most of the space. After some fancy salesmanship, he got Ford and General Motors to agree on the location. But Walter Chrysler balked, refusing to participate unless he could pick a site in the main area.

Whalen held his ground, telling him it was Transportation or nothing. Chrysler chose nothing, so Whalen divided the allotted space into halves instead of thirds and allowed Ford and GM to go hog wild with their pavilions. Chrysler eventually changed his mind, but by then space was gone. Voorhees and his crew took out their erasers and created new space in a smaller area originally designated for a comfort station.

By August, the Administration Building was completed. Grover and his staff, which now numbered over six hundred, vacated their offices in the Empire State Building and followed a convoy of twenty-five moving vans to the fairgrounds. Three days later, at a dedication ceremony for the site of the Theme Center, Whalen stood under a broiling sun and proudly announced that 86 percent of exhibition space had been "spoken for," including participation by thirty-one American states.

By now his declarations of peace, and of the role his World's Fair would play in it, were becoming ubiquitous. When a reporter dared ask him, "Wouldn't a European war completely ruin the Fair?" Whalen shot back, "There'll be no war. That's all newspaper talk." The Theme Center, he said at the dedication, was "a new layout for life. . . . The World's Fair will predict, may even dictate, the shape of things to come."

---

* Heinz eventually settled on an odd, domed-shaped building in another section of the Food Zone. But the pickles didn't disappear entirely—they appeared on the lapels of every visitor who picked up a free pickle pin after visiting the exhibit.

In fact, Whalen began to speak so often about world peace that, as in the Rothstein affair, many people believed his Fair would single-handedly solve the growing disturbance overseas. "My personal investigation in Europe has conclusively proved to me that there'll be no war," he asserted triumphantly. "A wave of enthusiasm for the World's Fair is sweeping Europe. That's what Europe is thinking of now—not war."

Of his trip abroad, he added, "It is the hope of many to whom I spoke that New York's World's Fair of 1939 will provide a peace table around which the powers of the world may sit and develop a worldwide peace program." Straight-faced, he also declared at a business luncheon that several countries were even considering sending "peace ships" to the Fair.

This was no mere salesmanship; Grover Whalen honestly believed that the dazzling model of the world he was creating—the World of Tomorrow—could potentially charm the dictators of the world into seeing the futility of war.

In addition to construction, the Whalen promotion machine went into high gear. In 1938, he convinced Governor Lehman to allow the words NEW YORK WORLD'S FAIR 1939 to be stamped on every automobile license plate in the state. (To make room for it, the actual license numbers had to be reduced by almost a quarter in size.) Most citizens took the news in stride, yet if there was any advance indication of New York's flippant attitude about the Fair, it came in the grumblings of drivers who wondered why they were being forced to carry free advertising on their cars.

One particular cynic, a forty-two-year-old mechanic from White Plains named Martin McBohin, expressed his displeasure by covering up the offending ad with electrical tape and subsequently got himself arrested for defacing a license plate. Before his trial, he announced to the press, "Next thing you know the State will compel us to advertise someone's corn flakes."

On the flip side, *The New Yorker* reported spotting a truck driver who, having lost his original plate and while waiting on a replacement, had hand-drawn his number on a piece of cardboard and had even taken great care in printing NEW YORK WORLD'S FAIR 1939 in block letters above it.

Whalen the salesman knew a good thing when he saw it, and the Theme Center logo was rapidly becoming famous. That summer, the uniforms of every New York Yankee, New York Giant, and Brooklyn Dodger ballplayer featured a different kind of "ball and bat"—the Trylon and Perisphere. Then he took the promotion a step further, wondering why, in addition to all the free advertising he was getting, the public couldn't be persuaded to actually *pay* for it. Promotion aside, he recognized that a good portion of pre-Fair revenues could be made from the sale of goods featuring the T&P. In an age when most labels were meant to be worn on the inside, Grover Whalen expanded the concept of branding to a new and larger audience. "I saw no reason why manufacturers should not profit by the advertising we received," he explained, "and at the same time pay for that advertising. We began selling licenses to those manufacturers who wanted to tie up with us."

After unraveling a bolt of fabric for one reporter, he pointed to the Theme Center pattern and smiled broadly. "We get a royalty on every yard of goods that man sells," he bragged. "And that's just one item. There are thousands of others tied up in a similar way with the Fair, and we are being paid for all of them."

Still, he may have gotten carried away with the idea. "We may even change the shapes of rolls and frankfurters," he went on. "Unless I'm disappointed, our visitors will be able not only to devour the Trylon and Perisphere with their eyes, but also with their mouths."

Throughout 1938, there was a dedication, a ceremony, or a groundbreaking every week, it seemed. In January, La Guardia, Moses, and Whalen presided as the cornerstone was laid for the New York City Building, one of only two structures erected to be permanent. (The New York State Marine Amphitheater, eventually to become more famously known as the Aquacade, home of Billy Rose's water-ballet extravaganza, was the other.) Moses attended only because he wanted to use the building as an indoor ice-skating rink when the Fair was torn down. Grumpy in the foul weather, he told reporters, "Only the brave deserve the Fair."

In April, the steel framework of the Trylon and Perisphere began rising. U.S. Steel chairman Myron Taylor echoed Whalen's peace mission by stating that the Fair was a place where "the peoples of the nations of the earth will repair to commune together as friends. It will have an unquestionable influence upon future amity." Whalen took the opportunity to speak about the future without realizing how prophetic he was being; the ceremony took place under a torrential downpour.

When he heard that Howard Hughes was planning a round-the-world flight, Whalen sold him on the idea of naming his plane the *New York World's Fair*. In July 1938, Hughes carried the message of the Fair, and the Trylon and Perisphere logo, to Paris, Moscow, Siberia, and Alaska in a record-breaking three days, nineteen hours, fourteen minutes, and ten seconds—cutting in half the record set by Wiley Post just five years earlier.

The massive press coverage continued. That summer, Grover Whalen was named the best-dressed businessman in the country. In September, the time capsule was buried. Shortly after, the first brick was laid in the Marine Amphitheater. And as winter settled in, local artists began painting the elaborate murals that would decorate the exteriors of several buildings in harsh, overly bright colors. Early spectators lucky enough to be given a preview may have scratched their heads, but the effect had been planned so that by midseason the following summer, the paint would fade sufficiently to its proper hue. For two years, the designers had been testing and developing new pigments to ensure their resilience to heat, wind, and rain.

At precisely midnight on January 1, 1939, the World's Fair made pyrotechnic history by setting off seven hundred aerial bombs that could be heard for miles around. Large, fiery portraits of President Roosevelt, Mayor La Guardia, and Grover Whalen lit up the sky, along with the words *Happy New York World's Fair Year 1939*.

But the biggest event of 1938 had been the World's Fair Preview celebration held on April 30, exactly one year before Opening Day. For that occasion, Whalen had organized a massive publicity parade from Battery Place in downtown Manhattan out to the fairgrounds in Flushing, a total of sixteen miles. For Grover Whalen, it was the triumphant culmination of everything he had accomplished in every celebration he had presided over, from Woodrow Wilson to Lindbergh, combined with the fervent anticipation of the year ahead and the two glorious seasons to come. Only this time he could rightfully claim his place as the bona fide star of the show.

The enormous procession included one hundred thousand marchers and more than three hundred animated displays, including, Whalen's press kit pointed out, "the most bizarre and interesting floats ever seen in a New York parade. Giants and midgets, huge cigarettes and candy bars . . . are among the features of this section."

There were so many participants that it took over three hours for all of them to pass any given point. More than a million people turned out to watch "the largest mechanized parade in New York history." Twelve hundred policemen and nearly every detective in the city were called out on duty, including, most likely, Joe Lynch and Freddy Socha. As a nod to his former role as police commissioner, Whalen ordered that the men in uniform be handed free hot dogs (in traditional rolls, alas!). The only hiccup in his way came from Robert Moses, who grumpily refused to allow the procession to cross over his Triborough Bridge on their way to Queens.

When the festivities kicked off at ten-thirty, "the sun was shining and a warm breeze was blowing," according to *The New York Times*. But by midafternoon the weather, offering its own preview of the World of To-morrow, did a complete about-face. The warm breeze bellowed into a freezing wind, followed by a thick rainfall that stopped the parade in mid-march. It got so cold that two women on the Florida Exhibits float, shivering in their skimpy bathing suits, required medical attention. One of them, Nellie Barrett, smiled through chattering teeth as she told a Fair physician that she actually hailed from a town called Frostproof.

By three-thirty, just as the marchers began filing past the reviewing stands out in Queens, the storm had grown into an incessant downpour. Less than a quarter of the parade had entered the fairgrounds when the order came for everyone to disperse, and a near riot ensued as tens of thousands ran for cover. Emergency squads from Brooklyn had to be called in to untangle the traffic jam of cars abandoning the makeshift parking lots.

An evening program of concerts and fireworks was canceled and rescheduled for the following day, but the bad weather continued for so long that the actual event took place a full week later, on May 8. World's Fair officials estimated the crowd at six hundred thousand; actual reports put the number at less than half that. Whalen was typically undeterred despite the fact that storm clouds still hovered overhead.

"The day was a big success, any way you look at it," he said in his speech. "With rain threatening all day . . .

"When we started the Fair we figured that forty million [visitors] would be satisfactory," Whalen continued. "After a year or so we revised our figures and gauged our efforts at getting fifty million. Now we are confident that there will be more than *sixty* million at the Fair in 1939!"

During the parade a week earlier, Mayor La Guardia had summed up all the hoopla of the three years prior and the three years yet to come. "Folks," he said in a radio address from the fairgrounds, "you ain't seen nothing yet! You just wait until May 1939, and you will see the greatest, most stupendous, the most wonderful and most marvelous site that you have ever seen."

A long and hearty cheer rose up from the crowd. La Guardia let them roar for nearly a minute, then roused them once more when he concluded, "Congratulations, Mr. Whalen!"

PART TWO

Dawn of
A NEW DAY

1939: The First Season

For more than three years, Mr. Whalen has been organizing an army, ruling it by diplomacy and governing it by consent. He has caused a City of Tomorrow to come into being at a time when many of us were afraid to think of tomorrow. The Fair he has built faces forward, toward the rising sun. It celebrates no twilight of the Western World.

—*New York Times* editorial, 1939

President Franklin Roosevelt addresses the crowd gathered in the Court of Peace on Opening Day, April 30, 1939. (© *Bettmann/Corbis*)

"THEY COME WITH
JOYOUS SONG"

As Opening Day approached, Grover Whalen spent the better part of the last week confined to his bed, bound and determined to rid himself of a nasty cold. The night before opening, he tossed and turned, running numbers in his head, going over and over the schedule of events the next day. President Roosevelt would officially dedicate the Fair that afternoon, on television no less. Whalen wondered what old FDR would say and then, worrying about it, decided instead to put that concern out of his mind and rehearse his own speech again. As the sun came up, he sat in his study and tried to concentrate, but something kept catching his eye.

He couldn't keep from smiling. On his desk sat an advance copy of that week's *Time* magazine, and this issue, like that of every other journal and newspaper in the city, was dedicated to the opening of the World's Fair. Except that the wise old editors of *Time* had decided to focus on him personally: Right there on the cover Whalen saw a rare full-color illustration of himself, grinning broadly and doffing his homburg, the letters *G.W.* clearly stitched inside. The Fair's Trylon and Perisphere Theme Center was merely a backdrop to his horse-toothed visage.

The morning of April 30, 1939, as Whalen had hoped, bloomed bright and promising as he hurried through breakfast and skipped his usual routine of calisthenics with his personal trainer. As he rode out to the fairgrounds, the unfettered sunshine warmed his car, a six-wheeled Imperial Parade Phaeton that had been built especially for him by Chrysler. It was early yet, not quite nine o'clock, and there was plenty of time; the gates wouldn't officially open until eleven.

Crossing over the Triborough Bridge on his way to Queens, Whalen read the weather reports and smiled again. The papers were all predicting an unusually warm day for early spring. From his private cockpit in the rear of the Phaeton, he peered through the car's uniquely curved windows and checked out the sky, noting an endless sea of blue and not a cloud in sight. If this kept up, it would be a record-breaking day.

From every point in the city, not a few others had the same idea. Special World's Fair trains began riding out to Flushing Meadows at nine, carrying excited passengers who hoped to be among the first to enter the New York World's Fair on Opening Day. They, too, had read the weather reports, and as such they donned their finest tweed suits and woolen dresses and left behind their sweaters and overcoats. Most didn't even think about carrying an umbrella.

At ten-fifteen, forty-five minutes before they were supposed to, the turnstiles nevertheless began spinning as the early birds burst forth from subway cars and shoved their way down the ramps to the entrance. They were a frantic-looking bunch, and so the order was given to let them in ahead of schedule, not only to ease the inevitable crowding, but also to avoid trouble.

Just inside the fairgrounds, they were met by equally frantic peddlers of peanuts and guidebooks and all manner of World's Fair–branded gee-gaws. Everything everywhere had that ever-present Trylon and Perisphere logo plastered somewhere across it—the slightly phallic image having been burned into American consciousness for over a year now. And the public craved it: They wasted no time buying up hand soaps, compacts, perfume bottles, Bakelite thermometers, sewing kits, hats, scarves, tablecloths, pencil sharpeners, kazoos, and Kan-O-Seats—walking sticks with fold-out seat attachments that allowed the footsore fairgoer a chance to sit down while waiting in long lines (however dubious its support structure seemed).

Even Superman and Batman saluted the T&P on a commemorative issue of World's Fair Comics.

This initial burst of buying done, the typical visitor hurried straight to the Theme Center—the magnificent "ball and spike," as *Time* magazine called them. The structures were indeed arresting, even at first glance. Harrison and Fouilhoux had started with the basic geography of a pyramid and sphere, advertised as representing the finite and the infinite. (Or the other way around—no one was ever quite sure.) But for many their visual appeal may have sprung from the more subliminal seduction of their undeniable resemblance to the male anatomy. E. B. White called the Trylon "the white phallus" (apparently without concern that he may have been referring to his own).

Some likened them to a vision of heaven; Grover Whalen said they were "a glimpse into the future, a sort of foretaste of the better world of tomorrow," and that their simplicity was "the keynote of a perfectly ordered mechanical civilization." Robert Moses saw it differently. "Barnum had his sacred white elephant and every Fair is entitled to at least one theme tower," he grumbled.

Built at a cost of $1.7 million, the Theme Center required that 1,272 piles, each a hundred feet long, be driven deep into the Flushing Meadows muck in order to support its crushing thirty-thousand-ton weight. Four thousand tons of steel had been used to construct its skeleton, but then the whole thing was covered in cheap gypsum in order to save money. In harsh daylight, its bumpy imperfections gave the Perisphere the appearance of an autumn gourd, but come nightfall hidden projectors spun clouds across its surface, making the globe appear to revolve slowly and majestically.

To complete the illusion, the Perisphere also seemed to float mysteriously in a reflecting pool—eight gushing, multicolored fountains hid its mirrored supporting columns, making them all but invisible to the casual viewer. Inside, occupying an area twice as large as the recently opened Radio City Music Hall, lay the exhibit everyone was hurrying to see.

"Democracity," as it was called, was a grand diorama that depicted a utopian landscape of the future—a dreamy vision of a world in which people lived in countrified splendor while having easy access to urban industry via convenient planning and a broad highway system. Five satellite towns (including "Pleasantville," which eerily predicted the suburb of the future) surrounded "Centerton," the industrial core. For the overcrowded city dweller as well as the isolated farmer, Democracity represented the ideal promise of a better world they so eagerly craved.

"As day fades into night," said the exhibit's narration, provided by the familiar and fatherly voice of CBS radio commentator H. V. Kaltenborn, "each man seeks home, for here are children, comfort, neighbors, recreation—the good life of a well-planned city."

Henry Dreyfuss, one of the most celebrated industrial designers of his day, not only had created a unique interpretation of a modern American city, but had devised an ingenious method for viewing it. After gliding up the "longest moving electric stairway in the world," you boarded "one of two revolving balconies which hung, seemingly unsupported, in space." The two platforms circled in opposite directions, and it took a full six minutes to make one complete revolution. No one, not even the most sophisticated New Yorker, had ever seen anything like it.

"The idea," said publicity man Dudley Britton, "is that you are two miles up in the air, on a magic carpet. . . . Spectators will find themselves cast in the role of the gods of old, from Olympian heights, to pierce the fogs of ignorance, habit and prejudice that envelop everyday thinking, able to gaze down on the ideal community."

Democracity, Kaltenborn's narration continued, was "a brave new world built by united hands and hearts. Here brain and brawn, faith and courage, are linked in high endeavor as men march on toward unity and peace."

Dreyfuss's vision painted so moving a portrait of the future that many visitors gasped at first glance. Their emotions were further stirred by its theme music, composed by an African American classicist named William Grant Still and conducted by André Kostelanetz. The total effect was mesmerizing. The show was timed so that after two minutes of wide-eyed gazing and slow progression, night began to fall and the tiny windows and streetlamps, painted with a new material called Poroseal, glowed under ultraviolet lights. Five hundred pin-dot holes in the exhibit's dome created the illusion of starlight.

Out of the darkness came a thousand-voice choir as images of marching men were projected overhead, "trooping from the distant skies until the whole arch of heaven is filled with towering figures, arms upraised, singing the song of tomorrow."

"Listen!" Kaltenborn's voice commanded. "From office, farm and factory, they come with joyous song." Just before exiting, spectators heard the symphony swell as the entire scene vanished behind drifting clouds. Then, suddenly, the music stopped and a great flash of polarized light ended the show. Blinking their way out of the Perisphere and into the blinding reality of the World's Fair itself, the crowd was noticeably hushed in a silent aura of wonder, already transported from their ordinary lives into the heretofore unimaginable World of Tomorrow.

From their vantage point at the height of the Helicline, the curved walkway leading downward out of the Perisphere, visitors could view the multicolored layout that divided the Fair into categorized "zones." Each had been landscaped according to color: "façades drenched in color, vistas as modulated in color, cocktails of color," as the guidebook described them. The observant may have also noticed that the Theme Center was the only structure painted pure white. Below them, extending outward like the spokes of a giant wagon wheel, three large avenues at forty-five-degree angles stretched outward in deepening tones of primary color.

To their right, facing east, the Avenue of Pioneers ran the gamut of blue, from pale violet to ultramarine; to their left, the Avenue of Patriots bloomed from canary yellow to deep gold; and directly in front of them, the multilaned Constitution Mall blushed from rose to burgundy. Intersecting each of these was the curving, appropriately named Rainbow Avenue, which connected all three spokes of the wheel and reflected their prismatic shifts in hue. All in all, it was an ingenious design; not merely decorative, the color-coded zones enlightened each fairgoer as to his or her exact location through the use of a similarly shaded map.

There were seven zones in all, and each housed its own particular wonder. Transportation held General Motors' Futurama, the second exhibit everyone wanted to see; Communications offered RCA and the new wonder of television; Production and Distribution featured General Electric, where spectators were literally shaken by its ear-splitting ten-million-volt lightning display.

They had so much to see. Over at Chrysler, you could don a pair of car-shaped glasses and watch a 3-D movie of an automobile being assembled by invisible workers. In the same building, designer Gilbert Rohde's exhibit offered a rocket ride to London (the moon not yet the focus of such excursions). At Ford, you could gasp at the daredevil exploits of stunt driver Jimmie Lynch, and after that you could catch your breath while admiring Kodak's enormous projections of their new color slide film or even pose while standing on top of a miniature version of the Trylon and Perisphere, where Kodak instructors would offer helpful hints for taking better photographs.

But for some, the most titillating exhibits were to be found in that staple of every modern American fair: the Amusement Zone, an overgrown midway set off of the man-made Fountain Lake at the southwestern quadrant of the grounds. At two hundred and eighty acres, the area was larger than the entire Paris International Exposition of two years earlier. As soon as they could, thousands of its eager male visitors headed straight for the risqué offerings of Dolores, "the Uninhibited Voodoo Dancer"; or the Sun Worshipers, an oddly zoological park that featured topless women cavorting outdoors as if that were their daily routine; or the "none too heavily clad" Amazon Warriorettes, which needed no explanation at all.

Picture taking was allowed in most of these exhibits. What you did with them afterward, including how you explained the film to your local developer, was your business.

And so, after a decent interval spent touring a few educational exhibits, husbands urged wives and children to visit the Borden Company's "Dairy World of Tomorrow," where Elsie the Cow was milked by the new "Rotolactor" vacuum method. Bachelors got loose from their dates and made appointments to meet up later, and the rather sheepish crowd slunk their way into what was winkingly referred to as "the Play Center." Unfortunately for the prurient-minded, on Opening Day more than half of the Amusement Zone exhibits weren't open yet. Actors from the unfinished Globe Theater smoked cigarettes and eyed the gawkers who at first feigned interest in Frank Buck's "Bring 'Em Back Alive" wild animal exhibit or Little Miracle Town's one hundred and twenty-five resident midgets, then chuckled knowingly as they headed straight for Oscar, the Obscene Octopus, a rubber creature who slowly "stripped" the bathing suits off of female swimmers.

For most of the morning, the weather held up nicely. In fact, it may have been a little too nice. As high noon approached, the prediction of an unusually warm day seemed an understatement. Men began to broil in their heavy suits, loosening their neckties and wiping their brows with handkerchiefs before returning their hats to their heads. Ladies wilted in the baking sun, while children begged to be taken indoors and treated to ice cream or sodas.

Grover Whalen, on the other hand, looked out the window of his office at the clear sky and then at the vista below him, wondering: Where are all the people? Pacing the halls of the Administration Building, he could see the long lines queuing up outside Futurama and the steady parade up the escalator to the Perisphere, but everywhere else, it seemed, the avenues and walkways were clear of all but the lightest foot traffic. Perhaps they were all indoors, Whalen mused, escaping the heat and enjoying the exhibits. Perhaps they were stuck in massive traffic jams on their way to his Fair. Then, reminding himself that it was Sunday, after all, Whalen tried to calm himself with thoughts that many potential ticket buyers had spent their morning in church; after the services were over, they would surely be coming his way.

For the first time, Whalen began to understand the tremendous responsibility he had taken on. In selling the Fair, first to an astounding number of foreign nations and then to Corporate America, he had never considered the idea that it was perhaps becoming too big and too expensive. The building he was now standing in had cost almost $1 million alone; his executive office looked to one observer like "a Hollywood scene representing a super-luxury hotel." The dining and conference rooms were walled in copper, and the paintings lining the various corridors gave "the effect of a modernist art gallery."

The corporation itself had estimated that the Fair needed fifty million visitors in order to turn a modest profit. That figure hadn't shaken Whalen's spirit; he personally expected at least that many would show up in the first year alone, plus another twenty-four million during the second season. And for Opening Day attendance, he had publicly predicted an inaugural gate of over one million wide-eyed, open-walleted guests. But unless there was a huge afternoon surge in late sleepers, that figure now seemed impossibly high.

Whalen's boast was an unfortunate but characteristic blunder—his inherent enthusiasm often burst forth in grandiose overstatements before he had a chance to check himself. In this case, if fewer than a million showed up, the Fair's Opening Day might appear to have been less than spectacular. Still, it was early yet, and the president was scheduled to speak that afternoon. Surely that would bring out the crowds. Readying himself for the formal ceremonies to come, Whalen may or may not have noticed one more crucial detail: the darkening shadows advancing on the Theme Center. A sudden blanket of angry clouds was turning the sky bullet gray.

As noon came and went, the weather got progressively worse. The rain was holding off, but a chilly wind began to kick up, carrying the spray of various fountains and giving nearby fairgoers a taste of what was coming. For NBC, however, the heavy cloud cover was a blessing in disguise: At precisely twelve-thirty, television was introduced to the country with a static view of the Trylon and Perisphere. The stark white structures silhouetted nicely against the darkened sky and made for a very fine transmission. Hundreds crowded around the two dozen receivers in the RCA Building* to squint at a two-inch-by-three-inch view they could have seen in real life if they had simply turned around.

It didn't matter; the public was hooked. Television sets were already on sale in several New York stores, selling for then astronomical sums of between $150 and $1,000.

Fifteen minutes later, at twelve forty-five, fairgoers gathered around

---

* Although television was most popular at RCA, both General Electric and Westinghouse also featured their own models. Perhaps envisioning its own version of the future, Ford had even installed one in its lounge—primarily to display its commercials.

the Theme Center to witness an extraordinary sight. A seemingly endless parade of flags emerged from the Perisphere like a multicolored string of yarn out of a big white ball. Standard-bearers from the armed forces were followed by the spectrum-filling parade of banners from sixty participating nations, and finally by the orange-and-blue theme colors carried by World's Fair staffers. This whirling, dizzying fan dance circled down the Helicline and then waited for the grand unspooling to finish.

But what began as a dignified procession ended in a footrace. The parade's grand marshal was an army man, Major General William Haskell, and he saw to it that all the pomp and finery was metered with military precision. But at the base of the Perisphere, another major, Allan Smith of the World's Fair Police (a special corps supervised by Whalen, who had again personally designed their uniforms, these with bright orange Bakelite buttons and batons), decided to step off on his own, leading his unit up the south walk of Constitution Mall. Haskell didn't like what he saw, and as soon as the rest of his marchers fell in, he took the opposing route and led them briskly along the north walk.

It turned out to be a good choice, since sections of the south side of the mall were still roughly paved and some stretches unfinished.* When Major Smith came across several lengths of rope that blocked his path, he showed the fortitude of any New York City cop: He pulled out his pocketknife, sliced through them, and marched on.

The procession was neck and neck until they reached Washington Square, where costumed groups representing the foreign nations joined them. One such group, the Armagh Patriotic and Benevolent Association, was led by a proud and burly Irishman named James Gorman. Seeing the diverse routes the two parade leaders were taking, Gorman instructed the men of Armagh, "in their sovereign kilts and Balmoral tams," to take the center path. This one, he noted, led directly to the grandstand from which President Roosevelt and other dignitaries would give their speeches.

---

* On the subject of the Fair's ongoing construction, Whalen would naturally spin it his way, stating that his Fair was "more nearly complete than any in history on opening day." In other words, he may have been unprepared, but he was less unprepared than anyone else before him. And that had to count for something.

As Gorman marched his men at the quickstep, the crowd around them, as if cheering on a horse race, clapped wildly and shouted words of encouragement for the Irish brigade to win the contest.

At the head of the parade's final section was Mayor La Guardia: short, squat, stocky, and not entirely comfortable in his top hat and striped trousers. Yet despite the tightness of his coat, he remained La Guardia, prancing ahead of Governor Lehman, Grover Whalen, and the remaining officers and directors of the World's Fair Corporation like a potbellied Pied Piper. The crowd, as always, loved him. And with each cheer, La Guardia gave them more and more to love, more of the Lou Costello arm swinging and head bobbing, until with every fourth or fifth step he was bowing at the waist in time to the festive music.

In the end, Haskell won the race, of course. And he waited, savoring his victory and shaking the hand of every official who marched up to the grandstand area. The major general was immensely proud of himself; his parade had ended precisely at one fifty-five. He had timed it to the minute.

A t two o'clock, just as the threat of rain seemed at its peak, Grover Whalen and an elite group of dignitaries began taking their seats around the presidential podium. A few minutes later, Eleanor Roosevelt came down the steps of the U.S. Federal Building, alone, sporting a brown silk dress patterned with the Trylon and Perisphere. Her matching hat and bag were similarly adorned. She may have felt a little silly in the outfit, but her namesake niece, Eleanor (who was trying to break into the fashion business), had designed it. Grover was delighted.

In front of them sat a sea of invited guests: high-end World's Fair bondholders, governors and mayors from around the country, and various foreign diplomats representing their nations' participation. Unfortunately for everyone else, the entire area surrounding the Court of Peace—an open-air mall wedged between two opposing corridors of the Hall of Nations, where countries that could not afford pavilions shared smaller exhibit space—was off-limits to the general public. This did not sit well with jaded New Yorkers who had paid their seventy-five-cent admission fee on the assumption that it would allow them full access to the president of the

United States. Fights broke out as the police struggled to turn away thousands of would-be spectators.

When the loudspeakers began announcing the festivities, Patrolman Bartholomew Nicastro was nearly crushed against the wooden sawhorse he was so avidly defending. A Queens woman, Mary Pease, decided to take matters into her own hands and climbed over a guard rope near the Lagoon of Nations, an oval pool in the center of the Government Zone. She fell and fractured her left leg. If not for the thickening rain clouds, there might have been a full-blown riot. It was the only good news the weather brought to the Fair that day.

For the next hour, the privileged crowd listened nervously as Whalen, Lehman, and La Guardia spoke, tilting their heads periodically at the sky and wondering whether their commemorative programs could serve as makeshift umbrellas. When the preliminary speakers were finished and back in their seats, the president's car drove up the ramp behind the grandstand.

The plan, as usual, had been carefully worked out in advance for FDR to "walk" as little as possible while seeming to have made the journey up to the podium by himself just the same. To complete this diversion, Secret Servicemen surrounded his car, ostensibly for the president's protection (although they were nowhere near as close when he actually spoke), and screened it from view.

Roosevelt's mother, Sara, left the car first; then John Roosevelt, FDR's youngest son, helped his father stand up out of the backseat and locked the braces around his knees that allowed him to stand for brief periods of time. The president would walk to the podium, as he always did, by utilizing the strength of his upper body—one hand gripped tightly on a cane he used as a crutch, the other leaning heavily on John's crooked elbow for support. By rocking from side to side in this manner, he managed a slow forward motion with the help of the steel grips around his legs.

This speech, like most of FDR's public appearances, would last no longer than fifteen minutes, the maximum amount of time he could spend on his feet. And it would not be the longest of the day; that honor would go to Whalen, whose own address had already clocked in at nearly twice as long.

Just as FDR got ready to speak, the clouds were at their most ominous, as if they were ready to burst at any second. A single RCA/NBC camera trained its lens on the podium from which, one news report boasted, "the televised image of the President will be carried within a radius of fifty-five miles in all directions from the Empire State Building." At that singular moment, television had indeed arrived.

The threat of rain notwithstanding, the speech itself was astounding, as much for what the president said as for what he didn't say. Despite the rise of Nazi aggression, the only war to which Roosevelt referred was the one Americans had fought with themselves seventy-five years earlier: "an internal war . . . which resulted eventually and happily in a closer union than before."

Leave it to 1930s optimism to put a positive spin on the Civil War. But Roosevelt took it further than that.

"The United States stands today as a completely homogenous nation," he stated, straight-faced and stern, "united in a common purpose to work for the greatest good for the greatest number, united in the desire to move forward to better things . . . and united in its desire to encourage peace and good will among the nations of the earth. Here at the New York World's Fair of 1939 many nations are represented, indeed most of the nations of the world, and the theme is 'The World of Tomorrow.' This general, and I might almost say spontaneous, participation by other countries is a gesture of friendship and good will towards the United States for which I render most grateful thanks."

From his seat directly behind FDR, Grover Whalen was beaming. He couldn't have written it better himself. The president of the United States was reaffirming the peacemaking promises of the World's Fair and declaring publicly that through this occasion, the nations of the world were coming together to stave off conflict. It was exactly what he'd hoped for, the justification of Whalen's status as statesman over salesman.

"All who come to this New York World's Fair will receive the heartiest of welcomes," Roosevelt continued. "They will find that the eyes of the United States are fixed on the future. Yes, our wagon is still hitched to a star. But it is a star of friendship, a star of international good will, and, above all, a star of peace. May the months to come carry us forward in the rays of that eternal hope."

Hope indeed. At the time, Roosevelt himself clung to the ideals of Einstein's previously derided isolationism as firmly and fervently as he held the podium's specially built grips upon which he depended for balance and support. Any slip threatened to topple him over, though very few in the crowd understood the full extent of his struggle, physically or morally. Just two months earler, Secretary of State Cordell Hull, during one of the weekly World's Fair broadcasts that used political speeches as a means to publicize the Fair, spelled out the administration's head-in-the-sand take on war:

"As a nation," Hull had stated, "we are convinced that there are no international differences which cannot be settled . . . by mutually fair and peaceful adjustment than by armed force."

Negotiation over action; words over guns. It would work as a national policy for two and a half more years. And no one, not even Albert Einstein, who was at that moment preparing to give his own speech at the Fair later that evening, could have imagined the magnitude of force that would soon be unleashed upon the world.

Nevertheless, Roosevelt's rays of eternal hope cheered the soggy crowd, as did his lighthearted reference to the repeal of Prohibition as "an unhappy trial of a few years." As FDR's words reverberated down the long corridor of the Court of Peace and echoed over the loudspeakers throughout the fairgrounds, his immediate audience, perhaps expecting that now, finally, he would acknowledge the situation in Europe, sat silently and waited for it. They waited some more, and more after that.

"And so my friends," Roosevelt said, wrapping it up, "I hereby dedicate the World's Fair . . ."

He stumbled briefly, having been standing for about as long as his physical endurance would allow. Behind him, John Roosevelt nearly jumped out of his seat, ready to catch his father should he begin to fall. He quickly thrust out his father's cane, then just as swiftly withdrew it before anyone noticed.

" . . . the *New York* World's Fair of 1939," FDR recovered, "and I declare it open to all mankind."*

For the first time since he had begun speaking, the crowd broke into a smattering of applause. War, it seemed, was not on the menu that day. Peace was, in the most ethereal forms imaginable. As a finale to the festivities, a chorus line of young women in white robes performed what was called a "Pageant of Peace." Then they mounted a rostrum called "the Altar of Peace" and waved flags symbolizing the Fair as an "Agency of Peace."

After that display, Roosevelt had apparently had enough. He left the podium at three-twenty, exactly twenty minutes after his car had arrived, and by four o'clock he and Eleanor were already chugging their way back to Hyde Park by special train.

---

* The correction was necessary. Out on the West Coast, San Francisco was hosting its own, significantly smaller World's Fair. A true Democrat, FDR was not about to ignore California.

Grover Whalen introduces Albert Einstein, whose speech was supposed to kick off the first nighttime lighting of the Fair. *(Courtesy of the New York Public Library)*

BLACKOUT

War aside, the World's Fair did not open without its own controversy. In another of his famous overstatements, Grover Whalen had boasted that the Fair represented "the sum total of almost all that man has produced since history began." Brushing off his critics, he also stated that "these acres have seen no strife" and that there had in fact been "exemplary cooperation among individuals and industries." Neither was true.

Just four weeks earlier, on April 3, New York City Council member James Burke, a Democrat from Queens, blasted the World's Fair as his neighborhood's blight and declared that the city itself had become "the victim of the greatest con game in history." He wasn't quite done. The real slogan of the World of Tomorrow, he said, should be "Never give a sucker an even break." Whalen, Burke went on, was a P. T. Barnum who "put the city in hock . . . for the purpose of insuring fat dividends for the bondholders of a private business venture known as New York World's Fair 1939, Inc."

His wasn't the only voice claiming unfair practices. Another council member, Salvatore Ninfo, representing the Bronx, questioned the Fair's employment policy. He specifically wanted to know why the Fair was importing workers from outside the city while thirty-one thousand civil service applicants had been turned away. In response, the World's Fair

Corporation tried an end run, asserting that it could not be investigated by the City Council because it was a private company.

Ninfo was left to shake his head and wonder publicly how any agency could be called private while it was availing itself of $70 million in city investment.

The naysayers continued right through Opening Day. At two o'clock, just before the speeches started, about two hundred African Americans showed up to picket the Fair. They were all from the Greater New York Coordinating Committee for Employment, and they marched specifically in protest against Grover Whalen and his "discrimination against Negro workers." A month earlier, on March 16, the National Association for the Advancement of Colored People charged that "negroes" had been excluded "from all employment with the New York World's Fair, except in the capacities of maids and porters."

The criticism stung Whalen deeply. Performers like Hattie McDaniel, who costarred that year as Mammy in *Gone With the Wind*, and Eddie "Rochester" Anderson, the gravel-throated, perennial foil to Jack Benny ("Mistah Benny! Mistah Benny!"), had been relegated to those same menial roles in Hollywood for years. Why were they picking on his Fair?

Whalen knew that racism existed in many parts of the country, despite Roosevelt's assertion of a "completely homogenous nation." Yet as early as January 1937, he had addressed more than five hundred members of the New York Urban League in Harlem and stated proudly, "I know that you people do not want to be set apart from the rest of the world, and I again promise you that the managers of the Fair will give you your just representation."

The "you people" part may have stung somewhat, but the audience felt his sincerity and cheered him loudly.

Nevertheless, some of the charges of discrimination were blatantly true. Whether or not Whalen knew about them is another matter. One such example (that clearly no one in New York could have approved) was a set of "Sales Instructions" from a Milwaukee-based travel agency that called itself "World's Fair Tours." In a company memo, the agency had no trouble assuring its staff that "the specific article we are selling is a prearranged tour for white people." Moreover, the agency stressed that it would not be offering any tours to what it not so subtly referred to as "the general public."

On the subject of ethnic representation, the Fair itself was of two minds. On the one hand, Henry Dreyfuss had chosen William Grant Still to compose the theme music for Democracity; and the courtyard of the Contemporary Arts Building showcased an imposing sculpture called *The Harp*, created by African American artist Augusta Savage and featuring an all-black choir.

Conversely, when a photograph of two African American Cub Scouts at the Fair was distributed to the press, the Publicity Department made sure to stress that blacks appearing in official photographs was "extremely unusual."

And then there was the middle ground—the murky subtext of racism that was both accepted and ignored (by both blacks and whites) at the time because its appearance was everywhere. The Fair's most popular show was *The Hot Mikado* at the World's Fair Music Hall. The musical's headliner was Bill Robinson, whose roles as a slave-era, nappy-headed servant in Shirley Temple films like *The Little Colonel* and *The Littlest Rebel* had made him a Hollywood star. Robinson, better known by the minstrel-tainted nickname "Bojangles," was portrayed on the program's cover with the wide white eyes and red pulpy lips of a lawn jockey. And no one protested, or even noticed. Not even the NAACP.

But protests weren't Whalen's foremost concern at the moment. The opening ceremony was over, it was nearly four o'clock, and still the massive crowds he had predicted had yet to show. Worse, the rain had finally kicked in, alternately drizzling and then coming down in heavy sheets. Thunder echoed off the buildings like a warning: This was only going to get worse. Frantically, Whalen headed back to his office and called for reports. What he heard made him sink lower into despair.

A policeman monitoring traffic along both the Queens and Northern boulevards reported that it was actually "lighter than last week's." The big city parking lot, with spaces for some twelve thousand cars, wasn't more than one-quarter filled. Each of the other five fields, all of them able to hold five thousand cars apiece, were said to contain no more than a few hundred.

By four-thirty, visitors were seen streaming up the exit ramps to already crowded trains. By five, it became a rout.

The second major ceremony marking the opening of the Fair (this one, mercifully, open to the public at large) was the dedication of a sixty-five-foot-tall statue of George Washington (thanks to Joseph Shadgen). The statue dominated Constitution Mall, standing like a watchful guardian between the Theme Center and the Court of Peace. At five o'clock, Governor Lehman officiated at a reenactment of the first inauguration, with Washington himself being portrayed by a local cartoonist named Denys Wortman. This was to be the culmination of a ceremony that had begun at Mount Vernon, where Wortman had stepped into a one-hundred-year-old coach-and-four for his long journey to Flushing Meadows. Now he was ready for his close-up. Costumed in a homespun suit but sporting a dress sword, Wortman rode up to the imposing statue and dismounted just as a fresh downpour began. The meager crowd that had awaited his arrival suddenly broke for cover, as if the sight of him had frightened them all away. Distraught and drenched, Wortman's Father of Our Country took the oath of office in front of only a handful of admirers.

A short time later there was a break in the weather, and once again fairgoers came out of exhibit lobbies into the open, checking to see if the storm was over. It wasn't. If ever the gods seemed to be directly mocking Grover Whalen and his World's Fair, it must have come at the moment when the still hopeful remnants of the crowd looked up and saw an ominous sight: While the sky just *outside* the perimeter of the fairgrounds looked bright and sunny, directly over their heads a dome of clouds hung low and heavy, like a mood-killing spaceship. It was as if everyone else in New York were enjoying a fine Sunday afternoon, while those at the Fair were being dumped on.

By that time, most of them had had enough. After a day that had blown first hot and then chilly, humid and then soaking, another mass exodus began heading home to change out of their wet clothes and process the scenes of wonder that had been laid out before them. Those who did remain dawdled in restaurants or revisited exhibits they'd already seen in a desperate attempt to get out of the rain.

In an effort to keep them all from leaving, Whalen ordered the engineers in charge of the Perisphere to begin projecting the multicolored images across the great white globe that were normally reserved for nighttime viewing. As they did so, the Perisphere's theme song began to play, a mournful dirge with the now ironic title "Rising Tide."

The music, one observer noted, added a "sad note, slightly morbid under the circumstances."

At seven o'clock, darkness fell and the final ceremony of the long day began. Albert Einstein, in his role as scientific adviser, was already frustrated with the Fair's rejection of true science in favor of gadgets and trickery. Against his own better judgment, he had reluctantly agreed to give a speech explaining cosmic rays to what remained of the Opening Day crowd. In typical World's Fair fashion, his words were just a prelude to the real fireworks—the dramatic turning on of the nighttime lights of the Fair. It was to be the first public demonstration of fluorescent lighting, and they were expecting a big show.

The plan was to "capture" ten cosmic rays from outer space at the Hayden Planetarium on Manhattan's Upper West Side. Each ray that arrived would be signaled by a beam of light that one by one rose up and illuminated the stately Trylon, accompanied by the ringing of the great bell wire at the base of the Perisphere. (Also known as "the Voice of the Perisphere," the amplified piano wire played every night from hidden speakers, filling the fairgrounds with an eerie-sounding, science-fiction-like melody.) At the arrival of the tenth ray, the lights would turn on everywhere, finally ending the gloom.

Also typically, the Fair's planners had requested that Einstein limit his speech to five minutes. At first he was furious, not out of any sense of ego or the fact that no such limitations had been placed on any other speaker that day. It would take volumes to even *begin* to explain the subject, he protested, and probably no one would understand it anyway, least of all the laymen in attendance. No, he indignantly refused the request; he would not do any such thing.

Fortunately, the Fair's director of illumination, Bassett Jones, could be as persistent as he was creative. Jones hounded Einstein, barraging him with phone calls, pleading letters, and telegrams, until the scientist finally gave in. For several weeks before Opening Day, he angrily scribbled notes on cosmic rays, all the while wondering why he was wasting his time with such nonsense. Angry and frustrated, Einstein wrote and rewrote his speech until he had shortened it to what he considered was a ridiculous seven hundred words.

"I'm very sorry," he apologized halfheartedly. "But I can't cut it down any further."

In the end, Einstein's rays, hopeful or not, never got off the ground. As he rose to the same podium where FDR and others had spoken earlier, he could see all around him a smattering of spectators, but he couldn't see their faces. Most of the remaining fairgoers held copies of the *World's Fair News* over their heads in an effort to stay relatively dry.

Grover Whalen gave a brief introduction and tried to make light of the situation. "I just apologized to Professor Einstein for the weather," he said, looking dapper as ever in a dark suit and bow tie. "And he said it's all right, it's just water."

Einstein laughed politely at the joke, then got immediately down to business.

"If science, like art, is to perform its mission truly and fully," he began, "its achievements must enter not only superficially, but with their inner meaning, into the consciousness of people."

Only a few words into his speech, the rain-soaked loudspeakers crackled with static, garbling his heavily accented English and further confusing the crowd. If they couldn't follow his explanation under ordinary circumstances, now they were completely in the dark.

Not that it mattered much. Here was Einstein, the great, eccentric scientist they had read and heard so much about; the man whom "laymen" scratched their heads over but grinned at in appreciation anyway. The oddball who talked about bending light and relativity and something called mass-energy equivalence, about which they knew nothing at all, but whose crazy white hair and funny clothes had made him an icon of intelligence. He was as puzzling and entertaining to them as the young egghead contestants on the popular radio program *Quiz Kids*. They had no idea what he was talking about, but they knew it was something important, and they listened reverently despite all the distortion and the wind that carried his words away as quickly as he had spoken them.

Their rapt attention pleased Einstein as much as it confused him. Years later, he would ask, "Why is it that nobody understands me, but everybody likes me?" It would never be truer than on this night.

By the time he got down to the mechanics of his speech—"If a metallic conductor is isolated completely by means of an electric insulator, an electroscope for instance"—the crowd was hopelessly lost. Nevertheless Einstein pressed on, reading from his translated German text and taking up his full five minutes of allotted time. They had come to hear an explanation of cosmic rays, and like it or not, they were going to get one.

When it was over, he politely shook Whalen's hand and took his seat, waiting to see what would happen next. With great flourish another voice, louder and more distinctly American, barked over the public address system: "Give us ten cosmic rays!"

In response, the voice of Dr. W. H. Barton, who was manning the apparatus that trapped the rays at the Planetarium, responded with an equal modulation of drama: "Here comes the first ray!"

The spectators, tired and drenched but eager as children, craned their necks upward as if to witness something akin to a shooting star. By now the remaining streetlights had been turned off, and the twilight effect was dramatic. The bell wire rang suddenly as the first tier of light struck the Trylon. A majestically higher note of music accompanied each progressively taller bolt of color that lit up the tower layer by layer, as if it were materializing by magic before their very eyes. And between the fervent countdown, the booming of the bell wire, and the illumination of the rays, both cosmic and electric, the anticipation grew to near frenzy. The crowd echoed each called number: " . . . eight, nine . . ."

Then, just as the day had proved weatherwise—with the future, both of the world and of the World's Fair, darkened by ominous clouds that held off hope—these particular rays proved equally unreliable and uncertain. When the tenth ray was captured and Einstein threw the switch to light up the final tip of the Trylon and the fluorescent lights, the electrical system overloaded and caused a total blackout.

Instead of making the Fair as bright as day, brighter than the day in fact had been, the power failure returned it to near complete darkness.

Whalen turned frantically to his aides for answers. Einstein probably chuckled at the irony of it all. Light apparently not only bent, it sometimes broke. The crowd didn't know what to think.

After several minutes, Whalen gave the order to set off the fireworks that had been planned for later on, when the main fairgrounds closed for the day. As roman candles began bursting over their heads, fairgoers turned their attention away from Einstein and his fluorescent dawn to the wonders exploding in the sky. It was an easy transition, a mere shift in perspective from science to spectacle, from light to dark to light of a different, albeit noisier, kind. "One they could applaud," as one astute reporter put it.

Einstein left the podium shaking his head, amused by what he had seen. He was escorted to his car for the long drive back to Peconic and his lakeside summer home. The speech, he noted mischievously, had been worth it after all.

Back in his palatial office in the Administration Building, Grover Whalen sat at his enormous Empire desk and tried to sum up the triumphs and follies of the day. Throughout the evening, he had been wooing every reporter he could find and then grilling them on their first impressions of his Fair, and every one of them seemed wowed by the show. He expected glowing reviews in the papers, but he also braced himself for criticism. He knew his "one million visitors" prediction would come back to haunt him; nevertheless, he'd continued to brag to everyone within earshot that the day's attendance would still exceed six hundred thousand.

(The next day, a reporter speculated that one reason the crowds stayed away was that "people were frightened by advance notices of the tremendous numbers expected on Opening Day." Which made Whalen's boast a double-edged miscalculation: Not only had the number doomed the day to failure under any circumstances, it may have actually scared away what might have been a decent-size crowd.)

Now, looking at the early returns, he slumped in his chair: If they were true, fewer than two hundred thousand had actually paid for admission. How could that be possible? Atop the forty-foot-tall National Cash Register building, whose digits were supposed to tally each day's attendance, the numbers had been fudged to reflect his inflated six-hundred-thousand figure. Whalen had instructed that they count every guest, speaker, and employee, and had even demanded that staffers leave the grounds several times a day and return, each ticket punch counting as a new visitor.

Although the press had never really been his friend, *Time*, in its cover profile, called him "the Magnificent Whalen" and the greatest salesman alive; but he was smart enough to recognize the thinly veiled challenge that concluded the article: "[Whalen] has got the circus into his tent. Now he has to get the public into his circus."

No kidding. He understood that the fortunes of the World's Fair, and its place in New York history, rested squarely on his shoulders.

Whalen spun around in his chair and looked at the gigantic "Time Tears On" calendar he'd installed in his office exactly one year ago. Each page had counted down the days, one by one, as a constant reminder of exactly how many were left before this one. Now he saw that it was empty, and it left him feeling nostalgic. So much of this Fair was about time and new beginnings. Its theme song was "Dawn of a New Day," and if ever anybody needed one, it was Whalen at that moment. The World's Fair simply could not be allowed to fail.

Typically well-dressed visitors viewing Futurama from the comfort of their two-seated "opera boxes"
(Courtesy of the New York Public Library)

14

"I HAVE SEEN THE FUTURE"

The next morning, May 1, Grover Whalen rose early after a fitful half night of semitortured sleep. For the past two years, he had been practically living at the Fair, working as long as sixteen hours a day and then retiring to a bedroom he had specifically designed and built for himself in the Terrace Club, his exclusive lounge and restaurant for VIP investors. And while the noise of construction had never seemed to disturb him—he may have been lulled into happy dreams by the incessant hammering and riveting as his World of Tomorrow rose—the quieter din of the maintenance crews kept him tossing and turning until dawn. More than eight hundred men and women had been working all night on the mess left over from Opening Day.

"I hadn't reckoned on the terrible noise cleaning operations made early in the morning—washing the streets down and so on," Whalen said. "These started at one a.m., and after a couple of nights of it I always went home to bed. To me, the most exciting thing about the Fair was . . . its plans."

He got up at six-thirty and, still recovering from his exhaustion and the fierce cold that had kept him bedridden the week before, decided on a massage instead of his usual appointment with his personal trainer. At eight, he grabbed a rare moment for himself and snuck away, all alone, to ride over the fairgrounds on the bicycle he kept just outside his office door. Other than the street cleaners and gardeners, he had the main area all to himself as he pedaled, circling up Petticoat Lane to Rainbow Avenue and stopping for a moment at the tip of Constitution Mall.

The sight never failed to give him a thrill: Behind him lay the Lagoon of Nations and beyond that the Court of Peace, where that afternoon he would host Prince Olav and Crown Princess Märtha of Norway as they dedicated the Norwegian Pavilion. Surrounding him on every corner stood *The Four Freedoms*, statues representing freedom of speech, religion, assembly, and the press. Whalen took a moment to admire them all before finally letting his gaze rise upward to the towering figure of George Washington and, beyond him, the gleaming Trylon and Perisphere, "the stupendous, awe-inspiring heart of the Fair," as he described them. "The tenth wonder of the world."

How could anyone stop in the middle of all this wonder and not feel a tremendous burst of pride in his country, so evidenced by what had been created here? "I rejoice that I was born in this country," Whalen had told a reporter, "and especially that I was born on the Lower East Side of New York, where I witnessed the immigration . . . of people from all nations and learned the opportunities for freedom of religion, freedom of speech, and freedom of action."

For Whalen, the Fair represented everything his own life had come to symbolize, the ability of the "Everyman" so often spoken of here to rise up out of his native circumstances and achieve whatever he desired through dedication and hard work. "My father himself was a so-called foreigner," he lamented wistfully. "I didn't have blue blood to get along. Just red blood."

Only three years earlier, the very spot where he stood had been a festering eyesore of refuse and the discarded waste of a city. Today, it was a gleaming model of the future, the promise of a better life to come risen, like a phoenix, out of the ashes. How could so few have shown up yesterday to witness its unveiling?

"The trouble is some people just don't get the idea," he had admitted a year ago. "It's too big for them. Think of it—high-class people from all parts of the world. Force for international peace. Think of the moral lesson to foreigners in *The Four Freedoms*. It's too big for small minds."

Then again, maybe that was the trouble.

But for Whalen, the Theme Center alone was worth the price of admission. "Think of this huge ball, thousands of people inside of it, seeming to float on tons of colored water bubbling beneath it," he would describe it, mimicking with his hands the fountains that hid the Perisphere's support columns. Everything it stood for, everything it represented, excited him beyond measure. For the life of him, he could never understand how others could fail to share his passion, the stirring call he felt whenever he set his eyes on them. Already there were grumblings about the seventy-five-cent admission fee. Hell, he believed it was worth $25 just to get in.

Continuing his ride around Lincoln Square and down the Avenue of Labor, he could hear the early bustle and curses of workmen scrambling to complete construction in the Amusement Zone. At first the delay in finishing "the Loop," as he called it (Whalen had officially banished the term *midway* because it reminded him of a hick-town country fair), had enraged him. Half the zone wasn't even paved yet, and an electrical tug-of-war was going on: The Illumination Department sucked up so much juice just keeping the lights on until two in the morning that some of the rides were stalling from lack of power.

But maybe it was a blessing in disguise. The cold weather had already killed off a hundred primates on Frank Buck's Monkey Mountain, and the Amazon showgirls in "No Man's Land" were said to be turning blue in their revealing gladiator costumes. So Whalen had decided to postpone the official opening of the Amusement Zone until Saturday, May 13, hoping the occasion would create another boost in attendance. Yesterday was disappointing, surely, but now as he giddily rode around and around the Theme Center, passing between the Court of Power and the Court of Communications, Whalen liked what he saw. The weather, at last, seemed finally to be on his side. After the previous day's freakish storm, nothing more sinister than a light cover of clouds hovered over the fairgrounds. It was a cool, crisp spring morning, truly the dawn of a new day.

The exercise felt good. After his third trip around City Hall Square, past the glass-brick-walled New York City Building, where Moses, who had built his career by skating on thin ice, wanted his indoor rink, Whalen rode over the Bridge of Wings into the Transportation Zone. Firestone was to his left, an eggshell-white structure trimmed in blue that looked like three separate buildings squashed together: an S-shaped main area cornered by a tire-shaped circle that curved into a second wing for some reason designed to look like the fuselage and tail of an immense aircraft.

Despite its odd character, Whalen loved this building because it featured an authentic, working American farm complete with livestock and animatronic farmhands. Sheep grazed in a city field for the first time since Moses himself had them banished from Central Park five years earlier, along with cattle, pigs, chickens, and ducks. What it all had to do with Firestone products was anyone's guess, as was the Singing Color Fountain, although the main exhibit area did feature a working factory that turned out a new Tire of Tomorrow every four minutes.

The Aviation Building, just beyond, was likewise an example of architecture gone mad—the enormous airplane hangar with an arrow-shaped protrusion jutting out made the sexual symbolism of the Trylon and Perisphere seem tame and innocent. At least the façade of the Marine Transportation Building made sense; the twin prows of two enormous ships flanked either side of its entrance, sixty feet high.

Whalen rode on, past Ford, Chrysler, and General Motors, then back over the Grand Central Parkway on the Bridge of Wheels. It was nearing nine o'clock, another hour until the gates reopened, and Whalen checked the traffic: heavy on the westbound lanes heading into Manhattan for an ordinary Monday commute, light coming eastward out toward the Fair. It was early, but he stood there a moment, admiring the skyline of the city, *his* city, almost willing them to come—if not for Olav and Märtha today, then for Crown Prince Frederick and Princess Ingrid tomorrow, when they would dedicate the Danish Pavilion. Or for television or Benny Goodman or designer Norman Bel Geddes's Futurama behind him or Geddes's other creation, the Crystal Lassies (or Crystal Asses, as some crude critics called them), where you could peer through two-way mirrors at a naked girl reflected sixty times over. He didn't care what reason they chose, just as long as they came.

Whalen rode on, hanging a left at Masterpieces of Art and returning to the Administration Building, where he could shower, take a shave in the private barber's chair he'd had once again installed in his office, and get ready to meet the Norwegian royalty and whatever else might come his way that day.

The lines of people waiting to get into Futurama, the General Motors exhibit, snaked down the curved pathways leading up to the building's entrance. Since the Fair had opened its doors that morning at ten a.m., they had been spilling out halfway down to the Bridge of Wheels.

Futurama was the dream of Norman Bel Geddes, a onetime Broadway set designer who, like Whalen, had developed a reputation as a man who never let financial considerations get in the way of his vision. In 1929, after abandoning the theater in favor of industrial design, he had laid out plans for what he called Air Liner Number 4, a nine-story flying hotel with sleeping accommodations for more than six hundred passengers, a three-story atrium, five dining rooms, several cocktail lounges, a gymnasium complete with tennis courts, and a library. He figured it could be built for around $9 million; whether it could fly was another matter.

"His head is in the clouds, but his feet are certainly not on the ground," one of his friends remarked.

Short, thick-bodied, and wild-haired, Geddes also carried eccentricity to the extreme. Every Easter he picked out several friends and sent them pregnant rabbits, laughing for weeks at his own joke. Nurturing a lifelong fondness for American Indians, he often greeted guests in his Park Avenue apartment wearing nothing more than a loincloth and a pair of moccasins. Some said he was obsessed with sex; for several years, his hobby was filming all sorts of wildlife in the act of copulation. He kept more than two thousand reptiles in his apartment and delighted in running blue movies of them in midcoitus to whichever dinner companions had made it past the loincloth.

He also considered himself something of an expert on the future. In 1931, he had written an article for the *Ladies' Home Journal* entitled "Ten Years from Now," in which he'd predicted such science-fiction-like ideas as double-decker sidewalks and controlled rainfall, but which had also foreseen startling future realities such as photoelectric cells that would automatically open doors, television as the main conduit for national news, and a combination Dictaphone and typewriter that would eliminate the need for stenographers.

Geddes developed his idea for Futurama after advertising giant J. Walter Thompson hired him for an ad campaign involving traffic problems in a fictional city twenty years hence. When the World's Fair came along, he set out to sell a similar concept to General Motors, who promptly turned him down on the basis of expense. For New York's Fair, GM vice president Richard Grant explained that the company was going to replicate the assembly line exhibit it had displayed at the Century of Progress exposition.

"Can General Motors afford to spend two million dollars to admit it hasn't had a new idea in five years?" Geddes asked at a meeting with Chairman of the Board Alfred P. Sloan.

He finally convinced its president, William Knudsen, by promising to bring the whole thing together for around the same $2 million they had spent in Chicago. Unfortunately, he couldn't keep his promise. At a preview for the New York press several days before opening, Knudsen good-naturedly admitted, "It cost us six million, seven hundred thousand dollars. I hope you like it."

Operating expenses, and Geddes's $200,000 fee, brought the total up over $7 million.

Geddes not only designed Futurama, he personally supervised its construction in an old movie studio in upper Manhattan. The enormous diorama featured five hundred thousand miniature buildings, more than one million trees, and, naturally, fifty thousand cars, ten thousand of which moved along motorized tracks. His obsession for detail became legendary among his workmen when Geddes insisted on exact scale dimensions of such minor details as patties of cow manure.

Even the building itself was something to see. Designed by the architectural firm of Albert Kahn, Inc., it was situated on seven and a half acres in the Transportation Zone. And given the size of GM's financial investment, Whalen had made sure it received one of the Fair's prime spots in terms of foot traffic. Visitors entering through the Corona Gate were deposited almost at its front door; it was directly adjacent to the New York

City Building in the main area and clearly visible from those descending along the Perisphere's Helicline.

Two monumental entrances had been designed to arrest anyone's attention. The entire structure was painted a glossy, futuristic silver gray. The northwest façade was simply an enormous, hook-shaped wall that rose from forty feet to more than ten stories high, at the end of which were projecting vertical letters spelling out "Highways and Horizons," the technical name of GM's entire exhibit, of which Futurama was only one part. Two sinewy, ascending ramps led up to a narrow slit accented in bright vermilion two-thirds of the way up the hook, allowing entrance into the building.

On either side as you passed through the narrow cleft were the huge, sculptured initials "G" and "M." No other ornamentation could be found along the wall, and the imagery was both imposing and stark. "The conception was one of immense power," noted *Architectural Record*.

Finally inside the building (the waiting time in line fluctuated between one and three hours throughout the run of the Fair), visitors, walking two by two, descended into a sixty-foot-high chamber, dimly lit as if in "an eerie blue twilight." Geddes had designed the lighting in order to hypnotize the audience into hushed reverence after the long, probably overheated wait in line. Slowly, a sixty-by-one-hundred-and-ten-foot map floated into view. The room was virtually silent; extra-thick carpeting had been laid to hush even the sound of footsteps. Then a soft, intimate voice, "as though it were a friend at [your] shoulder," explained the current problems of traffic congestion as shown on the map, followed by the imposition of superhighways designed to relieve the pressure.

Continuing in the half-gloom, the guests, always in pairs, stepped onto a platform moving at the same speed as a row of winged, double-seated chairs (often likened to love seats or opera boxes) opposite them. They sank deep into the plush blue velour upholstery, and then the real show began.

Futurama itself was a thirty-six-thousand-square-foot scale model of an American landscape as Geddes imagined it would look in 1960. He had based his re-creation on aerial photographs of actual cities and towns captured by, among others, Eddie Rickenbacker, the World War I flying ace.

The eighteen-minute ride simulated a flight of several hundred miles over mountains, countryside, industrial centers, farms, and half a dozen towns and cities.

Through changes in the model's scale and lighting (and by periodic rises and dips of the ride itself), the chairs seemed to fly at various altitudes, swooping low over the details of an agrarian community and then climbing high above jagged mountain peaks, where artificial frosting on the observation window completed the illusion of altitude. "You somehow get an almost perfect illusion of flying," said *The New Yorker*.

From tiny speakers embedded in the upholstery, a resonant, whispery voice (*Business Week* likened it to "a disembodied angel") began the narration: "Now we have arrived in this wonder world of 1960. Sunshine, trees, farms, hills and valleys, flowers and flowing streams—this world of tomorrow is a world of beauty. . . . But man has forged ahead since 1939. New and better things have sprung from his industry and genius. . . . Here we see one of our 1960 express motorways."

It came as no surprise to the jaded viewer that the first glimpse of GM's interpretation of the future was a fourteen-lane superhighway (seven in each direction) featuring streamlined, teardrop-shaped cars. On the four outermost lanes, bordered by three-foot-tall partitions, speed was limited to fifty miles per hour; in the next two lanes, you could push it to seventy-five; and on the inner lane, you could zoom along at one hundred miles per hour—safely, since the distance between cars was monitored by "radio-activated beams" sent from the lead car's bumper to the instrument panel of the car following behind it.

"Directly ahead is a modern experimental farm and dairy," the narrative continued. "Note the terraced fields and strip planting. The fruit trees bear abundantly under individual glass housings.* Strange? Fantastic? Unbelievable? Remember, this is the world of 1960!"

The ride flew on, past an aeration plant and a university, usually accompanied by some unique development in adjacent roadways. After a few

* "How will the little boy climb it?" complained E. B. White. "Where will the little bird build its nest?"

minutes, the scene dimmed as the sun began setting and lights went on in isolated farmhouses and a small town off in the distance.

"Night falls on the countryside and wives are serving supper to hungry families and farm hands," the soft, authoritative voice went on. "The highway surface is automatically lighted by continuous tubing in the safety curbing, which evenly illuminates the road surface. But what's this just ahead? An amusement park in full swing! A merry-go-round, a Ferris wheel, boys and girls shrieking with glee on a pretzel-like sky ride. Here's fun and merriment in this world of tomorrow!"

They passed a monastery, a steel town, and an enormous dirigible hangar suspended in oil so that it could be turned to meet any wind direction. Riders heard, "You are now at fifteen thousand feet," as beneath them, dawn broke over snowcapped mountains. The "flight" descended to show the detail of a winter lodge complete with ski run. As night faded, the ghostly spires of a white city gleamed in the distance. "Look far—far across the valley! The city is forty miles away. . . . This is the metropolis of 1960."

For a brief moment, the scene disappeared in a thick cover of clouds, and then, as if by magic, the city of the future came into close-up view. People moved on sidewalks elevated fifteen feet above street level so that cars could move freely without pedestrian interference. An elaborate system of ramps and escalators carried passengers from vehicle to walkways and building entrances. The skyscrapers were also domed in glass, and most of them had landing spaces for "autogyros" and other flying commuter craft.

In the attraction's most brilliant feature, Geddes had designed the end of the ride to float just above a four-cornered intersection featuring an auditorium, a department store, an apartment house, and, of course, a GM dealership. Suddenly, the moving cars burst out of the building into the open air, where visitors stepped out of their chairs and found themselves standing in a life-size replica of the scene they had just "flown over"— a cross section of the city of the future featuring the exact same buildings in the exact same locations. Only now they were free to walk along it.

It was a big finish all right, and some who experienced it for the first time were spellbound, believing they had somehow been miniaturized and placed in the giant diorama themselves. Others were certain they *had* been magically transported to 1960. When they regained their senses, each was handed a little blue-and-white pin that read I HAVE SEEN THE FUTURE. Almost everyone was sure they had.

But Geddes's genius was not just that he had created "the largest and most lifelike model ever constructed" or even that he couched General Motors' obvious self-promotion in a display that would demonstrate how a broad-scale national highway system would allow for the gradual spreading out of the population across a more vastly appealing landscape. Nor was it the even subtler message that more highways would naturally create an even bigger demand for new cars to drive across them.

Geddes's grand design not only made *seeing* the future a grand spectacle, but the *process* by which they were allowed to view it was as futuristic as the model itself. The experience of flying was not a common occurrence for most visitors to the World's Fair. Popular science-fiction magazines of the day were obsessed with flight and with flying men. Superman had made his debut in Action Comics just one year earlier;* real-life aviators such as Lindbergh, Wiley Post, and Howard Hughes consistently captured the public's fascination, and their exploits had elevated them to godlike status.

Now, with Futurama, ordinary fairgoers could experience the same thrill, enjoying the same heroic perspective as they flew comfortably, in plush sofas, over GM's version of the World of Tomorrow. Geddes's innovation purposefully brought riders into the show itself, not only as *witnesses* to but as *participants* in the future unfolding before them.

Even the mechanism was startling in its ingenuity. The "carry-go-round" was a third of a mile long and contained five hundred and fifty-two chairs. (That it was essentially a moving conveyor belt was not lost on GM's production designers.) But what made it especially unique was the intricate sound system required to deliver narration in synch with the passing scenes. Each sequence had to be coordinated so that the first car passing a particular view got one loop of narration, while the next group

---

* He would also have his own event, Superman Day, on the afternoon of July 3, 1940.

of cars heard a description of their point of view. And so on across the entire oval track.

Designed by James Dunlop and built in part by Westinghouse, "the Polyrhetor," as it was called, was a twenty-ton contraption that pulled sound from twenty-one individual strips of movie film revolving around an eight-foot steel drum. Seven photoelectric beams divided the strips into one hundred and forty-seven units of sound, and each was picked up and transmitted to two cars at a time via seven corresponding trolley tracks that ran beneath the cars.

In other words, one hundred and forty-seven separate bits of narration were delivered simultaneously throughout the ride, on a continuous loop since the cars themselves never stopped revolving around the circuit. Each segment was calculated to the exact second and the precise amount of time two cars took to pass a certain point. Incredibly, despite the fact that the conveyor occasionally slowed down to accommodate large crowds, the system never fell out of synch.

More than thirty thousand people a day, the exhibit's capacity, visited Futurama. Within two weeks, it was voted the most popular show at the Fair. The Perisphere's own City of Tomorrow, Democracity, had fallen to second place once visitors learned that you had to pay a quarter to get into that one. Futurama, among all its other wonders, was free.

Still, despite its aspirations (and mostly rave reviews), the exhibit did not go without its critics—all those multilane highways were bound to set some folks off. Lewis Mumford complained that "the future, as presented here, is old enough to be somebody's grandfather" and wondered why the roads had no tollbooths. Other astute, ordinary citizens took notice of something else: Geddes had placed no churches in his World of Tomorrow. (The situation was rectified for the second season.)

Walter Lippmann delivered the harshest verdict, mostly because his observation was impossible to dispute: "G.M. has spent a small fortune to convince the American public that if it wishes to enjoy the full benefit of private enterprise in motor manufacturing, it will have to rebuild its cities and highways by public enterprise."

Toward the end of May, the company invited five thousand of its executives to the Fair to celebrate General Motors Day. GM vice president Charles Kettering responded to the critics by declaring, "All we are trying to do is to show people the world isn't finished . . . show the young people they have as much opportunity as they ever had." Echoing the Whalen mantra, he continued, "Our Futurama is aimed to give us a peek into the future—what we could do if we want to do it."

Then they crowned "Miss General Motors of 1960," a twenty-three-year-old stenographer from their Delco Remy plant. Good thing they hadn't come a week earlier, when one of the moving model cars careened over an embankment and caused a multivehicle pileup, stopping the show for about twenty minutes mid-ride.

The only other problem came on the day Whalen magnanimously offered free entry to the Fair to any U.S. Navy man in uniform. The ride's dim lighting and two-person love seats promoted some amorous behavior for sailors and their girlfriends. "There's a special kick in stepping into the chairs in 1939 and necking right into 1960," one of them winked.

Distinguished visitors to Futurama included Sara Delano Roosevelt, FDR's mother, who commented to the gentleman helping her out of the moving chair, "It's beautiful. I wish my son could see it."

"I loved it," said another woman who was moved to tears by the exhibit, "because I was so proud of my boy. His voice is so beautiful." She was the mother of Edgar Barrier, a member of Orson Welles's Mercury Theatre, who so aptly supplied the "angelic" narration.

The art deco splendor of the General Motors building, with its sinewy lines of fairgoers. Behind it lay the New York City building (still in existence today), the dome of U.S. Steel, and, on the horizon, the Parachute Tower.
(Courtesy of the New York Public Library)

VISIONS AND
DREAMSCAPES

Throughout May, there were so many formal ceremonies, buildings to dedicate, and foreign dignitaries to greet that Grover Whalen rarely had a chance to change out of his striped trousers and frock coat. Not that he minded much. The sight of him in full formal regalia became so commonplace that one morning, as he enjoyed a pleasant stroll around the fairgrounds in a plain blue suit, a World's Fair policeman didn't recognize him and failed to snap to a salute, something Whalen insisted on whenever he passed.

Grover immensely enjoyed having his own police force again. He had dressed them sharply and had even hired a public-speaking expert to give them lessons in grammar and diction. "Slang will have no place in the World of Tomorrow," said the instructor, Dr. Walter Robinson, who taught at St. John's University in Brooklyn. "Visitors must be made to realize that there is *some* correct speech in New York."

In fact, Whalen liked the transformation so much that he extended the requirement to concessionaires and even the tour guides who rode visitors around on bicycle carts. Then he hired army officers to teach information guides and ticket takers how to drill in formation, and pretty soon everyone, not just the police, was required to salute Grover Whalen.

"He expects that kind of thing and he loves it," one drill instructor informed his class.

"What about Mayor La Guardia?" a student asked him.

"Never mind about the mayor," he was told. Furthermore, "You may see a beautiful blonde coming along. The sun may be shining through her dress. She may be a very tasty dish. But no flirting!"

Some worried that Whalen was making it all a little *too* nice, a little too well mannered, for their taste. Signs planted to keep people off the grass contained only a single word: PLEASE. This was not the way New York talked, after all, and there was concern that, since the city "has its loathsome fascination for the provinces," visitors might offer more colorful reports back home if the Fair "just relaxed and let him have it on the chin."

On May 2, Whalen bit his lip as Prince Olav spoke pessimistically about the chances for world peace in the years to come, World's Fair or no World's Fair. Then, perhaps sensing that his words were a bit of a downer under the circumstances, he bucked up the audience to "hope against hope" that war wouldn't happen after all.

The Belgians weren't any help, either. At the dedication of their pavilion, Dr. Joseph Gevaert, high commissioner to the Fair, had the audacity to complain in his address about his building's electrical problems and actually canceled what was to be the highlight of their show, an exhibition of diamond cutting, "due to unforeseen circumstances." The circumstances were that Belgium had refused to cave in to some electrical workers' demands, so they cut off its current. The pavilion was able to open only with the weaker supply of juice from an auxiliary generator. Later that night, someone swiped its motor.

Belgium itself was posing all kinds of problems in 1939. Albert Einstein was becoming gravely concerned about the Germans buying up huge quantities of uranium from the Belgian Congo—he worried that Hitler was using it to develop new weapons to use against his enemies. Regardless, Count Robert van der Straten-Ponthoz, the Belgian ambassador, declared in his speech, "We maintain the open-door policy, and all nations may buy or sell in the Belgian Congo on an equal footing with the mother country."

Whalen was put off by all the shenanigans, but at least he could take comfort in the fact that he had personally fired that Belgian son of a bitch who claimed the World's Fair would never have existed without him. Al-though Edward Roosevelt had been given a cushy job as the Fair's ambas-sador to Latin America, Joseph Shadgen had been shuffled off to a small room in the early Empire State Building offices and left pretty much on his own. He was offered a salary of $625 a month for, as he described it, "sharpening pencils and coloring in maps" in the Drafting Department.

"I worked for the Fair Corporation from July 30, 1936, to May 28th of this year," he said in 1937. "I had nothing to do and sat at my desk from nine a.m. to five p.m. That was like being in jail for a man of my tempera-ment."

Despite the fact that he had been required to sign a quitclaim giving up whatever rights he may have had in thinking up the Fair, Shadgen felt that George McAneny had essentially stolen the idea from him, built the Fair where he said it should be built, and even borrowed concepts from the sketchy maps he had once laid out across the banker's desk. Shadgen promptly sued for $2 million in damages: $1 million from the Fair itself and another million tacked on for personal revenge against McAneny.

The case dragged on for more than a year, and Whalen did his best to suppress the story. Finally, six months before Opening Day, the corpora-tion offered Shadgen $45,000 to forget the whole thing. To their amaze-ment, he accepted the token offer, insisting that he had won "a moral victory" against the Fair. Immediately afterward, he vowed that he would never set foot in the place, and he never did.

"Friends tell me I am crazy," he lamented. "I . . . I have no wish to see it. To me it is sometimes like a bad dream. Other times, just one of those very, very funny stories that can happen in the big city."

But Belgium wasn't the only foreign pavilion complaining about the unions; in fact, just about every major exhibitor had had its share of problems with the workingmen of New York City. On May 2, 1938, all four hundred electrical union workers walked off the job and went on strike because General Motors had dared to perform a test run with power from its own generators. The electricians' demands were quickly becom-ing legendary.

"They wouldn't complete our building unless we paid union men twenty-six dollars a day to turn our lights off and on," complained Raphael Lopez, the Venezuelan commissioner. "I can't touch a switch! I couldn't plug in an electric razor without violating union jurisdiction."

It was true; according to their contract, only union men were allowed to touch a light fixture, "to guard against fire." And that included the changing of lightbulbs, a service for which they charged $8.81.* It got so absurd that a married pair of mural painters, ironically named Mr. and Mrs. Short, discovered that electricians at the end of a workday were removing all the fuses in whatever building they worked, preventing the couple from turning the lights back on themselves. The host building had to hire a union man to sit around until the Shorts were done for the day so that he could personally and professionally flick the lights off himself.

The conflict came to a head on June 30, when six thousand construction workers from the Building Trades Union joined the electricians and began publicly picketing the fairgrounds. Their main complaint was that the New York Telephone Company was using its own employees to pull cables, a job they considered to be rightfully their own. The walkout completely suspended construction on more than forty buildings, and it lasted for eighteen days. Whalen finally stepped in and settled the matter by neatly dividing the work between the warring factions: Construction men would pull the cables from manholes into the buildings, and the Telephone Company men would pick up the work from there. All at extra cost, of course.

Right through the Fair's opening, the various unions hired by the corporation continued their onslaught. After Norman Mackie of the Old Masters exhibit hired eight experienced frame hangers to professionally display his artwork, he was forced to employ eleven members of the upholsterers union, at $175 a week, "to drive occasional nails into the wall." Romania had to pay $900 to union men who moved a small statue, a total of two hours' work.

Nevada withdrew from the Fair after the electricians demanded to completely rewire a five-ton working model of Hoover Dam. One con-

---

* In today's dollars, imagine paying someone about $100 to change a lightbulb.

tractor submitted an estimate of $600 to the New York Zoological Society to move a small aquarium across a room, declaring the job would require six men for six days. A second contractor did the job in half an hour and charged them $7 and change.

The unions struck back through sabotage and bomb threats, sending Detectives Lynch and Socha out to the fairgrounds so many times that they became familiar with the layout a year before the Fair was open. Union workers also had a habit of disappearing on the job. "I find them resting, sometimes asleep, or somewhere strolling in the grounds," said a specialist at the Netherlands' pavilion. "Occasionally a stranger turns up [and] tells me he is coming to see that his men are not working too hard."

All of this made certain that the buildings and exhibits would never be ready by Opening Day without huge payouts in overtime. *The New York Times* estimated that, in the end, costs for the foreign exhibits alone had soared more than $10 million over budget; local companies and concessionaires saw their costs increase by 50 to 100 percent.

Whalen, although he was fuming inside, did his best to minimize the controversy's importance. "We have had only the usual amount of labor problems that any project such as this would have." He shrugged in reluctant acceptance. "Many of these were caused by jurisdictional disputes over which we had no control."

(The statement would come back to haunt him as he courted and cajoled and begged European countries to return to the Fair in 1940, despite the fact that war had, as Prince Olav feared, broken out and there was no more hope to hope against.)

Yet as the Fair settled in to its first month of business, most of the reports coming back to Whalen were positive. People loved the architecture, the layout, the "carnival of color" that was spread out before them. And if they thought it was something to see in the daytime, by nightfall the entire fairgrounds came to life.

Bassett Jones, the director of illumination who had badgered Einstein into giving his speech on cosmic rays, designed two impressive fireworks displays for the Lagoon of Nations and Fountain Lake. Just after dusk, the lagoon erupted in a "Ballet of Fountains": Fourteen hundred nozzles shot twenty tons of water a hundred and eighty feet into the air, while four hundred flaming gas jets, almost six hundred multicolored drum lamps, and five giant spotlights danced and swirled in time with original music scores, all accompanied by roman candles bursting overhead. And the shows went on every night, free of charge.

Jones had also instructed that several hundred trees be illuminated from the ground with ultraviolet rays, to make them appear luminous. He banned floodlights on all buildings except the Trylon and Perisphere, designing instead a method that made them seem to emit light from within. "As darkness falls," said Lewis Mumford, "a dream world becomes a reality. Then the buildings one by one awake with color and light; then the Perisphere is a blue moon hovering over the water; then the tower of the Glass Center shines crisply and the blue flanges of the Petroleum Building spread outward like an inverted pagoda. . . . The effect becomes just what a carnival should be—a splendid riot."

"I've kept the intensities down," Jones said. "You get an almost fairy-garden quality at night."

If people complained about anything at all, it was the size of the place. The grounds were enormous, and at first, overwhelmed by it all, a lot of folks found themselves wandering around, not lost but seemingly without direction as they consulted their watches and guidebooks and tried to decide which exhibits they absolutely couldn't miss seeing and how many they could squeeze in for their seventy-five-cent admission fee.

One woman, recording her voice on RCA's MAKA Record (or "Make a Record") machine, was asked how she was enjoying the Fair. "Well, my feet hurt," was her first response. Quick to capitalize on the situation, Dr. Scholl's and other companies began advertising remedies for sore feet in many of the trains headed out to the fairgrounds.

Grover Whalen had insisted that the Fair maintain a festive attitude, regardless of its intention to educate and enlighten. So the bright blue-and-orange trams that carted the sore-footed visitor around joyfully played "The Sidewalks of New York." There were bands everywhere, and usually a dance floor thrummed with jitterbugs or kids from a local junior high school offering a tango exhibition. Rounding them out were dozens of clowns, jugglers, and strolling banjo and harmonica players, and crowds seemed to gather around wherever they went.

Jitterbugging in the Amusement Zone was one thing, but sometimes the connection between performer and location made little sense. A pair of "negro minstrels" was spotted sashaying in front of the Belgian Pavilion one afternoon, accompanied by a third playing an accordion.

"We're not familiar with your country's music," one fairgoer called out, assuming, naturally, they had been imported from Belgium. "What was that number you just played?"

The accordion player, without missing a note or cracking a smile, answered, " 'Hold Tight,' " a current popular hit by the Andrews Sisters.

And as much as the commercialism of the corporate exhibits rankled New York's crankiest critics, more folksy publications didn't seem to mind. *Life* magazine even declared it was "a magnificent monument by and to American business." And they meant it without irony. "It gets away from the immediate job of selling goods," *Harper's* agreed.

Most who attended the sponsored exhibits weren't bothered at all by the fact that they were being sold something; in fact, very few seemed to notice or care. Even those who did pick up on all the commercialism understood that the price of free admission was being met by having to listen to General Electric's talking appliances in the Kitchen of Tomorrow, or seeing how Firestone made the Tire of Tomorrow, or watching the parade of Lincoln-Zephyrs and Mercurys as they drove over Ford's Road of Tomorrow.

Tomorrow, of course, was everywhere you looked. "We shall eat the sandwich of Tomorrow," laughed *The New Yorker*. The Hall of Pharmacy even contained the Drug Store of Tomorrow, where you could enjoy a streamlined ice-cream soda at the Fountain of the Future. (Though what exactly constituted streamlined ice cream confounded even its soda jerks.)

And in case you didn't get the point, there was even a Town of Tomorrow in the World of Tomorrow. An attractive, orderly cluster of fifteen "Demonstration Homes," it was set in the Community Interests Zone along the edges of the Flushing River. If you swung north coming off the Helicline and headed up the deepening yellow path of the Avenue of Patriots, passing AT&T and RCA on your left, you couldn't miss it. (Of course, hanging a right onto the Avenue of Pioneers may have been a more popular choice, since along this blue-tinged route you would encounter General Cigar on your left, American Tobacco on your right, and, directly in front of you, at Lincoln Square, the oasis of beer known as the Schaefer Center.)

The main problem with the Town of Tomorrow was that not many of its visitors could ever hope to live there. The Board of Design had attempted to create truly low-cost housing by utilizing prefabricated material. But once building material manufacturers began sponsoring the houses, and major department stores began furnishing them (all with proper recognition and signage, of course), the home prices soared. The design team struggled just to keep six of them from costing more than $10,000 apiece, which was still well out of reach of three-quarters of Americans. The highest-priced homes cost between $22,000 and $35,000, which was not only beyond their reach, but also beyond even the wildest dreams of almost everyone who toured them.

What was worse, in the Production and Distribution Zone's Focal Exhibit, a graph spelled out in plain language just how poor everyone (or almost everyone) was at the time. Drawn from studies conducted by the Works Progress Administration, statistics showed an average family's yearly spending habits broken down into four levels: $800 was considered "subsistence"; $2,000 was "maintenance"; $2,500 was the minimum needed to enjoy "the good life"; and anything above $5,000 was considered "luxury."

The exhibit then went on to state that 90 percent of Americans fell into the "subsistence" category. Gardner Harding pointed out that 75 percent of people earned less than $3,000 a year, and complained that the Town of Tomorrow was "in point of fact a definite breach of faith."

Harding, writing in *Harper's*, went on to criticize the Fair's attitude regarding money, declaring that "the nickel is a coin no one recognizes at the Fair. . . . Hot dogs and hamburgers are all a dime. It would cost $14.10 to see all the attractions at the Fair."

It wasn't true, really. "The talk about the difficulty of getting food at reasonable prices is probably either Bolshevist or Nazi propaganda," responded *The Nation*. "There are plenty of resting places, drinking fountains and toilets."

As for the Focal Exhibits themselves, most people hadn't a clue what they were about, and several helpful journals advised their readers to skip them altogether. But they had been an integral part of the Board of Design's concept, an acting out of surrealism and outright pretension. The job of creating them fell to seven of the top industrial designers of the day, working closely with the Board of Design and the Theme Committee. Originally planned as an entrée into each of the seven zones, they introduced the commercial exhibits and were supposed to spell out the functions identified within each zone.

At least, that's what they were supposed to do. Raymond Loewy's design for the Transportation Zone's Focal Exhibit was probably the simplest and made the most sense. A large map with flickering lights demonstrated the distance you could travel in one day via various methods: car, train, and airplane.

Communications, designed by Donald Deskey, got a little weirder. On one end of the hall was a twenty-foot-tall plastic head that represented Man; on the other end, a *thirty*-foot globe represented the Earth. When Man spoke, telling of the glory of the postal service, for example, the globe lit up with images of a mail plane caught in an electrical storm. Its forward-thinking finale ended, ironically, with the globe turning into a gigantic TV tube. Viewers were left speechless—which, considering the focus, was probably not Deskey's intent.

Russell Wright's Food Zone exhibit featured a room painted entirely in dark red. At one end of a long hall, projected on a huge, sixty-foot egg, were images of an avocado (bedecked with jewels, no less) scaling a mountain. Then a flock of flying lobsters winged out of the sea and soared overhead, a cauliflower with a boxing glove pounded on a giant bug, and finally, a blinking eye and a clock racing backward inside of a dark can.

Gilbert Rohde had a solid idea for the Community Interests Zone's exhibit, but, so as not to be thought any less creative than the flying lobster inventor, he ended it with a bang. Simply, the exhibit attempted to show how much easier life had become since 1789, when George Washington had taken his oath. Lights rose and fell on five different theatrical sets, from an eighteenth-century colonial village to a modern suburban housing project. As the lights dimmed on the last scene, a narrator summed up the pleasures and pitfalls of 1939:

"At last man is freed—freed in time and space," the deep, sonorous voice called out as the room faded to complete darkness. Suddenly a spotlight flashed across the length of the hall, shining directly on two words:

"For *what*?"

Bang. Big finish.

The odd thing about the Community Interests Zone is that it seemed to be a catchall place for anything that didn't exactly fit in the other six zones. Visitors had their choice of the American Radiator Company or the Christian Science Building, the Electrified Farm or the House of Jewels, Gardens on Parade or the Palestine Pavilion, which Albert Einstein would officially open at the end of May. Whalen had even placed his future employers, Maison Coty, here, conveniently right next to the Hall of Fashion.

There were other Focal Exhibits, of course, but word of mouth quickly spread about these bizarre visions and dreamscapes, with their floating crustaceans and their Freudian warnings, and after a while the Board of Design noticed something unusual: People weren't following the well-laid-out paths they had expected them to. Worse, they didn't seem to get the whole "landscaping as color-coded map" guide, and they had the absolutely appalling tendency to turn right as often as they possibly could.

Exhibitors with buildings to the left of main entrances would watch as swarms of visitors systematically refused to head their way. Moreover, the exhibits that were doing well—RCA, AT&T, and General Electric among them—seemed to attract even *more* business simply because people naturally flocked to wherever they saw a crowd or a long line. Thus, the snaking, slithering queue outside Futurama inevitably drew even more customers eager to stand around for three hours.

"The designers found out that the crowd's greatest pleasure is in the crowd," one reviewer noted.

Still, throughout May those crowds never came in the numbers that were expected; but it wasn't exactly a disaster yet, either. True, the Fair expected a minimum of three hundred thousand paid admissions per day, with attendance reaching as high as eight hundred thousand on weekends, and on its best Saturdays and Sundays, no more than a quarter million showed up. (Weekday attendance was typically less than half that. A *lot* less.) Through June 15, basically a quarter of the way through the season, Whalen reported that just under six million people had paid their way inside, with eight million total, including those on passes and invited guests. Which was still okay, he reckoned.

"Naturally, we've had a few kinks to iron out, a few changes to make," he stated optimistically at the one-quarter mark. "But that is all done with now. The Fair is firing on all cylinders. Everyone tells us we have a magnificent exposition!"

He went on to reassure the press that attendance thus far had come within 1.5 percent of preopening estimates. But this again had been calculated on fuzzy math, and like the population comparison with Chicago, it made an awful lot of assumptions based on nothing more than what they hoped was going to happen. And in any case, it had better happen soon.

Because most of the foot traffic showed up on weekends, and most of the early visitors were from New York, it was assumed that as summer settled in and the kiddies were let out of school, the weekdays would soon do as much business as the weekends, and the weekends themselves would explode. People would begin their summer travels, piling in their cars and heading north and east toward this great American World's Fair. There was no reason to panic yet, regardless of the fact that a six-million "gate" one-fourth of the way through meant only twenty-four million paid admissions in 1939 if things stayed the way they were. Which would be a disaster by anyone's calculations.

Suddenly the World's Fair Corporation's estimates of forty and then fifty million seemed impossible, and forget about Whalen's sixty-million boast. Even if business doubled over the next ninety days of summer vacation, between the middle of June to just after Labor Day, it still wouldn't equal forty million. Attendance in July and August alone needed to reach a staggering thirty million in order to make up for the slow start and anticipated drop-off when school started again in September. That equated to half a million people per day, every day, with a little padding thrown in over the long Fourth of July weekend.

"This Fair has already gone over the top," Whalen nevertheless insisted, smiling. Privately, he was worried. Not only weren't they coming, they weren't spending as much as he'd hoped they would when they got there—less than a dollar per person. It was about a fourth of what he'd thought they'd spend, and he worried that if they were cheapening out here, what was happening throughout the city, where the average visitor was expected to spend $56 on hotels, entertainment, and meals? The whole idea was to bring $1 billion, if not more, worth of business into New York. If you cut three-quarters out of that, you barely had an excuse to spend $160 million in the first place.

Whalen began to brood, watching the Fair wind down day after day, the nightly fireworks seeming more like a dirge for the end of something than a celebration of a happy, successful evening, with another just like it to come tomorrow. Time was tearing on again, only this time working backward, down to the Fair's closing in October.

He knew what was at stake. Regardless of how much the public loved his show, and whatever history would write of it, bankruptcy would taint his reputation for the rest of his life. There would be no more big parades, big spectacles, big projects ahead; this would be the absolute high point of his life. And unless he did something about it right now, it would be over in a year and a half. If that.

Two ideas came to him: He would authorize immediate payment of 5 percent of the debenture bonds as a show of good faith to investors and, subsequently, good reports in the newspapers; and he would get back out there and sell this Fair all over again. Hell, he'd sell the damn tickets himself if he had to.

Einstein and his sister Maja inspect the Haifa diorama in the Palestine Pavilion. The exhibit's trick-mirror effect perpetually fascinated him. *(Courtesy of the New York Public Library)*

PALESTINE VS.
PANCHO VILLA

Gerald Wendt, director of the American Institute of New York City, had put together the Science Advisory Committee to the World's Fair at the beginning of 1938 and immediately asked Albert Einstein to become its honorary chairman. Einstein accepted, though somewhat reluctantly. Science was taking a wrong turn in the 1930s, he and many others felt. In January 1939, in a speech praising Nobel Prize–winning novelist Thomas Mann, Einstein made several astounding statements that revealed his disappointment with the purely introspective life, particularly in the face of current events.

"The standard-bearers of intellect have grown weak . . . and the powers of darkness have been strengthened thereby," he declared. "Weakness of attitude becomes weakness of character; it becomes lack of power to act with courage proportionate to danger."

Moreover, corporate science, geared essentially toward the singular goals of new technology, new products, and a greater desire for consumerism, was the dominant force of the day. Right or wrong, science in general lost a great deal of prestige after the Depression hit. As Einstein had predicted several years earlier at Caltech, in 1939 as many as one in four unemployed Americans believed they had lost their jobs because a machine had taken it over.

Despite Wendt's assurances that Corporate America would not dominate the scientific approach at the World's Fair, it became obvious rather quickly that that wasn't going to be the case. Although the Theme Committee was full of designers, artists, and architects, it was sorely lacking in scientists. As early as 1936, Whalen had been fielding questions about how the World of Tomorrow was going to be conceived with "the apparent omission of science . . . in connection with the plans for the Fair."

Stephen Voorhees answered that science was to be recognized "only in its applications." Meaning what, exactly? Nylon? Fluorescent lighting? *Television?*

Whalen spun it in a better light. Science wouldn't exactly have its own exhibit per se, but the overall goal of the World's Fair was "to tell the whole story of modern scientific research instead of a single chapter," he said. "As far as practical, to add a working, scientific display to every major exhibit."

In other words, gadgets and magic.

Part of the difficulty came from the scientific community itself, which could never quite manage to get its ideas and meaning across in a way that everyone could understand. In the middle of 1937, Columbia professor Harold Urey attempted to enumerate what scientists were trying to do with their work: "We wish to abolish drudgery, discomfort and want from the lives of men and bring them pleasure, comfort, leisure and beauty."

"Well, yes!" one can imagine a Westinghouse executive pounding his fist on a conference table and shouting. "That's exactly what *we* want, too!" So it came as no surprise that in one of Westinghouse's live performances, an actress portraying "Mrs. Drudge" toiled to wash her dishes by hand while "Mrs. Modern" waited leisurely in comfort as her electric dishwasher did all the work.

Unfortunately, Wendt and the Science Advisory Committee were a little too late to effect any real influence on the World's Fair. "Any plan now presented must be a compromise," he reluctantly told its members, "since it must be constructed at a time when the major commitments of the World's Fair have been made."

At DuPont's Wonder World of Chemistry, a puppet show featuring the Tatterman Marionettes performed an elaborate pageant detailing how such modern innovations as Lucite and nylon helped to improve its audience's quality of life. Con Edison's City of Light offered a gigantic diorama (the Fair loved dioramas) depicting how the New York metropolitan area benefited from the power of electricity, gas, and steam.

"The whole city in miniature, from Westchester to Coney Island!" its advertisement read. "Subways in action, elevators darting up and down! Factories humming! 130,000 lights go on as thunderstorm darkens sky! 24 hours in the life of New York portrayed in thrilling 12-minute drama!"

No wonder the scientists were upset. The Hall of Industrial Science showed off Plexiglas; Lastex was the U.S. Rubber Company's "miracle yarn"; Carrier even constructed a seventy-five-foot-high Eskimo Igloo of Tomorrow to show off the wonders of air-conditioning. And to entice visitors inside (and remind them exactly how uncomfortable they were on any given summer day), twin forty-eight-foot-tall thermometers registered the temperature outside and the cooler, Carrier-controlled climate indoors.

At AT&T, a pretty young woman operated "the Voice Operation Demonstrator," or Voder—a musical organlike structure with keys and foot pedals that replicated the sound of a human voice. And while *The New Yorker* called it "creepy," Gerald Wendt succumbed to the lure of gadgetry by stating, "No listener can resist being profoundly moved by the ghostly human quality of this synthetic speech."

But when it came to pure spectacle, Westinghouse topped them all. Visitors came to know its building by the inverted cone of expanding circles surrounding an imposing tower out front—the structure looking very much like something out of Dr. Frankenstein's laboratory. The company featured two separate exhibits, the Hall of Electrical Power and the Hall of Electrical Living, featuring a riderless bicycle and the Theater of Tomorrow, but its show-stopper was Elektro, the Moto-Man. Scheduled performances throughout the day featured the robot, seven feet tall and apparently programmed with a snide sense of humor, responding to his operator's requests with comments such as "Okay, Toots!" He smoked, he talked, he counted, and he was the first robot to walk backward.

"That's the most remarkable thing I've ever seen," says an actor in *The Middleton Family at the New York World's Fair*, a promotional film put out by Westinghouse that takes place almost entirely at the company's exhibit.

Its message, however, was right on point: Young Bud Middleton is a preteen cynic who believes the future holds no great opportunity for him until Jim, a Westinghouse engineer from "back home," explains that scientists are creating new opportunities for growth in industry every day. In the end, after seeing his voice waves appear on-screen and even performing in front of a television camera, Bud gets the message.

After the ironic, and laughable, power failure on Opening Day, Albert Einstein retreated to his rented cottage in Peconic, Long Island, and settled in for a long summer of sailing and reflection. At Princeton, he had become something of a recluse. After the death of his stepdaughter Ilsa in Paris in 1934, his wife had returned to Europe alone, to accompany her surviving daughter, Margot, safely back to America. Margot's husband, Dmitri Marianoff, who had been an assistant to Einstein in Germany, had left her, and with no means of support she decided to take up residency with them in Princeton.

The trip, however, proved fateful for Elsa. Every possession of theirs, including those of their children, had been confiscated by the Nazis, and the death of Ilsa had left her literally heartbroken. In December 1935, Elsa entered Montefiore Hospital. One year later she was dead, the victim, it was reported, of an inflammation of the heart. She was fifty-eight years old.

By 1939, at the age of sixty, Einstein had been robbed of his home, his property, his savings, and his native country. Now he was a widower as well. As a result, Einstein rarely spoke publicly on any subject, preferring to comfort himself in solitude and professing to be hard at work on his unified field theory. To a certain extent, his involvement in the World's Fair, in particular his dedication of the Palestine Pavilion, forced him out of his internal existence of private thought and into the realm of politics and the world at large. That real world reaction may have had something to do with his fateful decision later that same summer.

On May 28, Einstein was invited to return to Flushing Meadows to dedicate the building. It was hardly an occasion he could turn down, since visiting heads of state customarily dedicated foreign pavilions. That Einstein was chosen as lead speaker (in the absence of any formal ambassador) over key Zionist figures such as Chaim Weizmann, president of the Jewish Agency for Palestine, signified that Einstein was in effect being recognized not only as a great scientist, but also formally as a leader of the Jewish people.

Still, it was an honor he may or may not have desired. His stern pacifism had been rooted in his disgust for military aggression of any kind, yet the plight of the Jews in Germany had caused him to retreat in spirit from the true doctrine of war refusal. And as biographer Ronald Clark noted, "He wanted to aid the Jews and he wanted to help keep the peace of the world. But whenever he was in danger of becoming too deeply involved, there was some new riddle of the universe that demanded attention."

But the events of that spring made it almost impossible for Einstein to remain silent. On May 17, the British government published its new policy regarding Palestine, which, it was hoped, would settle the twenty-year conflict between Arabs and Jews. The policy, issued as a white paper, did anything but. Among other things, it called for an independent Palestine to be governed by both Arabs and Jews, in direct conflict with Great Britain's former Balfour Declaration of 1917, which had named Palestine as "a national home for the Jewish people." Further, it restricted the number of Jewish immigrants to Palestine to seventy-five thousand over the next five years, at which point the Jewish population would be frozen at a one-third minority, and gave the British high commissioner the power to prohibit Jews from purchasing land in certain regions.

That only a fixed number of Jews would be allowed to escape Nazi barbarism to the Holy Land was indeed an abominable position for such a world power to take. Almost immediately, riots broke out in Tel Aviv, a twenty-four-hour general strike was called, and mass demonstrations were held in all Jewish towns. The next day, more than one hundred and eighty teenagers were wounded when police battled an angry mob of five thousand marchers at the district commissioner's office. The confrontation lasted more than three hours; when it was over, five British constables had been shot, one was dead, and the conflict showed no signs of letting up.

For Einstein, the timing was critical. A week before the pavilion's dedication ceremonies, Dr. Israel Goldstein, president of the Jewish National

Fund, called for Jews throughout the United States to flock to the World's Fair "as a demonstration of determination to stand by the ideal of a national homeland." Additionally, leaders of American Zionist organizations collectively called for a mass demonstration at the Fair to protest against Great Britain. Already a group of rabbis were chanting prayers in front of the British Pavilion.

All of this made the World's Fair itself a kind of symbolic epicenter of the global political scene—a stage upon which conflicting elements could act out their grievances and receive the appropriate attention each party felt it rightfully deserved. This wasn't exactly what Grover Whalen had had in mind for his World of Tomorrow, but in some major way it elevated the Fair's status from a mere exposition to a gathering place for the voices of dissent in the face of oppression—the world in miniature played out in a scale-model replica on the grounds of Flushing Meadows.

May was an especially dreary month when it came to harbingers of war. On May 1, May Day, Hitler addressed a million and a half Germans and thumbed his nose at the U.S. boycott of German goods. "I believe it would have been more rational to import German commodities rather than the most inferior German subjects," the Führer stated. "We can be only happy to get rid of them and are content to leave it to others to get on with them. We shall see to it that they do not threaten us, and I have made every provision in advance for such a contingency."

(The reference was clearly to Einstein and his former German compatriots. The threat of which he spoke may have had something to do with the significant events of the following Fourth of July.)

Two weeks later, Mussolini assured a crowd of fifty thousand uniformed men and women that an alliance with Germany would be signed by the end of the month in Berlin. Il Duce, it was noted, seemed to part the clouds with this speech; it had been raining for several days until just minutes before he appeared, when the sky cleared and remained bright until he had finished.

"Will there be war or peace?" he asked. "I answer this question by declaring that . . . there are not at present in Europe problems big enough or acute enough to justify a war." It may have been a gesture toward peace, but in response, only the women cheered. The men, all of them potential soldiers, were clearly disappointed.

And when Mussolini referred sarcastically to the supposed moral superiority of potential enemies, a single-worded cry of protest went up: "Palestine."

Nevertheless, Whalen tried everything he could to keep the situation in Europe from turning his World's Fair into a political stage show. In mid-May, he declared it was Tulip Week at the Fair when one million bulbs were sent from the Netherlands and planted throughout the grounds. Robert Moses dedicated the Gardens on Parade exhibit, but only because it was to become the nucleus of a botanical garden for his future Versailles.

On English Speaking Union Day (whatever that was), Tallulah Bankhead recited poetry to the accompaniment of the British Coldstream Guards Band. Orson Welles read another poem, of course titled "The World of Tomorrow," written by twenty-three-year-old Pearl Levinson, who was the winner of the $1,000 prize for an official "Poem of the Fair" contest. And because so many people were complaining about the high cost of food, Whalen announced that four new "popular priced" restaurants would open, the largest with more than two thousand seats. He also increased the number of hot dog and hamburger stands based on their strong daily business, and may have wistfully regretted his decision not to go forward with his idea for the Trylon-and-Perisphere-shaped snacks.

But not every big event was going his way, and some events were taking place that no one had planned. One afternoon that month, a 950-pound Mexican steer named Pancho Villa managed to leap over a five-foot fence in the Cavalcade of Centaurs, the Fair's fancy name for a good old-fashioned rodeo and Wild West exhibit in the Amusement Zone. Chased by a pair of brazen cowboys on horseback, Pancho staged his one-man running of the bull up and down streets, charging first at a group of barkers outside Cuban Village and sending them hurtling for cover. Then he turned his wrath on the "bobbies" of Merrie Old England and sent them scattering every which way, looking like a nineteenth-century version of the Keystone Kops.

In hot pursuit by Bud Nelson and Gregorio Acosta (who were loving every minute of it, whooping and hollering and whipping their reins back and forth across their horses' necks), Pancho ran past the shimmying, topless mannequins outside Crystal Lassies,* past the Infant Incubator and the spinning windmill of Heineken's on the Zuider Zee, all through the entire length of the Loop. Visitors stood in awe, not quite sure if what they were seeing was part of the everyday happenings at the Fair.

After several passes, the rampaging bull crashed through the World's Fair Boulevard Gate and escaped into the streets of Queens, crossing the Grand Central Parkway extension and charging up 111th Street, where he passed astonished policemen gathered outside their station house at Fifty-first Avenue. Jaws dropped and cigarettes fell from their lips as they saw first the bull, then the two "Yee-hawing" cowboys galloping after him. Nelson, swinging a lariat around his head, had actually roped the beast and almost got him under control when the bull renewed his charge and dragged the cowboy two city blocks before Nelson thought to let go of the rope.

But Nelson got right back up on his horse, followed by several mounted policemen who now joined the chase, plus a squad of motorcycle cops and even a police emergency vehicle. At Forty-sixth Avenue and 108th Street, *two and a half miles* from the fairgrounds, Nelson got his lasso around him again and held on as Acosta swung his own line around the bull's neck. Finally the animal stopped, exhausted but seemingly pleased with himself, after crashing into a peanut vendor's cart. They tied him to a fire hydrant until everyone got their wits and wind back, and when they saw the bull standing calmly on a city street and thought about what had happened, the rodeo men collapsed into a fit of laughter that no doubt amused Pancho Villa but confounded the hell out of the peanut vendor.

In a little while, regaining themselves, Nelson and Acosta returned the proud Pancho to his frontier prairie alongside Fountain Lake.

That same day, May 17, Whalen was looking to his original foreign backers, the Soviets, to draw in a capacity crowd for its opening ceremony. The USSR Pavilion was indeed magnificent, and you couldn't miss it. A

---

* "Inside she's real!" hyped the show's marquee.

seventy-nine-foot-tall statue, alternately nicknamed "Ivan" and "Worker Joe," perched atop a towering pylon. Next to the Trylon, the tower was the tallest structure at the Fair. Dressed modestly in work clothes, this stainless-steel Superman raised a shining red star above his head. He was pitched slightly forward as if in midstride during a revolutionary march, and one of his feet extended over the base that supported the statue, suggesting that the next step would stomp the crowd below.

The pavilion itself swept around the pylon in an open horseshoe shape, fronted on both ends of the semicircle with huge columns sporting bas-relief profiles of Stalin and Lenin—the two leaders facing each other, the latter featuring his quote "The Russian Revolution must in its final result lead to the victory of socialism." A pair of bright red flags displaying the hammer and sickle snapped obediently in the wind while the Red Army Ensemble of Singers rang out with stirring patriotic melodies at all hours of the day and evening.

It was quite a statement for a representing country to the World's Fair to make, but the structure's imposing nature drew thousands of the curious and open-minded into the vast expanse of its exhibit. The main outdoor area was large enough to display the Tupolev ANT-25, the airplane in which Valery Chkalov had flown a nonstop, fifty-five-hundred-mile flight from Moscow to Vancouver, Washington, in sixty-three hours—nineteen hundred miles and thirty hours longer than Lindbergh's historic flight a decade earlier.

The pavilion's interior was also roomy enough to show off a sixty-foot section of the Mayakovskaya station of the Moscow subway, dubbed "the palace subway" by Muscovites. (Take that, Manhattan!)

Whalen's old comrade and original money producer Constantine Oumansky officially opened his country's pavilion. Oumansky had recently been promoted to ambassador, a fact that delighted Whalen. His pleasure was short-lived, however. The speech started off well. After being introduced by Whalen and briskly shaking his hand, Oumansky assured the attentive crowd that Russia was and would continue to be a "good neighbor" to the United States and was anxious to preserve world peace in the World of Tomorrow. His statements were greeted by much applause and one of Whalen's trademark gleaming smiles.

It went downhill from there. Pounding on the podium in classic Soviet style, Oumansky went on to affirm that in the preservation of said peace, Russia's mighty army was more than ready to defend its borders against invasion.

"The Soviet people," he said, looking somewhat uncomfortable in an ambassadorial morning coat that fit him badly, "are not impressed by threats. Neither do they beg for alliances. They are prepared to cooperate on a basis of complete reciprocity and equal obligations with powers which are interested in the maintenance of peace."

Whalen's toothy smile faded slowly into a reluctant, tight-lipped acceptance. Yes, Oumansky continued, they would fight against German aggression in Eastern Europe; but, no, they wouldn't do it single-handedly. England and France had better live up to their obligations, he warned, quoting Stalin that "warmongers accustomed to having others pull chestnuts out of the fire for them" could forget it.

Whalen looked down at his hands, fervently hoping that Oumansky would end this on a high note. He didn't, instead promising that the USSR would deal "a double blow for every blow" it received from anyone who violated its republic.

Exhausted and satisfied that he had gotten the message across, Oumansky took his seat to a smattering of applause and a brace of astonished expressions. For the first time in his life, Whalen was speechless. He looked up at the clear blue sky, felt the warm sun on his face tempered by the breezes that helped to cool hot tempers, and once again wondered where the hell everyone was. The Soviet Pavilion was the largest and most impressive damn building on the lot, but by the end of the day, paid attendance would still total under a hundred thousand.

Later that afternoon (a historic day all around, it seemed), the Federation of Jewish Women's Organizations met at the Fair's Temple of Religion, at the edge of Community Interests and directly opposite the Palestine Pavilion. Rabbi David De Sola Pool, president of the Synagogue Council of America, praised the fact that this gathering could only have been held in such a great democratic country as America, then launched into a by now almost rote denunciation of Great Britain's white paper.

The British government, he said, had broken its pledge to the Jewish people. Worse, he spelled out the real fear that was on everyone's mind: that the policy "barred the doors of the Holy Land to Jewish refugees from Germany." Some fifteen hundred people, crowded wall to wall in the sweltering Temple of Religion, wept and nodded in quiet, saddened acknowledgment.

On Tuesday, May 23, to practically no one's surprise but to everyone's dismay, the British House of Commons approved its government's new position on Palestine by a vote of 268 to 179. A Labor amendment, demanding that a stay of action be enforced until the League of Nations could be consulted, was defeated by one hundred votes. In response, the opposition, led by Winston Churchill, denounced the policy as "another victory for Hitler and Mussolini" and worried that it would taint their country's good relationship with the United States.

Out of that came an eerie premonition from Laborite Herbert Morrison, who warned, "The agents of Hitler and Mussolini seem to have the habit of lodging bombs in suitcases in various places. It has happened in Jerusalem and I gather it is happening in London."

Soon enough, it would happen in Flushing Meadows as well. And while it was true that a series of explosions had occurred in Palestine in protest, the details of the numerous suitcase bombs were left unexplained by news reports.

The night before dedicating the Palestine Pavilion, Einstein appealed to the Jewish National Workers Alliance to stop blaming Britain and for Jews the world over to look within themselves for answers. "England has, in part, ignored its sacred pledge," he said in a radio address to the meeting in Town Hall in Manhattan. "She gave her word then in a dire hour and she is acting now, too, in a dire hour. Remember, however, that in the life of a people . . . there can be only one source of security—namely, confidence in one's own strength and steadfastness."

In part, he was also concerned that making an enemy of the British might somehow weaken Europe's position in fighting the Nazi aggression against the Jews.

"Remember in the midst of your justified embitterment that England's opponents are also our bitterest enemies, and that in spite of everything the maintenance of England's position is of utmost importance to us," he warned. "Despite the great wrong that has been done to us, we must strive for a just and lasting compromise with the Arab people."

This could not have gone over well with his audience. As the anticipated gathering of more than one hundred thousand Jews—many of whom had traveled to New York specifically for this occasion—prepared themselves for bad weather (heavy rains were predicted for the next day's dedication), they now wondered exactly what Einstein's message at the pavilion's opening would be.

At eleven the next morning, May 28, the official party of thirty guests and dignitaries arrived at the World's Fair Gate and were met by the Haskell Indian cavalry guard. The American Indian brigade had become a familiar sight around the fairgrounds that spring, having been hired by Whalen himself to serve as his personal honor guard. Day after day, he could be seen trailing behind them in his open-topped limousine, the twenty-four dark-skinned horsemen dressed ironically in the Fair's blue-and-orange uniforms and carrying lances topped with fluttering pennants bearing the insignia of the Trylon and Perisphere.

Visitors must have been confused by the mixed imagery of the untamed West in full Fair regalia, but Whalen, forever a boy at heart and always the consummate showman, loved spectacle of any kind (especially when it brought him attention). When the confusion grew a bit too intense, he had the Publicity Department explain that the Indians symbolized "America's link to the heritage of the past." Though why they were here in the World of Tomorrow was the question. Perhaps, as one press agent noted, he "just liked having Indians and horses around."

Einstein and his party, including Chaim Rosenberg of the Palestine Labor Federation, Abraham Idelson of the Jewish National Council of Palestine, and George Back, president of the pavilion they were about to dedicate, among others, made a quick motorcade tour of the fairgrounds. After passing the Court of States and admiring the full-spectrum blossoming of flowers along Rainbow Avenue, they swung right on Constitution Avenue, drove around the Lagoon of Nations, and stopped first at Federal Hall. A massive, thirteen-columned structure (representing the original thirteen colonies), the building stood at the head of the Court of Peace and dominated the surrounding Hall of Nations. Two massive towers representing the legislative and judicial branches of U.S. government flanked the pillars, each adorned with statues depicting *Peace* and *Common Accord Among the Nations of the World.*

From there the motorcade headed west, retracing its route down the mall toward the great statue of George Washington, circling around the Theme Center and alighting briefly at the New York City Building, where Mayor La Guardia greeted them. The schedule was tight, so La Guardia kept his introductory remarks brief and everyone piled back into their cars, to be led by the dignified Haskell tribe up the Avenue of Patriots to the Palestine Pavilion. What Einstein made of his Indian escorts can only be imagined.

At eleven forty-five, a pre-dedication ceremony was held, marking the installation of an eternal light in front of a plaque commemorating those who had fought and died for Palestine. The flame, contained in an oil lamp designed to look like an ancient relic, had been lit at the Wailing Wall in Jerusalem ironically on Easter Sunday and had been carried to the Fair from a synagogue on Central Park West. A cantor's lone voice echoed reverently in prayer.

Given the heated tone that was expected for the rest of the day, the party enjoyed a few quiet minutes to themselves. The entire pavilion covered only half an acre but comprised ten separate halls, designed in eastern Mediterranean style, around a tranquil court complete with a lotus-blossomed pool and more than fifty varieties of trees and plants native to Palestine. Whalen had even seen to it that a sixteen-foot-tall palm tree, with fronds spreading as wide as its height, had been planted—a gorgeously incongruous sight smack-dab in the middle of New York City proper.

Einstein, clearly moved, was particularly fascinated by the Haifa Diorama. At the World's Fair, religion and reverence were one thing, but no exhibit, not even this one, could resist showing off a few technological tricks.* Designed to display the transformation of Emek Jezreel, the former Bedouin Valley of Death, into the fertile land of modern Palestine, the scene blinked instantly from barren wasteland to modern city before your eyes through the use of trick mirrors.

It was another gadget, of course, but Einstein was captivated, watching the change take place over and over again until the time came for them to leave. As they exited the building, each took notice of the restless crowd already gathered in front. What they couldn't see, off in the distance, were the more than twenty thousand chairs set up in the Court of Peace, where the speeches would take place in order to accommodate the expected masses. Each one had been claimed hours before the ceremony was to begin. An equal number of spectators stood impatiently around them, and more were arriving every minute.

At twelve-thirty, Whalen entertained his guests at a luncheon in Perylon Hall, another of his swanky, exclusive palaces where most of the Fair's official receptions and banquets were held. Situated adjacent to the Hall of Pharmacy, the private club was plushly carpeted, with copper walls and sleek art deco furnishings. Perylon (Whalen's own hybrid of Perisphere and Trylon) tended to impress even its most distinguished and powerful guests. The party relaxed and composed themselves for the main event of the day.

Whalen, uneasy with the tension yet buoyed by the largest crowd he had seen so far, excused himself briefly after lunch to tend to business. The reports were good; attendance was already estimated at nearing two hundred thousand, most of them paid. He took a moment to sip a cocktail (since Opening Day, he had eschewed his former teetotaling ways and often enjoyed a midday nip) as he checked out the weather. Despite the warnings of rain, he saw nothing but a clear blue sky. In fact, the ride back from the pavilion had been almost uncomfortably hot. Then he worried that maybe it was *too* hot, that the weather was playing another one of its

---

* And as a further nod to its surroundings, an inscription at the building's entrance read, "Holy Land of Yesterday—and Tomorrow."

nasty tricks on him, and that the broiling sun would only accentuate what were sure to be heated tempers once the voices of dissent against Great Britain began.

At two-fifteen, Einstein and the others regrouped in limousines and drove once again to the Court of Peace. Almost immediately, the crowd grew agitated. Seeing the procession arrive, they began swarming the cars and completely blocked the lane allowing the speakers entrance. There was a moment of panic before policemen stepped in and formed a protective cordon around the group. Pushing and shoving their way up the ramp, Einstein and the others were practically carried to the relative safety of the elevated platform.

Climbing to the podium, Whalen was awed by the largest crowd he'd seen yet, estimated at more than a hundred thousand in the Court of Peace alone. Even the section reserved for the press had been overrun by viewers demanding a front-row seat to the dedication and whatever political scene was to be played out. As he stood to begin the proceedings, a large group surged forward angrily, threatening to engulf and overrun them all. Once again, the police had to step forward and push them forcibly back behind the guardrails.

They had come from everywhere, up and down the eastern seaboard and as far away as Bolivia and Bombay. One car spotted in a parking lot bore a license plate from Alaska, as of then not yet even a state in the Union. Whalen, daunted, stumbled for a moment; for the first time, he felt uneasy in front of a large crowd. Summoning up his feelings for his Fair, he tried once more to play the peacemaker.

The World's Fair, he began, was first and foremost a forum for all nations and all people (he put particular emphasis on the word *all*) to tell of their plans "for a true world of justice, plenty and peace. The Fair has no dogma of its own." Then, as he was first and foremost a salesman, he decided to protect his interest, assuring whoever was listening and might be recording his words that the Fair also did not assume as its own the teachings of any of its participants. Business was business, and it, or rather he, could not afford to choose sides.

La Guardia was equally noncommittal. In an earlier speech he had stated, perhaps unaware of the ironic comparison with Flushing Meadows, that this pavilion was a demonstration "of what Jews have accomplished in reclaiming arid wastes" and that it "may point the way to similar work which fugitives from persecution can do in our country."

Bringing the metaphor full circle, on this day he said, "This pavilion is a token of thanksgiving from the people who . . . gave us the Ten Commandments." (Apparently, what one Moses had done in the Holy Land, another had accomplished here in Flushing Meadows. And Thanksgiving at least explained all the Indians.)

Finally, after more speeches, Whalen stood again and introduced the man of the hour. The crowd, lulled from anger to boredom by the blandness of the politicians, grew suddenly restive, eager to hear the words of their revered Einstein, that most famous exile from the most notorious oppressors. Yet the little scientist, Whalen noted, seemed undeterred by the masses; nothing, it seemed, could sway him from the intellectual bemusement he famously displayed under almost any circumstances.

"The World's Fair," Einstein began, "is in a way a reflection of mankind. But it projects the world of men like a wishful dream. Only the creative forces are on show, none of the sinister and destructive ones which today more than ever jeopardize the happiness, the very existence of civilized harmony. Such a presentation seems fully justified, though it be one-sided. Whoever has learned to appreciate and admire the positive side of man's aspirations is sure to be willing to protect and, if necessary, to fight with all his might in defense of what has been achieved."

And there it was. In a handful of sentences, the greatest mind of its era had encapsulated what Whalen had sought to portray—that the World of Tomorrow was a dream, surely; but it was a dream that was worth fighting for, one that had value regardless of its inherent need to succeed and function as a representative of democracy and capitalism. Once seen, by however many came in the end, the World's Fair stood if only as a realization of that great ray of eternal hope of which Roosevelt had spoken, and against the darkening clouds of whatever storm was yet to come.

"I am here entrusted with the high privilege of officially dedicating the building which my Palestine brethren have erected as their contribution to the World's Fair," Einstein continued. "[Palestine] is exposed to constant attack, and every one of its members is forced to fight for his very life. . . . Nothing of this shows here. We see only the quiet, noble lines of a building and within it a presentation of the Palestine homeland. . . . May the fine creative spirit of those who have built this structure find an understanding and appreciative public."

In the end, the ceremony turned out to be exactly what it should have been—an orderly demonstration of passive resistance to a great injustice. The afternoon had started out oppressively hot—in fact, nine visitors had to be treated for heat prostration—but as Einstein spoke, a wall of thick, dark clouds once again pushed across the sky and advanced on the Court of Peace. This time, miraculously, it was noted, "the storm blew over without spilling a single drop of rain on Flushing Meadows."

After the ceremony, the group returned to Perylon Hall and unwound with more cocktails. Einstein sat with his pipe. Whalen once again excused himself on business. He needed some other piece of news to lighten up the mood of the day in case things got too political, so just before five o'clock he hurried back to the World's Fair Gate and waited until he found what he was looking for. Whalen spotted the boy pushing through the turnstiles with his parents and younger brother, and instantly decided he was perfect.

With photographers and publicity men at the ready, Whalen pointed out a twelve-year-old freckle-faced kid and gave the signal. Two guides pounced on the family, who were at first startled into thinking they'd committed some sort of crime until they were happily told that little Douglas McMahon of Stamford, Connecticut, was officially the five millionth visitor to the World's Fair. Flashbulbs popped, hands were shaken, and the family was offered a free tour of the entire fairgrounds and VIP admission to all the shows Dougie wanted to see.

Whalen smiled, posed for the photo op, thanked the McMahons for coming (had he figured them for Irish?), and hurried back to Perylon Hall for the formal dinner that would finally cap this long and rigorous day.

Unofficially (Whalen was still sticking to his inflated Opening Day numbers), it was the largest paid attendance the Fair had seen in its entire thirty days of existence.

Police clash with protesters outside the German American Bund meeting at Madison Square Garden.
(© *Bettmann/Corbis*)

17

GERMANY YESTERDAY—
GERMANY TOMORROW

Grover Whalen's hoped-for collective of world peace efforts was disintegrating before his eyes. In bits and pieces, Czechoslovakia had fallen under Germany's command between October 1938 and mid-March of the Fair's inaugural year. Yet the country itself remained defiant, especially when it came to their pavilion at the World's Fair. Although the Nazis had stopped the shipment of exhibits to be displayed there, more than a third had already arrived. And with Mayor La Guardia's help, a committee was formed to complete its financing and fill in whatever gaps remained in the $600,000 building.

Despite Germany's demand that the pavilion be shut down, former president Edvard Beneš insisted that "Czechoslovakia is still alive. It will continue to live. . . . This pavilion is to be brought to a successful conclusion, just as will our struggle for our country."

On the west wall of the building, bronze letters spelled out "Begun by the Republic of Czechoslovakia. Although unfinished, maintained by its friends in America."

Scheduled to open on the same day as the Palestine Pavilion, the Czechoslovakia Pavilion was delayed for three days, until after Memorial Day, because of yet another strike by the concrete workers union. Although attendance after the four-day holiday weekend was predictably light—around sixty-eight thousand paid to get in—the speeches that day were to some degree more emotionally charged than those on Palestine Day. When Beneš got up to speak, La Guardia literally jumped out of his seat and applauded wildly.

The Nazis, Beneš declared, "can rule the country temporarily [but] cannot kill the spirit of the people." The crowd, many of whom were dressed in native costumes, stood as one and thundered their applause. Their country, Beneš continued, "cannot die. And she will not die."

After a prolonged ovation, La Guardia rose to speak. The afternoon was stiflingly hot and humid; all morning, a storm hovered over the horizon but held its rain in exchange for sopping humidity, and the mayor mopped his brow, wishing he could shed his formal coat. But he had been waiting for this moment. This pavilion was literally sticking it to the Nazis, and he was loving every minute of it.

"I have no apologies to make to anyone," he began, and the crowd renewed its applause and added whistles and hoots of laughter. As early as March 1937, La Guardia had used the World's Fair as an excuse to heckle Hitler. When a building dedicated to religious freedom was proposed, La Guardia stated that it should include a "chamber of horrors [containing] a figure of that brown-shirted fanatic who is now menacing the peace of the world."

In response, the German press called him a "dirty Talmud Jew" and a "Jewish ruffian." Eventually, Secretary of State Cordell Hull formally apologized, and La Guardia took the opportunity to make a joke out of it. "Secretary Hull and I have an agreement," he said later. "He attends to foreign affairs and I attend to cleaning the streets of New York. And when it concerns the relations with a certain gentleman in Europe, we're both dealing with the same commodity."

Punctuating his words in his peculiar nasal speech with fist pounding and head bobbing, La Guardia ended with the carefully chosen sentence "We are dedicating this temple to the cause of liberty and to the cause of a people who will not and who refuse to surrender their liberty."

President Roosevelt's invitation to participate in the World's Fair had been extended to every foreign nation, including Germany. Not surprisingly, this did not go over well with a great many New Yorkers. There were even some who talked of supporting La Guardia's reelection in 1937 if only because, with him as mayor, Hitler would never allow a German pavilion to be built. In an editorial titled "No Swastikas at the World's Fair!" *The Nation* issued a direct warning to Grover Whalen regarding his own political ambitions should he allow the Nazis to participate.

Summing up the tenor of the city's Führer furor, writer Oswald Villard asked, "Will any Jew set foot in the German exhibit? Certainly no self-respecting Jew. Will any Jews be *permitted* in the German exhibit? That may be for Hitler to decide."

Despite misgivings about a potential backlash against any sort of Nazi representation in Flushing Meadows, on December 30, 1937, Whalen had convinced Consul General Johannes Borchers to sign a contract for a one-hundred-thousand-square-foot pavilion, envisioned as one of the "major exhibits" at the Fair.

Almost immediately, there were doubts that the Germans intended to live up to their agreement. In February, Edward Roosevelt reported in a memo, "The Germans are not at all satisfied with their location." There had also been rumors that Hitler was still angry over La Guardia's "brown-shirted fanatic" comment and the fact that the Department of the Interior had recently refused the export of helium to Germany for use in its dirigibles.

Finally, on April 26, 1938, when with only a year to go before opening they would either have to begin construction or cut bait, Borchers sent a letter to Whalen formally declining participation. "The German government sincerely desired to accept your kind invitation and to participate in the World's Fair," he wrote. "As you know, several obstacles originally stood in the way. . . . However, the most important one remained, namely, the foreign exchange problem. . . . Because of this situation my government very much regrets its inability to actively participate as originally planned."

It was a pretty flimsy excuse; neither Italy nor the USSR was all that concerned with getting their money's worth, and Germany's investment was originally estimated to be about half their costs. Privately, bankers like Gibson and McAneny believed that Germany could come up with the money if they wanted to, but that the country was secretly building up a war chest against the day when cash would be needed for military supplies.

But even though Germany was out, there were some who believed that the country should be represented anyway. With some sixty-odd nations represented, the absence of Germany, even under current circumstances, would constitute a glaring omission in the World of Tomorrow. Every important power was represented; and after all, the country had existed long before the Nazis and God willing would continue on when Hitler's regime was long gone.

With that thought in mind, a small but distinguished group of New York's elite—including ex-governor Alfred E. Smith and his ex-protégé Robert Moses, Marshall Field, and, amazingly, even La Guardia—came up with a plan to erect what it called the Freedom Pavilion, with the subtitle "Germany Yesterday—Germany Tomorrow." (Like current movie heroine Scarlett O'Hara, this committee obviously preferred not to think about today.) Pulitzer Prize–winning journalist Herbert Bayard Swope got behind it. Even the State Department thought it was a good idea.

A letter to Secretary Hull spelled out its purpose: "We believe that as Germany will not be represented at the Fair, an exhibition comprising the creative efforts of many of Germany's most gifted artists and scientists . . . would be welcomed by the public." It was, among other things, to be a tribute to the culture that had netted America Einstein.

Hull's reply approved the idea (or, more specifically, didn't disapprove of it), and in the fall of 1938, McAneny assigned the project his blessing and Lot N-14, a thirty-thousand-square-foot space in the Government Zone. On January 13, 1939, the proposal made headlines, and all hell broke loose. The Nazi press called it a "Pavilion of Jewish Jetsam."

"Four days later," wrote Laura Z. Hobson in *The Nation*, "the whole project was dead." Hobson, who would go on to write the bestselling novel *Gentlemen's Agreement*, about anti-Semitism in America, stated, "Whalen won't let us do it. They've been getting to him. He won't let us have the site."

The truth was a bit more complicated and somewhat indicative of the split emotions regarding Germany, first as a nation of the world and then as a potential world dominator. At a luncheon at the River Club to raise money for the pavilion, a soft-spoken, eighty-two-year-old priest, Monsignor Michael Lavelle, voiced his opinion that the plan might be "loaded with dynamite. . . ."

"We don't want to do anything that is going to provoke a conflict," he added. "That's what I'm afraid of in anything of this kind. The smoldering end of a cigarette has often burned down many a towering building."

In contrast, the relatively youthful (at age sixty-five) Al Smith elucidated what was on everyone's mind at the time: "I have never believed and I never will believe that the present government of Germany is in keeping with the heart of the German people. Anything we can do to exalt Germany in the past, in the situation she now finds herself in, is a favor to the rank and file of the German people [who] someday are going to throw Hitler out the window."

Swope, who had been one of the project's earliest proponents, now stood and voiced his opinion against it. "This enterprise would be completely empty if it were even remotely to inflame a warlike spirit," he said. The next day, he gave the ad hoc committee the bad news. "I've been in constant touch with Al Smith and Grover Whalen. They think this will make trouble. Bobby [Governor] Lehman's against it. The Fifth Avenue store crowd is against it. . . . The World's Fair is supposed to be a pleasure place—controversial stuff's bad."

But while the Freedom Pavilion was never built, curiously the pavilions of Italy and Japan thrived during both seasons. The Italian Pavilion, a three-story palazzo offering an ingenious, if puzzling, synthesis of the architecture of classical Rome and modern Italy, was capped by a statue of the goddess Roma atop a two-hundred-foot tower. From her perch, and reflecting an Italian sense of both defiance and bravado, a waterfall cascaded down a long flight of steps and foamed into a pool featuring a monument to Guglielmo Marconi, the radio pioneer and noted Fascist. In the Salon d'Onore (Room of Honor), a statue of Il Duce stood defiantly facing the Court of Peace.

By contrast, Japan's pavilion was modeled after an ancient Shinto shrine, surrounded by gardens and pools and planted with Japanese trees and shrubs. Still, this was a world exposition, and understatements simply would not cut it. In what may have been the most outrageously ironic display at the Fair, the pavilion featured "the Million-Dollar Liberty Bell"— a replica of America's symbol of freedom re-created in a silver shell adorned with more than eleven thousand cultured pearls and four hundred diamonds.

The irony didn't end there. June 2 was officially declared "Japan Day" at the Fair, an event that "stressed the cordial relations existing between the United States and Japan." In a ceremony similar to Palestine's lighting of the eternal flame, a pretty girl named Akiko Taukimoto (for the purposes of the day, she was dubbed "Miss Japan") presented a "flame of friendship" to Grover Whalen. This particular flame had also traveled quite some distance to Queens, having been lit a month earlier at the eternal fire of Izuno, Japan's oldest shrine.

Japanese ambassador Kensuke Horinouchi solemnly declared that by sending the flame, "the Japanese people symbolize their ardent hope that the glorious tradition of peace and amity between America and Japan will remain as bright and eternal as the temple fire at Izumo."

To Whalen's utter delight, a member of the Japanese commission told him that the Fair was so well advertised in his country that the Trylon and Perisphere were seen everywhere, and that schoolchildren were especially obsessed with the symbols. Japan, he reassured everyone, was creating "a new civilization based on the harmonizing of the East and the West. That is the shape of things to come in the world of tomorrow as the Japanese conceive it."

Even in 1939, the Nazis were causing trouble in New York. Joe Lynch and Freddy Socha got in the middle of it in February when the German American Bund decided to hold a meeting in Madison Square Garden. Forty thousand of them were expected to show up, give their speeches, and raise all kinds of anti-American hell. Worse, they had chosen as their motto for the evening "True Americanism and George Washington Birthday Exercises."

The Washington connection could not have been lost on Whalen.

Lynch and Socha were drawn into the fray when La Guardia's office received an anonymous letter threatening that three time bombs would blow up the Garden if the meeting was allowed to take place. Chief Inspector Louis Costuma called Lieutenant Pyke, and two days before the event, the men of the Bomb and Forgery Squad spent hours combing through its seats and corridors and alleyways and finding, as usual, no trace of any such device.

But Pyke wasn't satisfied. If there was any occasion for a bomb to go off, this was certainly one of them. At first, to ease public tension, he reassured the press that the tip, like so many others his office was receiving these days, was almost certainly a prank. But then La Guardia couldn't keep his mouth shut about it. In Memphis for a conference, he had left New York City Council president Newbold Morris in charge as acting mayor, but Morris was a blue-blooded Yalie who was about as far removed from the dirty dealings of the city as La Guardia would have been from the privileged society Morris had grown up in.*

La Guardia, conscious of the turmoil that a Bund meeting would create, had nevertheless signed off on it, providing "it were orderly and no violence were advocated." On the day of the rally, he stunned New Yorkers in general and incensed Pyke personally by responding publicly to the threat and stating matter-of-factly, "If they bomb it, we'll catch the bombers." No one on the squad could believe he was being so cavalier about the idea.

Lynch, Socha, and the rest of Pyke's men were sent out repeatedly to make sure it was a hoax. If they allowed a bomb to go undetected and the damn thing went off and killed God knew how many—even if they *were* Nazis—the entire department would come under fire. Given the circumstances, the event was shaping up to be a black eye for the city and the police any way you looked at it.

Police Commissioner Valentine wasn't taking any chances, either. In addition to the bomb threat, anti-Nazi groups of all kinds were organizing various protests; the Socialist Workers Party began holding rallies the

---

* Morris, who ran unsuccessfully for mayor twice in the two terms after La Guardia, would eventually gain recognition as the man to succeed Robert Moses as city parks commissioner in 1960.

night before, a Friday, and was prepared to go right on demonstrating before amassing a group of thousands of Trotskyites at six o'clock the following evening, two hours before the event kicked off.

Valentine worried that it would spill over onto Eighth Avenue, that Bund members entering and leaving Madison Square Garden would cause trouble and endanger the usual hordes of people out for a nice evening at the theater. He had originally ordered almost a thousand police officers to be on duty; then on Friday he upped it to thirteen hundred. Pyke's men were part of a twenty-four-hour guard inside the building. Like it or not, Lynch and Socha were going to get a firsthand view of the Nazis strutting their stuff.

The Bund meeting sharply divided New York City along political and emotional lines. The American Civil Liberties Union and the National League for American Citizenship argued that the meeting should be allowed, if only to uphold the principles of American democracy. La Guardia again surprised everyone by supporting it: "If we are to have free speech, we have to have free speech for everybody," he said. "And that includes the Nazis."

On the other side, the New York contingent of the National Lawyers Guild stated, "We are outraged at the association of the Bund and the swastika with Americanism and the birthday of George Washington." The Bund was considered by many to be the local voice of the Nazi Party, determined to overthrow the government and install a Fascist dictatorship. It didn't help that some three thousand Bund members, dressed as storm troopers, would be acting as ushers at the evening's entertainment.

Newbold Morris himself got into the fray. "Why is it necessary for them to disport the storm trooper uniform, the symbol of a doctrine which stirs bitter resentment in the hearts of free people throughout the world?" he asked.

Worse, the uniforms themselves looked . . . well, actually, with their Sam Browne belts and snappy blouses, they looked amazingly similar to the uniforms Grover Whalen had designed for his police force way back when, leading Colonel Lewis Landes of the American Legion to worry that it would "mislead the people in the belief that these German-American Bund officials are wearing a part of the United States uniform."

The night of the rally started off orderly enough. Valentine, feeling the tension of the entire city coiled into an angry knot of resentment and barely repressed fury, was certain it would turn into a riot. Once more he upped the police detail to more than seventeen hundred, creating an almost impregnable fortress around Madison Square Garden. It may have been a wise decision, but the sight of so many civil servants called to duty in order to protect a gathering of Nazis only fueled the public's anger. For two blocks in every direction, the area around Fiftieth Street between Eighth Avenue and Broadway was cordoned off to pedestrians.

That was too much. Now the average New Yorker couldn't even walk on his own streets because the Nazis had commandeered a square mile of ground. "We have enough police here to stop a revolution," Valentine joked as the meeting kicked off at precisely eight p.m. The Socialists, needless to say, were not amused.

Inside the Garden, the meeting went pretty much as expected. Banners were waved exhorting members to "Smash Jewish Communism" and "Stop Jewish Domination of Christian America." A particularly tense moment occurred when, during a speech by Fritz Kuhn, national führer of the Bund movement, a young man in a blue suit (later identified as Isadore Greenbaum of Brooklyn) tried to rush the stage single-handedly. He was tackled by several burly cops but kept on pushing, somehow losing his pants in the effort.

Outside, however, there was chaos. Lynch and Socha had once again combed the Garden for any signs of a bomb in the hours before the meeting, and now Lieutenant Pyke called out his men for a different disturbance. Out of a second-floor apartment on Forty-ninth and Eighth, a loudspeaker could be heard blaring the message "Be American, stay at home!" and denouncing the Nazis. Pyke's contingent rushed into the building and kicked in the door. The sight of an alarm clock froze them, its ticking like the countdown of a bomb explosion they had all been dreading.

Frantically, they inspected the clock and found it had been set for seven fifty-five, about fifteen minutes earlier, yet no explosion had occurred. Pyke studied the setup and determined it had been wired to set off a record player, the source of the protest speech. They gathered the evidence and headed back out to the street, where spectators were already beginning to break through police lines. Fights broke out throughout the evening and escalated when the meeting concluded a few hours later.

It began as an ugly demonstration against the Nazis but somehow ended in a sorrowful protest against the police themselves. "You ought to be proud of yourself," said nineteen-year-old George Mason as he scuffled with a mounted patrolman. Charges of police brutality followed the next day. Isadore Greenbaum even became something of a heroic martyr when he showed up in court to defend himself against a charge of disorderly conduct.

"I went down to the Garden without any intention of interrupting," he explained. "But being that they talked so much against my religion and there was so much persecution I lost my head and I felt it was my duty to talk."

"Don't you realize that innocent people might have been killed?" Magistrate Andrews asked him.

"Do you realize that plenty of Jewish people might be killed with their persecution up there?" he answered, exasperated that the police had arrested *him* while the Nazis, who had thrown him to the floor and beaten him, were allowed to continue their meeting.

For days the papers talked of nothing else, especially the local tabloids in outlying boroughs with a mostly Jewish readership. On top of everything else Pyke's men were facing, now they were being placed in cahoots with the Nazis. The bad reputation Joe Lynch Sr. and Jr. had been experiencing throughout their careers had shown no signs of letting up; the public took every opportunity to berate its police force in the 1930s.

Published in 1939, John Steinbeck's blockbuster novel *The Grapes of Wrath* featured its Everyman hero, Tom Joad, waxing philosophically, "Wherever they's a cop beatin' up a guy, I'll be there"—effectively lumping all men in uniform as an enemy of the people. "The policeman is, and long has been, in very low repute with many Americans," *Scientific Monthly* reported in May. "That policemen are neither very intelligent nor well educated is painfully apparent."

That unfair assessment galled brave and dedicated men like detectives

Lynch and Socha, who could hardly believe their eyes in the face of such biased reporting. Valentine, in response to all the criticism, nevertheless did little to quell the renewed resentment against his men. "I think the results speak for themselves," was his only statement. "No comment is necessary."

An uncomfortable King George, along with Queen Elizabeth, signs the official guest book for a perplexed Grover Whalen. *(Courtesy of the New York Public Library)*

18

ROYAL FLUSH

Joe Lynch and Freddy Socha were called again to Flushing Meadows in June when King George and Queen Elizabeth came to visit the World's Fair. An enormous parade had been scheduled to welcome them, the size and pomp of which Whalen had become famous for. If the weather held out, the city was expecting a crowd even bigger than that which had come out to cheer for Lindbergh. More than a million school-children were to be dismissed from class early so that they could view the procession as the royal couple drove past in an open car.

But, as usual, there was also trouble. Another in a seemingly endless series of anonymous letters had come across Lieutenant Pyke's desk, threatening yet another bomb attack. This one was a bit more complicated, Pyke explained to his men. It had been written in pencil on the back of an application form for the Irish Republican Army, for one thing, instead of the more common practice of being crudely typed on an unidentifiable and ordinary piece of stationery. That meant a statement was being made. What kind of statement exactly was left up to the Bomb and Forgery Squad to decipher.

The bomb threat had taken a long and circuitous route to reach the desks of Lynch, Socha, and the other detectives on Pyke's team. Together, they stared at copies of it as Pyke explained that the letter had been mailed in Washington, D.C., to the British embassy; from there it had been turned over to the State Department and then finally up to New York, to Pyke's office for investigation.

Commissioner Valentine took it seriously enough to arrange a special conference with members of Scotland Yard, the U.S. Secret Service, and the U.S. State Department. Complicating the matter, the letter also listed fifteen individual targets in Manhattan, the Bronx, Brooklyn, and even Newark, New Jersey, where the plot was supposedly being hatched. The Bomb and Forgery Squad would have to check out every location.

As usual, Lynch and Socha worked as a team, running down addresses in their native Bronx and Brooklyn. When they hit the first address and found it was a saloon, both men took a breath. It was almost a sure bet that every other joint would turn out to be a bar, and as it turned out, they all were. Some idiot's or anarchist's idea of a joke.

Pyke's men relaxed, thinking they could go back to their normal routine, until new orders came through from Chief Inspector John Ryan, commander of the Detective Division. Practically every detective on the force was given special detail to search all the rooftops and any overhanging buildings along the parade route, from the Battery to Seventy-second Street, through Central Park to the East River Drive, and then over the Triborough Bridge. The extra duty ate up most of their days and kept Pyke's men from seeing their families except for the eight or nine hours they were allowed to return home and get a decent night's sleep.

Additionally, Lynch and Socha were among the one hundred and fifty detectives assigned to mingle with the crowds at the World's Fair and keep an eye out for suspicious activity while the royals were in attendance.

At nine-forty on the morning of Saturday, June 10, the royal couple boarded the United States destroyer *Warrington* for the largely ceremonial sail up the Hudson River, only a short excursion from Fort Hamilton in Brooklyn. Perhaps it was designed to make it look as though the king and queen had just alighted from the long sea voyage out of Dover, or maybe they just wanted to savor the majestic skyline of Manhattan. In either case, they started out the day disappointed; the morning was hot and hazy, and the tops of most of the city's famous skyscrapers were lost in the mist. Worse, La Guardia later reported that the king was disappointed in the chosen route north along the West Side Highway; he kept asking where Broadway was.

Grover Whalen got a kick out of that. He, too, was disappointed; he'd wanted to ride in one more spectacular parade, to hear the cheering and drown himself once again in the sea of confetti. But as official World's Fair host, he stayed put in Flushing Meadows to make sure everything went off perfectly. Then again, he comforted himself, there were no tall office buildings along this alternate parade route out of which workers could rain down the ticker tape, so he wasn't missing out on much.

That morning, about three and a half million New Yorkers came out to gawk at the spectacle. Whalen had been expecting the king and queen to come through the gates of the World's Fair at precisely eleven forty-five; but the enormous crowds slowed the procession to a crawl, and it was almost an hour later when the first car arrived. Whalen was frantic. He knew they were on a tight schedule; the entire visit was supposed to last only about five hours, with the royals leaving at four-thirty to board a train up to Hyde Park for a visit with the Roosevelts. Now it all had to be managed in less than four. The delay, unfortunately, was to have more serious repercussions as far as the king himself was concerned.

Whalen waited with his wife, Anna, at the entrance to Perylon Hall, nervously checking his watch over and over again. By the time word came that they had finally arrived, at twelve thirty-eight, he was a wreck. The weather was a steam bath. He had planned an official reception to start just after noon and end precisely at twelve-forty, exactly two minutes from now. Whalen had five hundred and sixty distinguished guests upstairs who had already been waiting for hours, and he had gone all out for this one. A million dollars' worth of tapestries, borrowed from the Metropolitan Museum, lined the walls of the reception area, along with priceless masterpieces of art and Louis XVI furniture. He had even built a special dais upon which the king and queen would receive their minions.

Now he had two minutes. He didn't even have that, actually. They were only at the gates, met once again by the oddly formal Haskell Indians and their World of Tomorrow tribal gear. Finally, after what seemed like an eternity, the royal party arrived. Whalen bowed, regaining his composure and displaying his impeccable skills at protocol. Without wasting any time, he directed George and Elizabeth into a private elevator with only himself and his wife as passengers. Immediately, Grover sensed something was wrong.

"When do we eat?" the king turned and asked him as soon as the elevator doors were shut.

Whalen responded that a state luncheon would take place as soon as the ceremony here was finished. The king, he noticed, did not seem pleased. He looked uncomfortable, a little strained, actually, as he took his seat on the dais and the photographers were brought in, along with the World's Fair guest book. King George signed it quickly, stiffly, as if peeved at all the fuss. In his formal clothes, despite the fact that he was now in air-conditioning, Whalen, decidedly *against* protocol, began to sweat.

Fifty young girls from the World's Fair staff, whom Whalen had chosen personally, ushered in the guests, ten at a time, to bow and curtsy and walk backward for the practiced six paces as they left the royal presence. The girls all wore matching blue dresses adorned with white Trylons and Perispheres, and when they escorted in the first group, Whalen nearly choked when Vice Admiral Giuseppe Cantu of Italy strode in and immediately stuck out his arm in the Fascist salute of the day.

"Who was that man?" the king demanded. Grover told him, noticing that George now looked even more miserable. And there were still five more groups to go.

The World's Fair board of directors came in next, and then the New York City Board of Estimate. Still waiting their turn were the city commissioners, including Robert Moses, and a host of others from all over the country who had traveled to the Fair strictly for an introduction to the king and queen. Whalen gave a slight hand signal to the Fair hostesses to speed things up a bit just as the British ambassador, Sir Ronald Lindsay, came forward and whispered in his ear, "His Majesty is leaving now."

"*What?*" Whalen spun around to face him, apoplectic. "He can't do that!"

Then, seeing the king heading for the door, Grover hurried to catch up. La Guardia raced forward and blocked him.

"What the hell are you doing?" he asked. "My commissioners haven't met the king and queen yet. Why are you ending it now?"

"Don't ask me, Fiorello," Whalen shouted back, running to the exit. "Ask him!"

They had been in and out of the building in less than fifteen minutes. Whalen knew his guests would be furious, but at least they were making up for lost time. Running out of Perylon Hall ahead of Lindsay and the others, he frantically signaled for the Trytons, the World's Fair band, to begin playing as the party approached the open cars for the ride up to the Federal Building, where the luncheon was scheduled. It was barely one o'clock, so if everything went smoothly from then on, he could relax again and make the most of what remained of the day.

But then, of course, it began to rain. Whalen silently cursed his luck. He couldn't have the royal couple drown on their brief tour of the fairgrounds, so he directed that the canvas tops be put up on the cars as quickly as possible. The king, impatient at yet another delay, stood noticeably fuming.

At last they all got in. As the car eased its way around the Theme Center, driving slowly so that its passengers could admire the view, the heat inside the closed windows grew insufferable. King George's face turned crimson; Whalen thought they would all suffocate. It was a rare instance when formalities failed him—opening the windows meant they might all be drenched by the time they reached the Court of Peace; leaving them closed threatened heat prostration.

Finally, just when the king looked as though he were going to have a stroke, George stopped the car and regally ordered the top down. Whalen closed his eyes and prayed. The weather couldn't ruin another occasion, not this one. And then, "as if by magic," he later described it, "the rain stopped at once."

The trouble wasn't over. George jumped out of the car at the edge of the Court of Peace and began hurrying up the south walk of the Hall of Nations. Troops from the U.S. Army, Navy, Marines, and Coast Guard went into a precision drill. Whalen had to race to catch up to the king.

"Your Majesty, the officer will now ask you to review the troops," he stated, nearly out of breath.

"I won't take the review," George answered. "When do we eat?"

Whalen was "shocked speechless." An aide stepped forward to inform the king that his refusal could be considered an insult to the United States armed forces. Apparently, he didn't care a whit.

"Which way is the Federal Building?" he demanded.

Dumbfounded, Whalen pointed in its direction, and George stormed off at the quickstep. An honor guard was standing at attention at the entrance, led by the U.S. commissioner to the Fair, Edward Flynn, and members of the president's military staff. Whalen, still flustered, began his formal presentation and then stopped midsentence when the king ignored them all and walked past them into the building by himself.

"What are you trying to do?" Flynn hissed as they both flew off in pursuit. Finally they got to the root of the problem.

"Where *is* it?" the king asked, looking completely desperate.

Whalen suddenly got it. The sail up from Brooklyn, the ceremony at the dock, and the long delay of the parade had left King George in dire straits intestinally. Grover pointed to a suite of offices on the left. The king, grateful at last, disappeared inside. Whalen took a seat on one of the benches and waited, hoping that at last the storm was over. When he thought about it, the whole thing was almost laughable. Grover had actually held entire *meetings*—scheduled conferences with the British diplomatic corps—on the subject of "relief" breaks for the king and queen. He had even wanted to set up a personal suite for them in Perylon Hall, where they could be assured the utmost royal privacy.

"*That*, Mr. Whalen," a diplomatic representative had told him stiffly, "will take place on British soil. In the British Pavilion."

Protocol, Grover mused, could get you in a lot of trouble sometimes.

After several long minutes, His Majesty emerged from the bathroom, looking much more relaxed and dignified.

"The gentleman who occupies this office must be bald," he said, attempting to gloss over the real reason for his haste. "There's no comb in there."

It's not my office, Flynn blurted out. Whalen shushed him with an elbow to the ribs.

The remainder of the day went much more smoothly. Whalen recovered himself and was the consummate host at lunch, though he swore Flynn to secrecy regarding the king's urgent need for "personal comfort." He would share the details only with those whose feelings had been hurt and who had been snubbed by the king's behavior (although later it would become one of his favorite anecdotes about his time at the World's Fair).

The royal couple went on to visit several other buildings in the Government Zone, almost all of them connected with the British Empire. And to show that they were good sports after all, they even took a ride on the "trackless train," the blue-and-orange trams that merrily played "The Sidewalks of New York" while sending pedestrians scurrying out of their way.

By the time the king and queen departed precisely at four-thirty, as planned, Whalen was drained. He ended the day by starting the music and color exhibition early in the Lagoon of Nations, and despite the fact that it was long before dark, he ordered the fireworks to go off. That afternoon, it included several hundred aerial bombs carrying both the British and American flags.

Not far away, Lynch and Socha heard the explosions and tensed a moment. Like the other detectives assigned to cover the fairgrounds that day, they had lingered all afternoon in the Court of Peace, pacing again and again from the British Pavilion down Continental Avenue to the League of Nations and back again to Federal Place. When they saw the fireworks go up, the partners eased back, checked their watches, and knew the show was about over. No terrorist bombs anywhere—not in the Bronx or Brooklyn or Newark, and definitely none in Flushing Meadows. For the time being, everyone could relax, though both men knew it was going to be a long summer.

General Electric's popular ten-million-volt lightning exhibit dazzled and deafened audiences.
(© Bettmann/Corbis)

19

"I NEVER THOUGHT
OF THAT!"

His previous two excursions to Flushing Meadows having been strictly formal affairs, Albert Einstein decided it would be fun to visit the World's Fair without having to make a speech. He chose Monday, June 12, an ordinary weekday when he figured there would be fewer people and he could hopefully spend a pleasant afternoon without too much fuss made over him. For company he brought along his sister, Maria, whom he called Maja, and his surviving stepdaughter, Margot. Their host for the day was Judge Irving Lehman, brother of the governor.

As usual, Einstein dressed casually: gray sweater over an equally plain gray sports shirt. And because he had been warned about the distances to be covered, he chose to forgo his usual sandals and padded around in soft-soled shoes. But no socks; Einstein hated wearing socks.

The judge had of course notified Grover Whalen of their arrival but repeated the scientist's firm instructions that there were to be no cere-monies involved, especially no Indians of any kind. They were allowed early entrance, and the party spent a pleasant half hour strolling around the grounds, happy to have the place for the most part to themselves. When the exhibits opened and the crowds began strolling in, Einstein di-rected his group to the Masterpieces of Art building over on the Street of Wheels.

Just across the bridge from General Motors and the Transportation

Zone, the simple, single-story structure was for some reason located in the Communications Zone (probably because they couldn't figure out anyplace else to put it). There had been quite a controversy about the display of art at the Fair; Whalen and his design team had waged a heated war for more than a year over whether or not such an exhibit should even be erected. Manhattan had plenty of art museums if that's what the customer wanted to see, Whalen had argued; and he doubted anyone would.

In the end, though, it had become enough of a public embarrassment for him to assign a small plot on the very edge of the Grand Central Parkway, in between Business Systems and the post office. But once it had to be done, Whalen decided to do it right; the three separate pavilions that made up the building contained more than $30 million worth of paintings and sculpture and was considered "one of the most important exhibitions of old masters ever displayed under one roof." Whalen made sure the guidebook said so.

It is impossible to know Einstein's itinerary on this casual visit, but it's likely he would have been interested in seeing General Electric's ten-million-volt lightning demonstration in Steinmetz Hall. Architecturally, the GE building itself was unremarkable. One part resembled an enormous Quonset hut, and the other presented a curved entryway fronting the large fountains and pools in the Plaza of Light. The exhibit's most noticeable, and arresting, feature was a freestanding spire forming the jagged dagger of a lightning bolt—except that this one exploded skyward, up from the earth toward the heavens. Made of stainless steel, the imposing sculpture rose taller than the four sixty-five-foot pylons that represented the four elements at the far end of the Court of Power and was topped by a gyroscope with a star dangling off of one end.

What did it mean? Stephen Voorhees, one of its designers, thought it represented the harnessing of electricity. Regardless of what anyone else, including Einstein, thought, the structure dominated the Production and Distribution Zone.

Inside the hall, spectators stood along a balcony and overlooked what might have been the engine room of a great steamship. Groups of black, shiny columns ringed with bright silver bands stood at either end of the hall; most of the equipment and a large panel between the columns featured the ubiquitous, scripted GE logo. In between was a network of wires and scaffolding and electrodes that shouted a futuristic vision reminiscent of Fritz Lang's *Metropolis*. Men in dark clothing raced back and forth, turning meaningless switches on a glowing instrument panel and shouting scientific-sounding gobbledygook to one another. Suddenly the lights faded and a single voice called out, "We are about to imitate Nature herself!"

It all sounded very dangerous and very intimidating; some of the ladies buried their heads in their husbands' lapels and covered their ears, readying themselves for the great explosion.

"We are going to have a bit of lightning and a spot of thunder," the voice teased. "Not enough to make your hair curl or deafen anybody, but enough for our purpose."

Then came the sales pitch. "By reproducing the conditions that exist in a real thunderstorm, General Electric tests its equipment," the narrator continued. "They keep on functioning, whether it storms or not."

Glass tubes suddenly began to glow; a shot rang out, and then another: the signal to get ready. With a tremendous crash of thunder, the lightning streaked across the thirty-foot gap between the columns. It was a startling sight, made even more beautiful by the clever addition of various salts to add color to the show. So it was not merely plain old everyday lightning that visitors saw—GE was doing more than "imitating" nature; they were enhancing it. The bolts arced in dazzling displays of orange, green, yellow, and blue. And they certainly made a terrific bang. Everyone agreed on that.

Most likely, Einstein and his party decided to skip the accompanying House of Magic, where steel bars floated in a sea of magnetic force and light talked. General Electric had taken the true science insult one step too far by featuring a "scientist-magician" who shook hands with his own shadow. It was a simple trick, but effective. An actor sat in front of a large screen coated with phosphorescent material. When the light was turned off, he got up and moved to a chair directly opposite, so that when the lights came back on, the image of his shadow remained in the space he had previously occupied. Then, by placing his hand in a similar position, he "shook hands" with it, slapped it on the back, and for a big finale he rolled it up and put it away.

Scientist-magician indeed.

But the Exhibits Hall displayed a huge mural by Rockwell Kent that was as brilliant as it was disturbing. Supposedly representing the progress mankind had made since the enlightenment of electrical power, a gleaming city—not unlike the Emerald City of that year's *The Wizard of Oz*—shone underneath the godlike figures of a man and woman touching fingers: God giving life to Adam; GE taking it from there.

From General Electric, it would have been a short stroll around Commerce Circle to Westinghouse, so it seems probable that Einstein would want to get a peek at the time capsule. The seven-foot-long, torpedo-shaped tube was made of copper alloy and was designed to last five thousand years. Inside, the capsule contained more than ten million words and over a thousand photos on eleven hundred feet of microfilm, plus a fifteen-minute newsreel featuring a speech by President Roosevelt, Jesse Owens winning the hundred-meter finals at the 1936 Olympics in Berlin, and, of course, a preview of the World's Fair with images of Mayor La Guardia and Grover Whalen.

There were also, owing to its source, a Westinghouse Mazda lamp, a Westinghouse electric razor and alarm clock, and several other items bearing the company's logo. Copies of *Life* magazine, the Bible, a woman's fashionable hat, a toothbrush, and other assorted ephemera rounded out the collection, all of it crammed into an "Immortal Well" buried fifty feet belowground but visible through a glass window (to prevent anyone from spitting down on it, one critic noted).

Grover Whalen had left a simple message beginning with, "We were thinking of you in the World of Tomorrow . . ." Thomas Mann was a bit more dour, warning, "Among you, too, the spirit will fare badly—it should never fare too well on this earth, otherwise men would need it no longer."

But Einstein, as usual, had taken it seriously. "People living in different countries kill each other at irregular time intervals, so that also for this reason anyone who thinks about the future must live in fear and terror," he had written the previous summer. (The time capsule was buried on September 23, 1938, during the Fair's construction.) "This is due to the fact that the intelligence and character of the masses are incomparably

lower than the intelligence and character of the few who produce something valuable for the community.

"I trust that posterity will read these statements with a feeling of
proud and justified superiority."

He may have been right about the intelligence of the masses, however
condescending it sounded. Burying a time capsule for five thousand years
was one thing, but in order to ensure that the cylinder would be found in
6939, several hundred copies of "The Book of Record of the Time Capsule," including instructions on how to find it and open it, were shipped to
universities and libraries around the world.

"I must say that the conception of the Time Capsule seems to us
somewhat infantile," said the chief curator of Belgium's Royal Library.
"We have received [the book] with a request to preserve it for five thousand years. That made us smile. . . . The skies today are full of hostile
planes, and nobody can tell what tomorrow will bring."

We can imagine, after a certain period of time, Einstein and his party
grew hungry. Maja, who professed a fondness for all living creatures, had
recently developed into a vegetarian, but she also had one weakness: She
loved hot dogs. It would seem a fitting picture to have them picnicking
somewhere on Whalen's manicured lawns, disregarding the PLEASE signs,
Einstein kicking off his shoes and sitting barefoot as all of them dug in.
For Maja's sake, her famous brother had decreed hot dogs to be a veg-
etable.

Certainly, at some point during his visit, Einstein would have visited
the Court of Peace, if only to pay silent homage to the little nook of the
Czechoslovakia Pavilion, dwarfed as it was by the USSR Pavilion on one
side and Japan on the other. Given that it had not yet been open when he
had dedicated Palestine on that fitful day a month earlier, almost certainly
the proud defiance of its building's existence now would have moved
something within him.

Walking along Congress Street, the pavilion of his beloved Belgium
to his left, he could look around and see the other nations that, unless
things changed radically over the next few years, would be overrun by
Hitler one by one. Poland was next, surely. Two days before the Fair

opened, Hitler had withdrawn from the German-Polish Non-Aggression Act of 1934. He wanted Danzig and he was going to get it, along with the rest of the country, and soon.

What, Einstein may have wondered, would the Court of Peace look like in 1940, when and if the World's Fair opened for a second season?

He appeared at the Fair several more times in the early summer, once on film with former Czech president Edvard Beneš and others in a documentary titled *World Leaders on Peace and Democracy*.

"Much blood will yet have to be spilled," Einstein warned. The film was shown daily in a small theater in the Science and Education Building.

On June 21, he returned in person to give yet another speech, along with Rabbi Stephen Wise, at a luncheon for Rho Pi Phi, an international fraternity founded by thirteen Jewish pharmacists who, in the face of anti-Semitism, formed their own nonsectarian group. Held at the symbolically named Café Tel Aviv, the crowning ceremony was the presentation of a trophy to "the World's Fairest Nurse."

In July, he turned up again at the Palestine Pavilion, this time unofficially. Perhaps the brief minutes before Whalen's formal lunch had not been enough for Einstein to appreciate the lush landscaping and the reflecting pool. Perhaps something else had brought him back. A pavilion worker reported watching "a gray-haired fairgoer who stood for almost an hour in front of the Haifa Diorama." He recognized Einstein but left the scientist in quiet bemusement, "trying to figure out how the designer rigged things so that a complete change of scene is effected, as if by magic."

To many of his colleagues, the Hungarian physicist Leó Szilárd was more than an enigma. If anything, he was closer in spirit to what Einstein might have become, if Einstein had not been ambitious. An outspoken and eccentric genius, Szilárd was widely regarded as a brilliant inventor, the quintessential mad scientist who rarely pursued his ideas to completion. When a new line of thinking entered his brain, he simply abandoned his current project and forged ahead with new ideas, often leaving others to claim credit for his inventions.

Working as a physics instructor in Berlin in the 1920s and 1930s, Szilárd had conceived plans for the linear accelerator and the electron microscope, both of which were later put into practical use without any formal credit given to Szilárd. In 1939, American physicist Ernest Lawrence was awarded the Nobel Prize for essentially improving upon Szilárd's early conception for what would become the cyclotron, a type of particle accelerator, and its application.

"Had he pushed through to success all his new inventions," said Dennis Gabor, one of Szilárd's early friends, "we would now talk of him as the Edison of the twentieth century."

Leó Szilárd also had the dubious distinction of being a coinventor, along with its namesake, of the Einstein Refrigerator—one of the few concepts for which a patent was actually filed, in 1930. It was at its root designed to be a machine without moving parts, and while their collaboration had lasted seven years, the product never reached consumers (although they did sell a couple of its innovations to Electrolux). The contraption was noisy, for one thing, and it used an awful lot of electricity. But the development of Freon and compressor refrigerators (with their sleek, aerodynamic, and, yes, streamlined design) effectively killed any chance of future riches to be made.

(Ironically, as it was to turn out, one other of their refrigeration-related inventions, the Einstein-Szilárd Pump, did eventually find a practical use: cooling nuclear reactors.)

Like Einstein, Leó Szilárd had fled Berlin and the Nazis, eventually accepting a position as a researcher at Columbia University in New York City. Unlike Einstein, he not only believed that atomic bombs were possible, he lived in constant mortal fear that Nazi Germany would develop them first. Szilárd was appalled by the lack of interest shown by the United States, especially after it was discovered that Germany had halted the sale of uranium ore from occupied Czechoslovakia.

In December 1938, a team of German chemists discovered nuclear fission, and Szilárd's worst fears set in. He suspected that the Germans would next go after uranium from the Belgian Congo, and if they got hold of enough of it, they could win what he now considered to be a race to develop atomic weapons. (Uranium was the key element needed to set off a nuclear chain reaction.) Szilárd talked it over with his close friend and fellow Hungarian Eugene Wigner, also a physicist, who happened to be working at Princeton. Wigner shared his concerns.

"Both Wigner and I began to worry about what would happen if the Germans got hold of some of the vast quantities of uranium which the Belgians had in the Congo," Szilárd would later explain.

What he didn't know was what to do about it. Part of the problem was Szilárd himself: His reputation as an eccentric preceded him, and he knew that if his concerns were to carry any weight at all, he needed a name attached to them.

"So we began to think, through what channels we could approach the Belgian government and warn them against selling any uranium to Germany," he said. "It occurred to me that Einstein knew the Queen of the Belgians." He was referring to Queen Elisabeth, whom Einstein had visited in his last months in Europe and with whom he often kept in touch by mail.

"And I suggested to Wigner," Szilárd wrote, "that we visit Einstein, tell him about the situation, and ask him whether he might not write to the Queen."

It began as simply as that. Einstein, in between his trips to the World's Fair, spent his days sailing on Long Island Sound in the little sailboat he had playfully named *Tinef*, Yiddish for "old piece of junk." It really wasn't much more than that. In 1933, to replace the one the Germans had confiscated, he paid $150 for the slightly decrepit, fourteen-foot boat, then promptly sawed off half the centerboard—a pivoting plank of wood that kept the craft from blowing sideways in a harsh wind.

"I sawed [it] so that I could sail in the shallow lake here in Princeton," he explained to a friend.

(According to Jack Moffly, commodore of the Princeton Yacht Club while Einstein was in attendance, the university dissuaded him from sailing alone for fear that he would drown—Einstein steadfastly refused to carry a life jacket.) Unfortunately, in the deeper waters of the Long Island Sound, the abbreviated centerboard sometimes left him stranded for hours, unable to tack against a headwind. Elsa would often have to keep dinner warm for hours while her husband drifted blissfully, deep in thought, until nature provided a breeze to carry him home again.

"We knew that Einstein was somewhere on Long Island but we didn't know precisely where," Szilárd recalled. They called his office in Princeton and were told he had rented a house on Nassau Point, in a little town called Peconic. It was near the larger village of Southold, and the owner's name was Dr. Moore. Wigner, unlike Szilárd, knew how to drive, and what's more he owned a car, a blue Dodge coupé that sported a perfectly flat windshield and was rather cramped inside for a vehicle of its size.

On Sunday, July 16, Szilárd and Wigner set off for the long journey out to the northern fork of Long Island. Driving from the city, the pair would have likely taken the Grand Central Parkway, where they would have passed the tall spire and bulging globe of the Trylon and Perisphere as they exited Queens and entered Nassau County. Like true, eccentric scientists, however, they promptly got themselves lost.

"We drove around for about half an hour," Szilárd said. "We asked a number of people, but no one knew where Dr. Moore's cabin was."

The houses all looked identical, gray-shingled and weather-beaten, and none bore any signs with the name of Moore. They were just about ready to give up and head back to the city when Szilárd spotted a young boy standing at a curb. Why not? he figured.

"Say, do you by any chance know where Professor Einstein lives?" Szilárd asked, leaning out of the window like a fan seeking an autograph.

The boy responded, Of course, everyone knew the house, although he had no idea who this Dr. Moore was. He climbed in the backseat and directed them through town to Old Grove Road, where he pointed out a small cottage at the end of the block. They were in luck; Einstein had just come in from a pleasant sail and was sitting on the front porch, chatting with a man named David Rothman.

The owner of a department store in town, Rothman had met Einstein when the scientist came into his store looking for a pair of "sundials." Einstein pointed to his feet, where his old pair of sandals were practically worn to shreds. The two became fast friends when Rothman revealed that he, too, played the violin. In the evening, they made music and discussed relativity, even though Rothman had only a grade-school education, or maybe because of it.

Einstein, surprised at the sight of his former student and colleague Szilárd, together with Wigner, stood and greeted them in his usual sailing attire: a dirty T-shirt and baggy pants tied at the waist with a string of rope. Rothman politely excused himself as Einstein invited his guests to come and join him on the screened-in porch. He asked Maja to make some tea.

As the trio sat and drank, conversing in their more familiar German, Szilárd began to explain, as Einstein remembered, "a specific system he devised, and which he thought would make it possible to set up a chain reaction."

"I never thought of that!" Einstein responded.*

He made Szilárd explain it again. Einstein was skeptical until the point was made that nuclear fission had been discovered not here, in America, but at the Kaiser Wilhelm Institute in Germany. Whether or not Einstein believed that atomic weapons might become a reality, he no doubt agreed with Szilárd that the Nazis could not be allowed to develop them first. And while he may initially have been hesitant about getting involved, his recent dedication of the Palestine Pavilion had forcibly thrust him out of the comfortable isolation of Princeton and into the World of Tomorrow, capitalized or not. Now, it seemed, there was no turning back. The future had just appeared on his doorstep.

They discussed what their next step should be. Szilárd mentioned Belgium and Einstein's relationship with the queen, but the idea was quickly discarded since all of them were technically foreigners and Einstein himself was not yet an American citizen. This was a matter for the State Department, they decided.

"Wigner suggested that we draft a letter to the Belgian government,"

---

* Again, the quote has been attributed in several incarnations. Szilárd later remembered Einstein saying, *"Daran habe ich gar nicht gedacht,"* or, "That never occurred to me."

Szilárd explained, "send a copy to the State Department, and give [them] two weeks in which to object."

Einstein, they all agreed, should write the letter, as he was the only one famous enough to ensure that it wouldn't be ignored. Einstein dictated a draft in German, and Wigner translated it. Without fully realizing what they had begun, Szilárd and Wigner got back in the Dodge and drove home to Columbia.

For the time being, Einstein thought no more about it. He had an engagement that evening to tackle a piece by Bach with his friend Rothman, the "sundials" merchant.

A few days later, their plans were switched again. "I decided to consult friends with more experience in things practical than we were," explained Szilárd, understanding that science and politics were two different worlds. One of those friends recommended that Szilárd talk to Alexander Sachs, who knew President Roosevelt personally. Sachs suggested that Einstein skip the State Department entirely and write a letter directly to FDR, promising that he would take it to the White House and hand-deliver it himself.

Another meeting was arranged on Long Island, only this time Wigner wasn't available to act as chauffeur. Instead, Szilárd enlisted another Hungarian companion, with a bigger car, to accompany him. Edward Teller, who in his lifetime would become famous as "the father of the H-bomb," owned a 1935 Plymouth.

"I believe his advice is valuable," Szilárd wrote to Einstein, scheduling the visit, "but I also think you might enjoy getting to know him."

On this second gathering in Dr. Moore's little cottage a week later, Einstein again dictated a letter in German, which Teller this time wrote out. The three of them drank tea and discussed exactly how much detail the final draft of the letter should go into.

"I wondered how many words we could expect the President to read," Szilárd said. "How many words does the fission of uranium rate?"

Back in New York, Szilárd wrote out two versions, a long and a short one, and left it up to Einstein to decide which was better. Possibly, the echo of the World's Fair's seven-hundred-word limit on his speech on cosmic rays came to Einstein's mind. He decided to sign both and leave it up to Szilárd, who chose the longer.

"Sir," the infamous letter began:

Some recent work by E. Fermi and L. Szilárd . . . leads me to expect that the element uranium may be turned into a new and important source of energy in the immediate future. Certain aspects of the situation seem to call for watchfulness and, if necessary, quick action on the part of the administration. I believe, therefore, that it is my duty to bring to your attention the following facts and recommendations.

. . . That it may become possible to set up nuclear chain reactions in a large mass of uranium, by which vast amounts of power and large quantities of new radium-like elements would be generated. Now it appears almost certain that this could be achieved in the immediate future.

This new phenomenon would also lead to the construction of bombs, and it is conceivable . . . that extremely powerful bombs of a new type may thus be constructed. A single bomb of this type, carried by boat or exploded in a port, might very well destroy the whole port together with some of the surrounding territory. However, such bombs might very well prove to be too heavy for transportation by air.

. . . In view of this situation you may think it desirable to have some permanent contact maintained between the administration and the group of physicists working on chain reaction in America.

Einstein ended the letter with two very specific recommendations for Roosevelt:

(a) To approach government departments, keep them informed of further developments, and put forward recommendations for government action, giving particular attention to the problem of securing a supply of uranium ore for the United States.

(b) To speed up the experimental work which is at present being carried on within the limits of the budgets of the university laboratories, by providing funds, if such funds be required, through his contacts with private persons who are willing to make contributions for this cause, and perhaps also by obtaining the cooperation of industrial laboratories which have the necessary equipment.

To make sure he got the message across, Einstein included a warning about Germany's activities: "I understand that Germany has actually stopped the sale of uranium from Czechoslovakian mines which she has taken over. . . ."

The letter was signed: "Yours very truly, A. Einstein."

Now it was up to Alexander Sachs to do his part and see that the letter got into Roosevelt's hands. With nothing further to do, the scientists waited. Einstein went back to sailing, back to his warm summer evenings playing music with Rothman and reading the newspapers to see which World's Fair pavilion Hitler might conquer next.

The exterior of DuPont's Wonder World of Chemistry (© *Bill Cotter, worldsfairphotos.com*)

20

"YOU TELL 'EM, MICKEY!"

As the first anniversary of Martha Hore's killing came and went, Joe and Easter allowed themselves the luxury of hope for the future again after a year of mourning and despair. Only one hurdle remained: the upcoming trial of Joe Healy, which would finally begin sometime in the new year. If all went well, Healy would be convicted quickly and they could get on with their lives. After all, they had another new baby, a third daughter named Mary, after Joe's mother, to look after.

It was summer before the case finally came to court. Healy had been sitting in jail for eighteen months, and as his trial approached he began to lose hope for a merciful judgment. On June 23, 1939, just as a jury was about to be chosen, Healy pleaded guilty to the lesser charge of second-degree murder in order to avoid the gas chamber. The 1930s had already seen more executions than any other decade in American history, an average of 167 per year. Joe Healy did not want to be one of them. Judge Koenig of the general sessions court accepted his plea.

On July 6, Koenig gave him the maximum allowable sentence: twenty years to life imprisonment. Calling the murder a "vicious crime," he justified his decision by stating that he believed Healy had killed Martha Hore deliberately, not merely as a result of the "holdup," but solely because he was afraid she would identify him to the police. Healy paled at the sentence, unable to believe his ears. He had befriended the head of the Probation Department, a man named Irving Halpern, who subsequently wrote a report detailing Healy's troubled childhood and the death of his mother at age nine.

Judge Koenig barely scanned it. He had not even allowed Grace, who by now had a sixteen-month-old boy to take care of, to enter the courtroom while the sentence was being imposed. Joe Healy's only ally that day was his father, Joe senior. The two of them did not exchange words as Healy was led away, back to the Tombs before being transferred to a state penitentiary for at least the next twenty years of his life.

When she heard the verdict, Grace bravely declared that she would wait faithfully for her husband while she worked to raise their son. The boy, she told reporters, was named Joseph Healy III.

In the middle of July, Grover Whalen began receiving the reports he had been dreading but still could hardly bring himself to believe. After recovering somewhat during a spectacular four-day Fourth of July holiday weekend, attendance at the Fair actually began to *drop*. The crowds he had envisioned would materialize as people gassed up their cars for their summer vacations were still, for whatever reason, not steering them toward New York. It was inconceivable, but there it was.

Once again, the critics came out in full force. The Fair was too "highhat"; the plain folk were worried they'd be laughed at; it was all over their heads anyway. Nonsense, Whalen sputtered. The Aquacade was playing to packed houses day and night. By July 15, General Motors was bragging that five million people had passed through its doors; Ford had already documented more than three million visitors.

Over at the AT&T building, which bordered the Theme Center on the north side of the Court of Communications, five free long-distance telephone calls were raffled off every half hour. An auditorium full of eavesdroppers listened in with earphones, thoroughly entranced by private conversations that stretched from the completely mundane to the occasionally hilarious.

"Hi, screwball!" said a kid brother to his sister and her boyfriend. "Have you hooked him yet?"

Another call, to a man from Seattle, was introduced by an operator with the greeting "Mr. Tompkins, this is the Telephone Company . . . calling you from the New York World's Fair."

"All right, all right!" Tompkins shouted. "I'll pay your damned bill!" and promptly hung up.

What was high-hat about that?

"It is evident that from now on the upswing of visitors from out of town will continue in line with our expectations," Whalen had stated hopefully on July 5, buoyed by the holiday rush. "Thousands of persons who have already visited the Fair and returned to their homes have begun to shower us with letters telling us that they were thrilled by the Fair and are advising all of their friends and acquaintances not to miss it."

Then he got in a dig at the critics: "In all of these letters there is a complete absence of complaint concerning food and other prices at the Fair."

The Whalen publicity machine went at it full force, flooding the airwaves with more than seven hundred radio programs carried over nineteen thousand stations. On the day when King George so desperately needed a bathroom break, more than sixteen hundred stations carried fourteen and a half hours' worth of coverage. Two hundred and thirty-six newsreels were produced for showing in theaters around the country. In one of them, Mayor La Guardia appeared with two movie stars, Mickey Rooney and Judy Garland, who had risen to the apex of their popularity by portraying All-American teenagers from small towns in the series of Andy Hardy movies and other pictures.

Mickey: "I have a lot of friends out where I live out on the Coast and they might come and visit the World's Fair. But I want to ask you if there's any place they can stay other than the Park Avenue hotels."

La Guardia: "Why, sure, Mickey! New York City's like every other town in this country! Except that we can give you better accommodations and better food for less money. . . . And if they come in groups, we can give it to them as cheap as fifty cents a night!"

Mickey: "Well, Mr. Mayor, that looks like we're gonna move in!"

La Guardia: "You move in! You tell the kids, Mickey!"

As for the newspapers, more than eighteen million column inches had been devoted in 1939 to spreading the news of the Fair all around the world. Many were reproduced word for word from press releases generated by Perley Boone and his team, and they were to a large extent positive. It was a massive undertaking. Publicity for the Fair was carried in more than one hundred and thirty million other types of outlets. The Trylon and Perisphere were featured on more than half a million Sears, Roebuck shipping cartons; three and a quarter million S. H. Kress paper bags and lunch counter menus; and two and a half million Child's restaurant menus. And, amazingly, one and a half million Bell Telephone customers found the Theme Center logo plastered across the tops of their phone bills.

During the first seventy-seven days of operation, nine hundred and sixty-three special events were held on the fairgrounds. Sixty-four conventions had their own "day" at the Fair. Fifty-six countries, thirty-three cities, and sixty-seven fraternal, patriotic, and civic organizations also got a day in their honor, including National Gastroenterological Association Day, Kalamazoo Day, Brooklyn Poetry Circle Day, and Brotherhood of Sleeping Car Porters Day. And that was only from Opening Day to July 11; over the remaining three and a half months of the first season, more than a thousand such events were scheduled to come.

"With respect to visitor reaction, the venture is an unqualified success," Whalen wrote in his president's report to the board of directors on July 20. "The people of this country accept the exposition as the greatest of its kind and are desirous of seeing it."

Still, he acknowledged what had to be acknowledged: "The one factor known to have mitigated against attendance thus far is the misconception of high prices in New York and at the exposition."

It was maddening. Despite the constant flood of Fair-generated reports to the contrary, wildly exaggerated tales of price gouging continued. "Don't believe these stories about hamburgers selling for a dollar and a half," La Guardia protested at a Chicago luncheon for seven hundred advertising men. "They cost a dime and they're not transparent or synthetic."

Time magazine, noting that the average daily attendance in July was

137,456 (only 6 percent better than Chicago's average for that month in 1933), listed six "guesses" as to why so many people just weren't coming:

1. Entrance fee too high;
2. Unfavorable reports of high food prices, etc. (An 85¢ dinner, 40¢ lunch, can be got at the Fair but its swank restaurants charge five times as much);
3. New York City itself is too much competition for any World's Fair;
4. Antagonism of country's press toward New York;
5. Absence of community pride among New Yorkers;
6. Hard times.

Pick one. Any and all of them probably applied. Worse, the billion-dollar boost in citywide business was also failing to materialize: July department store sales were up a mere 2 percent over 1938; most hotels were showing only a slight increase in bookings; and although total Fair attendance by mid-July was somewhere in the neighborhood of fourteen million (about three-quarters of them paid), only around three million were from out of town. Almost 85 percent of them had traveled less than five hundred miles to visit the Fair. In contrast with the original fears regarding Manhattan's blasé citizens, it wasn't the New Yorkers who weren't showing up; it was actually Mr. and Mrs. America, and their carloads of junior Americans. And as such their absence translated into relatively little new revenue coming into the city.

While at least publicly Whalen remained all smiles and good news, behind the scenes it was a different story. Reporters noticed that his perfect smile now had a tendency to fade all too quickly as soon as the cameras were put away. He began to look serious, even somber at times. His immaculate mustache became streaked with gray. And while he maintained his usual attire of blue suits, blue shirts, and natty ties, a handkerchief began replacing the ever-present boutonniere. For those who knew him well, the sight of Grover Whalen without a boutonniere was almost disturbing.

The Fair had begun with a working capital deficit of $3 million. As early as May 12, less than two weeks after the Fair had opened, construction costs, owing to the various delays caused by all the strikes, had exceeded estimates by $1.4 million. Concessionaires were for the most part bleeding money; even customers who did come didn't seem to want to part with any additional dough once they'd shelled out their admission fee. The price was too high, the midway operators complained. Why not cut it to fifty cents and see what happened?

Whalen wouldn't even consider it. Personally, he refused to believe that seventy-five cents was too much to charge for all this splendor; it would be a crime to lower it to, say, Chicago's standards.* How could they not see what a bargain they were getting?

Finally bowing to all the pressure, on July 13 Whalen appointed a special committee of three directors—Mortimer Buckner, Floyd Carlisle, and Thomas McInnerney—to examine the budget for the six-week period of July 20 through August 30 and present a plan to cut costs. They came back with an immediate 10 percent pay cut for any executive making more than $5,000 a year, including Whalen, who magnanimously volunteered to cut his pay by 25 percent, from $100,000 to $75,000.

The pay cuts didn't sting as much as the layoffs. Almost five hundred employees were dismissed on July 18, the bulk of whom were all three hundred of "Grover's Boys," the smartly uniformed "information cadets" he had trained as his personal corps of officers and who had gained fame and ignominy as his most ardent saluters. (Although the tale was almost certainly apocryphal, several reporters told of one cadet who saluted Whalen's empty car as it passed by, carrying only the president's top hat.) It was true, however, that on the day they were all dismissed, a large group of Grover's Boys yanked off their shirts and dived headfirst into the Lagoon of Nations, whooping and hollering to beat the band. Whalen hated to see them go.

Along with the cadets, Whalen's World's Fair police force was reduced from six hundred to four hundred and fifty. It was, he must have noticed,

* No U.S. World's Fair to date, including Chicago's, had ever charged more than fifty cents admission.

a bloodletting on his behalf—almost every personal whimsy, every attempt at finery he had brought to the Fair, was being discarded. He wouldn't have been surprised to see his private barber's chair carted off to be sold at auction. Nevertheless, the pay cuts and layoffs ultimately resulted in a significant reduction in operating expenses—approximately $415,000, or a little more than 15 percent.

What may not have registered in importance was an ominous move on the part of George McAneny, who formally resigned as chairman of the board at a directors meeting on July 20. That McAneny and Harvey Gibson had somehow collaborated on this decision was almost certain. For the moment, their motive remained a mystery, but Grover Whalen hadn't gotten this far by failing to recognize the obvious. Gibson was chairman of the finance committee. If the board of directors insisted on getting the Fair's money troubles under control, Gibson was the man they would choose to take over completely and do it for them.

In the wake of McAneny's resignation, two distinct camps began to form: those who supported Whalen and his dream Fair and those who felt that someone with a keener sense of a dollar ought to be in charge, namely Gibson. Whalen could sense it almost immediately as the executive committee meetings grew more contentious, and the minions who were ordinarily cowed by Whalen's leadership suddenly began questioning why, for instance, with the Fair losing so much money, the expensive fireworks display over the Lagoon of Nations was allowed to continue even during the slowest days of the week.

The smile faded further from Whalen's lips; the mustache seemed a little grayer. He was a long way from those early days at Wanamaker's, all those successful parades up Broadway. But no one ever had to pay admission to those. He'd never heard the Lindbergh crowd complain that the speeches and dinners and receptions were too high-hat. If they let Gibson take over, it would be a disaster. Gibson was a notorious tightwad, much worse than McAneny had been. He constantly badgered Whalen about expenses, even over the most ridiculous, meaningless sums. In August 1938, Gibson had written him a letter that Whalen saved as an example of just how petty the banker could be.

Dear Grover:

I received the attached single sheet of paper today as I have on various occasions heretofore, enclosed in a large manila envelope that
probably was ten times as heavy as the sheet of paper, with six cents
postage on it. . . . This is a small matter but I am afraid it indicates a
good deal of extravagance.

The president of Manufacturers Trust had taken time out of his day to
write and complain about an envelope and *six cents postage*. What the hell
would he do if he *was* placed in charge of the World's Fair? Whalen
couldn't bear to think about it.

But the truth was, they were already taking it away from him. The
concessionaires and practically everyone who ran an exhibit in the Amusement Zone were all screaming for prices to be lowered, so the board first
initiated a test run for a combination ticket good on weekends only: $1.00
bought you $2.25 worth of value in admission to the Fair (75¢), a choice
of five amusement concessions ($1.25), plus a light lunch worth around a
quarter. Then they thought it over and canceled it two weeks later. After
that, they lowered the admission price to forty cents after nine-thirty at
night, when visitors would have only a half hour to tour the actual fairgrounds before heading off to the Amusement Zone, which stayed open
until two a.m.

Finally, on July 31, after long months of harassment, Whalen agreed
to take a meeting with the finance and executive committees, as well as
representatives of a special committee of exhibitors who were pressing for
a lower general admission. The meeting began at three-thirty in the afternoon, and for an hour they listened as David French, chairman of the exhibitors committee, and others ardently pleaded their case.

After French and his cohorts left, the real fireworks began. Members
of the finance committee, including Harvey Gibson, demanded that admission be lowered to fifty cents. Whalen and his management team insisted that they keep it at seventy-five cents. What was the point in
lowering it, Whalen shouted, growing exasperated at this ridiculous mis-
comprehension of simple mathematics? Even if admission totals increased
by 50 percent, they'd still only break even on the price reduction.

Gibson's team argued just as strongly that more people coming through the gates meant more money that would be spent once they were inside. That's what the concessions were for, and why didn't *he* see *that*?

La Guardia stood up to voice his opinion that this ridiculous speculation was actually keeping people *away* from the Fair. An awful lot of potential fairgoers, he said sternly, were holding back because they were waiting to see if the price would be lowered. If you don't solve it immediately, he warned them, you're shooting yourself in the foot.

La Guardia left the meeting and the Administration Building at six forty-five, looking perfectly pleased with himself and joking with reporters who had been waiting for hours for an announcement. He was hungry, he'd missed his dinner, and he was nibbling on some licorice until he could get something more substantial to eat.

"Want a chew?" He held out a piece to a newsman.

At eight o'clock, La Guardia was told the meeting was still going on and was surprised to hear it. Whalen must be fighting for his life in there, he figured.

Finally, about half an hour later, the committee members began leaving in small, segregated groups. Whalen was the last to come out. At eight-forty, he called for Perley Boone to come to his office. Needing to blame someone for the financial mess the Fair was in, he abruptly fired Boone and replaced him with a hard-nosed reporter named Leo Casey. Casey knew how to talk to the masses, and the masses were what they needed if this thing was going to be turned around. Whalen appointed him director of public relations. He liked that title.

At nine o'clock, Whalen handed out written copies of a statement he had prepared himself. It was the first time he'd refused to speak to the press in person.

"The finance and executive committee," his statement read, "in joint session, unanimously voted a fifty-cent price of admission on Saturdays and Sundays for the remaining period of the Fair. On other days the price will remain seventy-five cents. This is the final decision of the joint committee." By which it was taken to mean there would be no more reductions as long as he was president.

He also announced the "resignation" of Perley Boone.

When word got around to the exhibitors committee, and eventually spread to the concessionaires and everyone in the Amusement Zone, the reaction was fierce.

"The announcement leaves me dumb and speechless," said David French. "I cannot understand the mental processes that could lead to such action. The [reduction] should have been applied to the bad days, not to the top days. Our top days have been Saturday and Sunday."

"I think the Executive Committee ought to resign," stated Joe Rogers, who was known as "the Mayor of the Midway." "They don't know what they're doing. To think it took them five hours to think up that bright idea. That's a very funny way of creating good will and bringing the masses to the Fair."

Rogers stomped around while an incensed group of amusement operators egged him on. "I wonder if any of those executives ever saw a show," he fumed. "It's a cinch they never produced one."

Grover Whalen retreated to his office until he was sure that everyone had left the building. Then he returned to the copper-walled sanctum of the boardroom and tried to assess his defeat. It was all so beneath him. Where there had once been filth and garbage, he had built a stately pleasure dome. Where he had once been concerned about what financial failure would do to his reputation, now he worried about what would happen to his Fair if that penny-pinching Gibson got his hands on it. Gibson would sell the copper off the walls if he thought he could get a good price for it. Everything Whalen had worked for seemed suddenly about to slip from his grasp.

"He had put so much of himself into the birth of the Fair that he was psychologically incapable of strangling his own baby," wrote Sidney Shalett, one of the Fair's most frequent commentators. And it was true. Whalen's heart and soul was in the place, and it showed. The sum total of his life was evident in its splendor and in its wonder.

For the first time since the Fair opened, Whalen considered taking a week off. Next Monday was the beginning of "Farm Week" at the Fair—decidedly not his idea. It was to be a true, down-home "get-together for folk from rural areas." Kicking it off was a parade including livestock, cows and chickens, and tractors. Farmers were going to be the principal speakers at the Court of Peace.

From Einstein to Elsie the Cow, Whalen brooded. It was a harbinger of things to come.

The Court of Peace in the Government Zone, bordered by the Federal Building (top) and the Lagoon of Nations
(© *Bill Cotter, worldsfairphotos.com*)

THE STORM CENTER
OF THE WORLD

After Alexander Sachs, the man considered to be the next best conduit to deliver Einstein's letter was Charles Lindbergh. It was an odd choice. There was, among certain circles, the belief that Lindbergh had Nazi sympathies. Only a year earlier, Hermann Goering had presented the aviator with the Order of the German Eagle, on behalf of Adolf Hitler. Perhaps the scientists, being scientists, were unaware of this. But for whatever reason, Einstein complied with Szilárd's request to write him a letter of introduction to Lindbergh.

"I would like to ask you to do me a favor of receiving my friend Dr. Szilárd and think very carefully about what he will tell you," Einstein wrote. "To one who is outside of science, the matter he will bring up may seem fantastic. However, you will certainly become convinced that a possibility is presented here which has to be very carefully watched in the public interest, even though the results so far are not immediately impressive."

Throughout the remainder of July and on into August, however, nothing was heard from either Lindbergh or Sachs. Szilárd grew restive with impatience. Einstein sailed and smoked his pipe.

Grover Whalen wasn't done yet. Not by a long shot. At the beginning of August, he began drawing up plans for yet another parade, this one carrying open-topped town cars and celebrities instead of tractors and Farmer Browns. Night after night, he sat at his desk, eschewing the air-conditioning as soon as the air grew cool enough to carry the breezes through his gauze curtains. He enjoyed hearing the happy sounds of fair-goers and fireworks.

To hell with them, he thought as the rockets continued blazing into the nighttime sky. It was still a damn good show and worth whatever thousands a night it cost. As the second weekend featuring the new fifty-cent admission fee came and went, attendance still didn't show a significant increase. All they'd done was lower the gate profits by a third. Of course Whalen wasn't exactly *happy* that paid admissions on a Saturday night were still under 170,000, but some part of him felt justified that his argument had at least held up in practice.

By mid-August, it became clear that the Fair knew only two kinds of weather: extreme heat and humidity, or rain. Sometimes both. On Sunday, August 13, the temperature reached ninety degrees as measured on the giant Carrier thermometer positioned just outside its incongruous Igloo of Tomorrow. Then it began to rain, a steady downpour that sent everyone scattering indoors. Then the sun came out again and steamed everyone like a plate of soggy clams.

A hundred and sixty-seven thousand paid to get in that day. Despite the price reduction, attendance was actually *lower*, by thirteen thousand, than the previous Sunday. For Whalen, every head that walked through the gates represented not the four bits they'd paid, but the quarter they hadn't paid. If he'd run Wanamaker's like that, they'd have been out of business by now.

The big idea, as Whalen saw it, was to get the Fair employees themselves involved in a drive to sell six hundred thousand tickets in two weeks. He called it "the Jubilee Campaign." It began the next day, on Monday, August 14, and Whalen got everyone involved—not just the six or seven thousand Fair employees remaining after the layoffs a few weeks earlier, but anyone who was even remotely connected with the Fair's financial success, including the exhibitors who now considered Grover

Whalen their enemy, from the girls who sold doughnuts to the midgets in Little Miracle Town to the lovely ladies who danced nude at the Cuban Village. Whalen felt certain that *they*, at least, were going to sell some tickets.

All told, some thirty thousand men and women would take part in the greatest sales campaign Whalen had come up with yet. At eleven a.m., two of the Fair's "trackless trains" left the fairgrounds carrying three hundred eager young bodies. To top off the show, Whalen added a parade of elephants and camels, plus a long line of swirling, twirling girls from the foreign pavilions, all of them decked out in their native splendor.

The parade headed up Queens Boulevard to the Queensboro Bridge, then into Manhattan at Sixtieth Street and down Lexington Avenue, then Fourth Avenue and Park Row, until they reached Whalen's old stomping grounds on Broadway, where they eventually gathered on Wall Street to place a wreath at the statue of George Washington—the spot where Joseph and Jacqueline Shadgen had read the original oath five years earlier. Bill "Bojangles" Robinson, to the delight of the crowd, got out of his car and did a shuffle step, one hand on his hip as he pranced and danced to the accompaniment of the Trytons playing in an open-topped, double-decker bus.

People jitterbugged in the middle of Broadway, jugglers juggled, the showgirls jiggled, and thousands of Whalen's ever-present lunchtime crowd gathered around and enjoyed the free show.

George McAneny, who had yet to be replaced, gave a speech. But since he was a banker at heart, everything he said came out sounding like a father's admonition to a child who had neglected his chores. Clutching the lapel of his jacket in one hand and a white straw hat in the other, he spoke in the disapproving cadence of a Chautauqua preacher.

"We want you all to come," he blustered, "and we know that most of you will. But because there are still some slackers among so many thousands, some of the Fair employees have come to tell you a bit more about the Fair."

Slackers. After that, the parade reversed its course and headed back up Broadway, traveled over the bridge, and returned to the fairgrounds. In three days, they sold 125,000 tickets. Whalen was elated. Maybe he could turn this thing around by himself after all, even with Gibson licking his chops and waiting in the wings.

On Wednesday night, Whalen had arranged for a different kind of parade, just to show them that he, too, understood that the common man must be reached in order to bring people into the Fair. He had once given a speech in a Harlem church, promising fairness for all races that wanted to work at the Fair. So once again, he called on Bill Robinson to lead a motorcade of nine cars and fifty Fair employees up through Seventh Avenue to 125th Street.

The Hot Mikado was still packing them in every night at the World's Fair Music Hall. Despite the fact that Robinson was performing three shows a night, seven days a week (with a fourth performance on Sunday afternoons), Whalen had pressured him to make this second promotional appearance on the premise that the entertainer owed him one. At a kickoff celebration for the Jubilee Campaign held in the Court of Peace, Robinson, Whalen felt, had openly mocked him.

"Ladies and gentlemen," Robinson had said, mopping his brow on yet another brutally hot afternoon, "I'm gonna sing a little parody on the World's Fair, and I think New York people will understand it. I don't know how the boss Mr. Whalen's gonna take it, but to me it's funny."

Robinson sang:

Just a little bit o' garbage fell, fell off a scow one day,
and it landed in a place I think they called it the Flushing Bay.
Then a little more garbage collected, in just a little while,
and it formed a great big piece of land that looked like Barren Isle.
Mr. McAneny got a great idea, and Moses thought it was swell,
so they planted a lot o' roses just to take away the smell.
Then they fronted it with a man named Whalen, to give the place a flair,
now it costs you seventy-five cents to get in—and they call it the World's Fair!

The Jubilee Campaign sold a lot of tickets, but it wasn't enough to stop the bleeding. By the third week of August, the Fair announced it had accumulated around $3 million in what it called "operating profits"—

meaning income left over after paying for the daily expenses of running the show. The problem was the Fair currently owed almost *$6 million*, most of it to contractors, plus another $1.7 million in overdue banknotes whose interest was growing daily. Worse, the Fair had sold about $3.5 million worth of advance sale tickets, so a good many of those heads that were now spinning the turnstiles represented no new cash. And in the wake of the price reduction, some people actually began *returning* their advance tickets for a refund, arguing justifiably that they had been overcharged.

Not only couldn't they get the people to come and spend money, now they were demanding some of that money *back*. The Fair was moving in the wrong direction financially. Plus, the contractors were threatening to shut down the Fair if they weren't paid immediately. The dream of the future was rapidly turning into a present-day nightmare.

As a result, the executive committee felt it had no choice. Gibson, who was enjoying a summer vacation in his native New Hampshire, got an urgent call to return to New York as soon as possible. Together with Bayard Pope, who was treasurer of the Fair corporation and secretary of the finance committee, Gibson devised a plan to call on the bondholders for mercy. As part of the original agreement, the Fair had been setting aside a percentage of its daily gate in order to pay off the debentures. To date, that came to around $1.2 million—hard cash the Fair desperately needed to keep the lights on.

Now Gibson had to convince them to let him have it back and forget about getting any future percentage of anything, probably for the remainder of 1939 and maybe on into 1940. That is, if they could even afford to reopen next season. According to revised estimates, total paid admissions for the 1939 season would be somewhere around twenty-five million— a far cry from the forty million originally expected. Yet by the time the Fair closed on October 31, the corporation would show a surplus of $274,291 after paying off all the operating expenses, all the contractors and other bills, and all banknotes.

What it didn't pay off was a single penny of the $28 million worth of debentures that would come due on January 1, 1941. Working his banker magic, Gibson convinced the bondholders to forgo the entire $2.8 million that had been promised to them in 1939, plus lend them back the $1.2

million already set aside for repayment. But it still wasn't enough. So Gibson then appealed to his banker cronies, who agreed to lend the Fair an additional $750,000.

Suddenly, in the eyes of the corporation, Gibson was the Fair's rainmaker and savior. In the ways and means of high finance, he had all but pulled off the impossible—as illogical as it sounded, he had borrowed enough money to pay off most of their debt.

"The house was now heavily mortgaged," Sidney Shalett noted, "but it was in order. Harvey Gibson went back to New Hampshire."

Where, no doubt, he patiently awaited the second call he knew would be coming.

As August wore on and Einstein sailed and Szilárd sweated, there was still no word from either Lindbergh or Alexander Sachs. Einstein, still not entirely convinced that atomic weapons would become a reality in the near enough future for Germany to use them against its enemies, was content to wait for the slowly spinning wheels of government to complete their revolution. Szilárd, on the other hand, could not be dissuaded from the idea that the Nazis were further along with their research than anyone realized, and that if the United States government didn't catch on very soon, the matter would be moot because Germany would have gobbled up all the uranium anyway.

As Labor Day approached, the situation in Europe looked bleak, if not hopeless. Poland seemed poised to fall at any moment. On Saturday, August 19, thirty-six thousand Polish Americans gathered at the World's Fair to celebrate Polish Falcons Day. The Falcons, members of a national Polish American social organization, took a solemn pledge to "sacrifice their lives for the sacred cause which Poland is ready to defend."

The Poles, many of them dressed in native costumes and more than twenty thousand of them in the blue uniforms of the Falcons, began arriving early that morning and took their seats in the Court of Peace. They smiled and clapped one another on the back as various chapters of the organization met members from such faraway places as Chicago, Baltimore, and Pittsburgh. Despite the solemnity of the occasion, it started out as a happy affair. Then, around eleven-thirty, they began to notice the sky. The rain began shortly after noon.

Undeterred, the Falcons held their ground, remaining in their seats even as the downpour grew more intense. They sat for hours, praying that the dances and military drills that had been planned for the afternoon would not be called off. But by five o'clock, it was hopeless. The ceremonies were canceled. After the formal announcement was made, many of them remained in their chairs, thoroughly drenched and weeping openly.

At the Polish Pavilion, instantly recognizable by its latticed brass tower fronted by a statue of King Jagiełło, the crowd, undeterred, stirred itself into a swell of national pride by a statement that was being cabled to Edward Rydz-Śmigły, commander in chief of Poland's armed forces, in Warsaw. "[We] send you cordial greetings from the World of Tomorrow, which will be a world of justice and democracy. We are proud that our Poland is again called by destiny to become the bulwark of democracy."

The cheering went on for several minutes, the crowd finally breaking up after an emotional singing of the Polish national anthem. After that, the organization promised to hold another Falcons Day at the Fair to present the pageant that had been canceled. The rain did not let up all afternoon and continued on into the night.

Five days later, Hitler and Stalin signed the Nazi-Soviet pact and began working out a plan for which piece of the Polish pie each would be allowed to carve up for himself. The so-called phony war was coming to an end; the Falcons never got their second "Day" at the Fair.

If there was any "good" news at all, at least for Whalen, a Gallup poll in late August showed that 83 percent of people who had visited the Fair responded that they "liked it very much." Another 14 percent said they "liked it moderately." Only 3 percent said they disliked it. Further, 84 percent stated they wanted to visit the Fair again. The overwhelming reason people gave for not visiting the Fair was that they "can't afford it."

But by this point, it didn't really matter much. Enough money had been secured to keep the doors open, but just barely, till the scheduled Closing Day at the end of October. Yet Grover Whalen's heart just wasn't in it anymore. Despite his earlier assurances, war was now a certainty, at least in Europe. He'd be lucky if they could manage another season without the Luftwaffe flying over the Trylon and Perisphere. More and more, Whalen chose to spend the afternoons sitting alone in his office, if only to stay dry.

The weekend after Falcons Day, yet another torrential rainstorm struck the city, forming puddles eight inches deep and raising the surface of Fountain Lake by nearly a foot. Performers in the Amusement Zone, where flooding was the worst, took the opportunity to shed most of their clothes and stomp around through the makeshift river that flowed through their streets. Then they stood, transfixed, when a flash of lightning ignited a series of fireworks set to go off that night, dazzled and delighted by a sputtering display of unexpected pyrotechnics.

Later, when they learned that the fireworks were part of a program called "The Three Little Fishes," the actors convulsed in laughter. Anything could happen at this World's Fair, and it usually did.

Not too many showed up that day, but those who did tended to gravitate toward the foreign pavilions, especially Poland. Parents of Polish descent took their children inside and gravely pointed out on the giant, illuminated maps the cities and towns where their relatives lived. The Polish Corridor, noted one observer that rainy afternoon, was "now the prospective storm center of the world."

The next day, the sky remained overcast, but the rain held off and more people came. Again, the talk seemed to have turned away from things like Futurama and Railroads on Parade and focused instead on politics. In the dining room at the Czechoslovakia Pavilion, several groups argued loudly whether Poland would soon suffer the same fate they had.

But life, at least at the Fair, went on. New Jersey hairstylists had journeyed to Flushing for "Beauty and Bustle Day," giving demonstrations on the latest styles, including "the bustle silhouette" and "the high-in-front hairdo." There was a "Jitterbug Jam" featuring Ben Bernie's Orchestra, and the National Association of Ice Dealers gathered in the Court of Peace to anoint the handsomest man in attendance. He was chosen by a pretty young girl and then made to sit on a throne carved out of an enormous block of ice. In the heat waves that rippled up from the concrete, he was probably the coolest customer in attendance.

The crowds, struggling hard to maintain their gaiety throughout it all, couldn't quite seem to muster the merriment and hang-it-all carefree spirit from the early days of the Fair. It all seemed too suddenly serious for such frivolity.

For Whalen, the ax came down on the last day of August. He had been expecting it for weeks, and now that the announcement came, he felt almost relieved.

In the agreement worked out by the board of directors, Whalen would keep his title as president of the World's Fair, but Harvey Gibson, whom the corporation now voted to be its new chairman of the board, would be running the show. Whalen would become largely a figurehead as far as day-to-day operations went. He hadn't even made it a full season. Now, at what should have been the pinnacle of his career, they were booting him out. In the end, he was no better than Joseph Shadgen, who Whalen suddenly wished to God had never heard of George Washington.

Gibson had asked for forty-eight hours to make his decision, fully aware that he would be taking command of a ship that was sinking fast and perhaps could not be righted again. No matter what strings he managed to pull, the World's Fair would almost certainly lose money in the end. It was now just a question of how much. But at least he would have the satisfaction of seeing that spendthrift Whalen get his comeuppance. There was some satisfaction to be had in that.

After two days, he sent the committee "a very long telegram," as one of them put it. Gibson must have thought it important; he didn't like wasting money on telegrams, especially long ones. The exact text was never made public, but one committeeman, who refused to be quoted, said it all came down to one thing. Gibson would take the job on one condition: Grover Whalen must be completely out of the picture.

At a meeting on August 31, the board of directors looked over the numbers "with considerable gloom." A silent pall hung over the boardroom. There was no surprise, just reluctant acceptance of a very sad state of affairs as the sheet of figures was passed around to every chair, showing exact paid attendance figures to date:

April 30–May 31: 3,699,038
June 1–30: 3,876,437
July 1–31: 4,263,241
August 1–30 [the figures as of twelve-thirty that morning]: 4,020,333

For a grand total of just under sixteen million. Twenty-four million short of what they'd hoped for in 1939, with two months to go. No, scratch that. Twenty-four million short of the *smallest possible* estimated attendance. The other, more grandiose estimates . . . well, it didn't pay to get into that. And with school starting and summer vacations over, you could bet the attendance for September and October was going to be less than the previous two months, even with the expected rush of visitors as people finally decided to show up before the Fair closed its doors for the winter. Possibly for good.

No one in the room blamed Whalen directly for the failure, though you could feel the disapproval of certain factions as thick as a dense fog. Everyone, including George McAneny, had agreed that the Fair would draw at least forty million, based on Chicago's attendance. It hadn't been Whalen alone beating the drum. But now he was sitting there taking the brunt of it.

The meeting, actually, was a formality. Gibson had already agreed to take charge. There would be an announcement as soon as it was over. The press boys had been told to be on alert for a big piece of news that afternoon. They were pretty sure they knew what it was.

Around six-thirty p.m., from the windows of the Press Building in the Communications Zone, they saw two figures emerge from the Administration Building and stroll across the Bridge of Tomorrow over the Administration Gate. One of them was dressed conservatively in a plain brown suit and dark necktie, and they had no idea who he was. The other was impeccably attired in a blue suit with a natty bow tie, a maroon boutonniere once again in his lapel, and a homburg perched on his head, and everyone recognized him. Neither man spoke to the other; in fact, they seemed to walk at opposite sides of the bridge, in step but physically as far apart as they could manage.

Grover Whalen took Harvey Gibson into the Press Building, walked him upstairs, and introduced him to the boys as the new chairman of the board of the World's Fair Corporation. No one said anything. No one even asked any questions.

"Haven't you received the statement yet?" Whalen, clearly exasperated, finally broke the ice.

The newsmen said they hadn't.

"Well . . ." Whalen stammered.

Suddenly Leo Casey burst in the door and frantically began handing out copies of the typewritten statement. The look on Whalen's face froze his blood. Thank God he wasn't the boss anymore.

The official notice didn't really say anything much, however. It gave the background about McAneny's resignation and some of Gibson's history as chairman of the finance committee and mentioned, almost in passing, that Whalen's duties at the Fair would "remain the same." But it neglected to answer the question that was on everyone's lips: Who was really in charge now?

Whalen answered first: "Mr. Gibson will give attention to fiscal matters and executive duties."

Gibson was quick to add that he would not take a salary for his services. For an instant, Whalen winced at the remark. His own exorbitant salary had been something of a sore point among those who felt that a civic undertaking should not be paying $100,000 a year to anyone.

A reporter asked whether Gibson planned on making any additional cuts to the payroll or laying off any more staff members. "I can't tell whether there will be further economies until I have had a chance to study the situation further," he answered. Although, as head of the finance committee, he damn well knew what the situation was.

Was the World's Fair in that much trouble? another reporter asked. Gibson smiled, denying that any kind of an "emergency" brought about this change with only two months left to go in the first season.

It was an uncomfortable moment for both men. Whalen was effectively being fired, and he knew it. So did everyone else in the room. But neither man let on that there had been any friction between them in the past; in fact, each seemed to go out of his way to compliment the other.

"The World's Fair is a pretty big job," Gibson went on. "I want to do everything I can to help Grover."

Whalen interjected, "I'd like to say that this help from Mr. Gibson has not just come today. It has been constant since the inception of the Fair."

What about the reports that Grover would leave for Europe soon to sign the foreign pavilions on again for next summer?

"I may go back to Europe at some point in the future," Whalen answered. "But I have no intention of doing so while the present war crisis still exists."

Gibson, a bit surprised at that, held his tongue. Without the foreign pavilions, what kind of a World's Fair would it be in 1940? With the European representation, what sort of World of Tomorrow would it really represent?

That afternoon, in fact, Whalen had called a meeting of the sixty foreign commissioners in order to determine their feelings about returning next season in the face of possible, if not probable, war. He was flabbergasted to learn that, while war was indeed a big factor in their determination, most of the commissioners were more concerned about a repeat of this season's labor problems and whether they'd get a break in their operating costs next year. Whalen came away feeling as if the whole world had gone mad—the real one overseas and its miniature representation here in Flushing Meadows. How could they talk about money while Germany was pointing a gun at their heads?

The conference over, Gibson and Whalen left the Press Building and walked back over to the Administration Building. The next day, Gibson would even be taking possession of Whalen's office. To Grover, it was as if he were handing over the keys to the whole shebang.

In the final stripping of Whalen finery, Gibson ordered that Perylon Hall be opened to the public; now, for a few measly dollars, anyone could dine where he had once entertained kings and scientists. There was no longer anything sacred about the place.

At ten-thirty the next morning, Whalen and La Guardia flew out of Newark Airport for a meeting with President Roosevelt in the White House. Whalen needed FDR to extend another formal invitation to the European nations to return next summer, and he wanted the president's assurances that the United States government would be behind him in his dealings with the various heads of state.

The date was September 1, 1939, and although neither of them was aware of it at the moment, World War II had just begun.

On Closing Day in 1939, the Perisphere was lit to look an enormous jack-o'-lantern, complete with blinking eye.
(© Bill Cotter, worldsfairphotos.com)

"S'LONG, FOLKS!"

That day, a Friday, the German army invaded Poland. Two days later, Great Britain declared war, joined quickly by Australia, New Zealand, France, Canada, and other nations. The anticipation of war had now become a reality.

"With bombs bursting in Poland yesterday," wrote *The New York Times*, "the impact of the general war that seemed to threaten Europe finally broke with full force in the International Area of the World's Fair, which such a short time ago was dedicated with brave speeches of international peace and good will."

That Friday was also the first sunny day at the Fair in almost a week. Not knowing what else to do in the wake of the war news, a record crowd turned out at the fairgrounds, which had once again become the gathering place for those who wished to congregate and commiserate over world politics. Most of them headed toward the foreign pavilions, which "acted as magnets" for those seeking comfort or solace or merely a reassurance that this representation of the world, at least, was not yet under attack. Not surprisingly, the pavilion they flocked to see was Poland.

All afternoon, families entering the building through its Court of Honor stood gazing reverently at a bronze portrait of Józef Piłsudski, the Polish chief of state who was a leader in the fight for his country's independence from Russia in the wake of World War I. That he had fought alongside Germany against the Russian Empire was duly noted and looked upon with great sadness and irony. Here they were, thirty years later, being invaded by their former allies in the fight for freedom.

The pavilion, it was noted, was designed to present the story of Poland "as she is today and as she intends to be in the future—an active, vigorous member of the family of nations." All day long, visitors streamed through the various halls, some of them teary eyed, the women holding handkerchiefs to their faces and the men putting on as brave a face as possible under the circumstances.

It was as close as anything yet to a preview of what was to come— finally, an all-too-accurate representation of the World of Tomorrow.

Joseph Jordan, the pavilion's manager, watched the sorrowful procession as long as he could before returning to his office, where he spent the rest of the day listening solemnly to radio broadcasts from Europe.

Even more ironic, almost unbelievable, the following day, September 2, had long been scheduled as Polish National Alliance Day. Again, it was a record turnout, the largest Saturday crowd so far: more than 312,000. A long parade kicked off at twelve-thirty and marched through the fairgrounds to the Court of Peace, led by a band playing first "The Star-Spangled Banner" and then the Polish national anthem, which, adding to the unreality of the occasion, translated into "Poland Is Not Yet Lost."

More than ten thousand members of the Polish alliance gathered in the court to hear speeches by La Guardia and Whalen, who stated, "We welcome you here with hearts full of understanding and sympathy, because we know you can't celebrate today without looking back home. . . . In the World of Tomorrow you are entitled as well as we are to happiness, peace and contentment."

"This is an hour of sorrow to the entire world," La Guardia said. "When the World of Tomorrow writes the history of today, the people of Poland will have a glorious page in that history."

Whalen shifted in his seat, looked at the same vista he had seen countless times in innumerable ceremonies like this one. The World of Tomorrow had been rewritten before his eyes; they were all confirming that today. If that was the case, then maybe he didn't want it anymore.

La Guardia then read a statement from President Roosevelt: "I have

today authorized an invitation to the foreign countries and nations participating in the New York World's Fair to continue their participation in
1940. I take particular pleasure in extending this invitation at this particular time.

" . . . The continuing hope of the nations must be that they will in-
creasingly understand each other. The New York World's Fair is one of
the many channels by which this continuing conception of peace may be
known."

For Grover Whalen, it was an echo of FDR's Opening Day speech.
Roosevelt's rays of eternal hope, apparently, still beamed. Like Einstein's
rays later that same night, climbing the Trylon, lighting the world. And
there was still the shining hope that they, too, wouldn't end in catastrophic
darkness.

B y mid-September, no progress had yet been made concerning Einstein's letter. With nowhere else to turn, Szilárd wrote to Lindbergh
again. Then, on September 15, America listened as the great aviator gave
a radio speech that was carried nationwide over all three major networks:
CBS, NBC, and MBS (the Mutual Broadcasting System). Many who
tuned in could not believe their ears.

"In times of great emergency, men of the same belief must gather together for mutual counsel and action. . . . We must not permit our sentiment, our pity, or our personal feelings of sympathy to obscure the
issue. . . .

"Much of our news is already colored . . . but we must ask who owns
and influences the newspaper, the news picture, and the radio station. If
our people know the truth . . . this country is not likely to enter the war
now going on in Europe."

In a letter to Einstein on September 27, Szilárd stated the obvious:
"Lindbergh is not our man."

To make matters worse, Alexander Sachs had now been holding on to
Einstein's letter for more than six weeks, and confessed to Szilárd that he
was still sitting on it. Finally, now that war had broken out, Sachs decided
to take action. On October 11, he stood in the Oval Office, and rather

than simply hand over the letter, which he feared "would be passed onto someone lower down," he read a summation of it that he had prepared himself.

"Alex," the president said after Sachs had finished, "what you are after is to see that the Nazis don't blow us up."

"Precisely," Sachs replied.

Immediately, Roosevelt sent for his secretary, General Edwin Watson. "Pa," he said, calling Watson by his affectionate nickname, "this requires action."

That same evening, a committee headed by National Bureau of Standards director Lyman Briggs was charged with investigating the military potentialities of nuclear fission. Begun by yet another Roosevelt, the ball, this ball, finally, was rolling.

G rover Whalen, who had seen enough of the World's Fair that year, sailed for Europe on September 16 to try to sell it all over again for 1940. If nothing else, at least it got him out of New York. Ten days later, he still hadn't been heard from. (Although his ocean liner, the *Statendam*, had been delayed by the British contraband control, he had nevertheless made no effort to contact anyone outside of his closest associates.)

Finally having his way without interference from Whalen, Gibson announced at the end of September that the fifty-cent admission fee would now be good for every day of the week until the Fair closed for the season on Halloween night. He also moved the forty-cent night admission up from nine-thirty to eight o'clock.

"More Fair for less money!" he declared happily.

A reporter asked him if the reduced fee would continue when the Fair reopened next May.

"Well," he shrugged, "I should think it would be pretty hard to put it back up."

Finally, the Mayor of the Midway, Joe Rogers, was happy. "It's pretty good," he admitted. "But they should have done it a long time ago."

The truth was, for a banker, Harvey Gibson had an odd idea of mathematics. He let it be known that according to his own calculations, every visitor to the Fair had received $35 worth of value for the price of three admissions. Reporters asked him to explain exactly how he'd arrived at that figure.

"It cost approximately one hundred and fifty million to build the Fair," Gibson said, counting off the points on his fingers. "Twenty million more to operate it; ten million for operating the exhibitors' buildings; and, say, another hundred million in advertising which was given to the Fair by the newspapers."

Reporters scratched their heads.

"That's two hundred and eighty million," he explained. "There will be approximately twenty-four million paid admissions, and we figure that each visitor attended on an average of three times, so that accounts for eight million individuals. Divide two hundred eighty million by eight million and you get the answer: thirty-five dollars."

They thought he had gone senile.

On Monday, October 2, Joe Lynch brought his family out to see the World's Fair. All policemen showing their badges that day were admitted free, and their children got in for a dime. Freddy Socha came, too, and brought his wife, Jennie. Joe and Easter, with the conviction of Joe Healy behind them, let each of the children pick out one exhibit they wanted to see.

For himself, for old times' sake and to revive his old Fordham University studies, Joe dragged them all, the kids protesting loudly, to the Hall of Pharmacy. At least it wasn't too far a walk; oddly, for such a mundane subject matter, Pharmacy was one of the seven largest buildings at the Fair, and it was right there beside the Theme Center where the Street of Wings dumped you into the Court of Power.

The kids were enthralled by the magic medicine chest, a mirror twenty feet tall and fifteen feet wide that alternately reflected your image and then let you see through it. Behind the giant sheet of glass, a puppet show brought everyday household drug products to life. But Joe thought it was a little silly. He was hoping for something a bit more instructive. Still, he took every piece of literature they offered and stuffed them in his pockets. Old interests die hard.

Naturally, they couldn't get out of there without passing through the Drug Store of Tomorrow and having a streamlined ice-cream soda at the Fountain of the Future. Joe gobbled his down and enjoyed watching his children blow straw wrappers at one another. Only Easter seemed anxious to leave. He caught glimpses of her in the counter's mirror, this one not magic, and then it came to him. The luncheon counter on Greenwich Street. He hurried the kids up, and they all consulted a map to see where to go next.

In the final ten days of the season, Gibson announced that the World's Fair of 1940 would be a "people's playground." And as if to prove it, a week later he declared Friday, October 27, to be "Children's Day" at the Fair. One hundred and fifty thousand New York City schoolchildren were given the day off and admitted for a nickel, and the result was even more disastrous than might have been expected.

According to the *New York Times* account:

At 10:03 a.m., fourteen-year-old June Higgins fractured her arm in a subway station crush.

At 10:17, a gas meter inspector made the mistake of stooping over to take a reading and was knocked flat by three well-placed kicks.

At 10:45, Frank Armour, the panic-stricken manager of the Heinz exhibit, shouted for guards to clear away what was left on the sample counters after kids had stormed the place and were cleaning him out. "Give 'em only pickle pins!" Mr. Armour roared.

At 2:00, a gang of kids had all but destroyed a replica of a New England merchant ship—tearing up the forward hatch, ripping out the pins, and throwing its flags into the water.

By late afternoon, the Perisphere was covered with sayings and dirty rhymes, and what looked like ten thousand names had been written across the base of George Washington's great statue.

The kids, the *Times* wrote, "managed to strip the World of Tomorrow of the last vestige of dignity it had managed to retain from the early, hopeful days of its opening."

Oh, it ended with a bang all right. On the last Saturday of the 1939 season, a northwest gale blew through New York City and ripped a sixty-square-foot chunk off the Trylon at a little past noon. Six-pound hunks of plaster, falling from a height of five hundred feet, had been carried as far as fifty yards away. Yet amazingly, nobody got hurt. Since August, when the movie opened in theaters nationwide, a lot of visitors had been comparing the World of Tomorrow with *The Wizard of Oz*. From a distance, the gleaming Trylon and Perisphere even made it look like the Emerald City. Now the winds were backing up that imagery.

For whatever reason, the decision had been made to close the Fair not on the last weekend in October, but two days later, on Halloween. On Sunday, the weather cleared somewhat, and more than four hundred thousand procrastinators finally showed up for what almost everyone, Fair officials included, considered to be the real Closing Day.

Two days later, it was a ghost town. Only around fifty thousand paid to get in, and most of the exhibits closed up early, fearing vandalism and souvenir hunters who would tear a piece of whatever they could get their hands on to keep as a memento. Eight hundred and twenty city cops and World's Fair policemen were on hand against any rowdiness, but they needn't have bothered. Rain and raw winds kept everyone from misbehaving—at least the visitors, anyway. Out in front of the Arctic Girls Tomb of Ice exhibit (informally known as "Frozen Alive"), which once again featured models in "abbreviated bathing suits," a couple of jokers hid behind its façade and periodically bombarded the rare passersby with chunks of ice.

To mark the occasion, as darkness set in the Perisphere was lit up like a giant jack-o'-lantern; every half hour, it winked its right eye and spooked the hell out of whoever happened to catch it. Of the concessions that did remain open, many were left understaffed; their employees, once again out of work, gathered in bars and drank toast after toast to the great summer folly in Flushing. For the first time all season, there was barely a line outside Futurama.

In the end, despite the financial losses, most of the exhibitors were happy. General Motors reported that more than five million people had traveled 1.7 million miles over Futurama, and an additional eight million, tired of waiting, had visited their other exhibits. Two million had ridden 350,000 miles over the Road of Tomorrow in shiny new Ford vehicles. Eight million saw GE's lightning show; six and a half million were awed by Elektro; and so on. Hostess sold a million cupcakes; half a million had ridden to the top of the Parachute Jump and made it safely down again (with only one well-reported anecdote about a couple who had been stranded at the top of the ride for several hours).

Planters wasn't very happy; they had sold $20,000 worth of peanuts, but it had cost them more than double that to do so. And Borden, even with Elsie the Cow, said, "There was some benefit, but it was necessarily general and not specific."

Out of all of them, Billy Rose was one of the few who came out of it financially smelling like . . . the shrewd theatrical producer that he was. The Aquacade had put on four shows a day since May 4, and even with a capacity crowd limited to ten thousand, he had sold more than five million tickets with a gross receipt of $2.7 million.

Ten million people, who probably regretted it later, had visited Japan's pavilion. As for Italy, George McAneny had assured the crowd on Italian-American Fete Day in late September, "There shall never in the course of our two histories be anything to change our friendship. . . . I believe no power on earth, certainly none in the heavens, will ever sever our cordial relations."

The USSR Pavilion had become a spooky place by the end of the summer. A frequent visitor named Edward Chalfant, who had become friendly with a Russian girl at the information booth, was now told by her that she could no longer speak with him; that he should leave and not come back. The pavilion itself did not return in 1940.

The last formal ceremony took place at four-thirty, under skies as soggy as those on Opening Day had been. A stumbling line of World's Fair troops marched by, taking swigs from flasks and barely managing to keep in step. Gibson said a few words no one listened to, and it was all over in ten minutes. Only one reporter showed up to mark the occasion, and he hadn't even brought a photographer.

The army band played "The Star-Spangled Banner" and then launched into "Auld Lang Syne," although no one sang along. As Gibson and the others filed out of the Court of Peace and headed off to the Administration Building, in a touring car but sans Indian brigade, a single audience member clapped, and a woman, standing ankle-deep in a puddle, summed up the emotions of the day.

"I'll bet they're going to eat," she said.

No one knew exactly what time the Fair officially closed its doors on the 1939 season, when the last person left, or when the gates were locked for the winter. Everyone was too busy trying to stay out of the rain.

A few days after the close, as he was wrapping up business for the long winter layoff, Gibson agreed to be interviewed in his new office, the one that had belonged to Grover Whalen and which still contained many of his souvenirs and mementos. It was, the reporter noted, "an eerie experience." Gibson sat behind Whalen's enormous desk wearing an ill-fitting brown suit and looking entirely uncomfortable in his new surroundings.

The office, oval-shaped, had been designed to conform with Whalen's notion of himself as president of the Fair. (Employees were under firm instructions to refer to him not as "Mr. Whalen," but only as "the president." All memos were similarly addressed.) The lavish décor irritated Gibson to no end.

"Grover Whalen is president of the Fair just the same as ever," he said, perhaps hedging his bets against taking full responsibility for its potential bankruptcy. "I have just come in to help him with some details which perhaps I am better at than he is."

Gibson also seemed to be making an effort to shrug off some of his banker's hard exterior, talking smoothly, trying to make friends. Visitors who came to the World's Fair in 1939 got "mental indigestion," he said, from too much free science and not enough free entertainment.

When asked if he would be as involved in next year's ceremonies as Whalen had this season, Gibson laughed. Distinguished visitors, if there were any, would still be met by Whalen and Mayor La Guardia.

"I don't know what we'd do without the Mayor," Gibson said. "I'm not very good at meeting people."

Then he hurried to explain, once again, the reason he had been given the top job, "as if," the reporter noted, "he thought [I was] going to get mad."

"If the bondholders felt any better with me devoting my full time to the business management of the Fair, I felt obliged to do so," Gibson stated matter-of-factly.

And what about the Manufacturers Trust Company? How were they managing in his absence?

Better than if he were there, he sighed.

Making one final effort to drum up some enthusiasm, Gibson launched into what was to become the mantra for the New York World's Fair in 1940:

"What we need is more of a carnival spirit." Gibson looked up, tried a smile, failed at it, and let his face turn serious again. "The wheels have already been set in motion, and next year, by God, we're going to *have* a carnival spirit!"

And so they did, to such a degree that those who came back could hardly believe the transformation.

PART THREE

For Peace and **FREEDOM**

1940: The Second Season

On behalf of the visiting Elmer from Kansas City,
Let's have a smile on me!
On behalf of the gentleman slicked-up and lookin' pretty
Let's make it two or three.

We're all gathered here on this auspicious day,
And, well, bless my soul, there's Elmer, what-cha say?
Let's have a smile on me!

—From the promotional song for "Elmer,"
official mascot for the World's Fair in 1940

Harvey Gibson shows off "Elmer," his "secret weapon" for the 1940 season.
(Courtesy of the New York Public Library)

"HELLO, FOLKS!"

I f there was ever any question about the differences between Grover Whalen and Harvey Gibson, the proof came on a spring day in 1940, as the World's Fair was sprucing itself up for its second and final season. Gibson, who was short and plump compared to Whalen's regal stature and rugged physique; who was white-haired and clean-shaven while Whalen sported a perfectly coiffed chestnut brown head and manicured mustache; who wore silver-rimmed spectacles and a stern expression in contrast with Whalen's sparkling, unfettered eyes and equally dazzling smile . . . well, if Whalen were dapper William Powell of the Thin Man movies, then Gibson was dowdy old Judge Hardy from the Mickey Rooney flicks of the sticks.

On that spring morning, Gibson left Whalen's old office and walked down to the basement of the Administration Building, where the employee barbershop was, to get himself a shave and a haircut in preparation for Opening Day 1940.

"Why don't you let me come to your office and shave you in the private chair that Mr. Whalen used to use?" the head barber asked him.

"Why," Gibson sputtered, "I've never sat in a private barber chair in my life! You'll never catch *me* using that thing!"

And so it was. Grover Whalen had built his version of a magnificent World's Fair on the idea that bigger (and, therefore, necessarily more expensive) was better. The grander the show, the more people would turn out to see it. Of course, it hadn't quite turned out that way. Gibson, on the other hand, was a cut-corners-wherever-you-can sort of guy. The adage "You've got to spend money to make money" was not in his lexicon.

Spend money to save money was more like it. One of his first initiatives was to hire local college boys to ride around the perimeter of the fairgrounds on bicycles in order to make sure no kids were sneaking in under the fences without paying.

As far as finances were concerned, Gibson knew there was no way in hell the Fair was going to break even at that point, let alone make any money. He also knew there would be hell to pay with Robert Moses, whose Parks Department had been earmarked to get the first $2 million in profits for building and beautifying Flushing Meadows Park after the Fair came down. But that was the least of his worries. Right now, Gibson's biggest concern was paying off as much of the World's Fair bonds as he could. Most of the investors were banker friends of his, and as things stood right now, they'd be lucky to get back fifty cents on the dollar.

But Gibson was ready. In fact, he had a "secret weapon" for turning around the fortunes of the World's Fair this season. On April 12, one month before Opening Day, he walked into the Press Building, where he had gathered newsmen from just about every major paper in the city, accompanied by a portly gentleman wearing a light gray suit and vest with an American flag stuck in his lapel, a blue bow tie (though not at all fashionable like Whalen's), and a gray farmer's hat planted firmly on the back of his head, good-ol'-boy style.

"How do you do, gentlemen!" Gibson said as he strode confidently into the room. "I want you to meet Elmer, the man who is going to bring millions to the Fair this year."

The newsmen gaped at them silently, suspecting that maybe it was a gag. Millions of what?

In true folksy fashion, "Elmer" stuck his thumbs in the armholes of his vest, smiled broadly, and said, "Well, I hope I bring millions!"

No one asked any questions. They didn't have any idea what to ask. So Gibson took off on his own.

"Mr. and Mrs. America were a little bit afraid of the Fair last year," he said, "because it was too formal, too stuffy. There were too many dedications and such, and too little emphasis on homey touches. It awed country boys like myself."

This from the president of the Manufacturers Trust Company. Gibson also unveiled a new poster, created by Howard Scott, a leading graphic artist who specialized in advertising. The poster, headlined with "Makes You Proud of Your Country," showed Elmer just as he now stood in front of the city's hardened newsmen. "This is Elmer. Sure, he's coming to the Fair!" the copy read.

"Elmer is the 'great American,' " Gibson explained, ignoring their openmouthed stares. "[He's] a composite of all the people in the country who we think can have a good time at the Fair."*

Then Gibson said something that absolutely floored his audience. Elmer, he announced, was going to be the Fair's "official greeter" this year. No wonder the banker seemed so pleased with himself. If he wanted to totally eradicate the imprint of Grover Whalen, to erase even his memory, surely this farmer—standing there tapping his foot to a record of patriotic music Gibson had put on to complete the All-American image, his light blue socks sticking up out of dark brown shoes—would do the trick.

Until, that is, Elmer opened his mouth. Recovering from their shock, the newsmen began peppering him with questions. In short order, they got him to admit that his real name wasn't Elmer at all but Leslie—Leslie!—Ostrander, and that, rather than a middle-American country boy, he had lived in Brooklyn all his life. He described himself as an actor and model, but admitted that the only job he'd had lately was portraying Joseph Stalin for a political poster some artist had drawn.

Stalin! The giggling reporters ate it up. Gibson winced. Better yet, as Elmer/Leslie went on to describe the gig, "another guy posed as Hitler, sticking a sword into a nude woman who was lying on the floor at our feet."

The newsmen were beside themselves, struggling to keep straight

* Gibson's publicity team actually went into great detail about "Elmer" in their press releases. He "has been married for sixteen years, has three kids: Joe, 14, who is going to college when he's a little older and if his high school marks get a little better; Mary Lou, 11, pretty as a picture; and Buster, 7, the baby, inclined to be spoiled by the rest of the family."

faces as they scribbled down the imagery. Gibson, embarrassed, furious, abruptly ended the press conference. Although he'd already announced that this Elmer was going to tour the country, speaking at local Kiwanis and Rotary clubs, showing up at American Legion gatherings, and tossing out the first pitch at Major League ball games, he was already making alternate plans as he hustled Ostrander out of there. They'd have to find another Elmer, and fast.

They did. A man named Ralph Bancroft was quickly hired, chiefly because he looked almost exactly like the poster portrait of "Elmer the First." Bancroft would become the "Road Elmer," traveling around the country and promoting the Fair, while Ostrander remained strictly in Flushing Meadows and was instructed to stroll around the fairgrounds and say absolutely nothing more than "Hello, Folks!" Along with a bevy of pretty "country gals," he also handed out paper badges that visitors could tie on their lapels. The badges, of course, also read, "Hello, Folks!" and had spaces underneath for fairgoers to write their names and where they were from. As though anyone in New York would care what your name was or where the hell you were from. Or as if it were all now just one great big jovial Shriners convention, minus the funny hats.

The Fair officially reopened at ten a.m. on Saturday, May 11, and true to form, within ten minutes there was a long line outside of Futurama. Experienced guards from last season had that "here we go again" look on their faces. Also true to form, Harvey Gibson's Opening Day ceremonies contained none of the high-hat hoopla of April 30, 1939. President Roosevelt didn't bother to show up but did send a brief message of welcome. Governor Lehman and Mayor La Guardia spoke, but they, too, kept their remarks to a minimum. There were no riots, no clamors to get into the Court of Peace, and come nighttime no Albert Einstein.

But at least they had the rain to remind themselves of the heady proceedings a year earlier. On opening night, it poured once again, and it was Gibson himself who went over to "the Great White Way," the newly renamed Amusements Area, and flipped a switch to light up the vastly improved overhead streetlamps that had been so spare and undercurrented last year.

Then, uncharacteristically, and perhaps in a further attempt to prove that he was at heart just a "country boy" banker, Gibson tossed his top hat into a thick, muddy puddle and waltzed with Mary Pickford, the onetime silent screen sensation, while a band played "Let Me Call You Sweetheart." Overall, there was nothing cosmic about it.

Total attendance for opening weekend was good: around three hundred and sixty thousand for both days, a little over three hundred thousand paid. Whalen had in fact done better on his Opening Day by about seventy-five hundred paying customers, but that was when the Fair was new, not a "twice-told tale," as its new administration liked to remind everyone.

"The transformation was almost totalitarian in its completeness," noted Sidney Shalett. "The high hat of the 1939 Fair was in the ashcan. The old stiff collar was completely wilted." The stuffed shirt was definitely gone, but in its absence, something else had gone as well. It felt, one observer noted, "as if the magic had been let out of it."

Gone, too, and rather quickly, were Elmers I and II. Within two weeks, Gibson had fired them both.

The changes were numerous indeed. Some of them made sense: Many of the exhibits were now "air-cooled," and railings had been added to the lines outside of Futurama for visitors to lean on while they waited. Other decisions didn't make any sense at all: There were eighty-six fewer restaurants, and many of them were charging higher prices "to keep the crowds away." Some were born out of necessity: The overall theme was now "For Peace and Freedom" rather than "Building the World of Tomorrow," for obvious reasons. Some just seemed to have been made in order to give the appearance of newness: "The Great White Way," for instance, now sat on "Liberty Lake," the new name for Fountain Lake.

And for whatever reason, perhaps to reinforce the idea that it was now, as Gibson described it, just one big "super country fair," he decided to get rid of the zones. Now fairgoers just wandered wherever they pleased as they saw fit. Ordinary folks didn't need to be told they were in this zone or that zone; they just wanted to know where Swift and Company was so they could see how bacon was made.

Norman Bel Geddes had spruced up Futurama with six hundred churches, since he had almost been crucified for forgetting about them in the first place. He also added a few gas stations, as people had questioned where all those cars were supposed to get fueled up. And to satisfy his own obstinacy, he threw in a few hundred extra moving cars, just to *utz* Walter Lipmann a little more.

Ford jazzed up its daredevil show, pairing stunt driver Jimmie Lynch with "two beauteous she-devils." The company also built a new $500,000 wing in order to stage a ballet-fantasy called *A Thousand Times Neigh*, which was, the press release reported without a trace of irony, "a history of Ford Motors from the viewpoint of a horse."

The horse in question was called Dobbin, and he had movable eyes, ears, lips, jaws, and tail. Together with forty-two dancers from the American Ballet Caravan, he jetéd for seventeen minutes, twelve times a day, until at the end he finally reconciled himself to the fact that the horseless carriage was here to stay.

Walter Dorwin Teague thought the whole thing up, and the grand finale featured a chorus of singers explaining the rather bizarre title:

> *Would he go back to an earlier day?*
> *Before the motorcar?*
> *Neigh, neigh, a thousand times neigh!*
> *And a horse laugh—HAR, HAR, HAR!*

In Gibson's world, classical ballet was fine as long as you "never once forgot that two men impersonating a horse are always good for a laugh," as *Time* noted.

Pedro the Voder could now speak several different languages, including Japanese. General Electric competed with Westinghouse's "Mrs. Modern" by introducing "Mrs. Cinderella," a marionette who turned from a ragged servant girl into a princess by the electrical appliances that helped her with her housework.

As for Westinghouse itself, Elektro the Moto-Man,* who had appar-

---

* "He looks like an amiable, attractive Frankenstein," the guidebook now described him. "And is proving to be the matinee idol of Flushing Meadows."

ently been lonely for moto-companionship, was given a robot's best friend by the name of Sparko, an "electric dog" who sat up, barked, and wagged its tail. Sparko actually turned out to be something of a face-saver for Westinghouse, who had already advertised "Mr. Nimatron," an "electrical brain" that would later become a prototype for automatic game players. To keep customers interested, he was also programmed to lose on occasion, but the device wasn't quite ready on Opening Day. As visitors kept asking where Mr. Nimatron was, embarrassed guides kept replying, "You wouldn't mean Sparko, would you? We've got a Sparko all right!"

Westinghouse also knew how to keep up with the times, and make old exhibits sound more exciting, by changing the name of its "Microvivarium"—a device that killed microbes with sterilizing rays—to "Microblitzkrieg."

Not surprisingly, the most obvious changes occurred in what used to be called the Government Zone, where the foreign pavilions were. Ten of the foreign nations could not make it back for the second season, including the Netherlands, Yugoslavia, and, most notably, the Soviet Union. That entire pavilion, so massive and imposing last season, had been crated up for shipping back to the USSR, along with Ivan.

In its place, the new administration had erected "the American Common," a two-and-a-half-acre monstrosity "dedicated to the perpetuation of an American idea." The "idea" was a kind of hybrid open-air market and amphitheater where native songs and dances were demonstrated, all of it designed to display "the greatest variety of racial strains getting along with each other and living at peace." Racial it was, along with strained; the whole thing came across as an ad hoc cacophony of desperation without a single unified concept, an afterthought in the "what in hell are we going to put in Russia's place?" confusion.

By midsummer, the Finland Pavilion, accompanied by the sad notes of "Finlandia," would also be closed. In addition to Czechoslovakia, the list of other invaded countries whose pavilions still stood now included Belgium, Denmark, France, Luxembourg, Norway, and Poland, whose pavilion was draped in black. Every evening, as dusk settled over the fairgrounds, the "Heynal" was blown from the top of its brass tower—a single, mournful horn bleating clear and loud and then ending, suddenly, on a broken note. The ceremony commemorated the fabled death of a Polish watchman who had saved the city of Krakow from invaders with just such an instrument, the musician silenced in mid-melody by an arrow to his throat.

Nevertheless, the pavilion's restaurant remained defiantly open, vowing to serve Polish ham and honey wine as long as supplies held out. In fact, most of the foreign nations' restaurants continued to operate, including Czechoslovakia's, whose main concern at the moment was finding an acceptable substitute for pilsner.

As for Japan, its pavilion's staff was eagerly and innocently preparing for the upcoming twenty-six hundredth anniversary of the founding of the Japanese Empire. Italy contented itself with the opening of a new spaghetti bar.

Much to Gibson's chagrin, Poland's nightly ritual cast a pall over his "super country fair." But, displaying some of Whalen's aplomb in turning a deaf ear to bad news, he set about reversing the Fair's fortunes with a series of promotional campaigns designed to appeal to the average American's two greatest desires: a new home and a new car.

"Those of you who are bondholders have two things to pray for," Gibson told a group of his cronies at the Wall Street Club. "One is good weather and the other is the success of the Golden Key."

Sponsored by a group of New York hotels, the contest seemed simple enough. Golden Key envelopes were given away to guests and contained a pair of keys that, it was hyped, would ensure "a car a day given away! Plymouth, Ford and Chevrolet!" The trouble was, as many people initially thought, you didn't simply walk up to a new car and try the keys in the ignition. Within the envelope was also a two-page set of rules and instructions for trying the keys in various "treasure chests" and other areas throughout the Fair, and the whole thing was so complicated that, as *Harper's* noted, "it would take almost a mathematical genius, armed with charts and maps and a convoy from the Explorer's Club, to discover what to do to win one of the cars."

In the end, despite the fact that a lot of cars were indeed given away, the promotion wasn't anywhere near as successful as Gibson had so obviously hoped it would be.

As for the new-home aspect of the American ideal, the Town of Tomorrow had recently been expanded by two new houses, each of which was to be occupied for a period of one week by forty lucky families selected by local newspaper promotions. The families, *The New Yorker* noted, "will consist of a father American, a mother American, and two little Americans, preferably a boy and a girl."

But the actual display itself was uncomfortable to look at, both for the viewers and for the chosen families. Visitors tended to rush past them with eyes averted, as if they were nothing more than Peeping Toms.

As June passed into July, the weather, the first element in Gibson's prayer, proved no more helpful. At his first press conference of the season, on May 28, the new chairman opened with an uncharacteristic joke: "Is the sun coming out?" The remark was met with a mixture of laughs and groans. It had rained on twelve of the first sixteen days of operation, and for eight straight days prior to the conference.

A miserable spring extended into a complete washout as the Fourth of July approached. On July 3, Superman Day at the Fair, even the Man of Steel looked about to rust.

Average net paid circulation for three months
Daily --- 1,950,000
Sunday - 3,500,000

DAILY NEWS

Copr. 1940 by News Syndicate Co. Inc. NEW YORK'S PICTURE NEWSPAPER Trade Mark Reg. U. S. Pat. Off.

FINAL

Vol. 22. No. 9 New York, Friday, July 5, 1940★ 44 Pages 2 Cents IN CITY LIMITS | 3 CENTS Elsewhere

BOMB AT FAIR KILLS TWO

PLANTED IN SUITCASE AT BRITISH PAVILION

— Story on Page 2

Victims of Fair Bomb. Bodies of two detectives, killed when bomb exploded near British Pavilion at World's Fair, lie where they were thrown by force of blast. The bomb, contained in canvas suitcase, was being carried from British Pavilion when it went off in rear of Polish Building. *Story on page 2; other pictures on page 20 and back page.* (NEWS foto by London)

"THIS LOOKS LIKE
THE REAL GOODS"

Police Commissioner Lewis Valentine and his troops were every-where at the Fair that spring, as were Lieutenant James Pyke and the men of his Bomb and Forgery Squad. The World's Fair itself, in ironic opposition to its "For Peace and Freedom" promise, had become instead a hotbed of political dissent and vehement protestation against the spreading war. At a rededication ceremony for Belgium's pavilion on May 18, former president Herbert Hoover summed up the change in the Fair's philosophy, at least as it was perceived by those who attended it. "This is not a celebration," he declared sadly. And it was true.

"This is not a dedication of a mere exhibit at a World's Fair," La Guardia reiterated in his speech. "This is a shrine dedicated to a twice-martyred nation."

In fact, war displays of one sort or another could now be found in most of the foreign pavilions. That same day, Portugal, which had already given up its pavilion and hoped to display some relic of its nationalism in the Hall of Nations, reluctantly withdrew from the Fair altogether. Later that month, the pavilions of nine Allied nations, seven of which were at war and three of which had already surrendered to the Nazis, took part in a massive prayer service held at Great Britain's pavilion. Extra security was ordered, and the police detail would remain in force throughout the re-mainder of June and on into July.

The bomb threat frenzy had begun in February, when Pyke's team had gotten word that the ocean liner *Britannic* was an intended terrorist target. Lynch and Socha, along with dozens of other men, scoured the ship for hours and came up empty-handed. The squad was now receiving more than four hundred written bomb threats each week, and the pairing of explosive expertise with forgery skills suddenly began to pay off. Most of the threats were deemed unworthy of investigation, but even the ones that had the remotest chance of turning out to be real were dug into. Day after day, Lynch and Socha found themselves digging around on hands and knees and finding nothing, then returning to the office and scouring an ever-growing stack of letters for clues.

Nevertheless, Pyke was insistent; they could not afford to miss the one warning that would turn out to be fatal.

Then, on June 20, the reason for Pyke's persistent uneasiness materialized. Without any warning whatsoever, two bombs exploded within an hour of each other, one on the eighteenth floor of 17 Battery Place at four-ten p.m. and the second at 35 East Twelfth Street at four fifty-three. The Battery Place building held the offices of the German Consulate General, but they were one floor below the explosion. The actual bomb went off at the Deutsche Handels und Wirtschaftdienst (the German Trade and Industrial Service). Yet the locations and appointments of both were written in German, and there was speculation that the saboteurs had mistakenly placed their bomb in the wrong office.

The second bomb went off in a building that housed a number of Communist agencies, including the *Daily Worker,* a popular Stalinist newspaper, and the New York headquarters of the Young Communist League. A handful of people had been injured at both sites, none of them seriously.

Pyke and his men began an immediate investigation. Routine procedure after a device had been detonated involved collecting material considered to be bomb fragments for analysis. It was a methodical job that meant scraping even the finest bits and pieces of suspect cloth and metal from floors, walls, even ceilings and furniture. Witnesses were quickly rounded up. An employee of the German agency reported seeing a young blond man who dropped a brown paper parcel in front of the office door. After the explosion, he was nowhere to be found.

At the Twelfth Street building, the bomb had been placed just outside the front entrance, but the blast was sufficiently strong enough to blow a hole through the bottom of the floor inside the doorway. Fragments of evidence were few and far between, but Deputy Fire Chief William Taubert speculated that it might have been a time bomb. Analysis of the findings would quickly prove they both had been.

Within hours, the police rounded up thirty suspects for questioning. None of them revealed any leads. Pyke and his men returned to their offices with an eerie feeling that this was only the beginning—a warning, perhaps a test run. Why the Germans *and* the Communists? The placement of the bombs seemed to suggest that the sabotage was "designed to create more sensation than damage," as one reporter noted, and the timing of the two explosions left little doubt that it was the work of the same man or agency.

Two days later, Pyke's office received notice of an anonymous phone caller who threatened that the Brooklyn, Manhattan, and Williamsburg bridges were about to be blown up. Although telephone threats almost always turned out to be hoaxes, the men of the Bomb and Forgery Squad were at it again, crawling all over the bridges for days to no avail. Still, Pyke was insistent. He convinced Commissioner Valentine to double the number of policemen guarding all piers, foreign consulates, and foreign-language newspapers, not wishing to be surprised next time by what he was convinced would not be a practice run again.

The World's Fair was now familiar territory for Joe Lynch and Freddy Socha. They had combed over the International Area and walked the perimeter of the Court of Peace so many times, they could do it blindfolded. Except for the absence of the USSR Pavilion the overall layout of this quadrant of the fairgrounds had changed little since 1939 (the shuttered pavilions notwithstanding). The Flushing River acted as a kind of barrier between it and the main area, except for the pavilions of Brazil, France, and Belgium, which fronted a somewhat less decoratively planted Rainbow Avenue.

Now they were at it again. On June 21, the day after the twin explosions in Manhattan, an operator in the Italian Pavilion got a call threatening to bomb the building. Security in the area was doubled. After yet another thorough, exhausting search, no bomb was found in the Italian building or anywhere else in the vicinity. Nevertheless, Pyke decided to send a regular crew of his detectives out to the fairgrounds on a rotating basis, just in case.

Aside from the Great White Way, which Gibson was hell-bent on promoting this season, the foreign pavilions were drawing the biggest crowds. The war brought them out to view what many New Yorkers considered to be the battlegrounds of Europe in miniature. Of particular concern was the fact that a Boy Scouts camp had been placed along the perimeter of the area at its northernmost point, just behind the U.S. Federal Building.

Thoroughly isolated and trafficked at all hours by the Scouts, along with their parents and visitors, the camp offered easy access and anonymity to potential saboteurs. Not to mention the safety issues for the constant stream of one hundred and sixty Boy Scouts who lived there for one week and then changed troops. There was simply no way to protect it.

Bomb hysteria was reaching a peak as summer officially began: A time bomb was discovered in the washroom of a Communist workers school in Philadelphia after an anonymous tip had been phoned in; another bomb scare shut down New York's Pennsylvania Station for several hours when an artillery shell was found abandoned in a Pullman car. It turned out to be a sample casing left behind by an absentminded and thoroughly mortified munitions salesman.

Again, Pyke took no chances. As the four-day Fourth of July weekend approached, he ordered all of his men to remain on duty whether or not they were required in the office. He needed to be able to reach them by telephone, if necessary, on a moment's notice.

On the afternoon of Thursday, July 4, 1940, Joe Lynch was sitting at home studying to take the exam for promotion to detective, first grade, which would almost certainly guarantee him a ticket out of the

Bomb and Forgery Squad. His wife would be grateful for that. Over the past few months, Easter had grown more and more worried now that an ever-increasing amount of Joe's time and responsibility was being consumed by the dangerous machinery of bombs rather than the subdued language of letters, however threatening their content.

The truth was that Lynch liked the squad, had great admiration for Lieutenant Pyke, and had grown close enough to Freddy to wonder why he and Jennie had not had any children yet, especially since Freddy had come from a large family himself. But the hard fact was that Joe needed the pay raise, now more than ever. His eldest daughter, Essie, was in St. Joseph's Hospital up in Yonkers. The little girl had just turned ten and was suffering from osteomyelitis, a bone infection for which the doctors at St. Joe had assured him they were doing everything they could. With proper treatment, her body would fight the infection and she would be fine. But it would take time.

Crowded as it was, the Lynch family's little Bronx apartment seemed empty without her. The hospital bills were a minor concern for Joe compared with Essie's health, but they were a concern nonetheless. Worse, the idea that his daughter had gotten so sick over a bacterial infection ate at the core of his sensibilities as a parent and protector. Whatever cut or scrape she'd received had gone unnoticed, apparently, until Essie's pain and fever became too great to ignore.

Joe had once studied pharmacy, yet he had been too busy with his police work to notice something as simple as an infected cut on his own child. With soap and water she'd have been fine. But there he was, scouring bridges and office buildings looking for evidence of damage when he should have been noticing it in his own household.

The weather, equal to his mood, had been miserable all week. At times this season, it seemed as if the rain would never stop, as if a day hadn't gone by since May when it didn't rain for at least an hour or two. Joe supposed he could take some comfort in that, being forced to remain at home and on call until he was officially off duty later that evening. The skies, heavy and overcast, were probably keeping everyone indoors anyway.

That evening, he planned on borrowing his sister's car and driving up to Yonkers with his wife to visit Essie. His mother was coming over to look after the other kids since they weren't allowed to visit the hospital, and now he worried over them and their cuts and bruises as if to compensate for his lack of attention with his eldest.

Joe tried to focus on the exam booklets in front of him but found himself distracted again and again. At a little after two o'clock, the doorbell rang; his mother was here, Easter told him. Since the murder of her own mother two and a half years ago, Easter had grown close to Mary Lynch. Throughout the early part of 1938, while Easter mourned her mother's violent death, Mary had stepped in to help her care for the children. Now that Mary was recently widowed, something about their mutual loss had brought them together.

Joe decided he'd best give up studying for the day, and the trio worked up a card game. It was too nasty outside to do anything else. They sat at a little table and played three-handed bridge.

Three days earlier, on July 1, another bomb threat was phoned in to the Fair, this time at the British Pavilion. An operator, Marjorie Rosser, picked up and heard a man with a muffled voice say, "Get out of the building. We are going to blow it up. Get everybody out before the box explodes!" She reported the call to Cecil Pickthall, the pavilion's commissioner general, who in turn immediately notified the police.

Pyke, although he thought it was probably nothing more than a repeat of the Italian threat, sent his team back out to Flushing Meadows. By now, the squad was making so many trips out to Queens, he thought they ought to at least get a discount train fare. October couldn't come soon enough.

Once again, his detectives found nothing. This was getting to be repetitive and frustrating. Sitting around and waiting for advance notice seemed pointless, an exercise in futility if ever there was one. Not to mention naïve. The two explosions that had gone off in the city had occurred without prior warning, so as an extra precaution, Pyke added two more detectives to the squad's regular World's Fair beat assignment. He instructed the men who pulled the duty to dress in ordinary street clothes, mingle with the crowds, and see if they could pick up on any suspicious activity. At least it was better than twiddling their thumbs while waiting for the phone to ring.

On Wednesday, July 3, an electrician named William Strachan noticed something that seemed a little strange. He was working on some wiring in the fan room of the British Pavilion, where the vents for the new air-conditioning system had been installed over the winter and which served as a sort of all-around control room for its electrical equipment. Up on one of the shelves, a small, tan-colored canvas bag caught his eye. It looked, he said later, like an overnight suitcase. Strachan assumed it had been left there by one of the building's employees, since the room itself was off-limits to the general public. Maybe, he figured, someone had packed it for a quick getaway on the holiday tomorrow. In any case, he decided not to bother with it.

It was there again when Strachan returned the next day, on the Fourth of July. This time, he leaned in for a closer look. The suitcase, he now discovered, was ticking. He looked at his watch; it was three-thirty in the afternoon, and the pavilion was swarming with visitors. Strachan, from the Bronx, was one of the few Americans who worked in the place, and he understood the fascination of coming here on the day his country was celebrating its independence from the British.

In fact, despite the bad weather, almost a quarter million people turned out at the Fair that day. And while many of them preferred the merriment of the midway, where an enormous fireworks show was going on all afternoon, the foreign pavilions remained as popular as they had been in recent months since the war. Great Britain, fighting bravely as the last great hope against the Nazis, had become the new focus of the crowd's fascination. It was estimated that throughout the afternoon, the number of visitors hovered somewhere between several hundred and a thousand at any given time.

Strachan, like many other of the building's employees and certainly most if not all of its visitors, had probably not been made aware of the bomb threat a few days earlier. Unlike the phone call to the Italian Pavilion, this one for some reason had not yet made the papers. Thinking there might be nothing more dangerous than a radio or something inside the bag that was making the noise, he nevertheless decided to turn it in, just in case. So he nonchalantly picked up the suitcase, carried it down the public stairway, and knocked on the office door of Cyril Hawkings, his boss.

Hawkings didn't know what to do about it, either. The suitcase was, he agreed, "ticking like a clock." That neither man panicked and ran for the cops is testament to either bravery or complete incomprehension and ignorance of what could be inside. What they did next seems to show evidence of the latter: Strachan picked it up again, and he and Hawkings walked through the crowded building in search of Sidney Wood, head of the pavilion's uniformed security.

It wasn't hard to find him. Wood, who was serious about his duties in protecting the priceless artifacts and historical documents that had been lent to the World's Fair for display, could most often be found in the Magna Carta Room. There, in front of the pavilion's most popular exhibit, one of four original manuscripts, they held the case up to Wood for inspection. Wood, apparently thinking no more about it than the other two, asked Commissioner Pickthall to join them.

All the while, the suitcase remained ticking in Strachan's hands.

Pickthall had the sense at last to call in the police. The two men on duty to patrol the area that day were Detectives Martin Schuchman and Fred Morlach. Morlach called in a report to his commanding officer, James Leggett, and they were quickly met by Detectives Joe Gallagher and Bill Federer. It was Morlach who finally, after the suitcase had been traveling around the pavilion for about half an hour, suggested they carry it outside the building and away from all the people. They left via a rear entrance and walked down an alley separating the British and Italian pavilions, then swung over on Continental Avenue to Poland's.

Morlach thought he knew a good spot behind the Polish Pavilion, about a hundred and fifty feet away from an open court where a small group of customers sat at tables under big umbrellas and sipped afternoon refreshments. There was a cyclone fence that marked the edge of the fairgrounds, but it gave them enough distance, and other than the bar patrons, the area seemed to be completely deserted.

Pickthall meanwhile had notified the World's Fair police, while Federer called Lieutenant Pyke's office. The four detectives convened on Front Street, where they nervously watched the suitcase and waited for the Bomb and Forgery Squad to show up.

At a little after four o'clock, the call came. Joe, Easter, and Mary Lynch were still playing cards. Joe looked at the phone and shook his head; in another hour or so, he was off duty and they could leave for Yonkers. He picked it up. It was Pyke, as he had feared. Something about a suspicious package found at the British Pavilion. Lynch needed to get out there and check it out.

Freddy's off today, he told his boss. Who do you want to go with me?

Get Hayias, Pyke told him. He's on home duty, same as you. The lieutenant hung up.

Lynch called Peter Hayias's number and got no answer. He tried again several minutes later. No answer. After cleaning up and changing into his uniform, he tried the number again. No answer. Now he wasn't sure what to do. Hayias was a good man who'd been on the force a lot longer than either him or Freddy Socha, and he knew his way around a bomb site. Lynch looked at the phone, thought it over, and then picked it up and called Freddy at home.

Sorry to call you on your day off, he said; it was a rotten break for the both of them. Socha shrugged him off. The crummy weather had kept him from heading out to the beach with his wife anyway. He had nothing else to do. Why not go out to the World's Fair and check out a bomb?

I'll pick you up, Joe told him, and hung up.

"I'll be back in an hour," he told Easter, heading out the door.

Lynch drove out on the Grand Central Parkway, hung a left on World's Fair Boulevard, and parked the car on Rodman Street. He and Socha entered the fairgrounds at the Flushing Gate; from there, it was a brisk walk across Federal Place to the Court of Peace to Continental Avenue and back behind Poland, where all the hubbub was. They came on the scene at around a quarter to five and found a pair of World's Fair policemen, John Sullivan and John McLaughlin, standing guard with Morlach and Federer.

They also saw another cop, who turned out to be Patrolman Emil Vyskocil, literally hovering over the suitcase. Morlach had assigned him to watch it until Lynch and Socha arrived, and he took the job seriously. Lynch relieved him of his immediate duty, and he and Freddy got down to work.

The suitcase was about twelve inches by eighteen by six, they measured, and hell, yes, it was ticking. How long had it been ticking? The electrician first heard it about an hour and a half ago. He hadn't noticed the sound yesterday.

Yesterday? How long had it been sitting around? About thirty hours, someone figured. At least that's how long it had been since Strachan first spotted it.

Lynch scratched his head on that one. Time bombs were set off by clocks, and clocks had the stubborn tendency to register the same time once every twelve hours. How in the hell could this one have been ticking for a minimum of two trips around the dial, maybe three?

They talked it over. Almost certainly, it had to be a hoax. Or if it was real, then surely it was a dud. No one had ever heard of a time bomb that couldn't tell time. But it was still ticking. So Lynch, recalling Pyke's new instructions on how to defuse bombs without completely destroying the evidence, decided to cut a small hole in the bottom of the suitcase in order to determine first whether there was, in fact, a bomb inside.

He and Freddy tipped the thing over. Morlach drew closer, angling in for a look. Gallagher and Schuchman stood nearby and waited for the verdict. Lynch took out his pocketknife and carefully cut away a two-inch strip off the bottom of the case. He and Freddy bent their heads down close to peer inside. They saw several sticks of dynamite bound together by cloth.

"This looks like the real goods," Lynch said, squinting up at Freddy. They were squatting knee to knee as they decided what to do next.

Morlach bit his lip and turned away to tell the others to get back. "It's the business," he warned them.

"What is it?" Sullivan asked.

Morlach never got a chance to answer. The last thing he remembered before hearing the explosion was the sight of Sullivan's hat being blown off his head.

Morlach felt the force of the blast at his back, and it shoved him forward, practically crashing him into Sullivan's chest as the two men were thrown to the ground. Morlach lay still for a moment, stunned but trying to regain his senses. Finally, he stood up and turned around. He saw a gaping hole in the ground where the suitcase had been sitting. Leaves from a tall maple tree were swirling in every direction, as if an early and angry autumn had descended suddenly, the tree itself having been blown bare by the bomb.

Morlach stared at it for a moment and then searched around for Lynch and Socha. He spotted what looked like the remains of two smoldering bodies on the ground, one with his knees raised upward, the other lying in a grotesque hunk of carnage. Two other officers, Federer and Gallagher, were crawling away from the crater on their hands and knees, their uniforms in tatters and smoke rising from their backs, dragging their mangled legs behind them.

Morlach, unable to contain himself, vomited into some weeds—the smell and the horror convulsing his body into great, heaving waves of nausea and sobs.

"It was terrible," said a waitress in the Polish Pavilion's café. "It came all of a sudden and shook everything in the place. I saw people running and then I saw people lying on the ground near the restaurant."

Another eyewitness, Josephine Chmiel, who worked as a salesgirl in the pavilion's candy shop but was on a break at that moment, broke down as she described the scene. "It was a terrible explosion," she cried. "I saw three men lying on the ground and two more were trying to crawl away. They were holding their faces. One tried to get up. Oh, it was horrible!"

Morlach ran toward the first body, Freddy Socha. The explosion had been so intense that it had blown him all the way to the fence line. Seeing that there was nothing to be done for him, he slowly approached Joe Lynch, or what remained of him. The bomb had stripped off his uniform and half of his face. He lay, arms outstretched, like the Savior on the cross. Hunched over the suitcase as it went off, he had been lifted straight up by the blast with a force so powerful that it had separated his legs from his feet, which clung to his ankles by strings of exposed tendons.

There was confusion everywhere. McLaughlin stood frozen, staring down at his left leg, wondering where all the blood was coming from. Customers who had been drinking in the Polish Pavilion café sat stunned; two windows in the rear of the restaurant were shattered, fifty yards away from the blast. Several others, farther away, began running toward the scene, followed by every other cop in the vicinity. Morlach recovered himself and took charge. A cordon was quickly set up; ambulances were called for the wounded and the dead. Within minutes, the crime scene was under control.

Detectives from the Bomb and Forgery, Alien, and Homicide squads were called in, basically anyone who could get there fast enough to collect all the evidence. They combed the area around the Polish Pavilion, and when that was done they moved on to the neighboring Netherlands and Venezuela buildings. Debris was found as far as one hundred yards away in every direction. Officers picked it up as carefully as they could and spread it all out on makeshift newspaper pallets, focusing first on items belonging to Detectives Lynch and Socha: money and coins, wallets, their firearms, fountain pens, and police notebooks.

Someone thought to measure the size of the hole the blast had left; it was a crater five feet wide and approximately three feet deep. Dynamite will do that, another remarked, blast as strong downward as in every other direction.

Commissioner Valentine arrived shortly after, followed by Lieutenant Pyke and the rest of his men. Pyke directed them to begin sorting out whatever appeared to be fragments from the bomb itself and store it carefully in boxes for transport to the Police Technical Laboratory for inspection. He personally collected several key fragments that he wanted to turn over to explosives experts at the DuPont plant in New Jersey.

Grover Whalen, dressed in an unfortunate white suit for the summer holiday, hustled over from the midway. For several minutes he stood silent and stared at the scene. This was his breaking point, the horrible coda to his career as Fair president and former police commissioner. He talked to the already gathering reporters with noticeable tears in his eyes.

At seven-thirty, La Guardia showed up, looking pale and frazzled; the men around him noticed that he wasn't wearing a hat. In fact, he had just driven in from his summer home in Northport, Long Island. It was normally about an hour's drive, longer on a big holiday like this one, but the mayor had made it in twenty minutes by having his driver blare the siren as he sped up the opposite direction on the Grand Central Parkway.

Knowing that he needed to make a formal statement, La Guardia chose his words carefully to avoid a panic.

"As to the accident itself," the mayor said, clearly shaken, "I must say that the very intelligent and courageous action of the police who handled this matter prevented what might have been an extremely serious calamity."

It was by no means an understatement. By later accounts, Joe Lynch and Freddy Socha, along with Fred Morlach and the others, had in all likelihood saved the lives of hundreds gathered in the British Pavilion that afternoon. Given the intensity of the blast, it was not inconceivable that the entire building might have come down.

"We get letters all the time threatening various kinds of outrages," La Guardia continued, "and we have had the Fair buildings of all belligerents covered by police since the Fair opened, just as their consulates are covered in Manhattan. In this instance the police did a splendid job in handling the bomb and staying with it, even to the point where Detectives Lynch and Socha lost their lives in consequence."

There was a noticeable murmur in the crowd. Most as of yet did not know that anyone had been killed in the blast. In fact, except for the few who had been enjoying a quiet afternoon drink on the terrace of the Polish Pavilion and had felt the force of the impact and the windows shattering behind them, almost everyone else at the World's Fair thought that the explosion they had heard was just more fireworks going off on the Fourth of July.

"There had been World's Fair fireworks in the vicinity about an hour before," said a coat checker who gave his name only as L. Morski, "and some thought it was more fireworks. But the explosion was much louder than that. It was like a cannon blow. The building was rocked."

All around the crime scene, the Fair was going on as usual, as if nothing out of the ordinary had occurred. Even Cecil Pickthall, who had heard the bomb go off while sitting in his office in the British Pavilion, thought it was part of the day's celebration.

After all, the suitcase found in his building was safely in the hands of the police. "I thought no more about it," he said.

Word began to spread, and within a couple of hours a crowd of ten thousand people stood around watching and whispering rumors to one another. The Irish Republican Army had done it; that's why it was in the British Pavilion. No, it had to be the Nazis—a symbolic strike against Great Britain in the face of war. What about Palestine? Revenge against the white paper? Didn't they read something about suitcase bombs going off in London?

La Guardia understood what was at stake. Two policemen had died here today, and out of sheer decency he felt he should at least close down the area, if not the entire fairgrounds. But what would happen to the World's Fair if he shut it down? Would anyone ever come out here again? On the other hand, what would it say to allow the celebrating to continue?

And then there was the worst consideration of all: What if another bomb went off?

"All the buildings involved are covered by our police," he reassured the press, "and I want to tell the public not to get panicky. The situation is pretty well covered, but I suppose that things like this will happen."

Of course, he had no way of knowing whether or not anything was sufficiently covered at that point. But there were still three and a half months left to go in the season; if he acted rashly now, the World's Fair would never recover. Worse, it would be tainted forever with the stain of saboteurs' blood. The Fourth of July could *not* become known as the day New York backed down to a terrorist act.

Darkness began to fall, and over in the Great White Way the frenzied celebrations were just getting into full swing. There would be more nighttime fireworks, the biggest show yet. Extra police details were called out for protection, but as the hours passed no order came to evacuate the area or the Fair itself. The risk of chaos was too great; there would be no safe method to control the panic. Sometime during that evening, the decision was made to allow the party to continue.

A police detail was sent out to Jennie Socha's apartment to tell her the news; the rest of Freddy's family found out over the radio.

Easter Lynch heard it from one of the priests at St. John's. When he left, she had a tough decision to make. She and Joe were supposed to drive up to the hospital that night. Easter decided to make the trip anyway, if only to make sure the nurses understood that in no way was Essie to find out that her father had just been killed.

Dressing for the visit became the hardest part. She couldn't wear mourning clothes, but she couldn't dress normally, either, out of respect for Joe. She finally settled on a plain brown dress and black stockings, hoping the child wouldn't notice.

"Who died?" Essie asked playfully as her mother walked in the room.

"It's just raining outside," Easter said. Where's Dad? He's on business. Where? At the World's Fair. She let it go at that.

Detectives went on swarming the foreign pavilions; now they were up on the rooftops and still finding and picking up bits and pieces of debris and evidence. When darkness fell, a large truck equipped with floodlights drove up and bathed the scene in light again. The men kept on working, digging the barren maple tree out of the ground and cutting away a section of the fence whose wire had been twisted and blown outward, when a lone bugler asked to be admitted to the scene. The officers, thinking he had come to blow "Taps" in honor of Joe and Freddy, lifted the cordon and let him through. The man raised his horn to his lips, and they heard the familiar notes that had been sounding out over the Polish Pavilion night after night. It was the "Heynal," and at the last note the bugler broke off, as he always did, in midnote. Without a word, he turned and left again.

It took several minutes for the officers to collect themselves and go on digging.

Sometime during that night, a detective handed Valentine a small piece of metal. It was twisted from the blast, but there was no mistaking it as a small brass cogwheel, the kind found in alarm clocks.

La Guardia finally left when Pyke reassured him that his men had combed every inch of the area and found no other suspicious packages. He would be back at the New York City Building early the next morning to give an address thanking the police department and minimizing the potential danger to visitors in the coming weeks and months.

"There will be a most thorough investigation, and there will not be any letup," La Guardia promised.

Before leaving, he was given a full report of the damages:

Detectives Lynch and Socha: killed instantly. The extent of damage to their bodies was too gruesome to detail.

William Federer: compound fractures of both legs; burns on his arms, face, and body; severe shock. Condition critical.

Joseph Gallagher: compound fractures of both legs; burns on his arms, face, and body. Condition critical.

Martin Schuchman: multiple abrasions and burns on his legs, body, and head. Condition fair.

Emil Vyskocil: multiple abrasions and contusions on both legs. Condition fair.

John McLaughlin: minor cuts to his face, mouth, and leg; treated at the scene and sent home.

Of all the officers on the scene, Detective Morlach was indeed the luckiest. Although he had been right beside Lynch and Socha as the suitcase was cut open, he had turned his back on the bomb and was walking away from it to give his observation of the dynamite when the suitcase exploded, and he had escaped, he'd thought, without any injury at all.

Morlach continued working through the night, the scene of horror keeping his anger and energy fresh. When he finally got home it was nearly sunrise. He took off his uniform jacket and then, after stripping off his shirt, stared blankly at the back of it. It was soaked in blood. He walked into his bathroom, turned around, and looked in the mirror. Using his fingernail, he dug a piece of metal about the size of a penny out of his shoulder. He hadn't felt a thing.

Mayor La Guardia *(seated)* and Grover Whalen
(in white suit) confer with the press at the
bomb site. *(© Bettmann/Corbis)*

Official reproduction of the World's Fair bomb
(without the Ingraham clock face) constructed
during the investigation
(Courtesy of the New York City Police Museum)

AFTERMATH

On Friday, July 5, the sun actually came out, and it looked as though it was going to be a nice weekend. It was, and over the four-day holiday, attendance at the Fair soared to 640,000. Harvey Gibson quietly ordered that the bomb crater be filled in, the dead tree replanted, the fence repaired, and every other visible evidence of the blast cleared away. The barriers stayed up while police continued to comb the area for clues, but it didn't stop the large groups of people who kept coming by all day and evening, hoping to get a look at the crime scene. Workmen had rushed to replace the windows of the Polish Pavilion, and the restaurant, it was noted, "did a rushing business all day."

Even the British Pavilion opened that morning, on time, and remained open throughout the weekend. Commissioner Pickthall reported that he saw no drop in business, which he attributed more to American pluck than morbidity. "I take my hat off to them," he said. Guards at the pavilion reported that they saw more visitors that weekend than they had since the Fair opened.

The same was true for the entire International Area. Gibson had worried that the explosion would cause people to shun the Fair, but "the reverse was the case." More people came than ever.

Security was tightened, but there wasn't much else they could do. A couple of hundred city policemen and World's Fair cops patrolled the buildings; Grover Whalen himself visited all of them and made sure they were checking all packages and purses and that the locks he had instructed to be placed on all interior doors had been installed properly.

After that, it was business as usual as far as the Fair went. Gibson bade a formal farewell to Borden's Elsie the Cow, who was off to Hollywood to star in a movie. Two new families moved into their homes in the Town of Tomorrow for their one-week residence, each from a small town and each with exactly one girl and one boy, as had been predicted. Eight thousand General Motors employees visited and named Miss Betty Crain the new "Miss General Motors 1960."

By Sunday, it was as if the tragedy had never happened. In fact, the only one still agitated about it was Emil Chodorowski, manager of the Polish restaurant, who actually filed a complaint with the police department because they hadn't finished wrapping up their business in the area where the bomb went off. Worse, they were taking suspicious-looking packages back there for examination, and customers were getting afraid. It was bad for business, he said.

On Sunday night, Gibson ordered the barriers taken down.

The night of the explosion, Commissioner Valentine stayed at the fairgrounds as long as he could, then returned to his office to make a few announcements in time for the morning papers. First, he ordered an immediate roundup of "agitators and other suspects . . . including Bundists, Fascists [and] members of the Christian Front." He knew it was a meaningless gesture—mostly the cops would rope in a few crackpots who hung around Columbus Circle and spewed their verbal garbage at anyone who would listen. But he also understood that his office would need to give off at least the appearance of doing *something*.

Then he took a more serious step and placed every available officer in the department on twenty-four-hour duty pending further notice. "We are mobilizing the entire police force of the City of New York," he announced, "not only to apprehend the perpetrators of this atrocious crime but also for the purpose of preventing any repetitions."

The situation, he knew, was dire. The city had been suffering from bomb fever for several weeks; a blast like this, on the nation's biggest holiday and at its most popular tourist attraction, could cripple business and create widespread panic. It wasn't just a matter of *solving* the crime; it was a matter of how *fast* they were going to solve it. Already, reporters were referring to the "war atmosphere" created by what they were calling "the World's Fair bomb."

Once again, Pyke wasn't wrong. First thing the next morning, the Capitol in Washington, D.C., had a police guard around it; tourists could still get in, but they now had to show identification and open all bags. Security made it clear that their actions were tied directly to the bombing of the British Pavilion.

The mystery of why the bomb hadn't gone off during the course of the two days it had spent in the fan room was apparently solved when the crime lab discovered that the brass cog found at the scene came from an eight-day Ingraham clock.

Then things got a little weird. The husband of Marjorie Rosser, the operator at the British Pavilion who had received the earlier bomb threat, reported that at eleven-thirty a few nights later, a man had phoned their apartment in Queens and asked to speak to her. Before Mr. Rosser could call her to the phone, the man shouted, "I'll kill her!" and hung up.

Valentine considered it a prank. Rosser's name had been in the papers, after all. Then someone pointed out that her name had in fact been misspelled as "Rossner." Further, after her husband described the man's voice, she said it sounded exactly like the original caller. Valentine picked up the thread again.

The pace was quickening, and for a while it seemed the entire city was on lockdown. Valentine rounded up more than one hundred "suspects" who were later questioned and released for lack of evidence. Extra police were sent out to the Fair and searched every building repeatedly. The French ocean liner *Normandie*, which had just sailed in to Pier 88, was guarded heavily and searched for bombs. All over the city, people talked about the bomb and about dirty Nazi sympathizers, looking at one another with a curious distrust that hadn't been there a few days ago.

When pressed for comment, Valentine, exhausted, finally admitted that he believed the whole thing was an inside job, that no one "but a person who had worked in the British building or had become intricately familiar with its plans would have known enough about the structure to plant the bomb in the strategic spot in which it was found."

Though it hadn't occurred to anyone at the time, the fan room was on the second floor and was in fact strategically located in the exact dead center of the building. Pyke had no doubt it had been left there for maximum impact on the structure. Not to mention the estimated five hundred to seven hundred people inside at the time of the blast. "It was only a miracle that hundreds of visitors to the British Pavilion were not killed," Valentine said, noting that the "dynamite shrapnel" was powerful enough to have blown away an entire wall of the pavilion and possibly its support structures. "Only conjecture can visualize the havoc that would have been wrought if the lethal device had exploded within the crowded building."

Police immediately began interrogating each of the more than one hundred employees who had worked there so far this year, as well as those in the surrounding pavilions. The most promising development in the case came during the arrest of a man named Caesar Kroeger, who had come under suspicion after several Bund members had been rounded up and questioned. When detectives came to the door of his apartment, Kroeger innocently invited them inside. On one wall of his room, they found a large world map with pins stuck in it. Kroeger shrugged it off and explained only that the pins represented cities with strong Communist factions.

Then, in a desk drawer, the officers found two German Luger pistols hidden under a copy of *Mein Kampf*. Kroeger was promptly arrested and after booking was found to be an illegal alien. That was enough to set the citywide Nazi fever ablaze all over again. For several days, the arrogant-looking German with the smug mustache became the face of the saboteur who had bombed the World's Fair.

After that, it got worse. A report that four sticks of dynamite had been stolen from a construction site in the Bronx sent panic throughout the neighborhood, until a supervisor confessed that, whoops, he had made a mistake in counting it. Two days after the bombing, a gift-wrapped box was found sitting on the glass case that housed the copy of the Magna Carta in the British Pavilion. Written on the paper was the directive, "Mail to the address inside."

Two men from Pyke's squad carted it quietly off to a men's room, where a portable X-ray machine showed it was probably empty. They carried it outside, opened it, and found a package of silk stockings and a ladies' handkerchief. Written on a note card was the message *"Danke Schoen."* Pyke was furious. With so much security in the area, how in the hell did someone manage to leave a box on top of the goddamn Magna Carta and go unnoticed?

At eight-thirty that same day, the night manager of a service station on West Sixty-sixth Street picked up the phone and heard a voice say, "This is just to tell you that we're going to blow up the gas tanks across the street." Over on Tenth Avenue, directly opposite the station, was a Con Edison electrical plant. At nine-fifteen, the same voice called again: "I'm not fooling. We mean business about the gas tanks." Police details were sent out to every Con Ed plant in the city, and a growing panic set in that the city's power supply was about to be sabotaged.

A pervasive feeling that New York was under attack began to spread, and the fear of more terrorism surged like wildfire. Reports of missing dynamite and suspicious packages tore up the phone lines; restaurants and bars suffered a noticeable layoff in business; hotels received numerous cancellations. Called to Philadelphia, Lieutenant Pyke found two bombs at the site of that year's Republican National Convention.

Valentine told reporters they were discovered "near the convention hall" a few hours before it started. Pyke, he said, had also found a third bomb "in a hall or a place where Communists gathered" and that "this bomb was in the course of destruction."

Yet despite the fact that an aide to Governor Arthur James, who had been nominated as a candidate for president, said that one of the bombs "was addressed to the Governor," the FBI issued a complete denial that any bombs had been found. No further investigation was made, and the entire matter was covered up. Pyke returned to New York, embarrassed and incensed.

On Monday morning, July 8, Grover Whalen, Harvey Gibson, La Guardia, Pyke, and Valentine attended a requiem high mass for Joe Lynch at St. John's Roman Catholic Church in the Bronx. Sixteen hundred mourners showed up, among them a thousand cops and firemen, and celebrities including Babe Ruth. Joe, who had been waked at home, was led by a formal procession to his funeral, accompanied by the police department's one-hundred-and-ten-piece band. Thousands of his neighbors and friends lined the sidewalks to see him go.

Before the service, in the Lynch apartment, La Guardia, near tears, pleaded with a detective, "I urge your boys to give all their spare time to this case. Do everything you can to solve it and it will be appreciated."

The next day, Freddy Socha, who was being waked in a funeral parlor in Brooklyn, would be buried in St. John's Cemetery in Queens. An equal number mourned at his services, lining the streets of Brooklyn in silent, tearful salute.

There were clues—a numbered piece of fiber in which the dynamite was supposedly wrapped; a chunk of metal made of an unusual iron alloy; even the tiny alarm clock wheel that was traced to a manufacturing plant in Bristol, Connecticut. But in the end, they added up to nothing. On Wednesday, July 10, Valentine, at his wits' end and emotionally spent, assembled a gathering of fifteen hundred detectives and ordered them to break the case. He was himself at the breaking point.

Monday morning, a commissioner in charge of Colonial Hall at the British Pavilion said he got a bomb threat over his private line, an unlisted number. On Tuesday, another call came through to an operator; this time a woman's voice said, "For God's sake, tell the police that the World's Fair is going to be bombed at two p.m. today!"

At ten forty-five she called back, but by this time the threats were getting so ubiquitous that the operator who took the call asked, "Have you told the police yet?"

"No," the woman answered.

"I'll connect you," the operator singsonged routinely, and nonchantly put the call through.

Valentine, frustrated at the public's indifference, told his men, "This is just the beginning. There have been a series of bombings in Europe. It is possible that we shall have more here. . . . Remember, you don't have to die to prove your courage."

VALENTINE WARNS OF MORE BOMBINGS, the next day's headlines read. Again, the city went on alert.

For a while, the fear and furor died down a bit. Then, in early August, paranoia flared up again when a Nazi flag was found by a night watchman in the British Pavilion. It had been curled up into a tight ball and stuck on a window ledge about fifteen feet from the fan room, and the panic rekindled. As the hot summer wore on, and as Germany continued its onslaught of Western Europe, anti-Nazi resentment grew into a hard and noticeable hatred. German Americans were no longer considered suspicious; now they were the enemy outright and no longer an ocean away. Thousands who had once preached isolationism and even pacifism began changing their tunes. The city had indeed taken on a war atmosphere, as the fairgrounds had on Independence Day.

In September, a Bund member, Edward Kangesier, was arrested by a special group of police officers known as the Espionage Squad and held for questioning in the World's Fair bombing. His apartment, it was noted, was "littered with Nazi pamphlets, a swastika flag and anti-Jewish banners and posters." Three days after the bombing, police noted, Kangesier was seen driving a new car, thought to be the result of a big payoff. After "hard" interrogation, however, both Caesar Kroeger and Kangesier were released; the cops could pin nothing on them.

Nobody on the force wanted the case to disappear, nobody wanted the public to forget about Joe and Freddy to such a degree that it would never be solved. But at this point, with so little evidence, most detectives understood that the only way the bombers were going to be caught was if someone turned in an accomplice in order to collect a reward. So the city voted to offer $25,000 to anyone who came forward with information. It was a lot of money; you could buy a house and car with it and still have plenty left over. Now all they could do was cross their fingers and pray.

Valentine kept the department's emotions running high. "If only the persons responsible for the bomb had seen the body of Joe Lynch," he told yet another gathering of detectives. "If we had them there, it was in our hearts to tear them limb from limb."

He paused a moment, struck by the comparison of his own words and the impact of the blast on Lynch's body, and let his anger spill over.

"We have got to get them!" The commissioner pounded his desk, tears streaming from his eyes, his voice all but gone. "Your professional reputations are at stake! We have got to *get* them, *convict* them and have them sentenced to the proper punishment—electrocution. There is only one punishment and that is *electrocution!*"

The Life Savers parachute tower in 1939 (© *Bill Cotter, worldsfairphotos.com*)

26

CURTAINS

The Briggs Advisory Committee on Uranium, as FDR's initial effort became known, had begun meeting in October 1939 in order to substantiate Einstein's claim that the discovery of a nuclear chain reaction could lead to "extremely powerful bombs." Present at the first meeting were Leó Szilárd, Eugene Wigner, and Edward Teller—all three of Einstein's summer guests—but no Einstein. Roosevelt had written him a note of thanks for bringing the matter to his attention, letting him know, "I have convened a board to thoroughly investigate the possibilities of your suggestion. . . ."

But that's about as far as the president, for the time being, was willing to go. Throughout the remainder of 1939 and on into 1940, FDR had approved the grand sum of $6,000 for research into uranium, and the committee was getting nowhere. So once again, Szilárd pressed Einstein to write yet another letter urging further action by the administration.

Another clarion call for research would not be sufficient. Instead, Einstein decided to focus on the threat that struck fear into everyone's heart—that the Nazis might be the first to develop atomic weapons, empowering them to wreak untold havoc on the world.

"Since the outbreak of the war, interest in uranium has intensified in Germany," Einstein therefore wrote to Alexander Sachs in March 1940. "I have now learned that research there is carried out in great secrecy. . . . Should you think it advisable to relay this information to the President, please consider yourself free to do so."

Once again meetings and conferences were held, and once again Einstein chose not to attend. Perhaps he suspected that he had already gone too far in promoting a new tool for war. Or perhaps, as he had desired so often in his life, he simply wished to be left in peace to work out the secrets of the universe. Whatever the motive, under the circumstances, Einstein would prove to be justified in refusing to get further involved—an FBI report submitted in July 1940 stated, "In view of [his] radical background, this office would not recommend the employment of Dr. Einstein on matters of a secret nature."

The report, among other things, cited the ridiculous protest made by the Women's Patriotic Organization that had called for Einstein to be denied an entry visa back in 1932. In addition to offering a number of bungled facts and conclusions, the FBI questioned whether "a man of his background could, in such a short time, become a loyal American citizen."

Which in fact Einstein promptly did, though not in response to any ridiculous FBI report. Having taken the citizenship test on June 22, he was sworn in on October 1, 1940. The ceremony took place a little more than one week after his final accolade at the World's Fair. On September 22, Einstein had been honored at the Wall of Fame as one of six hundred foreign-born Americans "who have made notable contributions to our living, ever-growing democracy, devoted to peace and freedom." That the Fair had jumped the gun by nine days in declaring him an American apparently went unnoticed.

"[Immigrants] are the only ones to whom it can be accounted a merit to be an American," Einstein stated in his message for the Wall of Fame, "for they have had to take trouble for their citizenship, whereas it has cost the majority nothing at all to be born in a land of civic freedom."

Bill "Bojangles" Robinson was also one of those chosen to be honored, and Einstein included in his statement the highly unpopular sentiment that the United States owed a debt to African Americans "for all the troubles and disabilities" that had been placed upon them and were still allowed to continue.

On the one hand, Einstein was being honored for his contributions as an American; on the other, his loyalties were being questioned and he was considered a security risk. Eventually the Briggs Committee came under the auspices of the more serious, and effective, National Defense Research Committee. And once again, it came about as a result of a letter from Einstein:

"I am convinced as to the wisdom and urgency of creating the conditions under which that and related work can be carried out with greater speed and on a larger scale than hitherto," he wrote. "Given such a framework and the necessary funds, it [the large-scale experiments and exploration of practical applications] could be carried out much faster than through a loose cooperation of university laboratories and government departments."

By the end of the following year, Einstein's multiple letters detailing the possibility of atomic weapons and his urging of formal action on the part of the U.S. government led to the creation of the Manhattan Project. The actual date of its official, though highly secret, launch was significant: December 6, 1941. A day before the Japanese attacked Pearl Harbor, the weapons ultimately used to defeat her would begin their conception.

By midsummer, once the Fair had seemingly recovered from the Fourth of July bomb and the curious onlookers began disappearing from the explosion site, the overall scene grew somewhat desperate. Boys who pedaled tourists around in bicycle "rickshaws" began taunting customers on weekdays when the crowd was almost nonexistent, racing their carts dead at them and then swerving away at the last minute just to amuse themselves. At night, leaning out the windows of the Press Building, bored reporters amused themselves by howling drunkenly at the moon. Concessionaires who sold the *Today at the Fair* newspapers goaded one another into shouting, "Don't buy these programs, folks! Absolutely nothing going on anyway!"

And what *was* going on turned out to be either disastrous or foreboding. At the end of July, a "Baby Crawling Contest" drew rampant criticism in the press. Reporters sent to cover it couldn't hide their disgust at the sight of seventeen infants crying and broiling under a hot sun for over an hour as they attempted to cross a lawn half a football field long. It ended only after one of the judges accidentally stepped on a contestant.

Then it was announced that the army's parachute troops would begin training in towers very much like the one set up in the Fair's Great White Way. What had once been a simple "thrill ride" now took on a more serious connotation for the young men who coaxed their dates into the two-seated benches. Worse, the ride itself began breaking down on a regular basis; on several occasions, it stranded panicky passengers for hours.*

At one such calamity, a reporter for radio station WOR was describing the scene on-air when a society photographer approached and asked him politely not to identify the stranded couple.

"Why not?" the reporter asked. "What's the matter with telling his name?"

"He's from Baltimore," the photographer responded, "and that's not his wife."

And then there was Robert Moses. Renewing his old habits of threats and timelines, he sent a report to La Guardia in August "reminding" him of the city's obligation to come through with the money for his vision of Versailles. The original agreement stipulated that the first $2 million in so-called profits be set aside for Flushing Meadows Park, and despite the bad news in attendance and revenues, Moses had somehow managed to have that figure doubled to $4 million. But even though everyone knew there weren't going to be any profits, Moses still wanted his money.

"The World's Fair made it possible to reclaim permanently this entire section of Queens with the development of a great park as the primary objective," Moses noted in his report. "Unless this work is started promptly, the entire area will be an eyesore and a shambles. . . ."

By "promptly," Moses meant October 28, the day after the Fair closed for good. He wasn't going to waste any time tearing this thing down, either. Within four months, he wanted the entire area cleaned out and hauled away so that come March 1941, he could finally begin the work he had set out to do in the first place. The New York World's Fair Corpora-

---

* The breakdowns became so well reported that Alfred Hitchcock added a scene to his 1941 film *Mr. and Mrs. Smith*, in which Carole Lombard and Robert Montgomery get stuck on the ride, in the rain, with the Trylon and Perisphere swaying behind them.

tion, he noted in the report, had set aside only $100,000 for demolition. No way was that going to cover it.

In response, the corporation's executive vice president, Howard Flanigan, took up an old, familiar argument. Not only had Chicago's Fair been cleaned up without its management having to spend a penny, he stated, but the contractor hired to demolish it had actually *paid* $28,000 to the Fair for the rights to the salvage left over from its buildings.

Chicago again. Moses threw up his arms. He had already placed the designated $4 million in the parks department's budget, and he intended to see every penny of it reclaimed and subsequently spent. Damn Whalen and his spendthrift ways. Way back in 1936, when all of this looked like such a promising dream, Moses had prompted Al Smith to write to the Fair corporation and urge them to put Grover Whalen in charge. "I suggest that there be no doubt as to the authority given him," Smith had stated. Now, four years later, Moses thought he must have been out of his mind.

I t was only August, yet already the thought on everyone's mind seemed to be Closing Day. Not wasting any time, Harvey Gibson decided to start selling off whatever pieces of the Fair he could. Everything from furniture to carpeting to lighting fixtures was suddenly up for sale to the highest bidder, as if the whole thing were already done with. He started by auctioning off the piano in the Terrace Club and the enormous copper-topped conference table in the board of directors office—two of Whalen's most prized possessions, naturally. Included in the long list, way down at the bottom, were forty-nine blue silk cummerbunds, leftovers from the high-hat finery of days gone by.

Bids would soon be going out to contractors for demolition estimates, and without a thought about public opinion, Gibson wanted everyone to know that the remnants of the World's Fair would be perfectly suitable for building the machinery of war. "In fact, Fair officials would like very much to see some of our materials used for national defense," he said through a spokesman.

Then he got an even better idea: Why not convert the entire fairgrounds into one great big army or navy camp when all was said and done? "Common sense will tell you that we shouldn't be tearing down millions of dollars' worth of structures when there is a possibility that the country will have conscription shortly, bringing on an urgent need for barracks," he said.

Conscription, of course, meant drafting young men into the armed forces in preparation for war. For a World's Fair that had done about as much as it could to be the purveyor of peace, Gibson was now publicly acknowledging that war would probably come to America and that the Fair could profit from it.

It was, of course, a dual slap in the face: one for Grover Whalen, whose former "World of Tomorrow" he would turn into an ironic location for a military training ground; and an even harder one for Robert Moses. "There is a serious possibility that actual demolition may be delayed sufficiently," Gibson acknowledged, putting a potential kibosh on Flushing Meadows Park for the foreseeable future. "To me it seems criminal to tear these buildings down with the state of the world as it is today."

This was Harvey Gibson at his best—acting as patriot when in fact his primary motive was to hand the government the keys to the World's Fair and let them deal with the expense of tearing it down—possibly even charging them a little rent money in the process. He could envision the lease being drawn up, the young soldiers drilling in the former Court of Peace, transforming Whalen's Terrace Club into a mess hall, using the Perisphere and Democracity as a giant map and strategy room. The irony of turning a world of beauty into a tool of war didn't matter a whit to him if the taxpayer could wind up footing the bill and paying off some of his debts.

Whalen, of course, was horrified at the thought. He stood witness as his dream was slowly dismantling before his eyes. The once glorious sight of the Trylon and Perisphere now held no great pull over him. If he tried, he could still see that glorious parade on Opening Day replaying itself—the long lines of multicultural marchers filing down the Helicline and up Constitution Mall, crisp in their uniforms, the flags of so many nations joined together and snapping in the wind as if they all represented a single, magnificent, unifying force.

So long ago; a different world entirely. It had been a coming together of peoples then, the country's wagon hitched to a star of freedom, of hope, and of peace. If Gibson had his way, men would be marching here again, but for an entirely different purpose.

In the beginning, when it was all coming together, Whalen was the only member of the corporation who attended every single meeting, believing in the Fair's purpose with every fiber of his being. Now, in the waning days of the Fair, he could barely force himself to attend a single one.

The fortunes of the Fair—not merely its finances, but the very real possibility that in the end it would be melted down into bombs and ships and fighter planes—had a profound effect on him. He began to gain weight, no longer taking his morning exercises and forgoing his ritual early morning bike rides and brisk walks around the fairgrounds. More and more he enjoyed his cocktails at lunch and found that he waited for the dinner hour when he could renew his imbibing. The lines in his face grew deeper, and his cheeks began to sink in even as his waistline expanded.

His name was hardly ever in the papers now, and his picture was almost nowhere to be found anymore. He still gave speeches on various occasions, since Gibson was admittedly never very good with the public, but he was almost never quoted. During a rare interview that summer, a reporter actually noticed the hint of a shine on his suit, indicating that Whalen no longer took such great care in his appearance. That summer, he was dropped from the list of best-dressed men in the country.

Only La Guardia seemed able to bring him out of it. Since he had grown nearly desperate for any kind of coverage, Whalen suggested that August 19 be declared Working Press Day. Gibson grudgingly gave him the okay, but only if it was held on a Monday, the emptiest day of the week. The day was to be a great big "thank you" to the newspapermen and columnists who had given the Fair so much praise over the years. And, true to Whalen's luck, it poured all afternoon.

For once, he decided not to let the weather spoil his fun. After a formal luncheon at Perylon Hall, where the booze flowed freely, the entire group toured the drenched fairgrounds in one of the sightseeing buses, whooping it up and raising all kinds of hell. Whalen had even arranged for a police escort just out of mischief, and when the reporters egged him on, he gleefully returned to the days of his commissionership and blared the lead car's siren repeatedly for them. It was a complete violation of World's Fair rules, but he honestly didn't care anymore.

La Guardia, out of sympathy for his old friend, agreed to play the role of a haggard, hard-drinking journalist in an impromptu performance the two of them put on during a dinner at the Terrace Club.

"Ho, hum!" the mayor began ad-libbing. "I wonder what that louse, Grover Whalen, is doing today? I gotta have a drink!"

Guzzling a Scotch and soda, La Guardia got in a dig at Whalen's nemesis. "Harvey D. Gibson. Who the hell is he? I asked Grover Whalen who he was, but Grover Whalen didn't seem to know. . . . He's the only man in public office who has been given sufficient notice before he is photographed to take a bath, have a face massage and get dressed up."

La Guardia and Whalen poked fun at the Fair, at the city itself, and at the treacly sentimentality of all this "super country" atmosphere. " 'Know your money,' " the mayor said in laughing reference to one of the films shown in the U.S. Federal Building auditorium. "This theme was dedicated to the bondholders of the World's Fair!"

They kept it up late into the night, drinking and laughing with the reporters at the wonderful spectacle of it all. Finally, after years of rebuke by the press, "Gardenia" Whalen had become one of the boys.

The weather remained abysmal, and heavy rains continued to keep attendance to a minimum. In between the storms, a heat wave pushed temperatures up into the mid-nineties. It stayed that way for eight days, until a fresh wave of showers soaked everything down again. By now, it was blatantly obvious that the only rise in business the World's Fair seemed to attract was from the war-torn countries and their native sons and daughters. Five thousand Polish Americans gathered again in the Court of Peace as a memorial to that nation's World War I veterans. The same afternoon was also National American-Hungarian Day.

The theme may have been "For Peace and Freedom," but if it weren't for the war, the Fair wouldn't be doing any business at all.

Needing a new enemy, Robert Moses was now battling openly with Harvey Gibson in the press, stating that the Fair was "bankrupt and busted, and everyone knows it." He accused Gibson of trying to save $750,000 for the bondholders by handing the site over to the government, but by the end of August, both the army and navy had turned down the idea of using the fairgrounds as a military encampment. Still, it didn't stop Moses from threatening to "find out why the Fair can't meet its obligations."

Desperate for cash, Gibson increased the fire sale of World's Fair items to include limousines and horses, flags and uniforms. He economized further by firing everyone he could and replacing them with cheap labor, leaving in his wake a steady stream of disgruntled workers who wondered when their turn would come. The message it sent seemed antithetical to the Fair's once-lofty purpose.

"Honorable Mr. Gibson," wrote Pablo Albortt, one of the disposed. "Tuesday the 13th I lost my job as porter at the American Jubilee. Myself and all other porters but three were suspended from the job and replaced with sanitation men. . . . Your Fair and your American Jubilee advocate freedom and peace. But how could there ever be freedom and peace . . . as long as we the negroes continue being discriminated in our own America the beautiful?"

Albortt enclosed two photographs of himself taken at the Fair and asked Gibson to sign one and keep the other for himself. Gibson, through a secretary, responded that there was nothing he could do and returned both photos.

By the end of the month, General Motors announced that Futurama, that glorious ride into the future, would not be preserved. Norman Bel Geddes's grand vision for 1960 was just too big, too intricate and delicate, "constructed like a jigsaw puzzle." Anyway, by that point, the future was no longer something to look forward to—except, perhaps, as a means to leapfrog over the next two decades, past a war that might conceivably last that long and into the bright vision of high-speed travel and the peaceful suburbia that awaited on the other side. As the Fair's second season ground slowly to a finish, many people who had "seen the future" most likely decided they wanted no part of it.

Only the bomb frenzy continued, nearly unabated. One week in August summed up the madness:

On August 6, La Guardia watched as Lieutenant Pyke carefully opened a ticking black suitcase that had been found under a bench in the Long Island Rail Road station. This one had been immersed in oil as a precaution, and, as Joe Lynch had done, Pyke sliced it open with a pocketknife while the mayor stood not ten feet away. Inside, they found an alarm clock and some travel clothes.

On August 9, six Bomb and Forgery Squad detectives scoured two freighters after a caller threatened that a bomb "might go off at any moment" on Pier 4 in Brooklyn.

On August 10, they were back at the World's Fair, where another suitcase had been found hidden in some bushes outside the Bell Telephone exhibit. Ignorant of the fact that water conducted electricity (and therefore might set off a bomb's timing device), the exhibit's director chucked it into a nearby pond just as its owner showed up to reclaim it.

"Hey, fellows, that's my bag," said Arthur Elder, a teenager who had hitchhiked from Dallas for six days to get to see the Fair. "Gosh, my only shirt and pair of pants!"

As recompense, Elder was given a free lunch and dinner and allowed to call his mother long-distance from the nearby exhibit at no charge (and with no one listening in).

On August 14, a series of calls came in threatening that "another bomb will be placed in the World's Fair today." Shortly after, a package found in a subway station was investigated and turned out to contain nothing more than garbage.

But the real scare occurred later that same afternoon when a "bomb-like" piece of iron pipe was discovered in Rockefeller Center. Certain that it contained nitroglycerin, more than twenty detectives, firemen, and army explosives experts took it carefully to DeWitt Clinton Park over on deserted Eleventh Avenue, where they babysat it for more than seven hours while trying to decide what to do with the thing. The iron casing prevented both a fluoroscope examination and the motor-oil-disarming tactic.

Commissioner Valentine finally stepped in and ordered that it be taken out to the Hudson River and dumped overboard. A reluctant procession of nervous officers carted it around on a feather pillow, took it aboard a police launch, and headed out for deep water. Two detectives, two firemen, and two of Pyke's bravest stood on deck and wondered how far duty called for them to sail before they could drop the thing gently into the river. A second launch followed "to pick up survivors if the bomb exploded on its way to sea."

When the crew finally decided they'd gone far enough, the pipe was gingerly lowered into the water. By the time the boats returned, full of emotionally spent but joyously relieved men, they learned that the supposed bomb actually belonged to an air-conditioning company that had been making an installation that morning. They had just given a ceremonial and terrifying burial at sea for a dollar's worth of mercury.

The hunt for the World's Fair bomber continued nonetheless. A suspect named Rudolph Klein, a restaurant worker at the Fair, was arrested and then released. Another mass was held for Joe Lynch and Freddy Socha, after which the Board of Estimate granted each of their widows an award of $3,200, the equivalent of one year's salary. Up until that point, Easter Lynch had received only $550 from the Riot Relief Fund; Jennie Socha was given only $300 because she had no children to feed.

In addition, each widow was awarded a pension of $1,600 a year for life, provided they never remarried.

One by one, the other detectives and policemen who had been injured in the blast began to recover. On the last day of August, Detective Bill Federer finally returned to his home. He had spent the summer recuperating at Flushing Hospital, just a few miles from the fairgrounds. He was thirty-six years old and would spend the remainder of that year on crutches, but he was alive. Aside from the other injuries to his body—his left leg was still in a cast from his hip to his ankle eight weeks after nearly being blown to bits—he was haunted by two sounds: a constant ringing in his ears that came as a result of his concussion; and the recurring sound of a suitcase full of dynamite exploding.

At night, unable to sleep, he didn't know which sound was louder.

The Administration Building, site of heated debates over the Fair's finances
(© *Bill Cotter, worldsfairphotos.com*)

WHALEN, GRAVISNAS, FORBINE, AND NOBILITY

In October, as if getting in one final snub at the idea of a World's Fair, a cold snap descended on the city and the temperature plummeted to near freezing for five straight days, setting a record low for that time of year. Nevertheless, perhaps finally sensing the Fair's importance, the crowds began turning out en masse, not wanting to tell their children and grandchildren that they had missed out on the greatest show the world had ever seen. Gibson made sure that even lower bargain rates would compete with their curiosity and compel them to come. He needed every customer.

Aside from all the buildings that needed to be pulled down, the problem arose as to what would happen to hundreds of foreign pavilion workers who no longer had homes to return to. In the final weeks, cooks, waiters, guards, and custodians gathered every day in cafeterias to bemoan their fates. Six Czechoslovakian employees and twenty Poles told reporters they would "forfeit their lives" if they were forced to return; and seventy-five Belgians, some of whom had wives and families who had not been heard from since the Nazi invasion, said they were driven "almost wild" over what to do next.

The Fair was scheduled to close for good on October 27, and with two weeks to go, Mayor La Guardia made one final pitch to his fellow New Yorkers to come out and see the show. "I can assure you that not in the lifetime of anyone living today will there be anything equal to the New

York World's Fair," he said. "When you come here you will wonder why millions of other people in other parts of the world are suffering the horror of war. . . . You will leave here with the conviction that here in America we have accomplished something. We believe we have done a great public service in presenting the World's Fair."

Tuesday, October 15, was declared "I Am an American Day" at the Fair. More than five thousand people gathered in the Court of Peace to recite the Pledge of Allegiance. In an effort to attract a crowd of half a million visitors, Gibson had issued a special bargain ticket that sold for $1.00 and offered $6.37 worth of value, including admissions to many attractions previously omitted from such promotions. Ticket takers at the most popular paid exhibits "literally prayed for rain to relieve the congestion."

At four o'clock, their prayers were answered and the skies opened. Only about a quarter of the estimate showed up.

Finally, on Closing Day, Gibson, Whalen, and the rest of the executives got what they had been looking for over the last two seasons: more than five hundred thousand showed up to bid farewell. To commemorate the occasion, Gibson had his paper badges reinstated, this time with "Goodbye, Folks!" printed on them. Paid attendance for the 1940 season reached 19,115,269, compared with 1939's 25,817,265. In all, almost forty-five million had paid their way into the World's Fair, far short of its goal and only six and a half million more than Chicago had attracted. But those who visited had witnessed a thing that, as La Guardia had stated, would not come again in their lifetimes, if ever.

There was little vandalism, but a lot of souvenir hunting. Plants and flowers were the most popular targets, along with some street signs and even wastebaskets. Special police patrols at the gates made the pilferers give everything back, and at every exit huge mounds of debris piled up as the guilty were made to empty their pockets of whatever goodies they might be carrying.

People scrawled their names along the base of George Washington's statue and gazed up in silent reverence one last time at *The Four Freedoms;* made out of plaster, they were scheduled to be among the first items to come down beginning the next morning. For many, the sight of the Trylon and Perisphere was just too difficult to look at; few could believe such magnificent structures were slated for demolition. Men and women were seen wiping their eyes and shaking their heads at the very thought of it.

The official souvenir hawkers, who had been so busy and so eager on Opening Day, clamored to make their final sales pitches and were met with a fervor equal to that which had first greeted them on April 30, 1939. Special yellow-and-blue flannel pennants bearing the affirmation, "I Was There on Closing Day, October 27, 1940" were the most popular item. Thousands of visitors snatched them up for a dime.

At four o'clock, Grover Whalen made his final appearance in the Court of Peace. A "retreat parade" reversed its original route, exiting this time from the U.S. Federal Building and marching down Constitution Mall toward the Theme Center—more than seven hundred members of the U.S. Army, Navy, and Marine Corps stepped bravely as twenty thousand gathered to watch.

Whalen, his voice catching, praised them all and began saying a few words about the Fair when the band surprised him by suddenly breaking into "For He's a Jolly Good Fellow." After that, he couldn't continue. He retreated first to Perylon Hall, where a group of his "old guard" staffers was waiting to toast him. Later he attended a dinner at the Terrace Club, where five hundred of the original executive members were fighting off their gloom with wine and cocktails.

At six p.m., Futurama spun around on its tracks for one last go-round. The honor of the last ride went to Robert Murray, chief maintenance engineer, and his crew. After the final car had exited into the open square, Murray, visibly in tears, led his men back inside the exhibit on foot. Each of them began stuffing their pockets with cars, trees, bridges, and anything else that wasn't nailed down. As the show at last went dark, they and a handful of GM executives headed for the nearest open bar and raised a glass to the *new* future, whatever that might be.

One final parade was scheduled for seven-ten in the Amusements Area. This one was meant to be a joyful, Mardi Gras–type celebration, sort of a funereal march that broke into song and dance in contrast with the gloomy event being celebrated. It never came off. The crowd in the midway was too big and had become somewhat unruly, many of whom were gleefully imbibing several of the one-dollar "Zombie" cocktails that were advertised as "one to a customer." To make matters worse, concessionaires, overwhelmed finally at the masses, had run out of food sometime that afternoon. At nine o'clock, word came down that the parade had been canceled.

Inside the Perisphere, an invited group of tipsy guests made one last pass around Democracity, led by Whalen. As the lights came up for the final time, one of Grover's friends drew a bottle out of his pocket, drained it, and leaned over the diorama's protective railing. He cocked his arm as if to smash it into the center of Henry Dreyfuss's utopian vision of America. Whalen, more than a bit tipsy himself at this point, threw his arms around him and held his buddy in a bear hug.

"Good old Grover," his friend said, grinning. The two men looked at each other a moment, then embraced again and walked down the Helicline arm in arm, simultaneously giddy and despondent.

As if it had a mind of its own (and a sense of humor to match), the New York World's Fair, a study in irony if ever there was one, declared for itself one final, victorious prank. On Opening Day, Albert Einstein had flicked a switch that blew out all the lights; at seven forty-five on Closing Day, a similar power failure struck the Great White Way, leaving most of it in darkness and stranding seven benches on the Parachute Jump in midair. The last of its passengers were eventually lowered by manual power, the workers slowly winching them back down to safety, and the ride was closed for good.

When the power came back on an hour later, the final Aquacade show began. Billy Rose stepped out into the spotlight and made a farewell speech. The man you should be thanking for all of this, he said, was Grover Whalen. He then led the audience in singing "Auld Lang Syne."

Perhaps the most dramatic scene of the night, at least publicly, was the grand finale fireworks show at the Lagoon of Nations. It was dedicated, appropriately, to "The Spirit of George Washington," and while the World's Fair band played stirring patriotic melodies, the spectacle of fire, light, water, and aerial bombs played itself out in front of fifty thousand viewers. As if that weren't enough to stir emotions, searchlights swept the sky overhead and then came to rest on the foreign pavilions in the Court of Peace.

The imagery was not lost, especially on those who had family in war-torn Europe, for whom searchlights and night skies held an entirely different meaning. And when the lights settled down to illuminate the British Pavilion—and beyond that Italy, and beyond that Poland; then swept right to flood the space where the USSR had stood, and next to her Czechoslovakia, and next to her Japan; then came full circle to Belgium and France—a hush fell over the crowd. Captain Eugene La Barre lifted his baton, and the band filled in the silence with "The Star-Spangled Banner."

When the music ended, the people, as if on cue, began wandering slowly toward the exits.

At the stroke of midnight, a lone bugler was supposed to play "Taps" from the top of the Helicline, signaling the formal closing of the Fair, but this too was thrown off schedule. By eleven p.m., with most of the exhibits already closed and the crowds streaming out (it was Sunday, after all, and tomorrow was just another workday), he stood, alone and without much of an audience, and played a final, if early, tribute.

It was over.

There were two men who had some final words to say. One was Dave Driscoll, a radio announcer for WOR who was known for his comic ability to speak in gibberish. From the dais at the Court of Peace, now almost empty, he addressed his microphone:

"In this vast amphitheater millions from all the Americas and from all corners of the world have heard addresses by statesmen, Whalen, gravisnas, McAneny, cabishon, Gibson, forbine, and nobility. Here was the pledge of peace which might well have been the fiederness, bedistran, and grodle of this great exposition. Now that pledge is forgotten. Sleedment, twaint, and broint furbish the doldrum all over the world. Alas!"

In short, he had inadvertently summed up the great folly that was the New York World's Fair with language as florid and incomprehensible as the Fair's original intent had been. Behind its beauty, there was a message that had somehow been missed, something of immense importance that no real words could capture. "Have you caught the magnificence of it all?" Whalen had asked a reporter exactly one year before Opening Day. When the newsman responded that, well, no, he hadn't, not quite yet, Whalen nodded. "Of course. Of course. It's too big. It takes time to grasp."

No one could understand it all, really. As he had once noted, in a way it was all too grand an undertaking.

The second set of last words came from Grover Whalen himself. In the late afternoon on the last day, after a "spirited" final lunch at Perylon Hall, he looked out the windows from atop the Hall of Pharmacy at the grand, skyward-reaching Trylon—the finite; and the endless, floating globe of the Perisphere—the infinite; and he spoke with great emotion of that which he had built.

Whalen was thinking of the day, eighteen months ago, when the lights first came on. "It was a crossword puzzle on paper up to that moment," he said, lifting his glass and gesturing out toward the fairgrounds below. "Then the lagoons caught fire and the buildings glowed in color and the trees were lighted with that mercury vapor.

"We dreamed dreams," he said, misty-eyed, "and the dreams all came true. We stimulated the world. We did our best to prove that nations can live in peace and freedom."

His eyes came to rest again on the Trylon and Perisphere, still bright in the October sun.

"I think we're stopping at the right time," he said. "But I've cried more than once, just thinking of it."

After the Fair, Flushing Meadows sat once again as a vast wasteland, lacking the funds to build Robert Moses's "Versailles of America." (© *Bill Cotter, worldsfairphotos.com*)

ASHES TO ASHES

In the end, it was a banker's Fair after all, and the numbers crunching went on for quite some time after the gates were closed for good. Although attendance for the second season was approximately 73 percent of the first—nineteen million as compared with twenty-six million (in round figures)—paid admission revenue in 1940 was only about half that of 1939. So on the one hand, Harvey Gibson's discounts might have cost the Fair about $2.5 million; then again, it's possible that many fewer people might have shown up if the price hadn't been dropped.

Several key facts are worth noting, however.

First, despite Gibson's insistence on promoting the concessionaires' need for business, the Fair grossed $500,000 *less* from these sources under his tenure than when Grover Whalen was in charge, despite the fact that the Fair took a much higher percentage of their profits in 1940.

Second, expenses for Fair-owned operations nearly doubled the second year, owing to such unprofitable new enterprises as the "American Jubilee" and "Streets of Paris" shows. And because of all the layoffs, the Fair eventually spent considerable sums of money for more expensive contract work that had previously been done by Fair employees.

Finally, since the comparison to Chicago's Fair was always on everyone's mind, the simple fact was that A Century of Progress had drawn twenty-two million visitors in 1933 and sixteen million—or exactly 73 percent—in 1934, Elmer or no Elmer.

But whatever the cause, the bottom line was undeniable: From its date of incorporation in 1935 to December 31, 1940, the World's Fair took in around $48 million and spent around $67 million—not including the foreign pavilions and corporate exhibits, which were paid for by their sponsors—a deficit of $19 million. Which meant that the bondholders were paid back an average of about forty cents on the dollar when all was said and done.

Both Gibson and Whalen agreed on one thing, however. Most of the investors were "very happy in their experience with the New York World's Fair," Gibson stated.

"The bonds, which paid forty-eight cents on the dollar," Whalen said, inflating the figures a bit, "were bought by companies that participated in the Fair. Those companies were more than repaid for their investment."

The city itself couldn't make up its mind about the Fair's overall benefit to business. The New York Convention and Visitors Bureau estimated that seven million out-of-towners traveled to the Fair over both seasons, spending around $40 each. Meaning the anticipated $1 billion in new business actually turned out to be only $280 million, still an impressive sum. Theater, nightclub, and restaurant owners weren't quite so thrilled, however, and griped that the competition had robbed them of customers. You just couldn't make everyone happy.

Least of all Robert Moses. In the first weeks after the Fair had closed, he enjoyed going out to the site and watching the wrecking crews do their work. In fact, he seemed almost as happy as he had been when they were clearing out the ash dumps four years earlier. One bright winter afternoon in 1940, strolling around the midway and still laying out park plans in his head, he spotted a concession booth where customers had once tossed baseballs at crockery, three for a nickel. Moses looked around, thought no one was watching, then scooped up an armful of rocks and smashed every last row.

He walked away grinning like a mischievous kid.

But that was before the New York World's Fair Corporation defaulted on its $4 million promise for Flushing Meadows Park. After scaling down his plans significantly, he settled on a few baseball diamonds and bicycle paths and laid out a football field where Futurama once stood. He did, however, finally manage to build his skating rink in the New York City Building; after the war was over, the building became temporary housing for the United Nations until the permanent structure was built along the East River in Manhattan. Then it returned as a skating rink again.

Moses, now disgusted with the whole affair, rarely visited the park. The sight of it left a bad taste in his mouth that would linger for two decades—until 1960, that magical year once envisioned by Futurama, when the prospect of another World's Fair arose and Robert Moses, as its president, set out to fulfill his great dream all over again.

As General Motors had announced, most of Futurama was destroyed, although a few sections of the diorama were preserved and displayed for a while at Rockefeller Center's New York Museum of Science and Industry. But because there was no simulated flight mechanism to whisk viewers over its peaks and valleys, visitors who simply stood and gaped at the now stationary highway system tried hard to remember what all the fuss was about.

Various parts of the Fair wound up all over the place. For several decades, visitors to the Bronx Zoo could still hear "The Sidewalks of New York" being tooted by the blue-and-orange tractor trains, and the sight and sound of them flooded former fairgoers with long-forgotten memories. Sixty of the American Express sightseeing chairs were bought by a resort in Long Beach, Long Island, for transportation along its boardwalk. The Parachute Jump was carefully dismantled and reassembled on the beach at Coney Island, where it continued to lift and drop (and occasionally strand) terrified passengers for years.*

Some of it just wound up in the garbage. In 1943, a reporter strolling

---

* The tower can still be seen there today, minus its benches and parachutes, next to the Brooklyn Cyclones baseball stadium.

along the junk shops of Lafayette Street noticed a large electrical device sitting on top of a scrap heap. He bent down to read the inscription: "Control Board, Fountain Fireworks, Lagoon of Nations."

But of course a lot of the wreckage, as Gibson had predicted and Whalen had feared, wound up in the service of war. The decorative Greyhound buses that had once shuttled future-fixated passengers around the World of Tomorrow were soon carrying draftees away from their hometowns and off to distant army camps. Lumber, electrical equipment, and plumbing fixtures were transported for use in army and navy stations up and down the East Coast. And after it had been stripped of its gypsum covering, the four thousand tons of steel that had gone into the construction of the Trylon and Perisphere went into the making of ships, shell casings, gun forgings, and the like.

In the end, the World's Fair would yield forty thousand tons of salvageable steel; almost all of it would go toward the war effort.

On December 7, 1941, listeners who tuned in to the CBS radio broadcast of the Japanese attack on Pearl Harbor heard a familiar voice: that of H. V. Kaltenborn, narrator of Democracity, telling them that America was now at war. Throughout the conflict, he would become one of its most famous commentators.

On April 15, 1941, Lord Halifax, the British ambassador, presided at a ceremony held at City Hall to honor the detectives who were killed and wounded in the Fourth of July bombing. Expressing his government's "profound thanks and deep respect," he presented Easter Lynch and Jennie Socha with an engraved silver plate.

"In the name of His Majesty's Government in the United Kingdom, I here salute the honored memory of those gallant officers who gave their lives in the public cause," the ambassador said.

Mayor La Guardia, in a statement that left no doubt as to who he thought was responsible, said, "The perpetrator of that crime, the maker of that bomb, the one who placed it there, must have enjoyed it in the same state of mind as the head of a government invading a defenseless Denmark."

Furious at what she considered to be a meaningless gesture, Easter wrote to the queen and told her what she could do with her "kitchen utensil." She never remarried.

In the wake of the explosion, Lieutenant James Pyke issued a report detailing better procedures for the handling and investigations of bombs. Subsequently, the La Guardia–Pyke Bomb Carrier was developed—a vehicle designed "to take a bomb from a congested area to a remote or suburban district and to do so in a manner that will protect the public and the police. In this way it will eliminate the risk that occurred at the World's Fair where an attempt was made to defuse the bomb in place. . . ."

Pyke's innovations, brought about by the heroics of Joe Lynch and Freddy Socha, led to countless improvements in the practice of defusing bombs, saving untold lives in the process.

On the ten-year anniversary of the explosion, Chief of Detectives William Whalen (no relation to Grover) reported that he was still working on the case, that the reward was still in effect, and that his file was "bulging with reports from every corner of the world."

No further arrests were ever made, and the case remains unsolved. On the Fourth of July 1964, a requiem mass was held for Joe Lynch and Freddy Socha in the Vatican Pavilion of the new New York World's Fair. Detective Philip Walsh, who had been a Police Academy classmate of Joe's, stood solemnly in attendance as a plaque was lowered into the ground just outside the New York City Pavilion.

THIS PLAQUE IS DEDICATED TO THE MEMORY OF DETECTIVES JOSEPH J. LYNCH AND FERDINAND A. SOCHA, BOMB AND FORGERY SQUAD, WHO WERE KILLED IN THE LINE OF DUTY WHILE EXAMINING A TIME BOMB TAKEN FROM THE BRITISH PAVILION OF THE WORLD'S FAIR IN FLUSHING MEADOW PARK AT 4:45 P.M. ON JULY 4TH, 1940.

The plaque is still there today. The reward, upped to $26,000, remains in effect.

Because he'd been named a security risk, Albert Einstein was never asked to contribute to the Manhattan Project. In December 1941, shortly after it had been created, one of the project's directors, Vannevar Bush, did ask his advice regarding the separation of isotopes. Einstein happily complied and handwrote a solution to the problem for Frank Aydelotte, the new head of the Institute for Advanced Study in Princeton.

"Einstein asks me to say that if there are other angles of the problem that you want him to develop," Aydelotte wrote in his conveyance of the solution to Bush, ". . . you only need let him know and he will do anything in his power."

But Einstein was never again asked, and he had nothing further to do with the development of the atomic bomb. In March 1945, Leó Szilárd again paid a visit to his friend and even pressed him to write another letter to FDR, this one with the opposite purpose—to dissuade the U.S. government from using the new weapon as a tool to end the war with Japan. This time, his letter was ignored. On August 6, 1945, the first of two atomic bombs was dropped on Hiroshima. When Helen Dukas brought him the news, Einstein, fresh from a nap, hung his head in despair.

"Oh, my God!" he said.

The following summer, in its Fourth of July issue, *Time* magazine featured an illustration of Einstein with a mushroom cloud in the background, the equation $E=mc^2$ superimposed on it. The issue was titled "Cosmoclast Einstein," and the magazine named him as "the father of the bomb."

"Had I known the Germans would not succeed in producing an atomic bomb," he sadly told *Newsweek* in 1947, "I would never have lifted a finger."

Even *Newsweek*'s cover featured Einstein, with the words, "The Man Who Started It All" headlined across it.

In 1954, near the end of his life, he admitted, "I made one great mistake in my life . . . when I signed the letter to President Roosevelt recommending that atom bombs be made."

G rover Whalen, his spirit broken by the calamity of the World's Fair, decided to take a long vacation to the Dominican Republic with Hugh Kelly, Anna's brother, to recuperate at his sugar plantation. "I wanted to go someplace where nobody would know me and where I could get a complete rest," he said, admitting that he felt "quite exhausted, physically and mentally."

After a long sail, the two men spent lazy afternoons on horseback, riding over the forty-thousand-acre plantation every morning and enjoying the sight of wild horses and cowboys. A few weeks into his visit, a herdsman rode up to Whalen, tipped his hat, and floored him with the greeting, "How are you, Commissioner?"

"Commissioner?" Whalen responded.

"Although I was born right here in San Domingo, I went up to New York and joined the cops," the cowboy told him.

"And how did you happen to come back here?"

"Well, when you were police commissioner you fired me," the horseman said, grinning.

"What for?"

"Numbers game."

"Were you guilty?"

The cowboy nodded. "I've been back in this damned hole raising cattle ever since."

The experience "made the Fair seem very far away," Whalen recalled. With renewed vigor, he returned to New York, to his new job at Maison Coty, and even reclaimed his volunteer duties as chairman of the mayor's reception committee. It was as if he were once again the Whalen of old.

In 1942, he organized a parade of half a million men and women, marching up Fifth Avenue (changing his old route so that it passed the headquarters of Coty, of course) in a salute to "New York at War." More than two million turned out to watch, and Whalen made sure the crowd understood that it was going to come off "rain or shine."

It rained.

Whalen continued on as New York City's "official greeter" through the 1950s, finally retiring to his Connecticut estate when it seemed as though the city, and the world, had fewer and fewer dignitaries worth greeting.

//"The little mind, confronted by too great a dream come true, usually has to take its choice between levity and madness," wrote *The New Yorker*, lamenting its own, as well as its native city's, wisecracking approach to the World's Fair. "When we speak flippantly of the miracles of order and beauty so casually wrought by Grover Whalen, it is with secret envy. . . . Life will probably always be like that—the men of vision creating, the little men carping, with terror and amazement in their hearts."

Whalen himself gave the last word on the Fair in 1951, asking, ultimately, what was the only serious and important question that remained to be asked: "Didn't they realize that we created a twelve-hundred-and-sixteen-acre dream city where there had just been a dump before?"

On March 1, 1962, he watched on television as astronaut John Glenn was honored with a ticker tape parade that was being described as reminiscent of Lindbergh's. The following month, on April 20, one day before the Seattle World's Fair opened, Grover Whalen passed away at the age of seventy-five. Robert Moses had just named him honorary chairman of the 1964 New York World's Fair.

Which would end in bankruptcy.

ACKNOWLEDGMENTS

Authors of nonfiction owe a debt of gratitude to a number of people who unselfishly devote their time and energy to the daunting task of seeing a book progress from concept to publication. In my case, that goes double. First and foremost, my thanks go to my vigorously talented agent, Scott Mendel of Mendel Media Group. You'll often hear that such-and-such project never would have happened without someone's input, but it was Scott who first suggested that I could, and should, write this as nonfiction rather than the novel I had originally submitted to him. That suggestion changed my life. His input was always spot-on, and he remains a true career mentor to this day.

As a first-time author, I could not have found a more perfect editor than Jill Schwartzman, who never grew tired of my ceaseless questions and who miraculously understood from the get-go exactly how this book should present itself. Whenever I was deep in the forest of confusion and frustration, she would always point the way home. It takes a hell of an eye and a great amount of talent to be able to do that. My thanks extend to the entire team at Random House and Ballantine: Libby McGuire, Lea Beresford, Becca Shapiro, David Stevenson, Susan Turner, and Dennis Ambrose, among others. All of them are the best at what they do and made this book the best that it could be.

A third big note of thanks must go to a true friend and the most intuitive business leader I have ever worked for, Jonathan Moffly, without whose support I would not have had the opportunity to actually sit down and write. Jonathan saw what this meant to me, and his generosity and patience added immeasurably to my being able to get this done in a timely manner. By extension, my thanks go as well to Jack and Donna Moffly, and to all the Moffly Media staff. The greatest compliment I can give them is that they put up with me. No easy task.

Gabe Perle, who literally wrote the book on publishing, gave me legal advice and an eyewitness account of the World's Fair. I cannot think of this book without the image of him dancing the tango there in 1939.

Several people helped me with the tremendous job of research. Debbie Celia of the Westport, Connecticut, library found numerous journals and obscure books I never could have unearthed on my own. Laura Ruttum and Thomas Lannon helped me navigate through the endless sea of material available at the Manuscripts and Archives division of the New York Public Library. Beth Spinelli of the New York City Police Museum devoted her time to shedding light on the details of the lives and careers of Joe Lynch and Freddy Socha. Mary Lynch Connolly, one of Joe's daughters, was instrumental in getting the whole thing started.

For visual references, I depended in part on the startling images provided by Bill Cotter and his terrific website, worldsfairphotos.com. He has also published several collections of images from both the 1939 and 1964 New York World's Fairs through Arcadia Publishing's "Images of America" series. Bill generously provided several key photographs for this book, and I bought several CDs loaded with fascinating glimpses of many World's Fairs from his site. Jason Kinch used all of his talents as a photographer to make me look reasonably human for my jacket photo, and lent his skill to improve the quality of several historical images throughout.

On a personal note, back to the other person without whom this book would never have been written: my wife, Heather, who, after reading some pages of a novel I had been working on, said to me, "This is what you should be doing." The rest, as they say, is history—in this case literally. She has endured every sacrifice, every writer's mood, and every physical manifestation of stress the human body can create for itself. (I count five as of this writing, and none of them are pretty.)

Finally, a note of thanks to two former professors who gave me the skills way back when: Richard Price, the novelist and screenwriter, who taught me how to write; and Edward Chalfant, the noted biographer of Henry Adams, who taught me how to *read*. Edward offered me solace and support after I confessed to him my abject terror in daring to take on a subject like Albert Einstein. Richard's work continues to haunt me to this day, and I often think of his advice over a seedy diner lunch: "There are stories in everything. The key is to find one and tell it."

Amen, brother.

NOTES AND SOURCES

There exists a multitude of reference material for anyone looking to find more information about the 1939 New York World's Fair. The best and most complete of these is the collection housed at the New York Public Library—literally hundreds of boxes of original documents, memos, minutes of board meetings, and the like. From these, one can extract the sum total of the history of the Fair in facts and dates, but the collection as a whole presents a somewhat detached, corporate picture (as it should, having been donated by the World's Fair Corporation). What was needed to round out this book was color: personal anecdotes, critical perspectives, the day-to-day follies of one of the most extraordinary events to take place in the twentieth century.

On the whole, actual visitor remembrances tended to be muddled by the passage of time, although occasionally a truly interesting detail would emerge. For the most part, then, anecdotal information had to be gleaned from accounts written while the Fair was active. The most helpful of these came from popular periodicals, including but not limited to *The New Yorker, Harper's, The Atlantic Monthly, The Saturday Evening Post, Time*, and *Newsweek*; as well as more obscure professional journals such as the *Kenyon Review, Spring 3100, Parnassus, Perspecta*, and *Vital Speeches of the Day*. Some newer academic journals, including *Design Issues, Cultural Critique*, and *Journal of the Society of Architectural Historians*, provided scholarly insight and analyses in startling detail, even if I did not always agree with the author's point of view. (Some folks had a rather interesting perspective when it came to that narrow slit of an entrance to Futurama, for example.) And notable cynics such as Lewis Mumford needed to be taken with a grain of snark. The New York elite in particular (to me, at least) seemed to have their guns out for Grover Whalen and the World's Fair and led me to believe that no exposition held in their esteemed city would have been good enough.

In researching material for this book, I therefore realized early on that most of the reading had to be done up front, before any serious writing was to begin. I needed to digest the sum total of what had been written and documented about the Fair, and then process those reports, before I could develop a true picture of what it was like to experience that particular place in that particular time. As such, I began by researching *everything*—checking every journal and newspaper account of the same events until it became obvious that at some point one has to stop and say, "Enough!" And out of the checking of multiple sources there also arose an interesting problem: Published accounts of identical events almost never matched exactly; the same with direct quotes, name spellings, and in some cases even the facts themselves. (Case in point: The original police reports of the Fourth of July bombing list different times, statements made, and even the spellings of Detectives "Morlock" and "Socka.")

No doubt this is due to the lack of recording devices available to journalists at the time; most scribbled quotes in shorthand and reported what they remembered hearing and seeing. For this reason, I have chosen to document most direct quotes from a singular source: *The New York Times*, the "paper of record." Therefore, in the following notes you will find an inordinate number of citations from that newspaper. In my retelling of events, however, I never relied on a single journal or account; details from newspapers are retraced from such varying sources as the *Daily News*, the *Herald Tribune*, the *Journal-American*, the *Brooklyn Daily Eagle*, and, for major news events, even *The Washington Post* (for a non–New York perspective).

As for Albert Einstein, my goal was to present a portrait of the man as a human being caught up in extraordinary, and probably exasperating, times. Yet Einstein's native German provides numerous examples of altered quotes relayed in different words even in his biographies and writings. Except in rare cases (as explained in the footnotes), for consistency's sake I've again relied on the *Times'* accounts when it came to reportage. For his speeches, however, I went to the original source: the Albert Einstein Archives at the Hebrew University at Jerusalem. They were most helpful in providing copies of original handwritten documents or typewritten notes edited in Einstein's own scrawl.

As for the notes that follow, I've cited as many quotes and facts as I felt necessary, including broad or controversial statements about the Fair or conclusions drawn after multiple points of view had been considered. The details are there for anyone who wishes to conduct further research, and some suggestions are made when it comes to further reading on the men who created and built the Fair—Grover Whalen in particular. His autobiography, *Mr. New York*, suffers from selective memory, while the all-too-biased press accounts are suspect for their puzzling vitriol. (Even the revered *New Yorker*, in an extensive, two-part profile published in 1951, grafted enormous ears onto his photo simply in order to make him appear foolish.)

Unjustly a forgotten man now, Whalen remains an enigma in the annals of New York City history. I hope I have done him justice.

As to the lives of Joe Lynch and Freddy Socha, the path to uncovering their stories was a bit more tricky. Documenting the everyday activities of ordinary workingmen involves deduction as well as investigation; suffice it to say I've had some rather interesting conversations with members of the NYPD who would prefer that I not bring up their involvement at all. Original documents provided by the New York City Police Museum helped round out their profiles. But I will say that interest in the case is still incredibly high, theories about the perpetrators are numerous, and an odd cloak of secrecy still surrounds a murderous act that at this stage can never be solved.

PROLOGUE: THIS BRIEF PARADISE

xv **On the Fourth of July** For Joe Lynch and Freddy Socha history, see *Spring 3100* (July 1940; July 1942); Mary Hosie, "Victim Answered Call to Fair on His Day Off," *Brooklyn Daily Eagle*, July 5, 1940; "Aftermath of World's Fair

Bombing," *Brooklyn Daily Eagle*, September 18, 2008; Maki Becker, "Remembering Ultimate Sacrifice," (*New York*) *Daily News*, July 25, 2000; and Bernard Whalen, "Easter Lynch," NY Cop Online Magazine, Fall 2002.

xvi **There were security issues** "Notes and Comment," *New Yorker*, July 15, 1939, p. 9.

xvi **nude and nearly nude models** The Fair was of two minds when it came to nudity in the Amusement Zone. On the one hand, Grover Whalen dictated, "No entertainment of the Sally Rand type will be permitted at the Fair": Joseph Mitchell, "Mr. Grover Whalen and the Midway," *New Yorker*, April 3, 1937, p. 22; on the other, the Cuban Village featured a "Miss Nude of 1939" contest: "Mayor Acts to End Nudity at the Fair," *New York Times*, June 3, 1939.

xvii **By June, the bombings turned deadly** "Bombing Is Third Within Two Weeks in City," *New York Times*, July 5, 1940.

xvii **a waste-management project** For a complete history of Flushing Meadows, see Benjamin Miller, *Fat of the Land: Garbage in New York—The Last Two Hundred Years* (New York: Basic Books, 2000), pp. 178–84; Robert Moses, *The Saga of Flushing Meadows* (New York: Triborough Bridge and Tunnel Authority, 1966); and Roger Starr, "The Valley of Ashes: F. Scott Fitzgerald and Robert Moses," *City Journal* (Autumn 1992).

xvii **In a novel** F. Scott Fitzgerald, *The Great Gatsby* (New York: Charles Scribner's Sons, 1980), pp. ix, 23.

xviii **"talks, sees, smells"** *Official Guidebook of the New York World's Fair, 1939* (New York: Exposition Publications, 1939), p. 203.

xviii **"cross-section of today's civilization"** Ibid.

xix **It was called many things** For descriptions and memories of the Fair, see Barbara Cohen, Steven Heller, and Seymour Chwast, *Trylon and Perisphere: The 1939 New York World's Fair* (New York: Harry N. Abrams, 1989), pp. 14–17.

xix **"It was the paradox"** Sidney M. Shalett, "Epitaph for the World's Fair," *Harper's Magazine*, December 1940, pp. 23–24.

xix **"the greatest salesman alive"** "In Mr. Whalen's Image," *Time*, May 1, 1939, p. 72.

xix **"an unforgettable opportunity"** Gardner Harding, "World's Fair New York," *Harper's Magazine*, July 1939, pp. 193–94.

xx **inventing the ticker tape parade** Grover Whalen, *Mr. New York: The Autobiography of Grover Whalen* (New York: Putnam, 1955).

xxi **"recognized on the street"** Elmer Davis, "Barnum in Modern Dress," *Harper's Magazine*, October 1938, p. 454.

xxi **The whole thing lasted** For detailed descriptions and analyses of the World's Fair, see John Peale Bishop, "World's Fair Notes," *Kenyon Review* (Summer 1939): 239–50; Joseph P. Cusker, "The World of Tomorrow: Science, Culture, and Community at the New York World's Fair," in *Dawn of a New Day: The New York World's Fair, 1939/40*, ed. Helen A. Harrison (New York: Queens Museum, 1980); Ed Tyng, *Making a World's Fair* (New York: Vantage Press, 1958), pp. 16–24; and David Gelernter, *1939: The Lost World of the Fair* (New York: Avon Books, 1995).

xxii **He celebrated the milestone** "Einstein Will Mark 60th Year Tomorrow,"

New York Times, March 13, 1939; "Einstein Has Quiet Birthday," *New York Times*, March 15, 1939.

xxii   **"unconditionally refuse"**   Otto Nathan and Heinz Norden, eds., *Einstein on Peace* (New York: Simon & Schuster, 1960), p. 95.

xxiii   **"Our results so far"**   William L. Laurence, "Einstein Sees Key to Universe Near," *New York Times*, March 14, 1939.

xxiii   **"one great mistake"**   Ronald W. Clark, *Einstein: The Life and Times* (New York: Harper Perennial, 2007), p. 752.

xxiii   **"ticking like a clock"**   "Aftermath of World's Fair Bombing," *Brooklyn Daily Eagle*, July 5, 2007.

xxiii   **Joe was in luck**   Mary Hosie, "Victim Answered Call to Fair on His Day Off," *Brooklyn Daily Eagle*, July 5, 1940.

xxiv   **"This is only the beginning"**   "Valentine Warns of More Bombings," *New York Times*, July 12, 1940.

CHAPTER 1: "WHY DON'T YOU DO IT, DADDY?"

4   **One in particular**   For details on Joseph and Jacqueline Shadgen, as well as Edward Roosevelt, see "Blame It on Jacqueline," *New Yorker*, June 26, 1937, p. 16; Davis, "Barnum in Modern Dress," p. 458; and John Bainbridge and St. Clair McKelway, "That Was the New York World's Fair," *New Yorker*, April 19, 1941.

4   **"Mr. Roosevelt"**   Bainbridge and McKelway, "That Was the New York World's Fair."

6   **"Well, what did you learn"**   Ibid.

7   **"Don't get the idea"**   "Blame It on Jacqueline," *New Yorker*.

7   **To date, there had been**   Gardner Harding, "World's Fair 1939: A Preview," *Harper's Magazine*, January 1938, p. 129.

7   **The very first**   For a brief history of World's Fairs, see George R. Leighton, "World's Fairs: From Little Egypt to Robert Moses," *Harper's Magazine*, July 1960; and Harding, "World's Fair 1939: A Preview."

10   **"Why don't you do it, Daddy?"**   "Blame It on Jacqueline," *New Yorker*.

10   **"I first began to think"**   "World's Fair Plan 'Scared' Its Author," *New York Times*, September 24, 1935.

11   **"Ed, this wine storage idea"**   Bainbridge and McKelway, "That Was the New York World's Fair."

11   **"New York lives"**   " 'Father of Fair' Never Visited It," *New York Times*, October 27, 1940.

11   **"I firmly believe"**   "World's Fair Plan 'Scared' Its Author," *New York Times*.

13   **"Flushing Meadows"**   Bainbridge and McKelway, "That Was the New York World's Fair."

14   **a seemingly endless series of luncheons**   Between September 17, 1935, and April 21, 1936, McAneny hosted twenty-three luncheons and ten dinners. New York World's Fair Archives (hereafter referred to as NYWF Archives), B9, F19.

14   **"Mr. Shadgen and Mr. Roosevelt"**   Bainbridge and McKelway, "That Was the New York World's Fair."

15 **"The subject of the site"** "New York to Hold World's Fair in 1939," *New York Times*, September 23, 1935.

16 **"We have a great idea"** Robert A. Caro, *The Power Broker: Robert Moses and the Fall of New York* (New York: Vintage Books, 1974), p. 654.

16 **"My God, that *is* a great idea!"** Ibid.

16 **"I am waiting for another"** Robert Moses, "From Dump to Glory," *Saturday Evening Post*, January 15, 1938, p. 74.

17 **"This was the logical place"** Ibid., p. 13.

17 **"An agreement was made"** Ibid.

17 **"This dream"** Moses, *Saga of Flushing Meadows*.

17 **"The miracle happened"** Ibid.

17 **"from the beginning"** Ibid.

18 **"thirty years of"** Ibid.

18 **"All my predecessors"** "392 More Acres Asked for the Fair," *New York Times*, October 12, 1935.

19 **"Rats"** Ibid.

19 **To his unending regret** In a letter dated April 22, 1936, former governor Al Smith, at the prodding of Robert Moses, wrote to the corporation's board of directors, "The period of debate and discussion must be ended. . . . I suggest that there be no doubt as to the authority given [Whalen]." NYWF Archives, B13, F2.

CHAPTER 2: MR. NEW YORK

22 **His was a curious boyhood** For biographical information on Grover Whalen, see Whalen, *Mr. New York*; Geoffrey T. Hellman, "For City and for Coty—I & II," *New Yorker*, July 14, 1951, and July 21, 1951, pp. 28–45; and Davis, "Barnum in Modern Dress."

22 **"My father started out"** Whalen, *Mr. New York*, p. 7.

23 **"My father was so grieved"** Ibid., p. 9.

23 **"I remember one house"** Ibid., p. 8.

24 **"I came to know"** Ibid., p. 22.

25 **There was more to do** For background on Whalen and Mayor John Hylan, see Davis, "Barnum in Modern Dress."

25 **"They sent for Mr. Lynn"** Whalen, *Mr. New York*, p. 26.

26 **"John F. Hylan may not be"** Ibid., p. 27.

26 **"He advised me"** Ibid., p. 33.

27 **"The various parades"** Ibid., p. 82.

27 **"I organized"** Ibid., p. 90.

27 **invented the ticker tape parade** "Hello & Goodbye," *Time*, April 27, 1962.

27 **"The Whalen welcomes"** Alva Johnston, "The Gilded Copper," *New Yorker*, January 12, 1929, p. 24.

28 **"Red Mike"** "Tammany Test," *Time*, July 8, 1929.

28 **"But I wouldn't want"** Johnston, "Gilded Copper," p. 23.

CHAPTER 3: A VOLUNTARY EXILE

31 **would assassinate Einstein** "Urged Murder of Einstein, Pays $16 Fine in Berlin Court," *New York Times*, April 8, 1921.

31 **"haven where scholars and scientists"** Clark, *Einstein: The Life and Times*.

32 **"Could I live on less?"** Ibid.

32 **"I am not abandoning Germany"** Walter Isaacson, *Einstein: His Life and Universe* (New York: Simon & Schuster, 2007), p. 398.

32 **"Sometimes the Americans"** " 'Nice People, Those Americans,' Says Einstein, Landing in Holland," *New York Times*, April 5, 1932.

32 **"Before you leave our villa"** Clark, *Einstein: The Life and Times*, p. 549.

33 **"Gone was the flustered"** Nathan and Norden, eds., *Einstein on Peace*, p. 124.

33 **"Do they think I am a prizefighter?"** Alva Johnston, "Scientist and Mob Idol—I," *New Yorker*, December 2, 1933, p. 24.

33 **"The Einstein of 1933"** Ibid.

33 **"Never before have I experienced"** Isaacson, *Einstein: His Life and Universe*, p. 400.

34 **"What is your political creed?"** "Einstein's Ultimatum Brings a Quick Visa; Our Consul Angered Him by Political Quiz," *New York Times*, December 6, 1932.

34 **"If we don't get that visa"** "Women Made Complaint," *New York Times*, December 6, 1932.

35 **"Wouldn't it be funny"** Ibid.

35 **"absolute pacifist"** Clark, *Einstein: The Life and Times*.

36 **"It has been assumed"** "Einstein's Address on World Situation," *New York Times*, January 24, 1933.

37 **"[I do] not intend"** "Einstein to Alter Status," *New York Times*, March 30, 1933.

37 **"Germany's contribution"** "Einstein Honored at Dinner Here," *New York Times*, March 16, 1933.

37 **"I decided today"** Nathan and Norden, eds., *Einstein on Peace*, p. 155.

38 **"But where the danger"** "Dr. Einstein Urges Hitler Protests," *New York Times*, March 17, 1933.

38 **"What do you think of pacifists"** Ibid.

38 **its firm stance on isolationism** One of the most profound analyses of 1930s isolationist America can be found in Raoul de Roussy de Sales's "What Makes an American," *Atlantic Monthly*, March 1939.

39 **he improvised ugly melodies** Alva Johnston, "Scientist and Mob Idol—II," *New Yorker*, December 3, 1933, p. 29.

39 **"A conflict between"** "Einstein Departs; Women Cheer Him," *New York Times*, March 19, 1933.

40 **"The raid on the home"** Clark, *Einstein: The Life and Times*, p. 562; "Nazis Hunt Arms in Einstein Home," *New York Times*, March 21, 1933.

40 **"Long live Einstein!"** "Einstein Foresees Dangers for Jews," *New York Times*, March 29, 1933.

40 **Two days after** "Nazis Seize Einstein's Funds in German Bank; Academy Refuses to 'Regret' His Resignation," *New York Times*, April 2, 1933.

40 **"a mass psychosis"** Clark, *Einstein: The Life and Times*, p. 569.

40 **"Surely there will come a time"** Nathan and Norden, eds., *Einstein on Peace*, p. 217.

41 **"All I ask"** "Einstein's Plan to Lecture Here Unaffected by Post in Madrid," *New York Times*, April 12, 1933.

41 **"What I shall tell you"** Nathan and Norden, eds., *Einstein on Peace*, p. 229.

41 **"It is beyond me"** Ibid., pp. 234–35.

41 **"Hitler's methods may be insane"** Ibid., p. 230.

41 **"Can you possibly be unaware"** Ibid., p. 231.

42 **he listed his address as *"ohne"*** "Commons to Rush Einstein Measure," *New York Times*, July 30, 1933.

42 **"When a bandit"** "Einsteins Plan Cruise," *New York Times*, September 9, 1933.

43 **"Be on your guard"** "Einstein, Guarded, Addresses 10,000," *New York Times*, October 4, 1933.

43 **"We must realize"** Ibid.

43 **"I am European by instinct"** "Einstein in Refuge on English Coast," *New York Times*, September 11, 1933.

43 **he remained in his cabin** "Einstein Is Silent on Ship at Halifax," *New York Times*, October 16, 1933.

44 **"He and Mrs. Einstein"** "Einstein Arrives; Pleads for Quiet," *New York Times*, October 18, 1933.

CHAPTER 4: THE GARDENIA OF THE LAW

47 **They weren't entirely wrong** For background on NYPD graft, gambling, and gangsters from 1910 to 1920, see Mike Dash, *Satan's Circus: Murder, Vice, Police Corruption and New York's Trial of the Century* (New York: Crown Publishers, 2007).

48 **Up for reelection** For details on Mayor Jimmy Walker and Arnold Rothstein, see Nick Tosches, *King of the Jews* (New York: Ecco, 2005).

48 **"I've got to make a change"** Whalen, *Mr. New York*, pp. 133–34.

49 **Whalen took office** For details on Whalen's term as police commissioner, see Johnston, "The Gilded Copper," pp. 21–24; Elmer Davis, "Our Island Universe: Reflections of a Resident of Manhattan," *Harper's Magazine*, November 1929, pp. 682–87; and Davis, "Barnum in Modern Dress," pp. 453–63.

49 **"the best on the market"** Davis, "Barnum in Modern Dress."

49 **"I'll have no use for that"** "Whalen Begins Shake-Up, Ousting Two Inspectors; Will War on Speakeasies," *New York Times*, December 20, 1928.

49 **"The city is in for"** "Whalen Abolishes the Homicide Squad; Carey Is Forced Out," *New York Times*, December 22, 1928.

49 **A newspaper cartoon** "In Room 349," *Time*, December 24, 1928.

49 **"He loves to design uniforms"** Davis, "Barnum in Modern Dress."

50 **"the two men responsible"** Whalen, *Mr. New York*, p. 144.

50 **"strong-arm squad"** "Whalen Spurs Raids on Speakeasies That Sell Poi-

son Liquor," *New York Times,* January 3, 1929; "Strong-Arm Corps Revived by Whalen to War on Crime; Policewomen Told to Aid," *New York Times,* December 27, 1928.

50 **"I told them"** "Whalen Begins Shake-Up," *New York Times.*

50 **"I want every"** Ibid.

50 **He also got rid** "New York's Whalen," *Time,* January 7, 1929.

50 **"A record of that kind"** Ibid.

50 **"certain major cases"** "Mayer Now Leads Search for Biller," *New York Times,* December 25, 1928.

50 **"There are certain types of places"** "Whalen Begins Shake-Up," *New York Times.*

50 **thirty-two thousand** "Buck-Passing," *Time,* September 9, 1929.

51 **several dubious films** Ibid.

51 **"poison liquor"** "Notes and Comment," *New Yorker,* January 12, 1929, p. 10.

51 **Just after New Year's** "Whalen Spurs Raids," *New York Times.*

51 **"those that sold a drink"** Davis, "Our Island Universe."

51 **"It seemed evident"** Whalen, *Mr. New York,* p. 150.

51 **"Red infiltration"** Ibid.

51 **frequently so violent** "The Week," *New Republic,* March 19, 1930, p. 110.

51 **"Mr. Whalen declared"** Davis, "Our Island Universe."

CHAPTER 5: NEW YORK WORLD'S FAIR, INC.

55 **"Well, we won the election"** Whalen, *Mr. New York,* p. 164.

55 **"would tolerate no interference"** Ibid., p. 138.

55 **"I lost his friendship"** Ibid.

56 **"This isn't Wanamaker's"** "Mulrooney for Whalen," *Time,* June 2, 1930.

56 **"It was your devotion"** Ibid.

56 **he had spent countless hours** "Be Seated!" *Time,* February 4, 1929.

56 **"Gardenia of the Law"** "In Mr. Whalen's Image," *Time.*

57 **"nineteen thirty-four"** Whalen, *Mr. New York,* p. 173.

57 **In the summer of 1935** For background on the World's Fair Corporation, see "Great World Fair for City in 1939 on Site in Queens," *New York Times,* September 23, 1935; Hellman, "For City and for Coty I & II"; and Bainbridge and McKelway, "That Was the New York World's Fair."

58 **managed to turn a small profit** For initial estimates regarding the Chicago World's Fair, see "Fair Investment Set at $45,000,000," *New York Times,* March 3, 1936.

58 **brought about $770 million worth** Shalett, "Epitaph for the World's Fair."

58 **On October 22** "Fair Papers Are Drawn," *New York Times,* October 20, 1935.

58 **"probably the most eminent group"** Harding, "World's Fair 1939: A Preview," p. 135.

58 **"The corporation is not organized"** "1939 World's Fair Now a Legal Fact," *New York Times,* October 23, 1935.

59 **"We had to find an idea"** S. J. Woolf, "The Man Behind the Fair Tells How It Grew," *New York Times*, March 5, 1939.

59 **"If the Galoshes Hall"** Bruce Bliven Jr., "Fair Tomorrow," *New Republic*, December 7, 1938, p. 121.

59 **"You had to have the soul"** Harding, "World's Fair 1939: A Preview."

60 **the desired minimum of fifty million** Minutes of the Promotion Council, January 24, 1938, NYWF Archives, B1, F7.

60 **"After we had the basic idea"** Woolf, "Man Behind the Fair."

60 **"That word, 'future' "** Ibid.

61 **a better life to come** "A World's Fair on New Lines," November 30, 1936, NYWF Archives, B9, F19.

61 **"It is evident that"** Bernard Lichtenberg, "Business Backs New York World's Fair to Meet the New Deal Propaganda," *Public Opinion Quarterly* (April 1938): 314–20.

61 **"compelling cause for hope"** Ibid.

61 **"the necessity of defending itself"** Gardner Ainsworth, "The New York Fair: Adventure in Promotion," *Public Opinion Quarterly* (October 1939): 695.

62 **"I wouldn't engage anyone"** Woolf, "Man Behind the Fair."

62 **"world war or World's Fair"** Forrest Davis, "Money Makes the Fair Go," *Saturday Evening Post*, April 15, 1939, p. 37.

63 **"I haven't the slightest idea"** "Navigable River to Pierce Fair Site," *New York Times*, September 26, 1935.

63 **In fact, the city** "392 More Acres Asked for the Fair," *New York Times*, October 12, 1935.

63 **"one step ahead of the lawyers"** "City Votes $200,000 for Early Fair Work," *New York Times*, October 24, 1935.

63 **"there has not been"** "1939 World's Fair Now a Legal Fact," *New York Times*.

63 **"The more I have thought"** "Navigable River to Pierce Fair Site," *New York Times*.

63 **"This is to be"** "City Votes $200,000," *New York Times*.

64 **"It was the judgment"** "Great World Fair for City in 1939," *New York Times*.

64 **From the beginning** For details on Robert Moses's involvement in the reclamation of Flushing Meadows, see Moses, "From Dump to Glory"; Moses, *Saga of Flushing Meadows;* and Starr, "Valley of Ashes: F. Scott Fitzgerald and Robert Moses."

64 **"the only site in New York"** Moses, "From Dump to Glory," p. 72.

65 **"A fighter of quick temper"** Cleveland Rogers, "Robert Moses," *Atlantic Monthly*, February 1939.

65 **The son of** For further biographical detail on Moses, see Caro, *The Power Broker;* Hilary Ballon and Kenneth T. Jackson, eds., *Robert Moses and the Modern City: The Transformation of New York* (New York: W. W. Norton, 2008).

66 **Nevertheless, he remained** For works by Moses, see Robert Moses, *Public Works: A Dangerous Trade* (New York: McGraw-Hill, 1970); Moses, "The Limits of Government," *Saturday Evening Post*, October 12, 1935; Moses,

"The End of Santa Claus," *Saturday Evening Post*, June 27, 1936; and Moses, "Slums and City Planning," *Atlantic Monthly*, January 1945.

66 **"Bob Moses is"**   Rogers, "Robert Moses."

66 **"If this Moses scheme"**   Hubert Herring, "Robert Moses and His Parks," *Harper's Magazine*, December 1937, p. 29.

67 **"Can't you realize"**   Ibid., p. 28.

67 **"The minute you put"**   Ibid., p. 26.

68 **"Robert Moses is a good man"**   Ibid., p. 36.

68 **"His most ferocious attacks"**   Herbert Kaufman, "Robert Moses: Charismatic Bureaucrat," *Political Science Quarterly* (Autumn 1975).

68 **Since January**   For details of Moses's various governmental battles, see "Robert (Or I'll Resign) Moses," *Fortune*, June 1938; and Rogers, "Robert Moses."

69 **"He acknowledged no one"**   Kaufman, "Robert Moses: Charismatic Bureaucrat."

69 **"too expensive"**   "Park No Place for Art Museum and 40-Cent Coffee, Moses Says," *New York Times*, March 12, 1935.

69 **"before he becomes a Mussolini"**   "Court Sees Moses in 'Mussolini' Role," *New York Times*, April 4, 1935.

69 **He followed that**   "Moses Defends Inwood Park Road," *New York Times*, March 23, 1935.

69 **"You tell him for me"**   "La Guardia Vexed by Moses Threat over Bridge Post," *New York Times*, June 29, 1935.

70 **It was one of the nicer**   For details on the Moses/La Guardia showdowns, see Caro, *The Power Broker*, pp. 446–67.

70 **On November 20**   For details on the original board of directors of New York World's Fair, Inc., see "McAneny Elected World's Fair Head," *New York Times*, November 21, 1935.

70 **In December, he warned**   "Moses Asks Speed in Plans for Fair," *New York Times*, December 24, 1935.

70 **"adopt an alternative plan"**   "Moses Again Warns of World's Fair Delay," *New York Times*, January 25, 1936.

71 **The Fair would proceed**   "Expects Millions at Fair," *New York Times*, January 31, 1936.

71 **Still unsatisfied**   "Moses Urges Grading on Fair Site and City Land Purchase at Once," *New York Times*, February 29, 1936.

71 **Whether or not it was true**   Ibid.

72 **At the end of March**   "Fair Halted by Delay in Grants," *New York Times*, March 24, 1936.

72 **"The loss of time"**   "No Fair Till 1940, Moses Now Fears," *New York Times*, May 1, 1936.

73 **the directors voted Grover Whalen**   "Whalen at Helm of World's Fair," *New York Times*, April 23, 1936.

73 **"Execution, rather than promotion"**   Ibid.

73 **He had already switched gears**   "Moses to Ignore World Fair Plans," *New York Times*, March 27, 1936.

74 **"despite scare headlines"** "World's Fair Funds Voted by Board," *New York Times*, May 2, 1936.

74 **"Do you mean that"** Ibid.

74 **"From the beginning"** Ibid.

CHAPTER 6: THE $8 MURDER

77 **"I started that"** "Whalen Reviews His Year in Office," *New York Times*, December 18, 1929.

78 **At a little after one o'clock** "Woman Is Slain in 'Village' Store," *New York Times*, November 27, 1937.

79 **When she finally** "Youth Admits Killing Woman Shopkeeper," *New York Times*, December 2, 1937.

79 **Then Martha grabbed** Ibid.

80 **At a little after four o'clock** "Woman Is Slain," *New York Times*.

81 **One detective posited** Ibid.

81 **On December 29** "Woman Hit with Cane Wins $500," *New York Times*, April 20, 1933.

82 **Steadying himself** "Youth Admits Killing," *New York Times*.

83 **Anna Tanzola identified** "Youth Sought in Slaying," *New York Times*, November 28, 1937.

83 **Without naming Healy** "Suspect in Killing Described," *New York Times*, November 29, 1937.

84 **Healy didn't show** "Youth Admits Killing," *New York Times*.

84 **Two days later** "Girl Wife Is Freed," *New York Times*, December 4, 1937.

84 **A grand jury** "Youth Indicted in Killing," *New York Times*, December 9, 1937.

85 **He would spend** "Changes Plea to Guilty," *New York Times*, June 24, 1939.

CHAPTER 7: WHY HAVE A FAIR?

87 **While all the controversy** For detailed information on the World's Fair design, concept, and development, see Pieter Van Wesemael, "New York World's Fair or 'Building the World of Tomorrow,'" in *Architecture of Instruction and Delight* (Rotterdam: 010 Publishers, 2001), pp. 445–558. Long out of print (but available from Amazon.com resellers and searchable via Google Books), this academic analysis provides startling details about the artistic development of the World's Fair. Also: Eugene A. Santomasso, "The Design of Reason: Architecture and Planning at the 1939/40 New York World's Fair," in *Dawn of a New Day: The New York World's Fair, 1939/40*, ed. Helen A. Harrison (New York: Queens Museum, 1980), pp. 29–42; and Larry Zim, Mel Lerner, and Herbert Rolfes, *The World of Tomorrow: The 1939 New York World's Fair* (New York: Harper & Row, 1988).

87 **In December 1935** Fair of the Future, NYWF Archives C 1.0.

88 **"If we allow ourselves"** Address to the New York Civic Club by Lewis Mumford, December 11, 1935, NYWF Archives PR 1.41.

88 **Taking the basic subtext** Michael Hare, "Why Have a Fair?" December 22, 1936, NYWF Archives PR 1.41.

88 **Industrial designers such as Teague** Roland Marchand, "The Designers Go to the Fair: Walter Dorwin Teague and the Professionalization of Corporate Industrial Exhibits, 1933–40," *Design Issues* (Autumn 1991): 4–17.

88 **the new style of streamlining** Norman Bel Geddes, "Streamlining," *Atlantic Monthly*, November 1934, pp. 553–63.

88 **were suddenly streamlined and bullet-shaped** Donald J. Bush, "Streamlining and American Industrial Design," *Leonardo* (Autumn 1974): 309–17.

89 **This committee** Fair of the Future, NYWF Archives C 1.0.

89 **their proposal was quickly adopted** Report of the Theme Committee, July 16, 1936, NYWF Archives A 1.13.

89 **Its general stated purpose** "Rival Art Groups Battle over Fair," *New York Times*, March 1, 1936.

89 **"If this World's Fair"** Ibid.

90 **"What are we going to do"** Ibid.

90 **"There is a way"** Ibid.

90 **"If the 1939 Fair"** Ibid.

91 **"Anyone who introduces"** Ibid.

91 **Impressed with Whalen's speed** "Whalen Elected President of Fair," *New York Times*, May 5, 1936.

91 **"headquarters will be established"** Ibid.

91 **notoriously bad reputation** Donald Moffat, "Mr. Pennyfeather on Manhattan," *Atlantic Monthly*, April 1936, pp. 385–94.

91 **"The big town"** Davis, "Money Makes the Fair Go."

92 **"We knew that our town"** Davis, "Our Island Universe."

92 **"So of civic pride"** Ibid.

93 **"A New Yorker is inclined"** Davis, "Money Makes the Fair Go."

93 **"It is infinitely"** Ibid.

93 **"to portray New York"** Davis, "Barnum in Modern Dress."

94 **"It is just like New York"** "Notes and Comment," *New Yorker*, January 4, 1936, p. 9.

94 **a gardenia-wearing stuffed shirt** "$156,000,000 Show: Eleven Gates Ready to Swing at the N.Y. World's Fair," *Newsweek*, May 1, 1939, p. 49.

95 **"The fashion amongst"** Davis, "Money Makes the Fair Go."

95 **"twentieth-century Barnum"** Ibid.

CHAPTER 8: 106 DEGREES IN THE SHADE

97 **"Time is of the essence"** "Two Low Fair Bids Rejected by Moses," *New York Times*, June 5, 1936.

97 **"I refuse"** "Moses Wins Fight for Fair Contract," *New York Times*, June 10, 1936.

98 **"The city cannot"** "Mayor Calls Police to Halt Razing of Ferry by Moses," *New York Times*, July 23, 1936.

98 **"All is quiet"** "Ferry Row Over, Service Resumed," *New York Times*, July 24, 1936.

98 **"the sun was hidden"** "Site Is Dedicated for World's Fair," *New York Times*, June 4, 1936.

99   **"the ground upon which"**   "La Guardia Runs a Steam Shovel as Work Starts on World's Fair," *New York Times*, June 30, 1936.

99   **"This is the way"**   Ibid.

100   **Already, crews**   For further details on the actual reclamation process, see Moses, "From Dump to Glory"; "Fair Bonds," *Time*, November 23, 1936; Victor H. Bernstein, "Dump and Swamp Areas Reclaimed for Fair," *New York Times*, August 16, 1936.

100   **"The scene there"**   "World's Fair Project in Construction Stage," *New York Times*, July 5, 1936.

101   **In July 1936**   "7 Die in and Near City," *New York Times*, July 10, 1936.

103   **"No flimsy riprap"**   Moses, "From Dump to Glory."

CHAPTER 9: PANIC IN TIMES SQUARE

107   **At first, the combined teams**   "Eight Detectives Moved in Shake-Up," *New York Times*, October 6, 1935.

107   **For the better part**   "Detectives Begin Cryptography Study," *New York Times*, February 12, 1935.

108   **Lieutenant James Pyke**   Richard Esposito and Ted Gerstein, *Bomb Squad: A Year Inside the Nation's Most Exclusive Police Unit* (New York: Hyperion, 2007), pp. 277–86.

108   **Hayias had refused**   "Lieut. Pyke Frees, Aids Relief Forger," *New York Times*, September 20, 1936.

110   **"I wouldn't arrest these people"**   Ibid.

111   **Socha, seeing another group**   "Windows Wrecked in Cleaners' Strike," *New York Times*, October 20, 1935.

111   **The boring part**   "K. of C. Sweepstakes Promoters Arrested on Mail Fraud Charge," *New York Times*, March 3, 1936.

111   **They also held**   "39 Seized in Raids on Race Tip Offices," *New York Times*, November 4, 1938.

111   **advanced to detective, second grade**   "9 Detectives Promoted," *New York Times*, December 25, 1937.

112   **In October, he got his name**   "3 Seized in Theft of City Tax Stamps," *New York Times*, October 20, 1938.

112   **Throughout the city**   "Theatre Is Bombed," *New York Times*, August 31, 1935; "Tear Gas Exploded in Six Theatres Again," *New York Times*, November 3, 1936.

112   **On one particular Thursday**   "225 Police in Hunt for Bombers Ring," *New York Times*, November 4, 1936.

113   **At three a.m.**   "Bombs Shatter Windows of 7 Fur Shops; West 29th St. Blasts Laid to Labor Trouble," *New York Times*, September 12, 1938.

113   **"I want thirty thousand"**   "Dynamiter Is Foiled in Hold-up of Bank; 31 Sticks of Explosive and Caps Are Seized," *New York Times*, September 9, 1938.

114   **"These bombs are crudely"**   "Roosevelt Aids Inquiry on Bombs," *New York Times*, April 13, 1936.

114   **he began devising a method**   James A. Pyke, "Some Notes on the Han-

dling of Suspected Bombs and the Investigation of Explosions," *Journal of Criminal Law and Criminology* (March/April 1942): 668–74.

CHAPTER 10: SELLING THE FAIR

117 **a salary of $100,000 a year** Ruth Brindze, "Grover Whalen's Mammoth Circus," *Nation*, December 10, 1938, p. 616.

117 **Board of Design** Tyng, *Making a World's Fair*, p. 25.

117 **"the definition of the main theme"** "Board of Design Is Named for Fair," *New York Times*, May 22, 1936.

118 **"The principal difference"** Woolf, "Man Behind the Fair," p. 15.

118 **"I wouldn't engage anyone"** Ibid., p. 3.

119 **"The New York World's Fair"** Report of the Board of Design, July 7, 1936, NYWF Archives, B2, F14.

119 **"I have now come to"** "Moses Quits Fair, But Split Is Denied," *New York Times*, October 9, 1936.

120 **"no difference of opinion"** Ibid.

121 **"I speak sincerely"** "Says Fair Bonds Are Sound," *New York Times*, December 22, 1936.

121 **"We believe"** Ibid.

122 **"If by some mischance"** "$460,000 Fair Bonds Bought by Macy's," *New York Times*, January 11, 1937.

122 **"Among other things"** "Truck Driver Buys $400 World's Fair Bond," *New York Times*, January 5, 1937.

124 **"conduct apparently contrary"** "Whitney & Co. Fails; Exchange Ex-Head Faces 3 Inquiries," *New York Times*, March 9, 1938.

125 **"The telephone operator"** Whalen, *Mr. New York*, p. 179.

126 **"The log jam was broken"** Ibid., p. 180.

126 **"I took the next ship over"** Ibid.

126 **"I called on"** Hellman, "For City and for Coty II."

127 **"As I entered"** Whalen, *Mr. New York*, p. 186.

127 **"I understand you served"** Ibid., p. 187.

127 **"Italy compete with Wall Street?"** Hellman, "For City and for Coty II."

127 **"The American people"** Whalen, *Mr. New York*, p. 188.

128 **"I said that participation"** Hellman, "For City and for Coty II."

CHAPTER 11: "FOLKS, YOU AIN'T SEEN NOTHING YET!"

131 **"We promised the world"** " 'Floating' Sphere to Dominate Fair," *New York Times*, March 16, 1937.

132 **"Wouldn't a European war"** Richard O. Boyer, "World of Tomorrow, Or Next Day," *New Yorker*, April 30, 1938, p. 38.

133 **"My personal investigation"** Ibid.

133 **"It is the hope"** "Whalen Returns, Hopeful for Peace," *New York Times*, September 14, 1937.

133 **could potentially charm the dictators** John T. Flynn, "World Peace for the World's Fair," *New Republic*, March 2, 1938, p. 100.

133 **"Next thing you know"** "Indignant Ambassador," *Time*, January 17, 1938.

134 **a different kind of "ball and bat"** Minutes of the promotion council, April 4, 1939, NYWF Archives, B1, F7.

134 **"I saw no reason"** Woolf, "Man Behind the Fair."

134 **"Only the brave"** "City Fair Building Gets Cornerstone," *New York Times*, January 20, 1938.

134 **"the peoples of the nations"** "Fair Starts Work on Theme Center," *New York Times*, April 9, 1938.

135 **World's Fair Preview** "235 Parades," *New Yorker*, April 30, 1938, p. 12.

137 **"The day was a big success"** "Fireworks Dazzle 600,000 at Fair Site," *New York Times*, May 9, 1938.

137 **"you ain't seen nothing yet!"** "Three-Hour 'Preview' Motorcade Gives City Glimpse of 1939 Fair," *New York Times*, May 1, 1938.

CHAPTER 12: "THEY COME WITH JOYOUS SONG"

143 **"ball and spike"** "Ball & Spike," *Time*, May 9, 1938.

143 **a vision of heaven** "Theme Center Idea Symbol of Heaven," *New York Times*, July 8, 1939.

143 **"Barnum had his sacred"** "Ball & Spike," *Time*.

143 **"Democracity"** For details on this exhibit, see Jeffrey Hart, "The Last Great Fair," *New Criterion*, January 2005, pp. 76–77; and "Stanley in the Perisphere," *New Yorker*, April 15, 1939, pp. 16–17.

148 **inaugural gate of over one million** "Fair Facts," *Time*, May 15, 1939.

148 **between $150 and $1,000** Daniel Lang, "Ike and Mike on the Air," *New Republic*, May 17, 1939, p. 43.

152 **"an internal war"** Franklin D. Roosevelt, "Opening of the New York World's Fair," April 30, 1939, in John T. Woolley and Gerhard Peters, *The American Presidency Project* [online], Santa Barbara: University of California (hosted), Gerhard Peters (database), accessed at www.presidency.ucsb.edu/ws/?pid=15755.

153 **"As a nation"** "Hull Warns World in Plea for Peace," *New York Times*, February 13, 1939.

CHAPTER 13: BLACKOUT

157 **"victim of the greatest con game"** "Attack on Fair Made in Council," *New York Times*, April 4, 1939.

158 **"from all employment"** "Negroes Protest to Fair," *New York Times*, March 16, 1939.

158 **"I know that you people"** "World's Fair Bans Bias Against Negro," *New York Times*, January 25, 1937.

158 **"the specific article"** Robert W. Rydell, "Selling the World of Tomorrow: New York's 1939 World's Fair," *Journal of American History* (December 1990): 968.

159 **the Fair itself was of two minds** Mentor A. Howe, "Come to the Fair!" *Phylon* 1, no. 4 (1940): 314–22.

159 **"lighter than last week's"** "Light Auto Traffic Surprise to Police," *New York Times*, May 1, 1939.

161 **"sad note, slightly morbid"** "Crowds Awed by Fair's Vastness and Medley of Sound and Color," *New York Times*, May 1, 1939.

161 **rejection of true science** Peter J. Kuznick, "Losing the World of Tomorrow: The Battle over the Presentation of Science at the 1939 New York World's Fair," *American Quarterly* (September 1994): 341–73.

161 **The plan was to "capture"** For a detailed analysis of the cosmic rays display, see Waldemar Kaempffert, "Science in the News," *New York Times*, April 30, 1939.

162 **"I'm very sorry"** "Einstein in New Triumph," *New York Times*, May 1, 1939.

162 **"I just apologized"** Archival newsreel, Movietone News, Inc., April 30, 1939, from "The World of Tomorrow," Tom Johnson and Lance Bird, prods. (CA: Direct Cinema Limited, 1992).

162 **"If science, like art"** Albert Einstein, "On Cosmic Rays," April 30, 1939, Albert Einstein Archives, 1–134.00. (Note: The handwritten text, heavily edited and with entire paragraphs penciled out, reveals exactly how Einstein struggled to accommodate his audience and his five-minute time limit.)

163 **"If a metallic conductor"** Ibid.

163 **"Give us ten cosmic rays!"** "Cosmic Rays Start Brilliant Display," *New York Times*, May 1, 1939.

163 **Einstein threw the switch** "156,000,000 Show," *Newsweek*, May 1, 1939, p. 46.

164 **"One they could applaud"** "Cosmic Rays," *New York Times*.

165 **fewer than two hundred thousand** Shalett, "Epitaph for the World's Fair."

165 **the numbers had been fudged** "Fair Facts," *Time*.

165 **"[Whalen] has got the circus"** "In Mr. Whalen's Image," *Time*.

CHAPTER 14: "I HAVE SEEN THE FUTURE"

167 **"I hadn't reckoned on"** Hellman, "For City and for Coty II."

168 **"the stupendous"** Boyer, "World of Tomorrow, Or Next Day."

168 **"I rejoice"** Hellman, "For City or for Coty II."

168 **"My father himself"** Ibid.

168 **"The trouble is"** Boyer, "World of Tomorrow, Or Next Day."

169 **"Think of this huge ball"** Ibid.

171 **Futurama was the dream** For details about Norman Bel Geddes and Futurama's design, construction, and experience, see Roland Marchand, "The Designers Go to the Fair II: Norman Bel Geddes, the General Motors 'Futurama,' and the Visit to the Factory Transformed," *Design Issues* (Spring 1992): 23–40; Christina Cogdell, "The Futurama Recontextualized: Norman Bel Geddes's Eugenic 'World of Tomorrow,'" *American Quarterly* (June 2000): 193–245; Robert Coombs, "Norman Bel Geddes: Highways and Horizons," *Perspecta* 13 (1971): 11–27; Adnan Morshed, "The Aesthetics of Ascension in

Norman Bel Geddes' Futurama," *Journal of the Society of Architectural Historians* (March 2004): 74–99; and Paul Mason Fotsch, "The Building of a Superhighway Future at the New York World's Fair," *Cultural Critique* (Spring 2001): 65–97.

171 **"His head is in the clouds"** Geoffrey T. Hellman, "Design for Living—I," *New Yorker*, February 8, 1941, p. 24.

171 **an expert on the future** Geddes also predicted that "car speed control will probably be by button on the wheel. . . . You will drive at forty or fifty or sixty or thirty, according to the button you push." Norman Bel Geddes, "What the Future Holds for Us," speech before the *New York Herald Tribune* Forum, October 26, 1939.

172 **"Can General Motors afford"** Geoffrey T. Hellman, "Design for Living—III," *New Yorker*, February 22, 1941, p. 29.

172 **"It cost us six million"** Ibid.

174 **"Now we have arrived"** Narration of Futurama taken from original recordings and "Futurama" promotional booklet produced by General Motors Corp.

177 **"the future, as presented here"** Lewis Mumford, "The Sky Line in Flushing: Genuine Bootleg," *New Yorker*, July 29, 1939, p. 39.

177 **"G.M. has spent"** Peter J. Kuznick, "Losing the World of Tomorrow: The Battle over the Presentation of Science at the 1939 New York World's Fair," *American Quarterly* (September 1994): 349.

178 **"All we are trying to do"** "General Motors Host to Employees," *New York Times*, May 29, 1939.

178 **"There's a special kick"** Meyer Berger, "At the Fair," *New York Times*, May 4, 1939.

178 **"It's beautiful"** Ibid., May 12, 1939.

178 **"I loved it"** Ibid., May 30, 1939.

CHAPTER 15: VISIONS AND DREAMSCAPES

181 **hired a public-speaking expert** "Oratory at the Fair," *New Yorker*, December 24, 1939, pp. 12–13.

181 **"Slang will have no place"** "Fair Aides to Begin Lessons in Diction," *New York Times*, October 29, 1938.

181 **"He expects that kind of thing"** "Orders," *New Yorker*, May 13, 1939, p. 14.

182 **"Never mind about the mayor"** Ibid.

182 **"has its loathsome"** "Notes and Comment," *New Yorker*, April 29, 1939, p. 16.

182 **"hope against hope"** Russell B. Porter, "5,000 Hear Prince," *New York Times*, May 2, 1939.

182 **"We maintain the open-door policy"** Ibid.

183 **"I worked for the Fair Corporation"** Bainbridge and McKelway, "That Was the New York World's Fair."

183 **"Friends tell me I am crazy"** " 'Father of Fair' Never Visited It," *New York Times*.

184 **"They wouldn't complete our building"** Charles Stevenson, "Labor Takes In the Fair," *Atlantic Monthly*, January 1949, p. 1.

184 **Whalen finally stepped in** "Strike Settled at World's Fair," *New York Times*, July 19, 1938.

184 **"to drive occasional nails"** Stevenson, "Labor Takes In the Fair," p. 6.

185 **"I find them resting"** Ibid., p. 9.

185 **"We have had only"** Ibid., p. 11.

185 **Bassett Jones** For details on the incredibly versatile Jones and his lighting of the World's Fair, see Geoffrey T. Hellman, "Day-Before-Yesterday-Man," *New Yorker*, April 29, 1939, pp. 24–30.

186 **"As darkness falls"** Lewis Mumford, "West Is East," *New Yorker*, June 17, 1939, p. 38.

186 **"I've kept the intensities down"** Hellman, "Day-Before-Yesterday-Man."

186 **found themselves wandering around** "Let's Go See," *Atlantic Monthly*, June 1939, p. 884–85.

187 **"We're not familiar"** Meyer Berger, "At the Fair," May 11, 1939.

187 **"We shall eat"** "Notes and Comment," *New Yorker*, April 29, 1939, p. 16.

188 **"a definite breach of faith"** Harding, "World's Fair New York."

188 **"the nickel is a coin"** Ibid.

188 **"The talk about"** Joseph Wood Krutch, "A Report of the Fair," *Nation*, June 24, 1939, p. 722.

190 **"The designers found out"** "Drama and Crowds—Direct Sources of and Materials for Design," *Architectural Record* (August 1940).

191 **"Naturally we've had"** "Fair 'Over the Top,' Whalen Holds, Predicting Unparalleled Success," *New York Times*, June 19, 1939.

192 **"This Fair has already gone"** Ibid.

CHAPTER 16: PALESTINE VS. PANCHO VILLA

195 **Science Advisory Committee** For a history of this committee and Gerald Wendt's involvement, see Robert W. Rydell, "The Fan Dance of Science: American World's Fairs in the Great Depression," *Isis* (December 1985): 525–42.

195 **Science was taking a wrong turn** Ten days before the Fair opened, on April 20, 1939, the California Institute of Technology's Robert A. Millikan gave a speech to the Merchants Association in which he predicted, among other misstatements, that "life in America fifty or a hundred years hence will not differ nearly as much from the life of today as the life of today differs from that of a century or even a half century ago"; and, "So far as tapping the energy 'locked up in the atoms' is concerned, we can count that out." Robert A. Millikan, "Science and the World of Tomorrow," *Vital Speeches of the Day*, May 1, 1939, pp. 446–48.

196 **"to tell the whole story"** "Science and the New York World's Fair," *Scientific Monthly*, April 1939, p. 587.

196 **"We wish to abolish"** Kuznick, "Losing the World of Tomorrow," p. 349.

196 **"Any plan now"** Ibid., p. 354.

199 **"He wanted to aid the Jews"** Clark, *Einstein: The Life and Times.*

200 **"I believe"** "Foes Are Warned," *New York Times,* May 2, 1939.

200 **"Will there be war or peace"** Herbert L. Matthews, "Speech Moderate," *New York Times,* May 15, 1939.

201 **"Palestine"** Ibid.

202 **The USSR Pavilion** For detailed descriptions of this pavilion, see Anthony Swift, "The Soviet World of Tomorrow at the New York World's Fair, 1939," *Russian Review* (July 1998): 364–79; "Russian Pavilion," *New Yorker,* May 20, 1939, pp. 15–16.

204 **"The Soviet people"** "Young Man Showing His Muscles," *New Republic,* May 31, 1939, p. 87; Russell B. Porter, "Russian Envoy Opens Nation's Pavilion at Fair as a 'Good Neighbor' of U.S.," *New York Times,* May 18, 1939.

204 **"warmongers accustomed to"** Ibid.

205 **"The agents of Hitler"** Robert B. Post, "Parliament Backs Plan on Palestine," *New York Times,* May 24, 1939.

205 **"England has, in part"** "Dr. Einstein Urges Patience on Jews," *New York Times,* May 28, 1939.

206 **"Remember in the midst"** Ibid.

206 **"America's link"** Frank Zachary, "The Fair That Was," *New Yorker,* April 11, 1964, p. 125.

206 **"just liked having Indians and horses around"** Ibid.

208 **Perylon Hall** For description, see "Perylonia," *New Yorker,* July 8, 1939, pp. 17–18.

209 **"for a true world of justice"** Frank S. Adams, "Spotlight at Fair Swings to Dedication of the Palestine Pavilion," *New York Times,* May 29, 1939.

210 **"of what Jews have accomplished"** "Officials Acclaim Palestine Exhibit," *New York Times,* May 13, 1939.

210 **"This pavilion is a token"** Adams, "Spotlight at Fair."

210 **"The World's Fair"** Albert Einstein, "Address at Dedication of Palestine Pavilion at N.Y. World's Fair," May 28, 1939, Albert Einstein Archives, the Hebrew University of Jerusalem, 28–490.00.

210 **"I am here entrusted"** Ibid.

211 **Einstein sat with his pipe** See Edwin Muller, "Einstein at Princeton," *Nation,* September 17, 1938, p. 267. Muller refers to the fact that Einstein eschewed alcohol but allowed himself three pipes a day.

CHAPTER 17: GERMANY YESTERDAY—GERMANY TOMORROW

213 **"Czechoslovakia is still alive"** Russell B. Porter, "Courage of Czechs Acclaimed at Fair," *New York Times,* June 1, 1939.

214 **"can rule the country"** Ibid.

214 **"I have no apologies"** Ibid.

214 **"chamber of horrors"** "La Guardia vs. Hitler," *Time,* March 15, 1937.

214 **"dirty Talmud Jew"** "La Guardia and the German Press," *New Republic,* March 17, 1937, p. 154.

214 **"Secretary Hull and I"** "Attack on Hitler Renewed by Mayor," *New York Times,* November 3, 1938.

215 **should he allow the Nazis to participate** NYWF Archives, B294, F13; a

report from Whalen to the executive committee, dated February 1, 1937, states, "Germany will participate if the exchange difficulty can be arranged."

215 **"Will any Jew set foot"** Oswald Garrison Villard, "No Swastikas at the World's Fair!" *Nation*, June 5, 1937, p. 648.

215 **one-hundred-thousand-square-foot pavilion** NYWF Archives, B294, F12; a handwritten, undated note states, "Industry will be prominently represented with cultural features—a restaurant is being considered."

215 **"The Germans are not at all satisfied"** NYWF Archives, B294, F14.

216 **"We believe that as Germany"** Laura Z. Hobson, "Freedom Pavilion," *Nation*, April 29, 1939, p. 492.

216 **"Four days later"** Ibid.

217 **"We don't want to do anything"** " 'Freedom Pavilion' at Fair Planned to Celebrate the Pre-Nazi Culture," *New York Times*, January 13, 1939.

217 **"I have never believed"** Ibid.

217 **"This enterprise would be"** Hobson, "Freedom Pavilion."

217 **The Italian Pavilion** Bishop, "World's Fair Notes," *Kenyon Review*, p. 245.

218 **"the Japanese people"** "Japan Dedicates Pavilion with 1,500-Year-Old 'Flame of Friendship,' " *New York Times*, June 3, 1939.

218 **"a new civilization"** Ibid.

219 **"If they bomb it"** "Bund Rally Bomb Rumor Fails to Worry Mayor," *New York Times*, February 21, 1939.

220 **"We are outraged"** "Bund Rally to Get Huge Police Guard," *New York Times*, February 19, 1939.

220 **"Why is it necessary"** "1,300 Will Police Big Bund Meeting," *New York Times*, February 20, 1939.

221 **"We have enough police here"** "22,000 Nazis Hold Rally in Garden; Police Check Foes," *New York Times*, February 21, 1939.

222 **"You ought to be proud"** Ibid.

222 **"I went down to the Garden"** "Bund Foes Protest Policing of Rally," *New York Times*, February 22, 1939.

222 **"The policeman is"** Read Bain, "The Policeman on the Beat," *Scientific Monthly*, May 1939, pp. 450, 452.

223 **"I think the results"** "Bund Foes," *New York Times*.

CHAPTER 18: ROYAL FLUSH

228 **"When do we eat?"** Whalen, *Mr. New York.*

228 **"Who was that man?"** Ibid.

229 **"What the hell are you doing?"** Ibid.

CHAPTER 19: "I NEVER THOUGHT OF THAT!"

234 **quite a controversy** Edward Alden Jewell, "Tomorrow, Inc.," *Parnassus* (October 1937): 3–8.

235 **a "scientist-magician"** "Man Loses His Shadow in World's Fair Exhibit," *Science News Letter*, August 12, 1939, p. 103.

236 **"We were thinking of you"** "People," *Time*, September 26, 1938.

236 **"People living in different countries"** Albert Einstein, "Message in the

Time Capsule," September 1938, in *Ideas and Opinions* (New York: Crown Publishers, 1954).

237 **"I must say that"** Russell Maloney, "6939 and All That," *New Yorker,* May 6, 1939, pp. 28–29.

238 **"a gray-haired fairgoer"** Meyer Berger, "At the Fair," *New York Times,* July 10, 1939.

238 **Leó Szilárd** For detailed information on Szilárd, see William Lanouette, *Genius in the Shadows: A Biography of Leo Szilard—The Man Behind the Bomb* (New York: Charles Scribner's Sons, 1992); and Leó Szilárd, *Leo Szilard: His Version of the Facts,* eds. Spencer Weart and Gertrud Weiss Szilárd (Cambridge, MA: MIT Press, 1980). Both works are long out of print but available via Amazon.com resellers.

239 **Szilárd had conceived plans** Valentine L. Telegdi, "Szilard as Inventor: Accelerators and More," *Physics Today* (October 2000).

239 **"Had he pushed through"** Gene Dannen, "The Einstein-Szilard Refrigerators," *Scientific American* (January 1997).

239 **Szilárd had fled Berlin** "Obituaries: Leo Szilard," *Physics Today* (October 1964).

240 **"Both Wigner and I"** Clark, *Einstein: The Life and Times.*

240 **"I sawed [it]"** Thomas Lee Bucky with Joseph P. Blank, "Einstein: An Intimate Memoir," *Harper's Magazine,* September 1964, p. 47.

241 **"We knew that Einstein"** Isaacson, *Einstein: His Life and Universe.*

242 **"Wigner suggested"** Clark, *Einstein: The Life and Times.*

243 **"I decided"** Ibid.

244 **"Some recent work"** Nathan and Norden, eds., *Einstein on Peace.*

CHAPTER 20: "YOU TELL 'EM, MICKEY!"

248 **The Fair was too "high-hat"** "A Cornflower for Mr. Whalen's Gardenia," *Saturday Evening Post,* September 2, 1939, p. 22.

248 **"Hi, screwball!"** Gelernter, *1939: The Lost World of the Fair,* p. 39.

249 **"Mr. Tompkins"** Bruce Bliven Jr., "Gone Tomorrow," *New Republic,* May 17, 1939, p. 42.

249 **"It is evident"** "Whalen Foresees Big Influx to Fair," *New York Times,* July 6, 1939.

250 **"With respect"** President's report to the Board of Design, July 20, 1939, NYWF Archives, B13, F11.

250 **"Don't believe these stories"** "Figures v. Dreams," *Time,* August 21, 1939.

254 **"Dear Grover"** Letter from Harvey Gibson to Grover Whalen, August 16, 1938, NYWF Archives, B13, F2.

255 **"Want a chew?"** "50¢ Week-End Fee at Fair Is Set as 'Final' Concession," *New York Times,* August 1, 1939.

255 **"The finance and executive committee"** Ibid.

256 **"The announcement"** Ibid.

256 **"I think the Executive Committee"** Ibid.

256 **"He had put so much of himself"** Shalett, "Epitaph for the World's Fair."

CHAPTER 21: THE STORM CENTER OF THE WORLD

259 **"I would like to ask you"** Clark, *Einstein: The Life and Times.*

261 **"We want you all to come"** Archival newsreel footage, Movietone News, August 14, 1939; from "The World of Tomorrow."

264 **"The house was now"** Shalett, "Epitaph for the World's Fair."

264 **"sacrifice their lives"** "Polish-Americans Defy Nazi Power," *New York Times*, August 20, 1939.

265 **"[We] send you"** Ibid.

268 **For a grand total** According to the annual report, year ended December 27, 1939, the actual paid attendance came to 25,817,265. NYWF Archives, B2, F11.

269 **"Haven't you received"** "New Economy Moves at Fair Seen in Choice of Banker as Chairman," *New York Times*, September 1, 1939.

269 **"Mr. Gibson will give"** Ibid.

269 **"I can't tell whether"** Ibid.

270 **"The World's Fair"** Ibid.

270 **"I'd like to say"** Ibid.

CHAPTER 22: "S'LONG, FOLKS!"

274 **"We welcome you here"** "Sympathy in Crisis Cheers Poles' Day," *New York Times*, September 3, 1939.

274 **"This is an hour of sorrow"** Ibid.

275 **"Lindbergh is not our man"** Isaacson, *Einstein: His Life and Universe.*

276 **"More Fair for less money!"** "Fair Cuts Its Rate to Flat 50 Cents for All October," *New York Times*, September 27, 1939.

276 **"I should think"** Ibid.

276 **"It's pretty good"** Ibid.

277 **"It cost approximately"** "World's Fair Aspires to the Title of 'People's Playground' Next Year," *New York Times*, October 21, 1939.

278 **"Give 'em only pickle pins!"** "Child Hordes Give Fair Wildest Day; 150,000 Stream In," *New York Times*, October 28, 1939.

279 **"managed to strip the World of Tomorrow"** Ibid.

280 **a couple who had been stranded** "Notes and Comment," *New Yorker*, July 22, 1939, p. 9.

280 **"There was some benefit"** NYWF Archives, B10, F3.

280 **"There shall never"** "362,522 Pack Fair on Its 2d-Best Day; Midway Sets Mark," *New York Times*, September 25, 1939.

280 **A frequent visitor** Interview with Edward Chalfant, January 11, 2009.

281 **"I'll bet they're going to eat"** "1939 Fair Closes; Seen by 26,000,000; Plans Laid for '40," *New York Times*, November 1, 1939.

281 **"Grover Whalen is president"** "Grover's Helper," *New Yorker*, November 4, 1939, pp. 12–13.

282 **"I don't know what we'd do"** Ibid.

282 **"If the bondholders"** Ibid.

282 **"What we need"** Ibid.

282 **could hardly believe the transformation** Sidney M. Shalett, " 'Hello Folks' Is the Watchword as Elmer Takes Over the Fair," *New York Times*, May 12, 1940.

CHAPTER 23: "HELLO, FOLKS!"

285 **"Why don't you let me"** Shalett, "Epitaph for the World's Fair."

286 **"How do you do, gentlemen!"** "Synthetic 'Elmer' 1940 Fair Greeter," *New York Times*, April 13, 1940.

286 **"Well, I hope I bring millions!"** Ibid.

286 **"Mr. and Mrs. America"** Ibid.

287 **"Elmer is the 'great American' "** Ibid.

289 **"The transformation"** Shalett, " 'Hello, Folks' Is the Watchword as Elmer Takes Over the Fair," *New York Times*, May 12, 1940.

289 **The changes were numerous** For an overview of the myriad changes in the 1940 Fair, see Russell Maloney and Eugene Kinkead, "Trylon, Trylon Again," *New Yorker*, May 11, 1940, pp. 36–42; and "Forty Fair," *Time*, May 20, 1940.

289 **"to keep the crowds away"** Maloney and Kinkead, "Trylon, Trylon Again."

290 **"Would he go back"** "Ballet for Ford," *Time*, June 3, 1940.

290 **"never once forgot"** Ibid.

291 **"You wouldn't mean Sparko"** Shalett, " 'Hello, Folks' Is the Watchword."

291 **crated up for shipping back to the USSR** "Pavilion in Crates," *New Yorker*, July 13, 1940, pp. 10–11.

292 **"Those of you who are bondholders"** Shalett, "Epitaph for the World's Fair."

292 **"it would take"** Ibid.

293 **"Is the sun coming out?"** "Gibson Is Pleased by Fair Finances," *New York Times*, May 29, 1940.

CHAPTER 24: "THIS LOOKS LIKE THE REAL GOODS"

295 **"This is not a dedication"** Sidney M. Shalett, "Hoover Condemns Nazis in Fair Talk," *New York Times*, May 19, 1940.

297 **"designed to create"** "Bombing Is Third Within Two Weeks in City," *New York Times*, July 5, 1940.

300 **"Get out of the building"** "Fair Gets New Bomb Scare from a Package of Cloth," *Washington Post*, July 7, 1940.

301 **an electrician named William Strachan** For the most detailed overall account of the bomb, from its discovery to explosion, see "Police Die in Blast," *New York Times*, July 5, 1940; and "Bomb from British Pavilion Kills 2, Hurts 5 at N.Y. Fair," *Washington Post*, July 5, 1940.

301 **It was there again** "Police Die in Blast," *New York Times*.

301 **three-thirty in the afternoon** Official report of James B. Leggett, commanding officer, 110-A Detective Squad, July 4, 1940, NYWF Archives, B1858, F10.

302 **"ticking like a clock"** "Aftermath of World's Fair Bombing," *Brooklyn Daily Eagle*, July 5, 2007.

302 **It was Morlach** Leggett, NYWF Archives.

302 **walked down an alley** Ibid. Leggett reports that Morlach (pronounced "Morlock") carried the bomb for a distance of about two blocks.

302 **The four detectives** Memo from Detective John H. Koester to the World's Fair director of public safety, July 4, 1940, NYWF Archives, B1858, F10.

303 **At a little after four o'clock** Ibid.

303 **Lynch called Peter Hayias's number** "Detective Hayias," *New York Times,* December 2, 1941.

303 **"I'll be back in an hour"** Maki Becker, "Remembering Ultimate Sacrifice: Memorial Eyed for Cops Killed at '40 World's Fair," *(New York) Daily News,* July 25, 2000.

303 **around a quarter to five** Leggett, NYWF Archives.

304 **Patrolman Emil Vyskocil** Ibid.

304 **twelve inches by eighteen by six** Koester, NYWF Archives.

304 **cut away a two-inch strip** Ibid.

304 **"This looks like the real goods"** "Death at the Fair," *Time,* July 15, 1940.

304 **"It's the business"** "Police Die in Blast," *New York Times.*

305 **Federer and Gallagher** Leggett, NYWF Archives.

305 **"It was terrible"** "Bomb from British Pavilion Kills 2," *Washington Post.*

305 **"It was a terrible explosion"** Ibid.

307 **"As to the accident"** "Mayor at Scene, Reassures Public," *New York Times,* July 5, 1940.

307 **"We get letters"** Ibid.

307 **just more fireworks** "Crowd Unaware of Bomb Tragedy," *New York Times,* July 5, 1940.

307 **"There had been"** "War Atmosphere Created by Blast," *New York Times,* July 5, 1940.

308 **"I thought no more about it"** "Police Die in Blast," *New York Times.*

308 **"All the buildings"** "Mayor at Scene," *New York Times.*

309 **"Who died?"** Becker, "Remembering Ultimate Sacrifice."

310 **"There will be a most thorough"** "Mayor at Scene," *New York Times.*

310 **Morlach continued working** "100 Examined in Bomb Round-Up; City Will Offer a $25,000 Reward," *New York Times,* July 6, 1940.

CHAPTER 25: AFTERMATH

313 **"I take my hat off"** "640,000 Throng Fair on 4-Day Week-End," *New York Times,* July 8, 1940.

313 **"the reverse was the case"** "Guarded Pavilions Visited by Crowds," *New York Times,* July 6, 1940.

314 **"Miss General Motors 1960"** Ibid.

314 **"We are mobilizing"** "All Police in City on 24-Hour Duty," *New York Times,* July 5, 1940.

315 **"war atmosphere"** "War Atmosphere Created by Blast," *New York Times.*

315 **"I'll kill her!"** "Experts Find Clue in Bomb Fragments," *New York Times,* July 7, 1940.

316 **"It was only"** James Pyke, "Handling of Suspected Bombs and the Investigation of Explosives," *Spring 3100*, July 1942, pp. 4–5.

316 **the "dynamite shrapnel"** "Dynamite Thief Sought in N.Y. Fair Bombing," *Washington Post*, July 6, 1940.

316 **arrest of a man named Caesar Kroeger** Ibid.

317 **"Mail to the address inside"** "Experts Find Clue," *New York Times*.

317 **"This is just to tell you"** "2 New Clues Found in Fatal Bombing," *New York Times*, July 8, 1940.

317 **a growing panic** "N.Y. Power Lines Guarded After New Bomb Threat," *Washington Post*, July 8, 1940.

317 **"near the convention hall"** "FBI Denies Convention Bomb Story," *Washington Post*, July 12, 1940.

317 **"was addressed to the Governor"** Ibid.

318 **Sixteen hundred mourners** For details of the Lynch and Socha services, see "City Votes $25,000 for Bomb Reward," *New York Times*, July 10, 1940.

318 **"I urge your boys"** "All Police Asked to Join Bomb Hunt," *New York Times*, July 9, 1940.

318 **"For God's sake"** "1,500 Detectives at Bomb Conference Today; Valentine Will Order Them to 'Break Case,' " *New York Times*, July 11, 1940.

320 **"If only the persons responsible"** "Valentine Warns of More Bombings," *New York Times*.

CHAPTER 26: CURTAINS

323 **"I have convened"** Isaacson, *Einstein: His Life and Universe*.

323 **"Since the outbreak of the war"** Clark, *Einstein: The Life and Times*.

324 **"[Immigrants] are the only ones"** Albert Einstein, "For 'Wall of Fame' of World's Fair New York 1940," Albert Einstein Archives, 28–529.00.

325 **"I am convinced"** Clark, *Einstein: The Life and Times*.

325 **"Don't buy these programs, folks!"** Shalett, "Epitaph for the World's Fair."

325 **"Baby Crawling Contest"** "Notes and Comment," *New Yorker*, August 3, 1940, p. 9.

326 **"Why not?"** Richard M. Ketchum, *The Borrowed Years: 1938–1941* (New York: Random House, 1989).

326 **"The World's Fair made it possible"** "Clear Site on Time, Moses Warns Fair," *New York Times*, August 15, 1940.

327 **"I suggest that there be no doubt"** Al Smith letter to NYWF board of directors, April 22, 1936, NYWF Archives, B13, F2.

327 **"In fact, Fair officials"** "Use of Fair's Steel in Defense Likely," *New York Times*, August 19, 1940.

328 **"Common sense will tell you"** "Gibson Backs Plan for Camp at Fair," *New York Times*, August 25, 1940.

328 **"There is a serious possibility"** Ibid.

330 **"Harvey D. Gibson"** "Mayor Gives Press a Few Tips at Fair," *New York Times*, August 20, 1940.

330 **" 'Know your money' "** Ibid.

331 **"bankrupt and busted"** "Inquiry into Fair Pledged by Moses," *New York Times*, August 27, 1940.

331 **"find out why the Fair"** Ibid.

331 **"Honorable Mr. Gibson"** Letter to Harvey Gibson from Pablo Albortt, August 16, 1940, NYWF Archives, B14, F2.

331 **"constructed like a jigsaw puzzle"** "Futurama, Hit of Fair, Will Not Be Preserved," *New York Times*, August 27, 1940.

332 **On August 6** "Penn Station Bomb Is Innocent Clock," *New York Times*, August 7, 1940.

332 **"might go off at any moment"** "Bomb Tip Proves Hoax," *New York Times*, August 10, 1940.

332 **"Hey, fellows, that's my bag"** " 'Bomb' Bag Is Ducked, Youth's Shirt Wilts," *New York Times*, August 11, 1940.

332 **"another bomb"** "3 Bomb Alarms Prove to Be False," *New York Times*, August 15, 1940.

333 **"to pick up survivors"** Ibid.

CHAPTER 27: WHALEN, GRAVISNAS, FORBINE, AND NOBILITY

335 **"forfeit their lives"** "Fair's Foreigners Face Crisis Oct. 27," *New York Times*, October 3, 1940.

335 **"almost wild"** Ibid.

335 **"I can assure you"** "Mayor in New Plea Invites All to Fair," *New York Times*, October 12, 1940.

338 **"Good old Grover"** Whalen, *Mr. New York*.

338 **power failure** "Rush As Fair Ends Brings Out 537,952, Its Biggest Crowd," *New York Times*, October 28, 1940.

340 **"Have you caught"** Boyer, "World of Tomorrow, Or Next Day."

340 **"It was a crossword puzzle"** Meyer Berger, "At the Fair," *New York Times*, October 28, 1940.

EPILOGUE: ASHES TO ASHES

343 **In the end** For a complete financial rundown of the World's Fair over both seasons, see Tyng, *Making a World's Fair*.

344 **"very happy in their experience"** Milton Bracker, "Profit of 1940 Fair Thus Far Is $696,118; 5% Payment on Bonds Is Likely in August," *New York Times*, July 10, 1940.

344 **"The bonds"** Hellman, "For City and for Coty II."

344 **The city itself couldn't** A. J. Liebling, "World of Five-Cent Hot Dogs," *New Yorker*, August 5, 1939, p. 34; "Curtains," *Time*, November 4, 1940; Shalett, "Epitaph for the World's Fair."

344 **One bright winter afternoon** "Whee!" *New Yorker*, December 7, 1940, p. 27.

345 **Various parts of the Fair** For details about the Fair's demolition and what became of some exhibits, see Eugene Kinkead, "Goodbye Folks!" *New Yorker*, May 31, 1941, pp. 38–44.

345 **In 1943, a reporter** "Plowshares into Swords Note," *New Yorker*, March 6, 1943, p. 9.

346 **"profound thanks"** "Heroes of Fair's July 4 Bombing Win British Government's Tribute," *New York Times*, April 16, 1941.

346 **"In the name of"** Ibid.

346 **"The perpetrator of that crime"** Ibid.

347 **"to take a bomb from"** For details on Pyke's innovations in bomb safety, see James A. Pyke, "The La Guardia–Pyke Bomb Carriers," *Journal of Criminal Law and Criminology* (September/October 1943): 198–205; Pyke, "Handling of Suspected Bombs," *Spring 3100*.

348 **"Einstein asks me"** Clark, *Einstein: The Life and Times*.

348 **"Oh, my God!"** Isaacson, *Einstein: His Life and Universe*.

348 **"I made one great mistake"** Clark, *Einstein: The Life and Times*.

349 **"How are you, Commissioner?"** Hellman, "For City and for Coty I."

350 **"The little mind"** "Notes and Comment," *New Yorker*, April 29, 1939, p. 15.

350 **"Didn't they realize"** Hellman, "For City and for Coty I."

350 **he watched on television** Michael Aronson, "Grover Whalen Welcome to New York City," *(New York) Daily News*, April 9, 1999.

BIBLIOGRAPHY

Applebaum, Stanley, ed. *The New York World's Fair 1939/40*. New York: Dover, 1977.

Ballon, Hilary, and Kenneth T. Jackson. *Robert Moses and the Modern City: The Transformation of New York*. New York: W. W. Norton & Co., 2007.

Brodsky, Alyn. *The Great Mayor: Fiorello La Guardia and the Making of the City of New York*. New York: Truman Talley Books, 2003.

Caro, Robert A. *The Power Broker: Robert Moses and the Fall of New York*. New York: Vintage Books, 1975.

Clark, Ronald W. *Einstein: The Life and Times*. New York: Harper Perennial, 2007.

Cohen, Barbara, Steven Heller, and Seymour Chwast. *Trylon and Perisphere: The 1939 New York World's Fair*. New York: Harry N. Abrams, 1989.

Committee for Federal Writers' Publications. *New York City Guide*. New York: Random House, 1939.

Cummings, Carlos E. *East Is East and West Is West*. New York: Buffalo Museum of Science, 1940.

Dash, Mike. *Satan's Circus: Murder, Vice, Police Corruption and New York's Trial of the Century*. New York: Crown Publishers, 2007.

Davis, Kenneth S. *FDR: Into the Storm, 1937–1940*. New York: Random House, 1993.

Doctorow, E. L. *World's Fair*. New York: Random House, 1985.

Einstein, Albert. *Ideas and Opinions*. New York: Wings Books, 1954.

Elliott, Lawrence. *Little Flower: The Life and Times of Fiorello La Guardia*. New York: William Morrow & Co., 1983.

Feldman, Burton. *112 Mercer Street: Einstein, Russell, Godel, Pauli, and the End of Innocence in Science*. New York: Arcade Publishing, 2007.

Fitzgerald, F. Scott. *The Great Gatsby*. New York: Charles Scribner's Sons, 1925.

Geddes, Norman Bel. *Magic Motorways*. New York: Random House, 1940.

Gelernter, David. *1939: The Lost World of the Fair.* New York: Avon Books, 1995.

Harrison, Helen A., ed. *Dawn of a New Day: The New York World's Fair, 1939/40.* New York: Queens Museum and New York University Press, 1980.

Heckscher, August. *When LaGuardia Was Mayor.* New York: W. W. Norton & Co., 1978.

Hillis, Marjorie. *New York: Fair or No Fair.* New York: Bobbs-Merrill, 1939.

Hodgson, Godfrey. *America in Our Time.* New York: Doubleday, 1976.

Isaacson, Walter. *Einstein, His Life and Universe.* New York: Simon & Schuster, 2007.

Jeffers, H. Paul. *The Napoleon of New York: Mayor Fiorello La Guardia.* New York: John Wiley & Sons, 2002.

Jerome, Fred. *Einstein on Israel and Zionism.* New York: St. Martin's Press, 2009.

———. *The Einstein File.* New York: St. Martin's Press, 2002.

Kessner, Thomas. *Fiorello H. La Guardia and the Making of Modern New York.* New York: McGraw-Hill, 1989.

Ketchum, Richard M. *The Borrowed Years: 1938–1941.* New York: Random House, 1989.

Lanquette, William, with Bella Silard. *Genius in the Shadows: A Biography of Leo Szilard, the Man Behind the Bomb.* Chicago: University of Chicago Press, 1992.

Lardner, James, and Thomas Reppetto. *NYPD: A City and Its Police.* New York: Holt Paperbacks, 2001.

Leuchtenburg, William E. *Franklin D. Roosevelt and the New Deal, 1932–40.* New York: Harper & Row, 1963.

Manchester, William. *The Glory and the Dream: A Narrative History of America: 1932–1972.* Boston: Little, Brown & Co., 1973.

Marquis, Alice Goldfarb. *Hopes and Ashes: The Birth of Modern Times.* New York: Free Press, 1986.

McDonald, Brian. *My Father's Gun: One Family, Three Badges, One Hundred Years in the NYPD.* New York: Plume, 2000.

Mitgang, Herbert. *Once Upon a Time in New York: Jimmy Walker, Franklin Roosevelt, and the Last Great Battle of the Jazz Age.* New York: Free Press, 2000.

Monaghan, Frank. *Going to the World's Fair.* New York: Sun Dial Press, 1939.

———. *New York: The World's Fair City.* New York: Garden City Publishing Co., 1937.

Monaghan, Sylvia Harris. *Going to the Fair: A Preview of the New York World's Fair 1939.* New York: Sun Dial Press, 1939.

Moses, Robert. *The Fair, the City and the Critics.* Pamphlet. New York: New York World's Fair 1964–1965 Corporation, 1964.

———. *Public Works: A Dangerous Trade.* New York: McGraw-Hill, 1970.

Mumford, Lewis. *The Culture of Cities.* New York: Harcourt, Brace & Co., 1938.

Nathan, Otto, and Heinz Norden, eds. *Einstein on Peace.* New York: Simon & Schuster, 1960.

Neffe, Jürgen. *Einstein: A Biography.* Baltimore: Johns Hopkins University Press, 2009.

Official Guide Book, New York World's Fair 1939. New York: Exposition Publications, 1939.

Official Guide Book, New York World's Fair 1940. New York: Exposition Publications, 1940.

Pais, Abraham. *Einstein Lived Here.* New York: Oxford University Press, 1994.

Rankin, Rebecca B., ed. *New York Advancing: World's Fair Edition.* New York: Publisher's Printing Co., 1939.

Rosenblum, Robert. *Remembering the Future: The New York World's Fair from 1939 to 1964.* New York: Rizzoli, 1989.

Shaw, R. P., dir. *Exhibition Techniques: A Summary of Exhibition Practice.* New York: New York City Museum of Science and History, 1940.

Teague, Walter Dorwin. *Design This Day: The Technique of Order in the Machine Age.* New York: Harcourt, Brace & Co., 1940.

Tosches, Nick. *King of the Jews.* New York: Ecco, 2005.

Tyng, Ed. *Making a World's Fair.* New York: Vantage Press, 1958.

Wendt, Gerald. *Science for the World of Tomorrow.* New York: W. W. Norton & Co., 1939.

Whalen, Grover (as told to Essie-Jean). *A Trip to the World's Fair with Bobby and Betty.* New York: Dodge, 1938.

Whalen, Grover. *Mr. New York: The Autobiography of Grover A. Whalen.* New York: G. P. Putnam's Sons, 1955.

White, Michael, and John Gribbin. *Einstein: A Life in Science.* New York: Dutton, 1994.

Zim, Larry, Mel Lerner, and Herbert Rolfes. *The World of Tomorrow: The 1939 New York World's Fair.* New York: Harper & Row, 1988.

INDEX

ABOUT THE AUTHOR

JAMES MAURO is a former editor of *Spy* magazine and executive editor of *Cosmopolitan*. Most recently he was editorial director for Moffly Media, publishers of the Connecticut periodicals *Greenwich, Stamford, Westport, New Canaan-Darien,* and *AtHome*. His writing has been featured in *Radar, Details, Spy, Psychology Today,* and a host of other publications. He lives in Connecticut, where he is at work on his next book. Visit him online at www.jamesmauro.net.

ABOUT THE TYPE

The text of this book was set in Janson, a typeface designed in about 1690 by Nicholas Kis, a Hungarian living in Amsterdam, and for many years mistakenly attributed to the Dutch printer Anton Janson. In 1919 the matrices became the property of the Stempel Foundry in Frankfurt. It is an old-style book face of excellent clarity and sharpness. Janson serifs are concave and splayed; the contrast between thick and thin strokes is marked.